A·N·N·U·A·L E·D·I·T·I·O·N·S

Educational Psychology
06/07

Twenty-first Edition

EDITOR

Kathleen M. Cauley

Virginia Commonwealth University

Kathleen M. Cauley received her Ph.D. in educational studies/human development from the University of Delaware in 1985. Her current research are student transitions to a new school, and the influence of assessment practices on motivation.

James H. McMillan

Virginia Commonwealth University

James H. McMillan received his bachelor's degree from Albion College in 1970, an M.A. from Michigan State University in 1972, and a Ph.D. from Northwestern University in 1976. He has reviewed and written extensively in educational psychology.

Gina Pannozzo

Virginia Commonwealth University

Gina M. Pannozzo recieved her Ph.D. in Educational Psychology from the University of Buffalo in 2005. Her current research examines the relationships among student engagement patterns in school and dropping out.

McGraw Hill Contemporary Learning Series

2460 Kerper Blvd., Dubuque, IA 52001

Visit us on the Internet
http://www.mhcls.com

Credits

1. **Perspectives on Teaching**
   Unit photo—© CORBIS/Royalty Free
2. **Development**
   Unit photo—© image100 Ltd
3. **Exceptional and Culturally Diverse Children**
   Unit photo—© PunchStock/Creatas
4. **Learning and Instruction**
   Unit photo—© Getty Images/Brand X Pictures/SW Productions
5. **Motivation and Classroom Management**
   Unit photo—© image100 Ltd
6. **Assessment**
   Unit photo—© CORBIS/Royalty Free

Copyright

Cataloging in Publication Data
Main entry under title: Annual Editions: Educational Psychology. 2006/2007.
1. Educational Psychology—Periodicals. I. Cauley, Kathleen M., *comp.*, McMillan, James H., Pannozzo, Gina M., II. Title: Educational Psychology.
ISBN-13: 978–0–07–351611–0   ISBN-10: 0–07–351611–2   658'.05   ISSN 0731–1141

Twenty-first Edition

Cover image © Digital Vision and Corbis/Royalty Free
Printed in the United States of America   1234567890QPDQPD9876   Printed on Recycled Paper

UNIT 3: Exceptional and Culturally Diverse Children

The Council for Exceptional Children
http://www.cec.sped.org/index.html

This page will give you access to information on identifying and teaching gifted children, attention-deficit disorders, and other topics in gifted education.

Global SchoolNet Foundation
http://www.gsn.org

Access this site for multicultural education information. The site includes news for teachers, students, and parents, as well as chat rooms, links to educational resources, programs, and contests and competitions.

International Project: Multicultural Pavilion
http://curry.edschool.virginia.edu/curry/centers/multicultural/papers.html

Here is a forum for sharing stories and resources and for learning from the stories and resources of others, in the form of articles on the Internet that cover every possible racial, gender, and multicultural issue that could arise in the field of multicultural education.

Let 1000 Flowers Bloom/Kristen Nicholson-Nelson
http://teacher.scholastic.com/professional/assessment/100flowers.htm

Open this page for Kristen Nicholson-Nelson's discussion of ways in which teachers can help to nurture children's multiple intelligences. She provides a useful bibliography and resources.

National Association for Multicultural Education
http://www.nameorg.org

NAME is a major organization in the field of multicultural education. The website provides conference informantion and resources including lesson plans, advice for handling touchy issues, and grant information.

National Attention Deficit Disorder Association
http://www.add.org

This site, some of which is under construction, will lead you to information about ADD/ADHD. It has links to self-help and support groups, outlines behaviors and diagnostics, answers FAQs, and suggests books and other resources.

National MultiCultural Institute (NMCI)
http://www.nmci.org

NMCI is one of the major organizations in the field of diversity training. At this Web site, NMCI offers conference data, resource materials, diversity training and consulting service information, and links to other related sites.

Teaching Tolerance
http://www.tolerance.org

This site promotes and supports anti-bias activism in every venue of life. The site contains resources, a collection of print materials, and downloadable public service announcements.

UNIT 4: Learning and Instruction

The Critical Thinking Community
http://criticalthinking.org

This site promotes educational reform through fair-minded critical thinking. The site also provides information and resources on critical thinking.

Education Week on the Web
http://www.edweek.org

At this page you can open archives, read special reports, keep up on current events, and access a variety of articles in educational psychology. A great deal of this material is helpful in learning and instruction.

Online Internet Institute
http://www.oii.org

A collaborative project among Internet-using educators, proponents of systemic reform, content-area experts, and teachers who desire professional growth, this site provides a learning environment for integrating the Internet into educators' individual teaching styles.

Teachers Helping Teachers
http://www.pacificnet.net/~mandel/

This site provides basic teaching tips, new teaching-methodology ideas, and forums for teachers to share their experiences. It features educational resources on the Web, with new ones added each week.

The Teachers' Network
http://www.teachers.net/

Bulletin boards, classroom projects, online forums, and Web mentors are featured on this site, as well as the book *Teachers' Guide to Cyberspace* and an online, 4-week course on how to use the Internet.

UNIT 5: Motivation and Classroom Management

Canada's Schoolnet Staff Room
http://www.schoolnet.ca/home/e/

Here is a resource and link site for anyone involved in education, including special-needs educators, teachers, parents, volunteers, and administrators.

I Love Teaching
http://www.iloveteaching.com

This site is a resource for new and veteran teachers as well as preservice teachers and student teachers. Information is broken out into various links such as "Encouraging Words," and "Classroom Management."

The Jigsaw Classroom
http://jigsaw.org

The jigsaw classroom is a cooperate learning technique that reduces racial conflict among school children, promotes better learning, improves student motivation, and increases enjoyment of the learning experience. The site includes history, implementation tips, and more.

North Central Educational Regional Laboratory
http://www.ncrel.org/sdrs/

This site provides research, policy, and best practices on issues critical to educators engaged in school improvement. A number of critical issues are covered.

Teaching Helping Teachers
http://www.pacificnet.net/~mandel/

This site is a resource tool for all teachers. It includes links to "Classroom Management," "Special Education," and more.

UNIT 6: Assessment

Awesome Library for Teachers
http://www.neat-schoolhouse.org/teacher.html

Open this page for links and access to teacher information on everything from assessments to child development topics.

Internet References

The following internet sites have been carefully researched and selected to support the articles found in this reader. The easiest way to access these selected sites is to go to our student online support site at *http://www.mhcls.com/online/*.

AE: Educational Psychology 06/07

The following sites were available at the time of publication. Visit our Web site—we update our student online support site regularly to reflect any changes.

General Sources

American Psychological Association
http://www.apa.org/topics/homepage.html

By exploring the APA's "PsychNET," you will be able to find links to an abundance of articles and other resources that are useful in the field of educational psychology.

Educational Resources Information Center
http://www.eric.ed.gov

This invaluable site provides links to all ERIC sites: clearinghouses, support components, and publishers of ERIC materials. Search the ERIC database for what is new.

National Education Association
http://www.nea.org

Something—and often quite a lot—about virtually every education-related topic can be accessed at or through this site of the 2.3-million-strong National Education Association.

National Parent Information Network/ERIC
http://npin.org

This is a clearinghouse of information on elementary and early childhood education as well as urban education. Browse through its links for information for parents.

U.S. Department of Education
http://www.ed.gov/pubs/TeachersGuide/

Government goals, projects, and grants are listed here, plus many links to teacher services and resources.

UNIT 1: Perspectives on Teaching

The Center for Innovation in Education
http://www.center.edu

The Center for Innovation in Education, self-described as a "not-for-profit, non-partisan research organization," focuses on K–12 education reform strategies. Click on its links about school privatization.

Classroom Connect
http://www.classroom.net

This is a major Web site for K–12 teachers and students, with links to schools, teachers, and resources online. It includes discussion of the use of technology in the classroom.

Education World
http://www.education-world.com

Education World provides a database of literally thousands of sites that can be searched by grade level, plus education news, lesson plans, and professional-development resources.

Goals 2000: A Progress Report
http://www.ed.gov/pubs/goals/progrpt/index.html

Open this site to survey a progress report by the U.S. Department of Education on the Goals 2000 reform initiative. It provides a sense of the goals that educators are reaching for as they look toward the future.

Teacher Talk Forum
http://education.indiana.edu/cas/tt/tthmpg.html

Visit this site for access to a variety of articles discussing life in the classroom. Clicking on the various links will lead you to electronic lesson plans, covering a variety of topic areas, from Indiana University's Center for Adolescent Studies.

UNIT 2: Development

Association for Moral Education
http://www.amenetwork.org/

AME is dedicated to fostering communication, cooperation, training, curriculum development, and research that link moral theory with educational practices. From here it is possible to connect to several sites on moral development.

Center for Adolescent Studies
http://www.indiana.edu/~cafs

This site provides information on research practices of instruction. Also included is a link to other resources.

Child Welfare League of America
http://www.cwla.org

The CWLA is the United States' oldest and largest organization devoted entirely to the well-being of vulnerable children and their families. This site provides links to information about issues related to morality and values in education.

Pediatric Behavioral Health Resources
http://www.earlychildhoodbehavioralhealth.com/index.htm

This Web site is dedicated to serving the needs of those working with young children and their families who are experiencing mental health or behavioral issues. Find information on Abuse & Neglect, Mental Health Disabilities, Classroom & Behavior Management, and Discipline Reactive Attachment Disorder.

The National Association for Child Development
http://www.nacd.org

This international organization is dedicated to helping children and adults reach their full potential. Its home page presents links to various programs, research, and resources into such topics as ADD/ADHD.

National Association of School Psychologists (NASP)
http://www.nasponline.org/index2.html

The NASP offers advice to teachers about how to help children cope with the many issues they face in today's world. The site includes tips for school personnel as well as parents.

Scholastic News Zone
http://www.scholasticnews.com

At this site, Scholastic Classroom magazines provide up-to-date information to children, teachers, and parents online to help explain timely issues.

Topic Guide

This topic guide suggests how the selections in this book relate to the subjects covered in your course. You may want to use the topics listed on these pages to search the Web more easily.

On the following pages a number of Web sites have been gathered specifically for this book. They are arranged to reflect the units of this *Annual Edition.* You can link to these sites by going to the student online support site at *http://www.mhcls.com/online/.*

ALL THE ARTICLES THAT RELATE TO EACH TOPIC ARE LISTED BELOW THE BOLD-FACED TERM.

UNIT 6
Assessment

The concepts in bold italics are developed in the article. For further expansion, please refer to the Topic Guide and the Index.

UNIT 5
Motivation and Classroom Management

The concepts in bold italics are developed in the article. For further expansion, please refer to the Topic Guide and the Index.

The concepts in bold italics are developed in the article. For further expansion, please refer to the Topic Guide and the Index.

UNIT 4
Learning and Instruction

The concepts in bold italics are developed in the article. For further expansion, please refer to the Topic Guide and the Index.

UNIT 2
Development

UNIT 3
Exceptional and Culturally Diverse Children

The concepts in bold italics are developed in the article. For further expansion, please refer to the Topic Guide and the Index.

Contents

UNIT 1
Perspectives on Teaching

The concepts in bold italics are developed in the article. For further expansion, please refer to the Topic Guide and the Index.

Preface

In publishing ANNUAL EDITIONS we recognize the enormous role played by the magazines, newspapers, and journals of the public press in providing current, first-rate educational information in a broad spectrum of interest areas. Many of these articles are appropriate for students, researchers, and professionals seeking accurate, current material to help bridge the gap between principles and theories and the real world. These articles, however, become more useful for study when those of lasting value are carefully collected, organized, indexed, and reproduced in a low-cost format, which provides easy and permanent access when the material is needed. That is the role played by ANNUAL EDITIONS.

Educational psychology is an interdisciplinary subject that includes human development, learning, intelligence, motivation, assessment, instructional strategies, and classroom management. The articles in this volume give special attention to the application of this knowledge to teaching.

Annual Editions: Educational Psychology 06/07 is divided into six units, and an overview precedes each unit, which explains how the unit articles are related to the broader issues within educational psychology.

The first unit, *Perspectives on Teaching,* presents issues that are central to the teaching role. The articles' authors provide perspectives on being an effective teacher and the issues facing teachers in the twenty-first century.

The second unit, entitled *Development*, is concerned with child and adolescent development. It covers the biological, cognitive, social, and emotional processes of development. The articles in this unit examine the issues of parenting, moral development, the social forces affecting children and adolescents, as well as the personal and social skills needed to cope with school learning and developmental tasks.

The third unit, regarding exceptional and culturally diverse students, focuses on inclusive teaching, serving students who are gifted, and multicultural education. Diverse students require an individualized approach to education. The articles in this unit review the characteristics of these children and suggest programs and strategies to meet their needs.

In the fourth unit, *Learning and Instruction*, articles about theories of learning and instructional strategies are presented. The different views of learning, such as information processing, behaviorism, and constructivist learning, represent the accumulation of years of research on the way humans change in thinking or behavior due to experience. The principles generated by each approach have important implications for teaching. These implications are addressed in a section on instructional strategies, covering such topics as instructional methods and technology, cooperative learning, and emotional learning.

The topic of motivation is perhaps one of the most important aspects of school learning. In order for teachers to be effective, they must find ways that help motivate students to learn and to behave in socially appropriate and responsible ways. How to manage children and what forms of discipline to use are issues that concern parents as well as teachers and administrators. The articles in the fifth unit, *Motivation and Classroom Management*, examine student motivation from various perspectives and discuss positive approaches to managing student behavior.

The articles in the sixth unit review assessment approaches that can be used to diagnose learning and improve instruction. The focus is on how high stakes assessment influence classroom assessment practices, student-involved assessment, formative assessment, and grading. Throughout, assessment is integrated with instruction to enhance student learning.

A feature that has been added to this edition are selected *World Wide Web* sites, which can be used to further explore the articles' topics. These sites are cross-referenced by number in the *topic guide.*

This twenty-first *Annual Editions: Educational Psychology* has been revised in order to present articles that are current and useful. Your responses to the selection and organization of materials are appreciated. Please complete and return the postage-paid article rating form on the last page of the book.

Kathleen M. Cauley

James H. McMillan

Gina Pannozzo

Editors

Editors/Advisory Board

Members of the Advisory Board are instrumental in the final selection of articles for each edition of ANNUAL EDITIONS. Their review of articles for content, level, currentness, and appropriateness provides critical direction to the editor and staff. We think that you will find their careful consideration well reflected in this volume.

FairTest
http://fairtest.org

This site is the homepage for the National Center for Fair and Open Testing. The main objective of this group is to end the misuses and flaws of standardized testing and to ensure that evaluation of students, teachers, and schools is fair, open, valid, and educationally beneficial.

Kathy Schrocks's Guide for Educators: Assessment
http://school.discovery.com/schrockguide/assess.html

Sponsored by Discovery School.com, this webpage has a comprehensive compilation of sites about classroom assessment and rubics.

Phi Delta Kappa International
http://www.pdkintl.org

This important organization publishes articles about all facets of education. You can check out the online archive of the journal, *Phi Delta Kappan,* which has resources such as articles having to do with assessment.

Washington (State) Center for the Improvement of Student Learning
http://www.k12.wa.us/

This Washington State site is designed to provide access to information about the state's new academic standards, assessments, and accountability system. Many resources and Web links are included.

We highly recommend that you review our Web site for expanded information and our other product lines. We are continually updating and adding links to our Web site in order to offer you the most usable and useful information that will support and expand the value of your Annual Editions. You can reach us at: *http://www.mhcls.com/annualeditions/.*

UNIT 1
Perspectives on Teaching

Unit Selections

1. **A Learner's Bill of Rights**, Charles H. Rathbone
2. **Teachers as Leaders**, Richard F. Bowman
3. **What Urban Students Say About Good Teaching**, Dick Corbett and Bruce Wilson
4. **Helping Children Cope With Loss, Death, and Grief: Response to a National Tragedy**, National Association of School Psychologists
5. **A National Tragedy: Helping Children Cope**, National Association of School Psychologists

Key Points to Consider

- What questions would you like to see educational psychologists study?

- Describe several characteristics of effective teachers. How is effective teaching viewed by different constituents?

- As we move into the twenty-first century, what new expectations should be placed on teachers and schools? What expectations will fade?

Student Website
www.mhcls.com/online

Internet References
Further information regarding these websites may be found in this book's preface or online.

The Center for Innovation in Education
http://www.center.edu

Classroom Connect
http://www.classroom.net

Education World
http://www.education-world.com

Goals 2000: A Progress Report
http://www.ed.gov/pubs/goals/progrpt/index.html

Teacher Talk Forum
http://education.indiana.edu/cas/tt/tthmpg.html

The teaching-learning process in school is enormously complex. Many factors influence pupil learning—such as family background, developmental level, prior knowledge, motivation, and, of course, effective teachers. Educational psychology investigates these factors to better understand and explain student learning. We begin our exploration of the teaching-learning process by considering the characteristics of effective teaching.

In the first article, the author describes the rights of the learner that all educators ought to endorse. In the next two articles, perspectives on effective teaching are presented, including the urban students' perspective.

The fifth article discusses the range of reactions that children and adolescents have experienced in response to tragedies such as the terrorism attacks of September 11, 2001 or the recent hurricanes, and suggests ways that educators can help them to cope and continue their schooling.

Educational psychology is a resource for teachers that emphasizes disciplined inquiry, a systematic and objective analysis of information, and a scientific attitude toward decision making. The field provides information for decisions that are based on quantitative and qualitative studies of learning and teaching rather than on intuition, tradition, authority, or subjective feelings. It is our hope that this aspect of educational psychology is communicated throughout these readings, and that, as a student, you will adopt the analytic, probing attitude that is part of the discipline.

While educational psychologists have helped to establish a knowledge base about teaching and learning, the unpredictable, spontaneous, evolving nature of teaching suggests that the best they will ever do is to provide concepts and skills that teachers can adapt for use in their classrooms. The issues raised in these articles about effective teaching, and the issues facing teachers in the twenty-first century, help us understand the teaching role and its demands. As you read articles in other chapters, consider the demands they place on the teaching role as well.

A Learner's Bill of Rights

In looking back at the progressive education movement, Mr. Rathbone identifies the rights of the learner that all educators should embrace and protect.

CHARLES H. RATHBONE

CELEBRATING its 35th year, the Fayerweather Street School of Cambridge, Massachusetts, is one of the few extant schools associated with the "open education" movement of the late Sixties.[1] Not only has the school flourished, but it has managed to stick to its original progressive principles. Fayerweather recently hosted a panel discussion on progressive education, which prompted me to write this article. Listening to the panelists discuss progressive education—its politics, its commitment to social responsibility, its emphasis on the individual learner as the maker of meaning—I found myself formulating a bill of rights, intellectual rights, that I imagine my progressive colleagues, past and present, might endorse.

The right to choose.

The progressive teacher acknowledges each student's right to make important decisions about what is learned, how it is learned, when, and with whom. As a British head (principal) once put it, "The basis for learning should be that the child wants to know, not that somebody else knows or that somebody says he ought to know."[2] Relevance, in other words, is to be determined by the learner herself. The pseudo-progressive teacher, while he may offer "choice time," presents only options chosen by himself and only at limited times. At worst, this teacher uses choice as a reward and withholds it as punishment.

The right to follow through.

An active learner often skips past conventional age- and grade-level expectations, ignoring the traditional boundaries of the disciplines and oblivious to the notion of social appropriateness. This means a progressive teacher cannot be skittish when the student shows an interest in sex, politics, religion, or rap. The entire world is available for exploration, with nothing predetermined, nothing censored, and certainly no one saying, "You mustn't learn that now because it is going to be taught later at some higher grade."

The right to take action.

Activity-based, developmentally appropriate learning by doing, using manipulatives, means noise, mess, and much active, often unplanned collaboration. This requires a flexible teacher prepared to share in decision making. Progressive teachers recognize that the right to take meaningful action is a logical corollary of the right to choose.

The right to remain engaged.

Full engagement of the mind is a desired educational objective. To interrupt a learner's focused attention risks teaching the student not to trust her own preferences, her own intellectual rhythms, her own mind. Though the teacher and school invariably have a program, a schedule, and a curriculum, the progressive teacher seeks also to honor the learner's interests, style, and tempo.

The right to wallow.

As David Hawkins eloquently explains in "Messing About in Science," some wallowing is worthwhile—perhaps even necessary—prior to that moment when the learner can articulate a question or define a pursuable problem.[3] When students are simply *given* all the problems, they never learn how to formulate one—a crippling intellectual restriction.

The right to err.

Answer-driven teaching and testing are anathema to those who want to foster genuine, personal learning. So long as one's self-esteem isn't on the line, error is a wonderful teacher. Moreover, as Hawkins points out in "I-Thou-It," inanimate materials provide immediate, objective, and emotionally safe feedback.[4] Progressives try to talk with students about their work without jumping to judgment. They seek to protect students against the debilitating effects of unsolicited criticism, and most would agree with British educator John Coe that all praise, to some degree, is condescending.

The right to concentrate.

So long as a student continues to learn new things, the progressive teacher trusts that this learning is likely to be worthwhile and does not worry that the student will somehow grow lopsided. Specialization often leads to deep understanding and powerful intellectual commitment. Progressives seem less anxious about curriculum "coverage," as they know that the clever teacher will find a way of merging the school's agenda with the child's. Moreover, they operate from an intrinsic optimism that the growing mind knows what it needs.

The right to take learning personally.

To the teacher who says it doesn't matter what the student writes about as long as she produces six sentences before the bell rings, the progressive teacher would respond, "What the student chooses to write is the *only* thing that matters!" Writing, inquiring mathematically, drawing, dancing, or thinking scientifically are all extensions of the self. For, as Sylvia Ashton-Warner and Elwyn Richardson remind us, it is those words nearest and dearest to the child's heart that she needs to learn, not an alphabetized list provided by a publisher.[5] The personal urge toward understanding is often linked to a drive to act upon newly acquired knowledge. A young child will simply want to share; an older student may wish to change the world. Either way, learning is both personal and social.

The right of collaboration.

So much of learning takes place within the communal group, especially in the younger years. Schools that provide opportunities for collaborative projects, for mixed-age grouping, and for cooperative performance capitalize on the social aspect of how children learn. Unfortunately, such approaches are susceptible to corruption: performance can promote competition and create a "star" culture; mixed grouping can place an enormous burden upon teachers who mistakenly think they must then teach two or three classes in one room.

The right to respect.

The unresolved problem and the unfinished thought are a very real part of learning, and they deserve the considered attention of a teacher who cares about the student's thought process as much as the end product. When there *is* a work product, it is seen as an extension of the student's thinking and therefore deserving of similar respect. Thoughtful, aesthetically pleasing displays of children's work honor that work and encourage everyone around to take it seriously. Teachers committed to progressive principles become students of their students, respectful researchers of how children think and what excites their imagination. The teachers then provision the environment accordingly.

The right of centrality.

"At the heart of the educational process lies the child," begins the *Plowden Report*.[6] When the learner's interests, needs, and intellectual style drive the educational enterprise, then scheduling, curriculum, teacher behavior, school architecture, and even budget decisions all fall, if not always into place, at least into perspective. John Dewey knew how important this was when he wrote:

> The change which is coming into our education is the shifting of the center of gravity. It is a change, a revolution, not unlike that introduced by Copernicus when the astronomical center shifted from the earth to the sun. In this case the child becomes the sun about which the appliances of education revolve; he is the center about which they are organized.[7]

THESE rights of the learner, like their constitutional analogs, are forever balanced in the real world against the greater good of the group. Naturally, there is a tension: just as free speech loses out to safety when an individual wishes to cry "Fire!" in a crowded theater, so the necessities of teachers to coordinate scheduling with specialists, of schools to maintain enrollments and not appear too wacko, and of publishers to sell their wares to nonprogressive schools all weigh against the undiluted implementation of these and other rights. Each time a compromise is made, however, I would want it to be publicly acknowledged and personally painful. I want teachers to flinch at each violation of a learner's rights. And I want the rest of us—like some shrill, educational ACLU—to point our fingers and demand that, if a right be restricted, it be with the least limiting restriction possible.

References

1. See Charles H. Rathbone and Lydia A. H. Smith, "Open Education," in James W. Guthrie, ed., *The Encyclopedia of Education*, 2nd ed. (New York: Macmillan Reference, 2003); and Lydia A. H. Smith, "'Open Education' Revisited: Promise and Problems in American Educational Reform (1967–1976)," *Teachers College Record*, vol. 99, 1997, pp. 371–415.
2. Roy Illsley, head, Battling Brook Primary School, Leicestershire, in Charles H. Rathbone, "Examining the Open Education Classroom," *School Review*, vol. 80, 1972, p. 535.
3. David Hawkins, "Messing About in Science," in *The Informed Vision: Essays on Learning and Human Nature* (New York: Agathon Press, 1974), pp. 63–75.
4. Hawkins, "I-Thou-It," in idem, pp. 48–62.
5. Sylvia Ashton-Warner, *Teacher* (New York: Bantam Books, 1963); and Elwyn S. Richardson, *In the Early World* (Wellington: New Zealand Council of Educational Research; New York: Pantheon, 1969).
6. Central Advisory Council for Education (England), *Children and Their Primary Schools* (known as the *Plowden Report*), vol. 1 (London: Her Majesty's Stationery Office, 1966).
7. John Dewey, *The School and Society*, 2nd ed. (Chicago: University of Chicago Press, 1915), p. 34.

CHARLES H. RATHBONE, *a former teacher and administrator, currently works with student teachers at Wheaton College, Norton, Mass. (e-mail: ceorathbone@comcast.net).*

Teachers as Leaders

RICHARD F. BOWMAN

In an era of dwindling resources, compelling student needs, burgeoning violence, and escalating performance expectations for students and faculty alike, classroom teachers are confronted with new demands that challenge their traditional roles as educators. The leap from a productive individual contributor, working essentially behind a closed classroom door, to a new identity of "teacher as leader" constitutes one of the most engaging transitions in teachers' professional lives. Learning how to accumulate informal power, exercise influence, and reconcile conflicting collegial interests requires nothing less than a profound identity shift for contemporary classroom teachers.

Why Lead?

Effective classroom teachers sense the positive changes they make in the intellectual, socioemotional, physical, and ethical lives of their students. This awareness gives meaning to their lives as professional educators. But to many teachers, leadership demands seem different—so different that many teachers shun the challenge of leadership opportunities altogether. Heifetz and Linsky argue, however, "when they look deep within themselves, people grapple with the challenge of leadership in order to make a positive difference in the lives of others" (2002, 74).

Ironically, when classroom teachers do embrace leadership challenges in his or her schools or school district, fellow teachers often chastise him or her for exhibiting a hunger for importance or a thirst for control. In truth, most professionals have a genuine need to feel impor-tant and have others confirm that authority (Heifetz and Linsky 2002). Moreover, many of those same professionals also feel they have a responsibility to transform their classrooms and schools for the better.

Instinctively, teachers fear taking leadership roles because the "essence of leadership lies in the capacity to deliver disturbing news and raise difficult questions in a way that moves people to take up the message without killing the messenger" (Heifetz and Linsky 2002, 74). Many teachers often are genuinely frightened to confront hard issues and embrace the sometimes painful solutions that will transform a school or a district (Heifetz and Linsky 2002). But for the teacher as leader, shrinking from these difficult challenges is ignoring one's responsibility as an effective educator. In one of his last addresses before his death, John W. Gardner, former secretary of health, education, and welfare, singled out the pathology of the comfortable indifference that affects too many reluctant leaders in organizational settings: "Who gave them permission to stand aside! I am asking you to issue a wake-up call to those people—a bugle call right in their ear" (Hesselbein 2003, 4). For teachers as leaders, learning to see is life's work. And learning to act upon what one sees is a limitless gift to others.

Teachers as Leaders

Successful teachers as leaders are adept at influencing constituencies over which they admittedly have no formal authority. These teachers as leaders are effective in doing so because they draw on diverse sources of power beyond formal authority: "expertise, appealing personal qualities, position in key networks, and visibility" (Johnson 2003, 10). Against the backdrop of increasingly interdependent professional relationships, teachers as leaders re-engage in workplace politics as they seek to create connections both inside and outside their schools. Perceptively, teachers as leaders recognize that everyday leadership dilemmas are laced with complex motives and are played out on an uneven political terrain (Badaracco 2002). However, they continue to believe that when organizations make an honest, open effort to determine the truth of a situation, the right decisions often become self-evident.

These education leaders create and sustain a developmental culture for their students and themselves by building a range of relationships with colleagues, parents, students, administrators, and community leaders. These relationships help establish and sustain systems that "reinforce a development mentality" within their individual school environments (Johnson 2003, 11). But teachers as leaders "simultaneously develop people and instill disciplined decision-making systems" in their classrooms and their schools, and they use similar techniques within their own classrooms (Belasco and Stead 1999, 15). The result is that teachers as leaders "infuse their entire decision-making process with the brutal facts of reality" (Stauffer 2003, 2).

To create and sustain such a developmental school culture, school leaders must teach not only students but also each other (Flaum 2003). Given that "almost a third of teachers leave the field within the first three years and a half before their fifth year," mentoring systems are increasingly important because they represent a supportive developmental system (Stern 2003, 13). Intensive mentoring for beginning teachers fosters productive development environments. In a school in Columbus, Ohio, for example, mentoring teachers are relieved of their teaching duties entirely to ensure they have time to focus on their caseloads of twelve to fifteen new teachers. Additionally, those mentors are "required to observe each new teacher 20 times in the classroom and schedule 10 conferences" (15). As teachers as leaders, the mentors are committed to creating success for the new teachers. This type of commitment builds relationships, increases job satisfaction, and further develops effective teaching techniques. In short, education leaders guide their colleagues by engaging in collective conversations, invoking symbolic gestures that reveal relationship, modeling professionalism beyond the label of

one's role, championing evocative ideas in both the classroom and the workplace, and being "in influence" as opposed to being "in control" (Ellinor and Gerard 1998, xxx).

Leadership: Powerful Processes

In their breakthrough study, *Geeks and Geezers,* Bennis and Thomas (2002) probed the powerful processes through which leaders emerge. They focused on the differences in leadership between those who grew up in the shadows of the Great Depression and World War II versus those who matured in the phosphorescent glow of computer screens. Their research findings suggest that true leaders of any age share a cluster of critical qualities: adaptive capacity, the ability to engage others in shared meaning, a distinctive and compelling voice, and a sense of integrity.

Adaptive capacity is "an almost magical capacity to transcend adversity, with all of its attendant stresses, and to emerge stronger than before" (Bennis and Thomas, 121). Although everyone faces obstacles, "the willingness to climb those walls and the ability to find ways to do so are the real measure of a leader" (92). For teachers as leaders, the core of adaptive capacity is the ability to grasp context. For example, at the conclusion of a recent student teaching observation, a clinical student inquired: "How well did I manage student interactions in class today?" His inquiry is significant on three levels. First, this student teacher internalized the fact that relationships are the key to classroom and organizational success. Second, he had transitioned from theory into practice. That is, he focused on managing relationships rather than individual student behavior. Third, he discovered that social context adds meaning to information. Like Saul Bellow's alter ego in the novel *Ravelstein* (2000), the clinical student was a first-class noticer.

Identifying relationships and skillfully managing them are the foundations for transitioning from teacher to leader. Related research by Bennis and Nanus (1997) suggests that teachers as leaders exhibit four common abilities:

Management of Attention
In Shakespeare's *Henry IV, Part I*, the Welsh seer, Glendower, boasts to Hotspur: "I can call the spirits from the vasty deep" (Knight 1968, 79-80). In response, Hotspur deflates Glendower with, "Why so can I or so can any man; But will they come when you do call them?" Like spirits, students return from the "vasty

deep" when the call is enticing enough. Teachers as leaders must devise and maintain an atmosphere in which students can succeed. Their calls must define purpose—a purpose that strikes a chord with students.

Human beings have an innate need to hear and tell stories because those stories provide a lens through which they can view things that happen to them. Stories ignite self-awareness and engender self-confidence. Teachers as leaders recognize the power of stories and often use them in the classroom to focus attention and frame purpose. Stories, metaphors, analogies, and evocative questions capture interest and sustain collective engagement.

Management of Meaning

At a fundamental level, learning, or meaning making, is a social activity. A school or classroom's culture is defined by the "emergence of shared meanings" (Block 1998, 89). Teachers who are adept at turning information into a shared experience lead in the classroom. This transformation is important because "… people change out of experience. They don't change out of words or techniques or manipulation of policies" (Ellinor and Gerard 1998, xi). Thus, effective teachers as leaders find ways to make meaning personal for students by creating a shared experience to which students can relate.

Management of Trust

Trust has two enemies: "bad character and poor information" (Prusak 2003, 12). Leadership is about character. Transparency and openness of action create trust in organizational settings. However, although trust is built over long stretches of time, it is often lost through a single thoughtless act. Teachers as leaders must always remember that "in a professional relationship, never be the cause of a surprise, because doing so inevitably erodes trust." Trust is inextricably linked to honesty and sincerity.

Management of Self

Teachers as leaders need to form a strong identity. Just as writers must find their voices, so too must classroom teachers. Teachers as leaders "must find an individual and persuasive voice, an authentic version of themselves that engages and recruits others. As long-time Girl Scouts of America CEO Frances Hesselbein observed, 'You lead by voice'" (Bennis and Thomas 2002, 137).

In their interactions with students, colleagues, and community, teachers as leaders must model integrity. In contrast, teachers with weak self-awareness or an exaggerated sense of entitlement, create difficulties for themselves because others will perceive their indulgences as neither right nor fair. Teachers who develop an authentic identity founded on genuine principles will become successful leaders.

Summary

The classic view of leadership is captured in the image of the leader of a band. The bandleader, as boss, barks commands, and followers march lock step. More recently, the role of a leader has been reflected in the representation of the conductor of a contemporary orchestra. Although many renowned orchestra leaders are still considered exceedingly autocratic, "they do not see themselves as the boss. They see themselves as the servant of the score" (Drucker 1996, 16). Thus, their authority rests on their ability to communicate with specialists in the orchestra. Today, the role of teacher as leader mirrors the playful novelty of a jazz band, in which leadership flows freely from player to player, refrain to refrain, inspiring others to new levels of achievement, service, and significance. In improvisational dialogue, teachers as leaders search for ways to collaboratively create a story that "wants to be born." Together, they sense that "an idea shared becomes a movement toward inevitable progress. An idea hoarded becomes filled with the stain of personal ambition and idiosyncratic desire" (Flaum 2003, 7).

In short, teachers as leaders do not inflate the importance of their leadership efforts or the likelihood of their success. Unlike heroic leaders who single-handedly save the world, teachers as leaders seek to lead from the middle-inconspicuously and without casualties. (Badaracco 2002).

Key words: developmental culture, leadership, management skills

REFERENCES

Badaracco, J. 2002. *Leading quietly*. Boston: Harvard Business School Press.

Belasco, J., and J. Stead. 1999. The five jobs of leaders. *Leader to Leader* 14: 15-17.

Bellow, S. 2000. *Ravelstein*. New York: Penguin Putnam.

Bennis, W., and B. Nanus. 1997. *Leaders: Strategies for taking charge*. 2nd ed. New York: Harper Business.

Bennis, W., and R. Thomas. 2002. *Geeks and geezers: How era, values, and defining moments shape leaders*. Boston: Harvard Business School Press.

Block, P. 1998. From leadership to citizenship. In *Insights on Leadership*, ed. L. C. Spears, 87-95. New York: John Wiley and Sons.

Drucker, P. 1996. The shape of things to come. *Leader to Leader* (Premier Issue): 12-18.

Ellinor, L., and G. Gerard. 1998. *Dialogue*. New York: John Wiley and Sons.

Etzioni, A. 2004. How character is built. *Kappa Delta Pi Record* 40 (2): 54-57.

Flaum, S. 2003. When ideas lead, people follow. *Leader to Leader* 30: 7-12.

Heifetz, R., and M. Linsky. 2002. A survival guide for leaders. *Harvard Business Review* 80 (6): 65-74.

Hesselbein, F. 2003. A bugle call right in the ear. *Leader to Leader* 30: 4-6.

Johnson, L. K. 2003. Accelerating the new manager's start. *Harvard Management Update* 8, no. 9 (September): 10-11.

Knight, C., ed. 1968. *Comedies, histories, tragedies, and poems of William Shakespeare*. 2nd ed. Vol. V. New York: AMS Press.

Mayer, J. D. 2004. Be realistic. *Harvard Business Review* 82 (1): 28.

Prusak, L., 2003. A matter of trust. *Trends and Ideas* 1, no. 1 (Fall): 11-12.

Stauffer, D. 2003. How to win the buy-in: Setting the stage for change. *Harvard Management Update* 8, no. 6 (June): 1-3.

Stern, S. 2003. The great escape. *Christian Science Monitor*, October 7: 13, 15.

Richard F. Bowman is a professor of educational foundations at the College of Education at Winona State University in Winona, Minnesota.

From *The Clearing House,* Vol. 77, No. 5, May/June 2004, pp. 187-189. Reprinted by permission of the Helen Dwight Reid Educational Foundation. Published by Heldref Publications, 1319, Eighteenth St., NW, Washington, DC 20036-1802. Copyright © 2004.

What Urban Students Say About
Good Teaching

Interviews with these inner-city adolescents show that they want to learn and have a vision of the kind of teacher who can help them excel.

Dick Corbett and Bruce Wilson

What can schools do to encourage students to care more about learning? Make sure that teachers act in ways that demonstrate how much *they* care! At least, that would be the answer of nearly 400 students we interviewed from inner-city, low-income middle and high schools. In fact, the students never wavered in identifying their teachers as the main factor determining how much they learned, and they spoke with one voice when describing good teachers. Good teachers

- Made sure that students did their work.
- Controlled the classroom.
- Were willing to help students whenever and however the students wanted help.
- Explained assignments and content clearly.
- Varied the classroom routine.
- Took the time to get to know the students and their circumstances.

Significantly, students did not confuse teachers' personal qualities with their professional ones. Interviewees described "mean" good teachers and "mean" bad teachers; "funny" good teachers and "funny" bad teachers; and "boring" good teachers and "boring" bad teachers. If a teacher had the six qualities that students identified as those of a good teacher, then demeanor, sense of humor, and charisma—as well as any other personal characteristic—were unimportant.

Interviewing Students About Reform Efforts

In an effort to include students' voices in education reform efforts being implemented in Philadelphia, we interviewed inner-city middle schoolers annually for three years while their schools were undergoing a districtwide reform known as Children Achieving. The adolescents,

selected to reflect a range of attendance and achievement patterns, attended six of the lowest-income schools in the city. Each year, we asked them to talk about their daily instructional routines, the classes in which they learned the most and least (and behaved the best and worst), how they preferred to learn and which classes accommodated this preference, what they thought good teaching was, and where in their schedules they encountered it. We hoped to discover through these conversations whether school reforms had actually changed the educational experiences of students.

We also followed many of the same students into high school. In a serendipitous occurrence, several of the middle schools fed into high schools that had adopted the Johns Hopkins Talent Development Model. Because of this fortunate timing, we were able to get students' descriptions of their high school experiences before and during this reform.[1]

Throughout the years that the students talked with us, they held fast to their view that good teaching was central to the quality of their schooling experiences.

Throughout the years that the students talked with us, they held fast to their view that good teaching was central to the quality of their schooling experiences. Moreover, when they talked about the value of education reforms (specifically, the Talent Development Model's block schedule), they judged such reforms on the basis of their effects on teacher behavior that aided student learning.

What Is a Good Teacher?

Students repeatedly invoked the six qualities of good teaching in answering almost any question we asked. Students talked approvingly about "strict" teachers—those who pushed students to complete their assignments and maintained an orderly classroom. Students added that good teachers were willing to help, explained assignments and content clearly, varied classroom activities, and tried to understand students.

Good Teachers Push Students

These urban students admitted that their default response to most assignments was to ignore them, which understandably gave the impression that they cared little about learning. Nevertheless, students liked teachers who successfully combated this habit. As two students explained (in their words and syntax),

> I like the ones that don't allow excuses. It's my turn to get an education. I need to have someone to tell me when I'm tired and don't feel like doing the work that I should do it anyway.

> If they don't keep after you, you'll slide and never do the work. You just won't learn nothing if they don't stay on you.

Teachers "nagged" students in many ways—by consistently checking homework, offering quiet individual reminders, giving rewards, and calling parents. As one student boasted, "He keeps pressing me until I get it right."

Good Teachers Maintain Order

According to students, their teachers varied tremendously in how well they were able to control students, and the ones who could not maintain control bothered them a lot. As one student succinctly explained,

> The kids don't do the work. The teacher is hollering and screaming, "Do your work and sit down!" This makes the ones that want to learn go slower. It makes your grade sink down. It just messes it up for you. The teacher is trying to handle everybody and can't.

Another student pointed out the difference between strict and not-so-strict teachers:

> Teachers that just let you do what you want, they don't get a point across. Strict teachers get the point across.

And, as was typical of almost everything students had to say about good teaching, everything came back to whether they learned:

> I want a teacher strict enough for me to learn.

Good Teachers Are Willing to Help

Just as research has demonstrated that students have different learning styles, the students we interviewed had different helping styles. Some wanted help after school, some during class, some individually, some through working with peers, some through whole-class question-and-answer sessions, and some without ever having to acknowledge to anyone that they needed it. Being omnisciently adept at knowing how and when to offer help was an indelible part of being a good teacher.

> A good teacher takes time out to see if all the kids have what they're talking about and cares about how they're doing and will see if they need help.

Teachers who offered generous help often hooked students who previously had been reluctant classroom participants into working.

> One boy in the class, he do all his work now. If it wasn't for my teacher, he wouldn't do nothing. At the beginning of the year, he don't do nothing; now he does…. [It's] 'cause the teacher took time out to help him and talk to him.

Teacher help also broke the cycle of failure that we heard about from so many students. One of them explained this phenomenon and the role of teacher assistance in ameliorating it:

> Say, for instance, I didn't come to school. The next day I came in, they went over something new. There wouldn't be like time to show me what they did [the previous day]. And the teacher wouldn't make sure I understood. So, I start moving with them, but I be behind. They should have given extra help…. They could pull me to the side and ask me if I want to do it. Then it would be my choice.

Good Teachers Explain Until Everyone Understands

Many students complained about teachers who moved too fast through material or explained it only once and in one way. They much preferred to have teachers who stayed on an assignment until everyone understood, who offered multiple and repeated explanations, and who, as one student said, "feed it into our head real good; they do it step-by-step and they break it down."

Students seemed most disturbed by teachers who allowed discipline problems to affect the quality of their explanations. For example, many students referred to teachers who would say a variant of "I've already told you this; you should have listened the first time" in response to repeated requests for clarification. Although the teachers may have been justified in feeling frustrated at the lack of attention that prompted the requests, to students this phrase meant "I refuse to teach you."

By contrast, students' faces brightened considerably when they were able to say something like the following:

> The teachers are real at ease. They take the time, you know, go step-by-step. We learn it more. It seems like they got the time to explain it all. We don't have to leave anyone behind.

Good Teachers Vary Classroom Activities

Different activities appealed to different students. Students' preferences included working in groups, listening to the teacher talk, reading from a book, doing worksheets, participating in whole-class discussions, and doing hands-on activities. However, students agreed that learning was the primary reason for liking a certain approach, as the following three statements illustrate:

> I prefer working in groups. You have more fun and you learn at the same time. You learn quickly. So, you have fun and you do the work.

> My favorite subject is math because she made our work into a game and I caught on real fast doing it that way.

> I prefer to work by myself because most people don't read on the same level. I don't like to listen to others read. I might be ahead or behind where they are, whatever the case may be.

Students appreciated teachers who made the effort to see beyond students' behavior and understand who they really were.

Good Teachers Try to Understand Students

Students applauded teachers who did more than just teach content to them. They especially appreciated teachers who made the effort to see beyond students' behavior and understand who they really were. One student explained:

> I heard teachers talking about people, saying "Those kids can't do nothing." Kids want teachers who believe in them.

Students particularly valued teachers who recognized the possibility that students' misbehavior was not automatically targeted at the teachers.

> Sometimes a teacher don't understand what people go through. They need to have compassion. A teacher who can relate to students will know when something's going on with them. If like the student don't do work or don't under-

stand, the teacher will spend a lot of time with them.

Good Teaching = More Learning

Students clearly expressed the belief that good teaching was important because it made them learn better. Understand that when they said "better," students sometimes meant that they learned "something." Unfortunately, it was not unusual for these students to spend a semester or an entire year in a core subject in which they learned nothing, most often because they experienced a revolving door of substitutes or a new teacher who was not equipped to meet the challenges of an urban environment. Indeed, one student's advice to an early-career teacher was, "She should quit this job—it's too hard for her."

Students defined learning "better" as "getting the work right," "understanding something that a teacher already tried to teach," and "getting stuff we haven't had before." Despite the lack of definitional sophistication, students voiced no doubt about doing better in some teachers' classrooms than in others.

And because they cared about learning, it mattered greatly to students how often they encountered good teachers. Nearly every student in all six Philadelphia middle schools could identify a teacher whom they considered to be good; and nearly every one could describe a classroom situation where little learning, if any, took place.

Students' Views on School Reforms

Because good teachers were central in determining students' school experiences, these same students judged the changes that adults implemented in their schools on the basis of whether the reforms increased the number of good teachers. Students were keenly adept at evaluating the effects of significant instructional changes that had been made in their schools in terms of whether these changes promoted better teaching and, by extension, learning.

In that respect, therefore, the students tended to adopt the kind of single-minded, uncomplicated focus on improved school and classroom practices that the experts frequently urge education stakeholders to use when making strategic decisions. An illustration of how students perceived the value of one such change occurred after our original middle school students had moved on to two high schools that adopted a block schedule.

The Block Schedule

The students we had talked to in the middle school project were in the 10th grade when their schools became Talent Development High Schools and switched all of the grades from the traditional seven-period day to a block schedule in which students took four classes each semester, with 80–90 minutes devoted to each class. They saw a difference between their 9th grade and 10th grade experiences. Time seemed to be the theme that ran through many of their comparisons:

> Teachers last year wouldn't take as much time to help you.

> Now the teachers take time with you, and let you know what's got to be done.

Students predictably complained about the length of the classes with this new arrangement. Class got boring, they said—they had to sit too long, and sometimes the teachers talked forever. However, when we asked whether they preferred seven periods to four, 107 out of 148 9th and 10th graders said that they wanted the latter. Of the 41 who did not, six were neutral, and not a single student said that he or she learned better in the shorter classes. Even as they rolled their eyes about the tedium of having to be with one teacher for so long, the students explained their almost reluctant endorsements of the block schedule:

> There is more time for the teachers to help you. They can explain the work. We get to also work in groups and if I don't understand, someone else can help me.

> You learn more with just four classes because the teacher has a longer time to explain it right.

> We get to do more things. We get to work by ourselves, we get to work together, and we get to go over the work more.

> I become more focused. With more classes, oh God, it drove me crazy.

> You can build a relationship with the teacher. We can have more one-on-one interaction.

Readily available help… good explanations… variety… focused attention… closer student-teacher relationships—the block schedule, students felt, had almost single-handedly created a school full of good teachers! In spite of students' complaints about the "boredom" of longer class periods, the implementation of block scheduling had changed teachers' behaviors to correspond more closely with students' notions of good teaching—and that result alone was enough reason for students to support the reform.

Students Do Care

The block schedule has been the subject of intensive debates. Adults argue passionately, relying on research that cannot conclusively bolster either side. Our students exhibited much more single-mindedness in deciding that they supported this change. Unlike adults, they did not raise financial, political, occupational, legal, bureaucratic, or philosophical reasons why something that promoted student learning was nevertheless inadvisable. All that the Philadelphia high school students knew was that with the advent of longer classes, their teachers had changed. Instead of telling the students something once and leaving it up to them to choose to work or not, the teachers prodded, aided, and clarified more. And, over time, students noticed the true benefit of this development—they learned better.

When adults ask what they can do to make students care more about learning, their question implies that students do not care enough now. Adults, quite understandably, allow scowls, yawns, misbehavior, disrespect, and refusal to work to persuade them that apathy is rampant.

But our interviews with students in high-poverty schools suggest that these adolescents do care. The students we talked with cared so deeply about having good teachers that they wholeheartedly embraced a reform about which many adults are deeply divided. Students simply wanted good teachers because such teachers made them learn—often in spite of themselves.

Do students care about learning? Perhaps the question we should be asking is What can schools do to support and reinforce adult actions that demonstrate to students that the adults care as much about learning as the students do? The students' definitions of good teaching provide an excellent starting point for identifying just what those actions might look like.

Note

1. Our discussions with middle schoolers are reported in detail in *Listening to Urban Students: School Reform and the Teachers They Want* (Wilson & Corbett, 2001, State University of New York Press). Additional material from the project that followed students to high school is available in *Students' Perspectives on the Ninth Grade Academy of the Talent Development High Schools in Philadelphia: 1999–2000* (Corbett & Wilson, 2000, Philadelphia Education Fund).

Dick Corbett (610-408-9206) and **Bruce Wilson** (856-662-6424) are independent education researchers. Their most recent book (with coauthor Belinda Williams) is *Effort and Excellence in Urban Classrooms: Expecting and Getting Success with All Students* (Teachers College Press, 2002).

From *Educational Leadership*, September 2002, pp. 18-22. Reprinted with permission of the Association for Supervision and Curriculum Development.

Helping Children Cope With Loss, Death, and Grief: Response to a National Tragedy

The security and safety that was a hallmark of our American society was shattered by the events of September 11th. Never before in our nation's history have so many lives been lost in a single day. Communities are impacted by multiple losses that stretch their capacities to cope. It is difficult to predict how students, adults and schools will be able to deal with the harsh realities of life in the coming weeks, months and years. Children who have experienced the loss of one or both parents, siblings, other relatives, friends, or neighbors are now suffering from profound grief.How can caring adults help these children deal with loss of this magnitude? How can we begin to understand and respond to the depths of their suffering? One thing we do know is that this will be an extremely difficult and painful task. Children and adolescents will need all the support they can get and they will require a long time to recover. Life may not be the same for anyone in this country, but those youngsters who have sustained personal losses may require significant assistance from trained, caring adults.

Expressions of Grief

Talking to children about death must be geared to their developmental level and their capacity to understand the related facts of the situation. Children will be aware of the reactions of significant adults as they interpret and react to information about death and tragedy. The range of reactions that children display in response to the death of significant others may include:

- *Emotional shock* and at times an apparent lack of feelings, which serve to help the child detach from the pain of the moment;
- *Regressive (immature) behaviors*, such as needing to be rocked or held, difficulty separating from parents or significant others, needing to sleep in parent's bed or an apparent difficulty completing tasks well within the child's ability level;

- *Explosive emotions and acting out behavior* that reflect the child's internal feelings of anger, terror, frustration and helplessness. Acting out may reflect insecurity and a way to seek control over a situation for which they have little or no control;
- **Asking the same questions over and over**, not because they do not understand the facts, but rather because the information is so hard to believe or accept. Repeated questions can help listeners determine if the child is responding to misinformation or the real trauma of the event.

Helping Children Cope

The following tips will help teachers and parents support children who have experienced the loss of parents or loved ones. Some of these recommendations come from Dr. Alan Wolfelt, Director of the Center for Loss and Life Transition in Fort Collins, Colorado.

- *Allow children to be the teachers about their grief experiences*: Give children the opportunity to tell their story and be a good listener.
- *Don't assume that every child in a certain age group understands death in the same way or with the same feelings*: All children are different and their view of the world is unique and shaped by different experiences. (Developmental information is provided below.)
- *Grieving is a process, not an event*: Parents and schools need to allow adequate time for each child to grieve in the manner that works for that child. Pressing children to resume "normal" activities without the chance to deal with their emotional pain may prompt additional problems or negative reactions.
- *Don't lie or tell half-truths to children about the tragic event*: Children are often bright and sensitive. They will see through false infor-

mation and wonder why you do not trust them with the truth. Lies do not help the child through the healing process or help develop effective coping strategies for life's future tragedies or losses.

- *Help all children, regardless of age, to understand loss and death*: Give the child information at the level that he/she can understand. Allow the child to guide adults as to the need for more information or clarification of the information presented. Loss and death are both part of the cycle of life that children need to understand.
- *Encourage children to ask questions about loss and death*: Adults need to be less anxious about not knowing all the answers. Treat questions with respect and a willingness to help the child find his or her own answers.
- *Don't assume that children always grieve in an orderly or predictable way*: We all grieve in different ways and there is no one "correct" way for people to move through the grieving process.
- *Let children know that you really want to understand what they are feeling or what they need*: Sometimes children are upset but they cannot tell you what will be helpful. Giving them the time and encouragement to share their feelings with you may enable them to sort out their feelings.
- *Children will need long-lasting support*: The more losses the child or adolescent suffered, the more difficult it will be to recover. This is especially true if they lost a parent who was their major source of support. Try to develop multiple supports for children who suffered significant losses.
- *Keep in mind that grief work is hard*: It is hard work for adults and hard for children as well.
- *Understand that grief work is complicated*: When death results from a terrorist act, this brings forth many issues that are difficult, if not impossible, to comprehend. Grieving will also be complicated by a need for vengeance or justice and by the lack of resolution of the current situation: Perpetrators may still be at large and our nation is at war. The sudden nature of death and the fact that many individuals were considered missing rather than dead further complicates the grieving process.
- *Be aware of your own need to grieve*: Focusing on the children in your care is important, but not at the expense of your emotional needs. Adults who have lost a loved one will be far more able to help children work through their grief if they get help themselves. For some

families, it may be important to seek family grief counseling, as well as individual sources of support.

Developmental Phases in Understanding Death

It is important to recognize that all children are unique in their understanding of death and dying. This understanding depends on their developmental level, cognitive skills, personality characteristics, religious or spiritual beliefs, teachings by parents and significant others, input from the media, and previous experiences with death. Nonetheless, there are some general considerations that will be helpful in understanding how children and adolescents experience and deal with death.

- *Infants and Toddlers*: The youngest children may perceive that adults are sad, but have no real understanding of the meaning or significance of death.
- *Preschoolers*: Young children may deny death as a formal event and may see death as reversible. They may interpret death as a separation, not a permanent condition. Preschool and even early elementary children may link certain events and magical thinking with the causes of death. As a result of the World Trade Center disaster, some children may imagine that going into tall buildings may cause someone's death.
- *Early Elementary School*: Children at this age (approximately 5–9) start to comprehend the finality of death. They begin to understand that certain circumstances may result in death. They can see that, if large planes crash into buildings, people in the planes and buildings will be killed. However, they may over-generalize, particularly at ages 5–6—if jet planes don't fly, then people don't die. At this age, death is perceived as something that happens to others, not to oneself or one's family.
- *Middle School*: Children at this level have the cognitive understanding to comprehend death as a final event that results in the cessation of all bodily functions. They may not fully grasp the abstract concepts discussed by adults or on the TV news but are likely to be guided in their thinking by a concrete understanding of justice. They may experience a variety of feelings and emotions, and their expressions may include acting out or self-injurious behaviors as a means of coping with their anger, vengeance and despair.
- *High School*: Most teens will fully grasp the meaning of death in circumstances such as the

World Trade Center or Pentagon disasters. They may seek out friends and family for comfort or they may withdraw to deal with their grief. Teens (as well as some younger children) with a history of depression, suicidal behavior and chemical dependency are at particular risk for prolonged and serious grief reactions and may need more careful attention from home and school during these difficult times.

Tips for Children and Teens with Grieving Friends and Classmates

Many children and teens have been indirectly impacted by the terrorists' attacks. They have learned of the deaths of people close to their friends and classmates—parents, siblings, other relatives and neighbors. Particularly in areas near the World Trade Center or Pentagon, it is not unusual to find several children in a given classroom who lost a family member—or even multiple family members. Additionally, all over the country, children have been impacted by the death of a family member at either the attack site or on board one of the four hijacked planes. Seeing their friends try to cope with such loss may scare or upset children who have had little or no experience with death and grieving. Some suggestions teachers and parents can provide to children and youth to deal with this "secondary" loss:

- Particularly with younger children, it will be important to help clarify their understanding of death. See tips above under "helping children cope."
- Seeing their classmates' reactions to loss may bring about some fears of losing their own parents or siblings. Children need reassurance from caretakers and teachers that their own families are safe. For children who have experienced their own loss (previous death of a parent, grandparent, sibling), observing the grief of a friend can bring back painful memories. These children are at greater risk for developing more serious stress reactions and should be given extra support as needed.
- Children (and many adults) need help in communicating condolence or comfort messages. Provide children with age-appropriate guidance for supporting their peers. Help them decide what to say (e.g., "Steve, I am so sorry about your father. I know you will miss him very much. Let me know if I can help you with your paper route…") and what to expect (see "expressions of grief" above).

- Help children anticipate some changes in friends' behavior. It is important that children understand that their grieving friends may act differently, may withdraw from their friends for a while, might seem angry or very sad, etc., but that this does not mean a lasting change in their relationship.
- Explain to children that their "regular" friendship may be an important source of support for friends and classmates. Even normal social activities such as inviting a friend over to play, going to the park, playing sports, watching a movie, or a trip to the mall may offer a much needed distraction and sense of connection and normalcy.
- Children need to have some options for providing support—it will help them deal with their fears and concerns if they have some concrete actions that they can take to help. Suggest making cards, drawings, helping with chores or homework, etc. Older teens might offer to help the family with some shopping, cleaning, errands, etc., or with babysitting for younger children.
- Encourage children who are worried about a friend to talk to a caring adult. This can help alleviate their own concern or potential sense of responsibility for making their friend feel better. Children may also share important information about a friend who is at risk of more serious grief reactions.
- Parents and teachers need to be alert to children in their care who may be reacting to a friend's loss of a loved one. These children will need some extra support to help them deal with the sense of frustration and helplessness that many people are feeling at this time.

Resources for Grieving and Traumatized Children

At times of severe stress, such as the trauma of the terrorist attacks on our country, both children and adults need extra support. Children closest to this tragedy may very well experience the most dramatic feelings of fear, anxiety and loss. They may have personally lost a loved one or know of friends and schoolmates who have been devastated by these treacherous acts. Adults need to carefully observe these children for signs of traumatic stress, depression or even suicidal thinking, and seek professional help when necessary.

Resources to help you identify symptoms of severe stress and grief reactions are available at the National Association of School Psychologist's website—*www.nasponline.org*. See also:

For Caregivers

Deaton, R.L. & Berkan, W.A. (1995). *Planning and managing death issues in the schools: A handbook.* Westport, CT: Greenwood Publishing Group.

Mister Rogers Website: *www.misterrogers.org* (see booklet on Grieving for children 4–10 years)

Webb, N.B. (1993). *Helping bereaved children: A handbook for practitioners.* New York: Guilford Press.

Wolfelt, A. (1983). *Helping children cope with grief.* Bristol, PA: Accelerated Development.

Wolfelt, A. (1997). *Healing the bereaved child: Grief gardening, growth through grief and other touchstones for caregivers.* Ft. Collins, CO: Companion.

Worden, J.W. (1996). *Children and grief: When a parent dies.* New York: Guilford Press

For Children:

Gootman, M.E. (1994). *When a friend dies: A book for teens about grieving and healing.* Minneapolis: Free Spirit Publishing.

Greenlee, S. (1992). *When someone dies.* Atlanta: Peachtree Publishing. (Ages 9–12).

Wolfelt, A.(2001). *Healing your grieving heart for kids.* Ft. Collins, CO: Companion.

A National Tragedy: Helping Children Cope

Tips for Parents and Teachers

Whenever a national tragedy occurs, such as terrorist attacks or natural disasters, children, like many people, may be confused or frightened. Most likely they will look to adults for information and guidance on how to react. Parents and school personnel can help children cope first and foremost by establishing a sense of safety and security. As more information becomes available, adults can continue to help children work through their emotions and perhaps even use the process as learning experience.

All Adults Should:

1. **Model calm and control**. Children take their emotional cues from the significant adults in their lives. Avoid appearing anxious or frightened.

2. **Reassure children that they are safe** and (if true) so are the other important adults in their lives. Depending on the situation, point out factors that help insure their immediate safety and that of their community.

3. **Remind them that trustworthy people are in charge**. Explain that the government emergency workers, police, firefighters, doctors, and the military are helping people who are hurt and are working to ensure that no further tragedies occur.

4. **Let children know that it is okay to feel upset**. Explain that all feelings are okay when a tragedy like this occurs. Let children talk about their feelings and help put them into perspective. Even anger is okay, but children may need help and patience from adults to assist them in expressing these feelings appropriately.

5. **Observe children's emotional state**. Depending on their age, children may not express their concerns verbally. Changes in behavior, appetite, and sleep patterns can also indicate a child's level of grief, anxiety or discomfort. Children will express their emotions differently. There is no right or wrong way to feel or express grief.

6. **Look for children at greater risk**. Children who have had a past traumatic experience or personal loss, suffer from depression or other mental illness, or with special needs may be at greater risk for severe reactions than others. Be particularly observant for those who may be at risk of suicide. Seek the help of mental health professional if you are at all concerned.

7. **Tell children the truth**. Don't try to pretend the event has not occurred or that it is not serious. Children are smart. They will be more worried if they think you are too afraid to tell them what is happening.

8. **Stick to the facts**. Don't embellish or speculate about what has happened and what might happen. Don't dwell on the scale or scope of the tragedy, particularly with young children.

9. **Keep your explanations developmentally appropriate**. *Early elementary school* children need brief, simple information that should be balanced with reassurances that the daily structures of their lives will not change. *Upper elementary and early middle school* children will be more vocal in asking questions about whether they truly are safe and what is being done at their school. They may need assistance separating reality from fantasy. *Upper middle school and high school* students will have strong and varying opinions about the causes of violence in schools and society. They will share concrete suggestions about how to make school safer and how to prevent tragedies in society. They will be more committed to doing something to help the victims and affected community. *For all children, encourage them to verbalize their thoughts and feelings. Be a good listener!*

10. **Monitor Your Own Stress Level.** Don't ignore your own feelings of anxiety, grief, and anger. Talking to friends, family members, religious leaders, and mental health counselors can help. It is okay to let your children know that you are sad, but that you believe things will get better. You will be better able to support your children if you can express your own emotions in a productive manner. Get appropriate sleep, nutrition, and exercise.

What Parents Can Do

1. **Focus on your children over the next week following the tragedy**. Tell them you love them and everything will be okay. Try to help them understand what has happened, keeping in mind their developmental level.

2. **Make time to talk with your children**. Remember if you do not talk to your children about this incident someone else will. Take some time and determine what you wish to say.

3. **Stay close to your children**. Your physical presence will reassure them and give you the opportunity to monitor their reaction. Many children will want actual physical contact. Give plenty of hugs. Let them sit close to you, and make sure to take extra time at bedtime to cuddle and to reassure them that they are loved and safe.

4. **Limit your child's television viewing of these events**. If they must watch, watch with them for a brief time; then turn the set off. Don't sit mesmerized re-watching the same events over and over again.

5. **Maintain a "normal" routine**. To the extent possible stick to your family's normal routine for dinner, homework, chores, bedtime, etc., *but don't be inflexible*. Children may have a hard time concentrating on schoolwork or falling asleep at night.

6. **Spend extra time reading or playing quiet games with your children before bed**. These activities are calming, foster a sense of closeness and security, and reinforce a sense of normalcy. Spend more time tucking them in. Let them sleep with a light on if they ask for it.

7. **Safeguard your children's physical health**. Stress can take a physical toll on children as well as adults. Make sure your children get appropriate sleep, exercise, and nutrition.

8. **Consider praying or thinking hopeful thoughts for the victims and their families**. It may be a good time to take your children to your house of worship, write a poem, or draw a picture to help your child express their feelings and feel that they are somehow supporting the victims and their families.

9. **Find out what resources your school has in place to help children cope**. Most schools are likely to be open and often are a good place for children to regain a sense of normalcy. Being with their friends and teachers can help. Schools should also have a plan for making counseling available to children and adults who need it.

What Schools Can Do

1. **Assure children that they are safe** and that schools are well prepared to take care of all children at all times.

2. **Maintain structure and stability within the schools**. It would be best, however, not to have tests or major projects within the next few days.

3. **Have a plan for the first few days back at school**. Include school psychologists, counselors, and crisis team members in planning the school's response.

4. **Provide teachers and parents with information** about what to say and do for children in school and at home.

5. **Have teachers provide information directly to their students**, not during the public address announcements.

6. **Have school psychologists and counselors available** to talk to student and staff who may need or want extra support.

7. **Be aware of students who may have recently experienced a personal tragedy** or a have personal connection to victims or their families. Even a child who has been to visit the Pentagon or the World Trade Center may feel a personal loss. Provide these students extra support and leniency if necessary.

8. **Know what community resources are available** for children who may need extra counseling. School psychologists can be very helpful in directing families to the right community resources.

9. **Allow time for age appropriate classroom discussion and activities**. Do not expect teachers to provide all of the answers. They should ask questions and guide the discussion, but not dominate it. Other activities can include art and writing projects, play acting, and physical games.

10. **Be careful not to stereotype people or countries that might be home to the terrorists**. Children can easily generalize negative statements and develop prejudice. Talk about tolerance and justice versus vengeance. *Stop any bullying or teasing of students immediately*.

11. **Refer children who exhibit extreme anxiety, fear or anger to mental health counselors** in the school. Inform their parents.

12. **Provide an outlet for students' desire to help**. Consider making get well cards or sending letters to the families and survivors of the tragedy, or writing thank you letters to doctors, nurses, and other health care professionals as well as emergency rescue workers, firefighters and police.

13. **Monitor or restrict viewing scenes** of this horrendous event as well as the aftermath.

For information on helping children and youth with this crisis, contact NASP at (301) 657-0270 or visit NASP's website at www.nasponline.org..

UNIT 2
Development

Unit Selections

Key Points to Consider

- How do biology and environment interact to produce an intelligent human being?

- Why is an accurate perception of self important to children's self-esteem?

- How can schools and teachers provide an environment that is conducive to adolescent development?

Student Website

www.mhcls.com/online

Internet References

Further information regarding these websites may be found in this book's preface or online.

Association for Moral Education
http://www.amenetwork.org/

Center for Adolescent Studies
http://www.indiana.edu/~cafs

Child Welfare League of America
http://www.cwla.org

Pediatric Behavioral Health Resources
http://www.earlychildhoodbehavioralhealth.com/index.htm

The National Association for Child Development
http://www.nacd.org

National Association of School Psychologists (NASP)
http://www.nasponline.org/index2.html

Scholastic News Zone
http://www.scholasticnews.com

The study of human development provides us with knowledge of how children and adolescents mature and learn within the family, community, and school environments. Educational psychology focuses on description and explanation of the developmental processes that make it possible for children to become intelligent and socially competent adults. Psychologists and educators are presently studying the idea that biology as well as the environment influence cognitive, personal, social, and emotional development and involve predictable patterns of behavior.

The perceptions and thoughts that young children have about the world are often quite different when compared to adolescents and adults. That is, children may think about moral and social issues in a unique way. Children need to acquire cognitive, moral, and social skills in order to interact effectively with parents, teachers, and peers. Human development encompasses all of the above skills and reflects the child's intelligent adaptation to the environment.

Today the cognitive, moral, social, and emotional development of children takes place in a rapidly changing society. A child must develop positive conceptions of self within the family as well as at school in order to cope with the changes and become a competent and socially responsible adult. In "Shaping the Learning Environment: Connecting Developmentally Appropriate Practices to Brain Research," the authors discuss the interaction of biology and environment. The article "The Importance of Being Playful" discusses the important role of play in the development of cognitive and social skills in children.

Adolescence brings with it the ability to think abstractly and hypothetically and to see the world from many perspectives. Adolescents strive to achieve a sense of identity by examining and questioning not only their own beliefs and values, but those of the adult world they are moving into. This questioning often leads to behavior that challenges authority and conflicts with parents and teachers as adolescents strive to establish a sense of autonomy. The articles in this unit discuss the unique needs of young adolescents in relation to their physiological and affective development, and also suggest ways in which schools and teachers can help meet these needs.

Shaping the Learning Environment: Connecting Developmentally Appropriate Practices to Brain Research

Connections are shown between recent findings in brain research and principles of Developmentally Appropriate Practices to explore the implications for early childhood learning environments and teaching practices. New research on how the growing mind learns appears to bear out the value of NAEYC's constructivist approach to early childhood education where environments are designed to gain the learner's attention, foster meaningful connections with prior understanding, and maximize both short- and long-term memory through patterns and active problem solving. Each unique learner needs to feel challenged, but not fearful, so that stimulating experiences result in an exchange of ideas and promote deeper understanding.

KEY WORDS: early childhood education; brain research; developmentally appropriate practices (DAP); learning environments.

Stephen Rushton and Elizabeth Larkin

INTRODUCTION

The past several years have seen an explosion of published articles, books, and documentaries as well as a proliferation of conferences and workshop seminars focused on connecting recent neuroscientific research findings relating the child's developing brain to educational strategies. President of the James S. McDonnell Foundation, Bruer (1998), questions the validity of this marriage, stating clearly that "brain science has little to offer education practice or policy" (p. 14). He is supported by others who warn the educational community that knowledge gleaned from today's brain science may well be out-dated in several years due to its rudimentary nature. Indeed, many educators are quick to exert pressure on the educational pendulum in order to substantiate their philosophical position. However, although brain science is relatively new, Wolfe (1998), an educational consultant and expert on brain research, postulates that the bridge between neuroscience research and education is not the job of neuroscientists, but instead, that of educators.

Studies about how the human brain learns need to be interpreted in light of the classroom environment, because children spend a great deal of their time in these settings at a critical period in their development, and expectations for our professional success carry high stakes. The good news is that new research appears to be affirming what many early childhood educators have always known about effective learning environments. The bad news is that we have yet to fully explore the implications of this rapidly expanding area of knowledge in terms of generating widely recognized practices in the field of early childhood education. This paper is a beginning attempt to draw some parallels between brain research and the early childhood classroom, and so it should be acknowledged at the outset that the connections we propose here are tentative.

The National Association for the Education of Young Children's position statement on developmentally appropriate practices (DAP) for children birth through age 8 (Bredekamp & Copple, 1997) originally stated two main objectives, namely, (a) to provide "guidance to program personnel seeking accreditation by NAEYC's National Academy of Early Childhood Programs"; and (b) to counter persistent beliefs in the prevailing traditional approach to early childhood education. The educational emphasis was on a didactic, teacher-centered approach to learning that encompassed primarily whole group instructional techniques (Bredekamp & Copple, 1997, p. v). Subsequently, DAP was revised to describe a philosophical orientation that now implies a constructivist approach to teaching young children. It is built on the premise that children are social learners who actively construct meaning and knowledge as they interact with their environment.

Research on what constitutes appropriate early learning experiences has focused during the past decade on both the social-emotional (Burts, Hart, Charlesworth, & Kirk, 1990; Hyson, Hirsh-Pasek, & Rescorla, 1990) and the cognitive (Dunn, Beach, & Kontos, 1994; Sherman & Mueller, 1996) development of young children. Studies indicate that children actively engaged in learner-centered environments score higher on measures of creativity (Hyson *et al.*, 1990), have better receptive verbal skills (Dunn *et al.*, 1994), and are more confident in their cognitive abilities (Mantzicopoulos; Neuharth-Pritchett, & Morelock, 1994; Stopek, 1993). Additionally, Frede and Barnett (1992) reported that children who attended developmentally appropriate programs in preschool performed better in first grade on standardized assessments of achievement. A study by Burts *et al.* (1993) indicated that children from low socioeconomic home environments who were enrolled in DAP kindergarten classrooms showed higher reading scores in first grade than their counterparts who attended more traditional classrooms.

Unfortunately, even with these studies, there exists a wide discrepancy between what research recommends and how children are currently being taught. Dunn and Kontos (1997) postulated that DAP programs are not the norm in early childhood programs as teachers have difficulty knowing how to implement such practices. They also reported that many parents are unaware of the significant benefits of a DAP program and therefore choose a more traditional learning environment for their children.

During the past decade a parallel body of literature has emerged, one that has potentially important implications for teachers and young children alike. Research in the fields of neuroscience (Diamond & Hopson, 1998; Fitzpatrick, 1995; Sylwester, 1997), cognitive psychology (Gardner, 1993; Goldman, 1995; LaDoux, 1996), and education (Caine & Caine, 1991, 1997; Jensen, 1998; Kovalik, 1994; Wolfe, 1998) has provided some new information for teachers to better understand the learning process with implications for how to create more effective classroom environments. Combining knowledge across these disciplines could benefit teachers seeking ideas about best practices in designing environments that are consistent with what we now know about how the human brain learns. Specifically, brain research will help provide educators with strategies that can stimulate specific areas of the brain (thalamus, amygdala, hippocampus, and the frontal cortex) in order to gain the learner's attention, foster meaningful connections with prior understanding, and maximize both short- and long-term memory.

Brain research also supports the importance of developing and implementing a curriculum that is appropriate for the learner's particular developmental age. Early childhood teachers have been acutely aware for some time now that certain periods in a young child's life are more receptive for some kinds of learning. It is exciting to observe how the literature also indicates that particular "windows of opportunities" for learning do exist when the brain's plasticity, or adaptability, allows for greater amounts of information to be processed and absorbed (Wolfe, 1998).

Many teachers who embrace the early childhood philosophy are already practicing brain research-based strategies. Rushton (in press) describes a typical early childhood setting, for example, encouraging verbal interaction, integrating curriculum content areas, and providing meaningful problem-solving opportunities. Brain research, in and of itself, does not introduce new strategies for teachers; however, it does provide very concrete and important reasons why specific approaches to teaching and certain classroom strategies are more effective than others. As we will show, brain research seems to affirm many DAP principles and the underlying early childhood educational philosophy. With each DAP principle and brain research corollary, examples are provided on how to create, organize, and/or implement a learner-centered classroom that is compatible with both bodies of research. Not all principles are addressed since clear connections are not always evident. Table I outlines the parallels between the DAP standard and what we termed Brain Research principle. Additionally, the chart provides a few classroom strategies [to] connect the two similar bodies of research.

DAP Principle 1

Domains of children's development—physical, social, emotional, and cognitive—are closely related. Development in one domain influences and is influenced by development in other domains.

Educators have known for some time that development in one area is either influenced by, or is influencing another area of development. For instance, Graves (1983), Adams (1990), Weaver (1990), and others have articulated how reading and writing are connected; as a child begins to explore letters, sounds, and writing the desire and capacity to interpret, recognize, and understand these symbols increases simultaneously. And of course, this is conditional on the child's ability to see and hear—two very separate, yet interconnecting physiological functions. With even younger children, becoming mobile increases their ability to explore and understand their immediate environment. This increased activity also helps to stimulate cognitive development as they begin to interact and make sense of their surroundings (Kostelnik, Soderman, & Whiren, 1993; Sroufe, Cooper, & DeHart, 1992).

Each region of the brain consists of a highly sophisticated neurological network of cells, dendrites, and nerves that interconnect one portion of the brain with another. New stimuli entering the body via the five senses are directed immediately to the thalamus. The thalamus acts as a sorting station and reroutes the sensory input to various parts of the brain that deal specifically with each sense. These portions of the brain, called lobes, consist of millions of cells related to the specific sense that is being stimulated. For instance, the occipital lobe relates to the receiving and processing of visual information, and is located near the rear of the brain. The temporal lobe relates to language development, writing, hearing, sensory associations, and, to some extent, memory. It is located in the mid-left portion of the brain. The parietal lobe relates to higher sensory, language, and short-term memory. Finally, the frontal lobe helps us in our ability to judge, be creative, make decisions, and plan. Learning does not take place as separate and isolated events in the brain—all these parts work together.

When a child is engaged in a learning experience a number of areas of the brain are simultaneously activated. Each lobe interacts cohesively, not as separate or isolated organs, but as interdependent collective units (Sylwester, 1997), and all of them are needed in order to read and write. For instance, reading a book requires that the child picks up a book (activating the motor cortex: movement); she looks at the words (activating the occipital lobe: vision); she attempts to decipher words (activating the temporal lobe: language); and finally, she begins to think about what the words mean (activating the frontal lobe: reasoning) (Sorgen, 1999).

We know that learning and memory are strongly connected to emotions, and thus, the learning environment needs to be both stimulating and safe. Classroom experiences can be designed to allow children to investigate, reflect, and express ideas in a variety of ways that are increasingly complex and interconnected. Gardner (1993) proposed that each individual draws on multiple intelligences and generally relies on some more than others. Thus, learners need ample opportunities to use and expand their preferred intelligences, as well as adapt to and develop the other intelligences, which are all interdependent within the one brain. Then, they need opportunities to express what they know and understand in a variety of formats.

Early childhood teachers need to recognize developmental characteristics among children in a group, as well as each learner's unique capabilities. Multiage grouping is one strategy that helps to facilitate learning for a range of abilities (Kasten & Clarke, 1993). Because all the children in the class are not the same age, children can recognize more readily how individual approaches to learning tasks are both distinctive and viable. Here, what a child knows and how he knows it is not so much a factor of age as of prior experience and learning meanings. In this, or any environment, teachers of all ages will want to foster a learning context that builds trust, promotes self-direction, and encourages students to freely exchange their feelings and ideas so that the social/emotional realm is connected positively to cognitive and physical experiences.

Table I. Different Strategies and Principles

DAP position[a]	BR principle[b]	Classroom environment[c]
1. Domains of children's development—physical, social, emotional, and cognitive—are closely related. Development in one domain influences and is influenced by development in other domains.	Each region of the brain consists of a highly sophisticated neurological network of cells, dendrites, and nerves that interconnect one portion of the brain to another. The brain's emotional center is tied to the ability to learn. Emotions, learning, and memory are closely linked as different parts of the brain are activated in the learning process.	Good curriculum naturally engages many of the five senses and activates more than one of Gardner's eight intelligences at the same time. Learning is a social activity, so children need opportunities to engage in dialogue. Multiage grouping is a strategy that can support and challenge a range of learning styles and capabilities. Good learning environments build trust, empower learners, and encourage students to explore their feelings and ideas.
2. Development occurs in a relatively orderly sequence, with later abilities, skills, and knowledge building on those already acquired.	The brain changes physiologically as a result of experience. New dendrites are formed every day, "hooking" new information to prior experiences. An enriched environment increases cell weight and branching of dendrites.	Hands-on activities stimulate the various regions of the brain, and active participation helps young children to form stronger associations with existing understanding. Different stages of play (solitary, parallel, associative, collaborative), for example, can be identified and appropriate activities designed to build increasingly complex ideas through play.
3. Development proceeds at varying rates from child to child as well as unevenly within different areas of a child's functioning.	Each brain is unique. Lock-step, assembly-line learning violates a critical discovery about the human brain: each brain is not only unique, but also is growing on its own timetable.	Environments should allow choices to accommodate a range of developmental styles and capabilities. Large blocks of time, and systems for planning and tracking work, can be organized for children to share responsibility for their activity choices. Teachers need to adjust expectations and performance standards to age-specific characteristics and unique capabilities of learners.
4. Early experiences have both cumulative and delayed effects on individual children's development. Optimal periods exist for certain types of development and learning.	Brain research indicates that certain "windows of opportunity" for learning do exist. The brain's "plasticity" allows for greater amounts of information to be processed and absorbed at certain critical periods (Wolfe, 1998). The critical period for learning a spoken language is lost by about age 10 (Sorgen, 1999).	Children need opportunities to use sensory inputs, language, and motor skills. Young children also require frequent opportunities to interact verbally with peers. Repeated opportunities to interact with materials, peers, and ideas are critical for long-term memory. Second language programs will be most successful before 5th grade and should start as early as possible.
5. Development proceeds in predictable directions toward greater complexity, organization, and internalization.	The brain is designed to perceive and generate patterns. The brain is designed to process many inputs at once and prefers multi-processing. Hence, a slower linear pace reduces understanding (Caine & Caine, 1997).	Finding patterns can be built into math, language arts, science, and other subject area curriculum. Learning environments need to be organized for both low and high order thinking skills. The use of metaphor, and repeated opportunities to compare and contrast through multiple modalities, allow children to differentiate increasingly complex schemas.
7. Children are active learners, drawing on direct physical and social experience as well as culturally transmitted knowledge to construct their own understanding of the world around them.	When a child is engaged in a learning experience, a number of areas of the brain are simultaneously activated. Children raised in nonacademically oriented environments have little experience in using decontextualized language. They are more inclined to reason with visual, hands-on strategies (Healy, 1990).	Learning should be presented in a real life context so that new information builds upon prior understanding, and then generalizes to broader concepts. Field trips, guest speakers, interactive technology, and multicultural units of study will help children better understand themselves and succeed in today's world. In environments where children can interact with diverse populations (various cultures and generations—including grandparents), and use language as well as visual-spatial strategies, their learning will be enhanced.

Table I. Different Strategies and Principles (cont.)

DAP position[a]	BR principle[b]	Classroom environment[c]
8. Development and learning result from interaction of biological maturation and the environment, which includes both the physical and social worlds that children live in.	Each of the senses can be independently or collectively affected by environmental factors that in turn will affect the brain's ability to learn. Enriched environments increase dendritic branching and synaptic responses (Diamond, 1998).	Environments should be carefully monitored for appropriate lighting, aromas, ionization (fresh air), and noise. Water and appropriate foods should be made available to children, remembering that each person's internal clock differs.
	The simple act of reading a book may be one of the most challenging tasks the brain must perform. Speech comes naturally, but reading does not (Sorgen, 1999).	Environments should offer a wealth of materials and activity choices to explore.
		Children need to understand the relevance of learning to read. Learning to read should be connected to the child's speaking and writing. Reading aloud and reading for meaning are two different processes, and children need opportunities to do both.
11. Children demonstrate different modes of knowing and learning and different ways of representing what they know.	"The mental mechanisms that process music (and rhyme and rhythm) are deeply entwined with the brain's other basic functions, including emotion, perception, memory, and even language" (Sorgen, 1999, p. 56).	A classroom should provide opportunities for individual children to learn via modalities other than just verbal/linguistic or logico-mathematical tasks.
		Rhyme and rhythm are memory aids.
	The most powerful influences on a learner's behavior are concrete, vivid images. The brain has a primitive response to pictures, symbols, and strong, simple images (Jensen, 1995).	Children should be able to express knowledge in a variety of forms. Dramatization, music, and the visual arts should be made readily available as modes of both learning and expression. Symbolic representation can easily be built into the arts.
12. Children develop and learn best in the context of a community where they are safe and valued, their physical needs are met, and they feel psychologically secure.	Brain research has clearly demonstrated that high levels of stress, or a perceived threat, will inhibit learning (Caine & Caine, 1997).	The classroom environment should connect learning experiences to positive emotions.
		Students need to make decisions and choices about learning that is meaningful to them.
	"The brain is primarily designed to survive. No intelligence or ability will unfold until or unless given the appropriate model environment" (Jensen, 1996).	The classroom culture should support risk-taking, and view failures as a natural part of the learning process.

[a]NAEYC's positions on Developmentally Appropriate Practices (DAP)

[b]What brain research (BR) suggests about how the brain learns

[c]Strategies that incorporate both BR and DAP

DAP Principle 2

Development occurs in a relatively orderly sequence, with later abilities, skills, and knowledge building on those already acquired.

DAP Principle 3

Development proceeds at varying rates from child to child as well as unevenly within different areas of a child's functioning.

We learn to sit before we crawl, and crawl before we walk. In this way, human development is ordered and sequential. Developmental psychologists have described how stages of physical, cognitive, and social development are stable and predictable over time especially in children during the first 9 years of life. Notable pioneers such as Piaget (1952) and Erikson (1963), for example, proposed different stages of play and socialization that, providing normal development, are observable, predictable, and measurable. In these hierarchies, no stage can be skipped over as the developmental process unfolds.

Wolfe and Brandt (1998) stated that the brain changes physiologically as a result of experience. As the child experiences an event for the first time, either new dendrites are formed, or the experience is associated with a similar past event hooking new information to old understanding. Much of our behavior and development is "hardwired" through a long history of human evolution (i.e., breathing, circulation, and reflexes). However, individual brains are also "softwired" in order to adapt and create new neurological networks in response to the unique environmental stimuli encountered in our individual lives. It is in the interplay between environment and genetics, hardwired automatic behaviors and softwired developing neuronetworks, that we need to be sensitive to differences among children.

Each child's uniqueness is expressed in a number of ways: personality, temperament, learning style, maturation, speed of mastering a skill, level of enjoyment of a particular subject, attention, and memory. These attributes help to identify how a particular child will learn and what style of teaching is best suited for him or her. Further, each brain's growth is largely dictated by genetic timing, and therefore is as individualized as DNA (Sylwester, 1995). In truth, there are no homogeneous groups of children; as no two children are the same, no two brains are the same. Wolfe (1998) put it succinctly when she stated: "The environment affects how genes work, and genes determine how the environment is interpreted" (p. 10).

IMPLICATIONS FOR PRACTICE

Early childhood teachers have learned that children progress through various stages of development, knowing that each child's rate of development (and each brain) is unique and different. Providing hands-on activities that both cater to the differences among children and stimulate various regions of the brain reinforces stronger associations of meaning and makes learning inherently more interesting. Teachers who are trained to observe each child's development can establish a responsive environment for different documented stages of play (solitary, parallel, associative), and carefully design appropriate activities for the child's level. Teachers of older students can pay attention to higher order thinking skills in a similar manner, challenging students with engaging problem-solving opportunities. Teaching complex skills too soon may impede learning, and conversely, not teaching children when they are ready may result in boredom and a lack of interest.

Activities that have different levels of complexity allow every child access both to the content ideas and to conversation with peers. Creating centers around the classroom with a range of problems to solve and materials to use can accommodate the differences among learners. A general overall theme may permeate the activities in each center so that the children see connections across subject areas. A center (Rushton, in press) approach can easily be adapted from preschool to third grade, using planning sheets and individualized contracts to help children discover for themselves what their particular strengths and challenges are.

Because each learner is so different, children should be able to choose activities that fit their level of development, experience, and interest. Thus, teachers will want to use a variety of teaching methods and materials to ensure that every child becomes interested in exploring ideas, so that their auditory, visual, tactile, or emotional preferences are accounted for. More important, teachers need to remember that each child's educational experiences inside the classroom play a part in shaping a lifetime of learning habits. Different children feel challenged by different problems, and threatened by different social circumstances, and these matter in what and how they learn.

DAP Principle 4

Early experiences have both cumulative and delayed effects on individual children's development. Optimal periods exist for certain types of development and learning.

Principle 4 suggests that each learning experience lays groundwork for future learning, either positively or negatively. The child's ability to learn and interpret new information is directly related to the frequency of prior experience with related ideas. Brain research also indicates that certain windows of opportunities for learning do exist (Sorgen, 1999). In some instances, it is vital to development that a particular sense be stimulated. For instance, it has been demonstrated that some animals have had their vision obscured at key times in their development and were unable to ever see again. The blueprint, so to speak, relating to vision simply cannot be reestablished if not stimulated to grow in the first several years (Wolfe, 1998). The same can be said for developing oral language. In extreme cases in which a child has been abused, neglected, and cut off from society, speech pathologists have been unable to help those individuals speak normally.

Language and motor development both require children to actively engage with others. Conversation and physical activity are extremely important for the development of the brain. To facilitate optimal development, young children require opportunities to interact with each other regularly, encounter new vocabulary, construct arguments, express emotions, and stretch their muscles. Thus, learning environments should encourage verbal interactions, moving around the room as children work on projects or pursue a line of inquiry, and plentiful occasions to use manipulative materials including gross motor equipment.

Second language acquisition is most successful prior to fifth or sixth grade when the necessary structures in the brain for language learning are still in place. Young children seem to be particularly adept at mimicry, especially when language is rhythmic and rhyming. Also, the brain looks for patterns and connections, and repetition is critical for long-term memory. Introducing young children to more than one language is extremely beneficial, even if they do not yet understand how language is structured grammatically or written down. This early learning creates a foundation for later, more formal, study of another language.

DAP Principle 5

Development proceeds in predictable directions toward greater complexity, organization, and internalization.

The brain is designed to perceive and generate patterns and is constantly seeking to place new information into existing neurological networks. If no prior network exists, then new dendrites will be formed. Each layer of learning builds upon former networks. It has been suggested that the myelin sheath that surrounds the axons (the long tentacles of a dendrite) thicken with repeated exposure to a thought, idea, or experience. The greater the complexity of an experience, the thicker the myelin becomes. The belief is that thicker myelin results in faster recall of an event and greater memory (Diamond & Hopson, 1998). If this is true, then repetition of activities helps to thicken the myelin and thus, reinforce students' understanding.

Since no two children learn at the same rate, it is crucial that children be given repeated opportunities and ample time to explore, play, and socialize while they work in various curriculum areas (paint, blocks, dramatic play, listening center, water table, science). A typical K–3 classroom covers content in reading, writing, and mathematics, and time permitting, social studies, science, and the arts. Curriculum is often presented as separate subjects in distinct units with little overlap. Information would be better presented in a context of real life experiences where new information can build upon prior knowledge, so that learners understand how it is meaningful to them. Field trips are an excellent strategy to connect new learning to real world applications. When studying pollution, for example, students might visit the landfill, clean water treatment center, recycling plant, or local municipal garbage collection center rather than just viewing pictures and reading texts about the subject. The learner should be able to connect new information to well-established conceptual frameworks in an experiential manner, not as isolated bits of information that have no meaningful connection.

DAP Principle 7

Children are active learners, drawing on direct physical and social experience as well as culturally transmitted knowledge to construct their own understanding of the world around them.

DAP Principle 8

Development and learning result from interaction of biological maturation and the environment, which includes both the physical and social worlds that children live in.

The environment in which a child learns, both the explicit physical surroundings (people, manipulative materials, books) and the implicit cultural norms (alphabet, numerical symbols, values), shapes that child's understanding of the meaning of his or her experiences. Bredekamp and Copple (1997) stated that "young children actively learn from observing and participating with other children and adults" and that they need to "form their own hypotheses and keep trying them out through social interaction, physical manipulation, and their own thought processes" (p. 13).

The human brain is constantly seeking information from a variety of stimuli. These data are interpreted through all the senses and are then organized by the brain. Since each of the senses can be independently or collectively affected by environmental factors, they will affect the brain's overall ability to learn. Therefore, it stands to reason that the learning environment should make children physically comfortable—they need good lighting, fresh air, and a reasonable level of noise. In addition, children cannot learn when they are hungry or tired because their minds will be focused on the body's signals to eat or sleep. They need to move around to oxygenate their blood and exercise their muscles.

The social environment in a classroom relies heavily on language, and the simple act of reading is one of the most challenging tasks the brain performs. But the brain perceives patterns, and so we can help children develop language skills by looking for letter patterns in words, word patterns in sentences such as rhyming or alliteration, patterns in story sequence, and the like. Most importantly, we need to help children see the relevance of learning language and becoming competent readers, so that their motivation to learn and attention to the challenge are both high. The learning environment can reflect children's interests by including them in conversations about which books will be read.

Children who have been raised in nonacademically oriented environments have less experience using decontextualized language than their peers. In other words, they are less apt to rely on words to describe events to others outside the context where they occurred, and oral language skill development will affect later reading ability (Snow, Tabors, & Nicholson, 1995). These children may communicate more readily through using visual images, physical activity, and symbolic representation.

The curriculum can include practice in storytelling as a way to develop oral language skills and to make connections with children's real world experiences at the same time. The more children are exposed to and talk about experiences that are new to them, the more connections they can make to what they already know. Children also need opportunities to express ideas and understanding in physically active ways, such as through visual and dramatic arts. Repeated practice helps children to recall information and master physical tasks. As new information builds on prior understanding, children are able to generalize their own experiences to broader concepts.

DAP Principle 11

Children demonstrate different modes of knowing and learning and different ways of representing what they know.

Gardner's (1993) work in multiple intelligences and assessment has pointed to the need for classrooms to provide more occasions for children to use music, bodily-kinesthetic, visual-spatial, and interpersonal domains to learn and express understanding. Brain research has indicated that the "mental mechanisms that process music (and rhyme and rhythm) are deeply entwined with the brain's other basic functions, including emotion, perception,

memory, and even language" (Sorgen, 1999, p. 56). If music and movement can be used to build children's social/emotional experiences in the classroom, and to reinforce memory, language development, or even mathematical skills, we are likely to reach more kinds of learners than we would if we relied solely on narrowly defined subject areas.

Jensen (1998) has said that the most powerful influences on a learner's behavior are concrete, vivid images. The brain, he added, has a primitive response to pictures, symbols, and strong, simple images. It follows, then, that our systems of symbolic representation (the alphabet and numbers) are learned better if they can be connected to concrete, vivid images such as pictures and expressive motions. Children's memories are helped by physically representing what they know in addition to using language, so the arts should hold an important place in the curriculum. Children can draw, paint, construct, and dramatize what they know and understand.

DAP Principle 12

Children develop and learn best in the context of a community where they are safe and valued, their physical needs are met, and they feel psychologically secure.

Research on the brain and learning has clearly demonstrated that high levels of stress, or a perceived threat by the child, inhibits learning (Caine & Caine, 1997). It is the brain's principal job to ensure survival. The brain's emotional center is tied to its ability to learn. The amygdala checks all incoming sensory information first to see if it fits a known impression of danger. If a threat is perceived, the ability to learn is greatly impeded as the entire body automatically gears up to defend itself.

Teachers have a central responsibility to create a learning environment that feels relaxed enough to allow children's attention to focus on the curriculum, and challenging enough to excite interest. Evaluation is one component of the educational milieu, and thus, all assessment situations need to avoid generating a perceived threat. Clearly, using a variety of methods for collecting data enhances the likelihood of matching an individual learner's ways of knowing, and provides a more complete picture of what is known and understood.

Emotions, learning, and memory are closely linked as different parts of the brain are activated in the learning process. It is crucial, especially during the first several years of the child's life, to provide a rich and safe environment that lays groundwork for this neurological network to develop. Early childhood programs ought to invite children to make choices about what and how they learn so that they are more willing to take risks and view their experiences as both relevant and positive. Children need to explore, play, and discover, in a safe and healthy environment, using all of their senses in making connections from one part of the curriculum to another.

CONCLUSION

Technological advancements during the past decade have seen the development of some sophisticated equipment that has helped to better understand the functions of the human brain. This technology and subsequent understanding of the brain, albeit overwhelming for most educators, supports many of the philosophical tenets of constructivism, rooted in the philosophy of Dewey (1964). He believed that children learn best when interacting in a rich environment. He also believed that children constructed meaning from real life applications, and further, he knew that when various senses were used simultaneously, the probability of learning would be greater. Our modern educational terminology—such as integrated curriculum, whole language, hands-on learning, authentic assessment, and developmentally appropriate practices—not only echoes brain research, but also, we believe, contains many of the underpinning beliefs, thoughts, and tenets of Dewey.

Brain research helps to explain further why constructivist educators such as Dewey (1964), Piaget and Inhelder (1969), and Vygotsky (1967) still prevail. It is hoped that with new understanding about how the brain works, combined with the tenets of Developmentally Appropriate Practice, our ability to educate future generations will be greatly enhanced. The neuroscientist's job is to better understand the workings of the mind and brain; it is our job, as educators, to carefully sift through their findings and connect them to what we know empirically about how children learn best.

REFERENCES

Adams, M. J. (1990). *Beginning to read: Thinking and learning about print.* Urbana-Champaign, IL: The Reading Research and Education Center.

Bredekamp, S., & Copple, C. (1997). *Developmentally appropriate practice in early childhood programs* (Rev. ed.). Washington, DC: National Association for the Education of Young Children.

Burts, D., Hart, C., Charlesworth, R., & Kirk, L. (1990). A comparison of frequencies of stress behaviors observed in kindergarten children in classrooms with developmentally appropriate versus developmentally inappropriate instructional practices. *Early Childhood Research Quarterly, 5,* 407–423.

Burts, D., Hart, C., Charlesworth, R., DeWolf, D., Ray, J., Manuel K., & Fleege, P. (1993). Developmental appropriateness of kindergarten programs and academic outcomes in first grade. *Journal of Research in Childhood Education, 8*(1), 23–31.

Caine, R. N., & Caine, G. (1997). *Education on the edge of possibility.* Alexandria, VA: ASCD.

Dewey, J. (1964). The relation of theory to practice in education. In R. Archamault (Ed.), *John Dewey on education: Selected writings* (pp. 313–338). New York: Random House.

Diamond, M., & Hopson, J. (1998). *Magic trees of the mind: How to nurture your child's intelligence, creativity, and healthy emotions from birth through adolescence.* New York: Penguin Putnam.

Dunn, L., Beach, S., & Kontos, S. (1994). Quality of the literacy environment in day care and children's development. *Journal of Research in Childhood Education, 9*(1), 24–34.

Elkind, D. (1981). *The hurried child.* Reading, MA: Addison-Wesley.

Erikson, E. H. (1963). *Childhood and society.* New York: Norton.

Fitzpatrick, S. (1995). Smart brains: Neuroscientists explain the mystery of what makes us human. *American School Board Journal.*

Frede, E., & Barnett, W. S. (1992). Developmentally appropriate public school preschool: A study of implementation of the High/Scope curriculum and its effects on disadvantaged children's skills at first grade. *Early Childhood Research Quarterly, 7,* 483–499.

Gardner, H. (1993). *Multiple intelligences: The theory in practice.* New York: Basic Books.

Graves, D. (1983). *Writing: Teachers and children at work.* Portsmouth, NH: Heinemann.

Hirsh-Pasek, K., Hyson, M., & Rescorla, L. (1990). Academic environments in preschool: Do they pressure or challenge young children? *Early Education and Development, 1,* 401–423.

Hyson, M., Hirsh-Pasek, K., & Rescorla, L. (1990). The classroom practices inventory: An observation instrument based on NAEYC's guidelines for developmentally appropriate practices for 4- and 5-year-old children. *Early Childhood Research Quarterly, 5,* 475–494.

Jensen, E. (1998). *Teaching with the brain in mind.* Alexandria, VA: Association for Supervision and Curriculum Development.

Kasten, W., & Clark, B. (1993). *The multi-age classroom: A family of learners.* New York: Richard C. Owen Publishers.

Kostelnik, M., Soderman, A., & Whiren, A. (1993). *Healthy young children: A manual for programs.* New York: Macmillan.

LaDoux, J. (1996). *The emotional brain: The mysterious underpinnings of emotional life.* New York: Simon & Schuster.

Piaget, J. (1952). *The origins of intelligence in children.* Toronto: George J. McLeod.

Piaget, J., & Inhelder, B. (1969). *The psychology of the child.,* New York: Basic Books.

Rushton, S. (in press). A developmentally appropriate and brain-based compatible learning environment. *Young Children.*

Sherman, C., & Mueller, D. (1996, June). *Developmentally appropriate practice and student achievement in inner-city elementary schools.* Paper presented at Head Start's Third National Research Conference, Washington, DC. (ED 401 354)

Sorgen, M. (1999, June). *Applying brain research to classroom practice.* Materials presented at the University of South Florida Brain/Mind Connections Conference, Sarasota, FL.

Spodek, B. (Ed.). (1993). *The handbook of research on the education of young children.* New York: Teachers College Press.

Snow, C. E., Tabors, P. O., & Nicholson, P. A. (1995, Fall/Winter). SHELL: Oral language and early literacy skills in kindergarten and first grade children. *Journal of Research in Childhood Education, 10,* 37–48.

Sroufe, L. A., Cooper, R. G., & DeHart, G. G. (1992). *Child development: Its nature and course* (2nd ed.). New York: Knopf.

Sylwester, R. (1997). The neurobiology of self-esteem and aggression. *Educational Leadership, 54*(5), 75–79.

Vygotsky, L. (1967). Play and its role in the mental development of the child. *Soviet Psychology, 12,* 62–76.

Weaver, C. (1990). *Understanding whole language: From principles to practice.* Portsmouth, NH: Heinemann.

Wolfe, J., & Brandt, R. (1998). What we know from brain research. *Educational Leadership, 56*(3), 8–14.

Stephen Rushton and Elizabeth Larkin are from the University of South Florida at Sarasota

Correspondence should be directed to Stephen Rushton, University of South Florida at Sarasota, 5700 N. Tamiami Trail, PMC 217, Sarasota, Florida 34243; e-mail: srushton@sar.usf.edu

From *Early Childhood Education Journal*, Volume 29, No. 1, 2001, pp. 25-33. Copyright © 2001 by Kluwer Academic Publishers. Reprinted with kind permission from Springer Science and Business Media.

The Importance of Being Playful

With the right approach, a plain white hat and a plate full of yarn spaghetti can contribute to a young child's cognitive development.

Elena Bodrova and Deborah J. Leong

Educators have always considered play to be a staple in early childhood classrooms. But the growing demands for teacher accountability and measurable outcomes for prekindergarten and kindergarten programs are pushing play to the periphery of the curriculum. Some proponents of more academically rigorous programs for young children view play and learning as mutually exclusive, clearly favoring "serious" learning and wanting teachers to spend more time on specific academic content. But do play and learning have to compete? Research on early learning and development shows that when children are properly supported in their play, the play does not take away from learning but contributes to it (Bergen, 2002).

As researchers studying the ways to scaffold the development of foundational skills in young children, we have never met a teacher—preschool, Head Start, or kindergarten—who disagreed with the notion that young children learn through play. At the same time, many teachers worry that children's play is not valued outside of the early education community. These teachers must increasingly defend the use of play in their classrooms to principals, parents, and teachers of higher grades.

Early childhood teachers admit that the benefits of play are not as easy to understand and assess as, for example, children's ability to recog-

nize letters or write their names. Teachers also tell us that they feel obligated to prove that play not only facilitates the development of social competencies but also promotes the learning of pre-academic skills and concepts. We believe that a certain kind of play has its place in early childhood classrooms and that the proponents of play and academic learning can find some much-needed common ground.

Effects of Play on Early Learning and Development

Play has been of great interest to scholars of child development and learning, psychologists, and educators alike. Jean Piaget (1962) and Lev Vygotsky (1978) were among the first to link play with cognitive development. In a comprehensive review of numerous studies on play, researchers found evidence that play contributes to advances in "verbalization, vocabulary, language comprehension, attention span, imagination, concentration, impulse control, curiosity, problem-solving strategies, cooperation, empathy, and group participation" (Smilansky & Shefatya, 1990). Recent research provides additional evidence of the strong connections between quality of play in preschool years and children's readiness for school instruction (Bowman, Donovan, & Burns, 2000; Ewing Marion Kauffman

Foundation, 2002; Shonkoff & Phillips, 2000). Further, research directly links play to children's ability to master such academic content as literacy and numeracy. For example, children's engagement in pretend play was found to be positively and significantly correlated with such competencies as text comprehension and metalinguistic awareness and with an understanding of the purpose of reading and writing (Roskos & Christie, 2000).

How Play Evolves

Make-believe play emerges gradually as the child moves from infancy to preschool. In the beginning, children are more focused on the actual objects that they use when they play. Later, they focus on the people who use the objects in social interaction. Whereas a toddler might simply enjoy the repetitive action of rocking a baby doll, an older child engaged in the same activity would call herself "Mommy" and add other mommy behaviors such as using baby talk when talking to the doll. These preschoolers depend heavily on props and may even refuse to play if they think that the props are not sufficiently realistic.

By the time most children turn 4, they begin to develop more complex play with multiple roles and symbolic uses of props. Many preschool- and even kindergarten-age children, however, still play at the toddler level. We define this kind of repetitive, unimaginative play as "immature play" to distinguish it from the "mature play" that is expected of older preschoolers and kindergartners. Mature play contributes to children's learning and development in many areas that immature play does not affect (Smilansky & Shefatya, 1990).

As children grow older, they tend to spend less time in pretend play and more time playing sports and board or computer games. In these activities, children have to follow the established rules and rarely have a chance to discuss, negotiate, or change those rules—an important skill that contributes to the development of social competence and self-regulation. When learning to play games takes its natural course (see Piaget, 1962; Vygotsky, 1978) and builds on the foundation of well-developed pretend play, children get an opportunity to both develop and apply their social and self-regulation skills. When pretend play is completely replaced by sports or other organized activities, however, these important foundational skills might not develop fully.

Characteristics of Mature Play

Teachers often disagree about what constitutes mature play. Some think that the play has to have more sophisticated content, such as playing archaeological dig or space station; others believe that children play in a mature way when they don't fight with one another. We, however, consider play to be mature only when it has the following characteristics, which we have extracted from research and best practices.

Imaginary situations. In mature play, children assign new meanings to the objects and people in a pretend situation. When children pretend, they focus on an object's abstract properties rather than its concrete attributes. They invent new uses for familiar toys and props when the play scenario calls for it. Sometimes children even describe the missing prop by using words and gestures. In doing so, they become aware of different symbolic systems that will serve them later when they start mastering letters and numbers.

Multiple roles. The roles associated with a theme in mature play are not stereotypical or limited; the play easily includes supporting characters. For example, playing "fire station" does not mean that the only roles are those of firefighters. Children can also pretend to be a fire truck driver or a phone dispatcher.

When children assume different roles in play scenarios, they learn about real social interactions that they might not have experienced (not just following commands but also issuing them; not only asking for help but also being the one that helps). In addition, they learn about their own actions and emotions by using them "on demand." (I am really OK, but I have to cry because I am playing a baby and the doctor just gave me a shot.) Understanding emotions and developing emotional self-control are crucial for children's social and emotional development.

Clearly defined rules. Mature play has clearly defined rules and roles. As children follow the rules in play, they learn to delay immediate fulfillment of their desires. A child playing "customer" cannot take an attractive toy if the toy—a scale or a cash register—is the prop for the role of the "checker." Thus, mature play helps young children develop self-regulation. To stay in the play, the child must follow the rules.

Flexible themes. Mature play usually spans a broad range of themes that are flexible enough to incorporate new roles and ideas previously associated with other themes. When children play at a more mature level, they negotiate their plans. For example, when playing "hospital" or "store," children can create a new play scenario in which a doctor goes to the grocery store to buy medicine for the hospital or a cashier in a grocery store gets sick and is taken to the hospital. By combining different themes, children learn to plan and solve problems.

Language development. A mature level of play implies an extensive use of language. Children use language to plan their play scenario, to negotiate and act out their roles, to explain their "pretend" behaviors to other participants, and to regulate compli-

ance with the rules. In doing so, they often need to modify their speech (its intonation, register, and even choice of words) according to the requirements of a particular role or as they switch from talking in a pretend way to talking for real. As the repertoire of roles grows, so do children's vocabulary, mastery of grammar and practical uses of language, and metalinguistic awareness.

Length of play. Mature play is not limited to one short session, but may last for many days as children pick up the theme where they left off and continue playing. Creating, reviewing, and revising the plans are essential parts of the play. Staying with the same play theme for a long time allows children to elaborate on the imaginary situation, integrate new roles, and discover new uses for play props.

How Teachers Can Support Imaginative Play

In the past, children learned how to play at a mature level simply by being part of an extended multi-age group within their own family or in their neighborhood. Unfortunately, with children spending more time in age-segregated groups, that is no longer the case. TV shows and computers, even with carefully selected educational content, cannot replace live play mentors. The teacher needs to take the primary role in helping children develop and maintain mature play.

Some teachers go overboard and become too involved so that the play loses its spontaneous, child-initiated character and changes into another adult-directed activity. Other teachers prefer to limit their interventions in play to the situations in which children get into fights or fail to communicate. They do not intervene when children's play remains stereotypical and unexciting day after day. Thus, children miss opportunities to expand the scope of their play. Teachers can maintain a balance between supporting mature play and keeping it truly child-initiated. To do so, they need to provide specific support for each of the key characteristics of mature play.

Create Imaginary Situations

A good way to guide children in the development of imaginary situations is to provide multipurpose props that can stand for many objects. For example, instead of placing specific dress-up costumes in the dramatic play area, stock it with bolts of differently colored and textured fabrics. Children can then use the same piece of lace to play Sleeping Beauty and Cinderella, wear the same white hat when playing a nurse or a chef, and drape themselves in a piece of fabric with an animal print when playing different animals. Instead of buying plastic food for a pretend restaurant, teachers might use generic paper plates and have children draw food on them or use other objects to represent food (for example, packing peanuts look like marshmallows, and pieces of yarn make great spaghetti).

Some children may not be ready to make their own props and will not play without realistic props. If many children are at this stage, teachers can combine multipurpose props with realistic ones to keep play going and then gradually provide more unstructured materials. At the same time, teachers can use additional strategies to help children create and maintain the imaginary situation. During small-group time, teachers can show the children different common objects and brainstorm how they can use them in different ways in play. For example, a pencil can be a magic wand, a thermometer, a space ship, a stirring spoon, or a conductor's baton. Teachers should always encourage children to use both gestures and words to describe how they are using the object in a pretend way.

Integrate Different Play Themes and Roles

Left to their own devices, children rarely come up with truly imaginative play scenarios because they lack knowledge about the roles and the language needed. As a result, play themes in most classrooms are limited to family, hospital, or store, with few roles to play.

Teachers should use field trips, literature, and videos to expand children's repertoire of play themes and roles. Children rarely incorporate the new themes into their play scenarios, however, if these resources are not used properly and the teacher focuses children's attention on the "things" part of the field trip or video—what is inside a fire station or what happens to the apples when they become apple cider. Instead, teachers should point out the "people" part of each new setting—the many different roles that people have and how the roles relate to one another. Learning about the new roles, language, and actions will help children reenact them later in their play.

Sustain Play

Teachers can support mature play by helping children plan play in advance. Planning helps children communicate about the roles and describe what the person in each role can and cannot do. Children benefit most from advance planning when they record their plans by drawing or writing them. By using these records later as reminders of their play ideas, they may be stimulated to create new developments in their play scenario.

TV shows and computers, even with carefully selected educational content, cannot replace live play mentors.

Children who put effort into planning their future play tend to stay longer with their chosen play theme and get less distracted by what is happening in other areas of the classroom. Teachers see fewer fights in the classrooms when children draw pictures of what they want to play first. For instance, when Monica wants to be the cashier in a pretend bakery, Isabella shows her the plan in which she drew herself at the cash register, so Monica agrees to choose a different role.

Positive Effects of Mature Play

As we worked with preschool and kindergarten teachers on scaffolding children's literacy development (Bodrova & Leong, 2001; Bodrova, Leong, Paynter, & Hensen, 2002; Bodrova, Leong, Paynter, & Hughes, 2002), we noticed that teachers achieved the best results when they focused on supporting mature play. Children in these classrooms not only mastered literacy skills and concepts at a higher rate but also developed better language and social skills and learned how to regulate their physical and cognitive behaviors (Bodrova, Leong, Norford, & Paynter, in press). By contrast, in the classrooms where play was on the back burner, teachers struggled with a variety of problems, including classroom management and children's lack of interest in reading and writing. These results confirm our belief that thoughtfully supported play is essential for young children's learning and development.

References

Bergen, D. (2002). The role of pretend play in children's cognitive development. *Early Childhood Research and Practice, 4*(1). [Online]. Available:http://ecrp.uiuc.edu/v4n1/bergen.html

Bodrova, E., & Leong, D. J. (2001). *The Tools of the Mind Project: A case study of implementing the Vygotskian approach in American early childhood and primary classrooms.* Geneva, Switzerland: International Bureau of Education, UNESCO.

Bodrova, E., Leong, D., Norford, J., & Paynter, D. (in press). It only looks like child's play. *Journal of Staff Development, 2*(24), 15-19.

Bodrova, E., Leong, D. J., Paynter, D. E., & Hensen, R. (2002). *Scaffolding literacy development in a preschool classroom.* Aurora, CO: Mid-continent Research for Education and Learning.

Bodrova, E., Leong, D. J., Paynter, D. E., & Hughes, C. (2002). *Scaffolding literacy development in a kindergarten classroom.* Aurora, CO: Mid-continent Research for Education and Learning.

Bowman, B., Donovan, M. S., & Burns, M. S. (2000). *Eager to learn: Educating our preschoolers.* Washington, DC: National Academies Press.

Ewing Marion Kauffman Foundation. (2002). *Set for success: Building a strong foundation for school readiness based on the social-emotional development of young children.* Kansas City, MO: Author.

Piaget, J. (1962). *Play, dreams, and imitation in childhood.* New York: Norton.

Roskos, K., & Christie, J. F. (Eds.). (2000). *Play and literacy in early childhood: Research from multiple perspectives.* Mahwah, NJ: Erlbaum.

Shonkoff, J. P., & Phillips, D. A. (Eds.). (2000). *From neurons to neighborhoods: The science of early childhood development.* Washington, DC: National Academies Press.

Smilansky, S., & Shefatya, L. (1990). *Facilitating play: A medium for promoting cognitive, socio-emotional, and academic development in young children.* Gaithersburg, MD: Psychological and Educational Publications.

Vygotsky, L. (1978). *Mind in society: The development of higher psychological processes.* Cambridge, MA: Harvard University Press.

Elena Bodrova is a senior consultant with Mid-continent Research for Education and Learning, 2550 S. Parker Rd., Ste. 500, Aurora, CO 80014, and a research fellow for the National Institute for Early Education Research; ebodrova@mcrel.org. **Deborah J. Leong** is a professor of psychology at Metropolitan State College of Denver, P.O. Box 173362, Denver, CO 80217, and a research fellow for the National Institute for Early Education Research; leongd@mscd.edu.

From *Educational Leadership*, Vol. 60, No. 7, April 2003, pp. 50-53. Reprinted with permission of the Association for Supervision and Curriculum Development. © 2003 by ASCD. All rights reserved. The Association for Supervision and Curriculum Development is a worldwide community of educators advocating sound policies and sharing best practices to achieve the success of each learner. To learn more, visit ASCD at www.ascd.org

What Empathy Can Do

Students respond to us because we care—and because they like us.

By Ernest Mendes

With pursed lips and a furrowed brow, Julie strode into my second-period social studies class. She sat down, slammed her books on the desk, and said, "I hate this class!" I stood at my podium, reviewing my notes for the next period. On hearing her remark, I looked up and saw that Julie was not happy. I took a deep breath and walked slowly toward her. I squatted down next to her desk.

"Julie, you're really upset. What's wrong?" I asked.

"It's not fair. I hate this!" She paused. I waited. "We had a stupid pop quiz in math last period. I didn't have time to study last night because we had to pick my grandma up from the airport and got home late."

I acknowledged her frustration, took another deep breath, and said,

Julie, just hang in there today. Do whatever you can. It's tough to have that happen first thing in the morning.

I walked back to my podium. By now, most of the sophomore students had arrived.

As class began, I noticed that Julie sat dazed at her desk. After about 15 minutes, she opened her notebook and began to participate in class. When the bell rang, she left without a word, which wasn't unusual for her; she rarely spoke when she entered my class and never made eye contact.

The next day, Julie was the first to arrive in class once again. As she passed by my podium, she smiled at me, her eyes bright, and said exuberantly, "Good morning, Mr. Mendes."

"Good morning, Julie," I replied.

"So, what are we going to do today?" she asked. I gave her a thumbnail sketch. When class began, she actively participated. When class was over, she passed by me and said enthusiastically, "Have a good day, Mr. Mendes." The next day—and every day thereafter—she greeted me, participated in class, and

left with a goodbye. She raised her grade from a C to an A that semester.

What happened here? Am I suggesting that my empathetic response during a brief conversation influenced her behavior that dramatically? Dozens of variables were present in Julie's life during that time. I know from my 23 years of teaching, however, that Julie's change was not an exception, but rather the rule. Every student with whom I consciously made an effort to establish a rapport or a caring relationship demonstrated dramatic changes in behavior, effort, and performance.

Positive responses create an emotional bank account that can absorb relational difficulties that occur along the way.

Students do respond just because we care—and because they like us. Some educators want students simply to respect rather than like their teachers. But earning the respect of students is not enough. Students must perceive that we care, and even that we like them deep down, as people. As it turns out, they will work harder for someone they like than for someone they simply respect. And in our professional adult capacity, we can maintain both friendship-like qualities and our leadership role.

Having rapport means that two people are alike physiologically, emotionally, or cognitively, even if the similarity is temporary. Knowing students' interests and concerns is one sure way to build rapport. Being physically on the same level when talking with students—matching their rate of speech and their tone when it is positive—can help build rapport. Using students' names during lectures and acknowledging all responses in some way during class discussions are also part of building rapport.

What does it take to build rapport? The teacher needs a genuine desire to build a connection with students and strategies for reframing experiences so that they elicit a student's interest rather than frustration.

Nurture and Structure

Moustakas (1994) asks student teachers to draw from personal experience to create a profile of an effective relationship with a caring adult and then work to replicate this relationship with their students. Students feel special, for example, when the teacher affirms their interests and needs and makes suggestions rather than impositions. Psychologist Carl Rogers (1951) described the ideal therapeutic relationship as one in which the therapist is genuine and nonjudgmental, providing unconditional positive regard. Teachers can develop these characteristics of a good therapist to create healthy teacher-student relationships.

Developing caring relationships does not negate the need for limits and structure in the classroom. Students need both structure and nurture, and the ways in which the teacher responds to these needs in the classroom are crucial. Caring teachers succeed in managing their classrooms effectively, including maintaining discipline, solving problems, and setting expectations, limits, and rewards (Gootman, 1997). Caring classrooms are home to warm, supportive, stable relationships and to the social and ethical dimensions of learning (Lewis, Schapps, & Watson, 1996).

Emotional Intelligence

Self-awareness and self-management are crucial elements of emotional intelligence. Self-awareness entails identifying your own emotional state—knowing when you feel frustrated, for example, and why. Self-awareness includes being able to distinguish between your own feelings and those of others.

Self-management is the ability to manage your emotions and use them to move toward a desired outcome. Self-managing behavior might include taking some deep breaths or calming yourself with internal suggestions, such as "Relax" or "I can handle this." Once you have achieved self-control, it is easier to listen and respond to others with *I-messages*, stating how the other person's statement is affecting you.

Earning the respect of students is not enough. Students must perceive that we care, and even that we like them deep down, as people.

When we are aware and in control of our own emotions, we also need to be aware of other people's emotions so that we can make appropriate choices about how and what we communicate. Training and coaching can help develop this skill in reading between the lines.

In a study that measured the emotional intelligence of 49 high school teachers, I found that a teacher's ability to accurately identify emotions was directly related to the number of years that the teacher had taught (Mendes, 2002). This finding is consistent with other research on emotional intelligence (Mayer, Caruso, & Salovey, 2000). Classroom teachers must possess these competencies if they are to succeed with students.

Choosing Empathy

Sometimes empathy can serve multiple purposes. For example, viewing a situation empathetically can lead to a calmer internal state, which can influence the response of the teacher. In the case of Julie, I thought about how awful it is to feel that angry and almost out of control. That insight influenced my behavior. In addition, my observation allowed me to perceive Julie's upset state. This ability to read and identify emotions works together with self-management and leads to the optimal timing of responses.

In the classroom, we might be excited about a great activity for our students. But if a student is having a bad day, how do we respond? Do we perceive the student as apathetic and as having a negative attitude? Do we stick to our behavioral management plan and give the student a warning, soon to be followed by a set of consequences?

How do we discern, in the moment, what state the student is in and what course of action would be best? It's not always an easy task. The observation skills required to make these quick daily decisions are part of empathy.

The Adolescent Brain

Every time I read about neuroscientists' findings about developmental stages, I am amazed that adolescents can function in a classroom at all. The adolescent's brain is undergoing a state of reorganization, and the frontal lobe region, which is crucial in controlling impulses and making healthy decisions, has not finished developing (Giedd et al., 1999). Further, uncontrollable temper outbursts and violence may be due to mini-seizures in the temporal lobes (Amen, 1998). When making important decisions, the amygdala, an emotional trigger, gets activated more frequently in an adolescent brain than in an adult brain. Hormones magnify the intensity of moods and behavior (Amen, 1998). A bad family situation, for example, may be wreaking havoc inside the student's head.

These difficulties are not excuses for student performance and behavior, but they represent some of the factors that play into the observable behavior you see every day. When I remember these mitigating factors, I feel more empathy.

How to Build Relationships

- Acknowledge all responses and questions.
- Mention students' names, skills, ideas, and knowledge in your presentations—without mentioning weaknesses or confidential information.
- Use self-disclosure when appropriate. Be a real person.
- Use responses beginning with "I agree," "I appreciate," and "I respect."
- Ask students about their interests. Collect an information card at the beginning of the year and have students update it regularly. Pay attention to students' nonverbal responses and make adjustments as you capture their interest or hit neutral ground.
- Build on what you hear from students by sharing stories, interests, and worries.
- Display empathy with individuals and with classes by communicating what you think their needs or feelings might be.
- Listen actively. Match students' expressions and conveyed moods. Paraphrase their message, when appropriate. Know your students' world and go there first to open the relationship door.

Opening the Relationship Door

Gottman describes people's attempts to make connections with others as *bidding* (Gottman & DeClaire, 2001). We make numerous attempts at interpersonal connections throughout the day, in all of our relationships, and people can respond to our bidding in one of three ways: toward the bid, away from it, or against it.

For example, if a person in your proximity commented on the warm weather, and you asked him to pass the newspaper, you would be moving *away* from response. If instead you agreed that a heat wave is in the making, you would be moving *toward* the attempted bid for connection. You would be making an *against* response if you replied, "What are you, the weather man?" Relationships that include many *toward* responses are more durable than those with many *away* and *against* responses. Positive responses create an emotional bank account that can absorb relational difficulties that occur along the way.

Bidding takes verbal and nonverbal forms. Depending on the relationship, a glance, a touch, or a verbal "hey" may be appropriate. When a student asks a question that is out of context and unrelated to the classroom discussion, we have choices: We can ignore it; acknowledge it and suggest another time to address it; or make a sarcastic response. Every response is either making a deposit to or a withdrawal from our relationship account. When an individual, either in a group or one-on-one, risks sharing an idea or thought with you, you have an opportunity to deposit or withdraw. Which will you choose?

Students need both structure and nurture, and the ways in which the teacher responds to these needs in the classroom are crucial.

We may need to practice making clear, recognizable bids to others. When we do not clearly communicate with students, they may misinterpret our intention. For example, an after-class conversation regarding a student's behavior may start out harshly and set the conversation on a downward spiral:

> Jessie, knock it off. I'm tired of your wisecracks in class. You're being a smart aleck, and you're going to be sorry if you don't stop.

Instead, the teacher should ask the student what's going on:

> You didn't seem your usual self today in class.

The student explains. The teacher uses self-control:

> When you said, "This class is stupid," I became defensive and felt angry because I thought you were attacking me in front of the class. I want to know where that comment came from.

The student explains. The teacher responds:

> In the future, if you're angry with me or at something else, I want you to take out a piece of paper and write me a note describing your feelings and why you feel that way. Then you can share it with me later. How does that sound?

The student comments. The teacher finishes:

> OK, I'll talk with you more tomorrow.

This dialogue is only one of the typical, ongoing bidding scenarios we face daily. How we bid and respond to bids has a cumulative effect.

To open the relationship door, teachers need to understand their students' world. To build relationships in the classroom, teachers need to know their students, their own strengths and limitations, and how to connect with students by demonstrating genuine interest in them.

References

Amen, D. G. (1998). *Change your brain, change your life*. New York: Random House.

Giedd, J. N., Blumenthal, J., Jeffries, N. O., Castellanos, F. X., Liu, H., Zijdenbos, A., Paus, T., Evans, A. C., & Rapoport, J. L. (1999). Brain development during childhood and adolescence. *Nature Neurosciences*, 2(10), 861-863.

Gootman, M. (1997). *The caring teacher's guide to discipline: Helping young students learn self-control, responsibility, and respect*. Thousand Oaks, CA: Corwin.

Gottman, J., & DeClaire, J. (2001). *The relationship cure*. New York: Crown Publishers.

Lewis, C., Schapps, E., & Watson, M. (1996). The caring classroom's academic edge. *Educational Leadership*, 54(1), 16-21.

Mayer, J., Caruso, D., & Salovey, P. (2000). Emotional intelligence meets traditional standards for an intelligence. *Intelligence, 27*(4), 267-298.

Mendes, E.J. (2002). *The relationship between emotional intelligence and occupational burnout in secondary school teachers*. Ann Arbor, MI: ProQuest Information and Learning Company.

Moustakas, C. (1994). *Phenomenological research methods*. Thousand Oaks, CA: Sage.

Rogers, C. (1951). *Client-centered therapy: Its current practice, implications, and theory*. Boston: Houghton Mifflin.

Ernest Mendes is an education consultant and President of Mendes Training and Consulting, 374 E. H St., Ste. A, PMB-314, Chula Vista, CA 91910; erniemendes@cox.net; www.erniemendes.com.

The Biology of Risk Taking

For help in guiding adolescents into healthy adulthood, educators can look to new findings in the fields of neuroscience and developmental psychology.

Lisa F. Price

I celebrate myself,

And what I assume you shall assume,

For every atom belonging to me as good belongs to you.

—Walt Whitman, *Leaves of Grass*

Adolescence is a time of excitement, growth, and change. Whitman's words capture the enthusiasm and passion with which teenagers approach the world. Sometimes adolescents direct this passion toward a positive goal, such as a creative essay, an art project, after-school sports, or a healthy romance. At other times, they divert their passions to problematic activities, such as drug experimentation, reckless driving, shoplifting, fights, or school truancy.

Why do adolescents take risks? Why are teens so passionate? Are adolescents just young adults, or are they fundamentally different? Advances in developmental psychology and neuroscience have provided us with some answers. We now understand that adolescent turmoil, which we used to view as an expression of raging hormones, is actually the result of a complex interplay of body chemistry, brain development, and cognitive growth (Buchanan, Eccles, & Becker, 1992). Moreover, the changes that teenagers experience occur in the context of multiple systems—such as individual relationships, family, school, and community—that support and influence change.

Educators are in a pivotal position to promote healthy adolescent growth. Understanding the biological changes that adolescents undergo and the behaviors that result can provide the foundation for realistic expectations and effective interventions.

The Impact of Puberty

The hormonal changes of adolescence are often considered synonymous with puberty. The word *puberty* comes from the Latin term *pubertas*, meaning "age of maturity." As implied by the word's etymology, the changes of puberty have long been understood to usher in adulthood; in many cultures, puberty and the capacity to conceive continue to mark entry into adulthood. In contrast, puberty in modern Western culture has become a multistep entry process into a much longer period of adolescence (King, 2002).

Hormonal changes of adolescence include adrenarche, gonadarche, and menarche (Dahl, 2004; King, 2002). Adrenarche refers to the increased production of adrenal hormones and occurs as early as age 6-8. These hormones influence skeletal growth, hair production, and skin changes. Gonadarche refers to the pulsatile production of a cascade of hormones and contributes to driving the growth spurt and genital, breast, and pubic hair development. Menarche refers to the beginning of girls' menses, which generally occurs late in girls' pubertal development.

The Stages and Ages of Puberty

The clinician J. M. Tanner developed a system for classifying male and female pubertal growth into five stages (Tanner I-V). In the 1960s, he identified a trend of progressively earlier age at menarche across cultures (1968). Since then, investigators have identified similar trends of earlier arrival of other markers of puberty, such as breast and pubic hair development (Herman-Giddens et al., 1997). These trends have diverged across race in the United States, with proportionately more African American girls experiencing earlier-onset puberty than white girls. The implications of these trends have ranged from debates over the threshold for premature puberty to investigations into factors that contribute to earlier-onset puberty (Kaplowitz & Oberfield, 1999).

Boys who enter puberty at an earlier age experience certain advantages, including higher self-esteem, greater popularity, and some advances in cognitive capabilities (King, 2002). These same boys may also be more likely to engage in risk-taking behavior, possibly because they often socialize with older boys (Steinberg & Morris, 2001). Girls, on the other hand, often have more problems associated with earlier entry into puberty, including lower self-esteem and elevated risk for anxiety, depression, and eating disorders. These girls are also more likely to engage in risk-taking behaviors, including earlier sexual intercourse.

Don't Blame It On Hormones

In the past, hormones were believed to be in a state of great flux, which presumably caused adolescents to be dramatic, erratic, intense, and risk-prone. Evidence suggests, however, that only minimal association exists between adolescent hormone levels and emotional/behavioral problems (Buchanan et al., 1992; King, 2002). Youth with higher levels of hormones do not appear to be at higher risk for emotional or behavioral problems (Dahl, 2004).

> **Adolescence is a time of excitement, growth, and change.**

Today, adolescent specialists view emotional intensity and sensation-seeking as normative behaviors of adolescence that are more broadly linked to pubertal maturation than to hormone levels. Pubertal stage rather than chronological age is linked to romantic and sexual pursuits, increased appetite, changes in sleep patterns, and risk for emotional disorders in girls. One group of investigators studying teen smoking and substance use found that increased age had no correlation with increased sensation-seeking or risky behavior (Martin et al., 2002). Instead, they determined that pubertal maturation was correlated with sensation-seeking in boys and girls, which, in turn, led to a greater likelihood of cigarette smoking and substance use.

Pubertal stage was clearly linked to difficulties that Derek began experiencing in school. He had been a solid student in 6th grade who scored in the average range and generally turned his homework in on time. He socialized with a group of same-age friends and was teased occasionally because he was skinnier and shorter than his peers. By 7th grade, however, he had begun his growth spurt. He was now a few inches taller and had developed facial hair. Although he appeared more confident, he also seemed more aggressive and was involved in several fights at school. He began to spend part of his time with a few 8th grade boys who were suspected of writing graffiti on a school wall.

A teacher who had a good relationship with Derek took him aside and spoke with him about the change in his behavior from 6th to 7th grade. Derek was able to talk about his own surprise at the changes, his wish for more respect, and his ambivalence about entering high school—he was worried about what teachers would

expect of him. Derek and the teacher agreed to talk periodically, and the teacher arranged for Derek to meet with the school counselor.

The Adolescent Brain

Neuroscientists used to believe that by the time they reached puberty, youth had undergone the crucial transformations in brain development and circuitry. Data obtained through available technology supported this view, identifying similar brain structures in children and adults. The adolescent brain seemed entirely comparable to the adult brain.

This view of adolescent brain development has undergone a radical shift during the last decade, with the identification of ongoing brain changes throughout adolescence, such as synaptic pruning and myelination. People have the mature capacity to consistently control behavior in both low-stress and high-stress environments only after these neurobiological developments are complete. This maturation does not take place until the early 20s.

Synaptic pruning refers to the elimination of connections between neurons in the brain's cortex, or gray matter. In the 1990s, researchers determined that during adolescence, up to 30,000 synapses are eliminated each second (Bourgeois & Rakic, 1993; Rakic, Bourgeois, & Goldman-Rakic, 1994). The removal of these redundant synaptic links increases the computational ability of brain circuits, which, in turn, enhances a function intricately connected to risk taking: the capacity to regulate and rapidly stop activity. Myelination, which refers to the wrapping of glial cell membranes around the axon of neurons, results in increased speed of signal transmission along the axon (Luna & Sweeney, 2004). This facilitates more rapid and integrated communication among diverse brain regions.

Synaptic pruning and myelination, along with other neurobiological changes, facilitate enhanced cognitive capacity as well as behavioral control, also known as *executive function*. Executive function is the ability to interact in a self-directed, appropriate, organized, and purpose-

ful manner. The prefrontal cortex plays a vital role in guiding executive function, which is also influenced by such areas of the brain as the hippocampus (which coordinates memory), the amygdala (which coordinates emotional processing), and the ventral striatum (which coordinates reward-processing). The prefrontal cortex is less mature, however, in young adolescents than in adults.

Given these three factors—an inability to completely regulate and refrain from certain activities, an absence of fully integrated communication among the various regions of the brain, and a less developed prefrontal cortex—it is not surprising that adolescents biologically do not have the same capacities as adults to inhibit their impulses in a timely manner.

Biology and Thrill-Seeking

By their mid-teens, adolescents appear to have achieved many decision-making abilities seen in adults (Steinberg & Cauffman, 1996). In fact, studies have found that teens can identify the same degree of danger in risky activities that adults can—driving while intoxicated, for example (Cauffman, Steinberg, & Woolard, 2002). However, certain methodological flaws in studies of adolescents may have prevented investigators from accurately assessing adolescent risk taking (Steinberg, 2004). These flaws include evaluating teens individually rather than in the context of a group, within which most risk-taking behavior occurs; asking teens to evaluate theoretical situations, which may not sufficiently represent the challenges of actual situations; and evaluating teens in settings that reduce the influence of emotion or induce anxiety rather than generate the exhilaration associated with risk taking.

One result of these flaws may be that measures of adolescents' cognitive abilities—particularly their evaluation of risk—do not adequately reflect their actual cognitive and emotional processes in real time. Consequently, teens *appear* to have the cognitive capacities of adults yet continue to engage in more risky behaviors.

The emotional lives of adolescents also appear to shift during these years. Adolescents seek more intense emotional experiences than children and adults do. They appear to need higher degrees of stimulation to obtain the same experience of pleasure (Steinberg, 2004). Developments in an area of the brain called the limbic system may explain this shift in pursuit and experience of pleasure (Spear, 2000).

> **Teenagers generally thrive in reasonable, supportive environments that have a predictable, enforced structure.**

Ongoing cognitive development and emotional shifts result in a biologically based drive for thrill-seeking, which may account for adolescents' continued risk taking despite knowledge of the accompanying hazards. Some interventions attempt to reduce the potential for risky behavior through external means—laws and rules, for example—rather than placing sole emphasis on the practice of educating teens in risk assessment (Steinberg, 2004). Others have considered teens' ability to reason well in "cool" circumstances but their failure to do so when in "hot" situations that arouse the emotions. Providing adolescents with sufficient scaffolding, or a good balance of support and autonomy, may be particularly important (Dahl, 2004).

This kind of scaffolding would be especially effective with a student like Shauna. Shauna raised the concerns of school faculty soon after she started 9th grade. Her attendance, class participation, and assignment completion were erratic. She had also run away from home during the summer and received a warning for shoplifting. The school counselor learned that Shauna's parents had separated over the summer and that her mother was struggling to set limits in the absence of Shauna's father. The school counselor, several teachers, and the vice principal decided to meet with both of Shauna's parents.

Although tension between the parents was evident, both parents agreed that Shauna should come home immediately after school instead of going to the mall, which she had recently started to do. Both parents also felt strongly that she needed to regularly attend school and complete assignments. The parents arranged to meet with Shauna together to discuss their shared expectations for her. The parents and teachers agreed to stay in contact with one another regarding Shauna's attendance and homework. The group also decided that a home-based reward system might encourage Shauna's success at school. The reward system would involve outings to the mall and to friends' homes, with incrementally less adult supervision and more autonomy as she continued to succeed.

The Role of Educators

These new findings suggest some beneficial approaches that educators might follow to guide adolescents into healthy adulthood.

- *Ensure that schools provide adolescents with vital support.* School bonding provides a protective influence for youth. The mentorship of a teacher can make the difference in a teen's course.
- *Keep a long view.* Researchers have found that the benefits of successful interventions may disappear for a few years in adolescence to reappear in later adolescence (Masten, 2004). Other teens are late bloomers whose troubled earlier years are followed by success.
- *Prioritize your concern.* The junior who has never been a problem and gets into trouble once is at a different level of risk than the 7th grader who has a long history of worrisome behaviors, such as fights, school truancy, mental illness, exposure to trauma, loss of important adult figures, or absence of stable supports. Act early for adolescents with long histories of risk taking.
- *Remember that puberty is not the same for all teens.* Some adolescents enter puberty earlier than others, giving them a perceived social advantage as well as possible disadvantages. There may be a biological drive to risk taking in teens, which is expressed by individual teens at different ages.
- *Remember that teens are not adults.* Having the scientific evidence to support the view that teens are not adults can be helpful to educators working with families, adolescents, or other professionals who may have unrealistic expectations for adolescents.
- *Take advantage of adolescent passion.* Direct adolescents' enthusiasm toward productive ends. A teen's passion can become a bridge to learning about such topics as music theory, history, politics, race relations, or marketing.
- *Reduce risk with firm structure.* Although teenagers dislike rules, they generally thrive in reasonable, supportive environments that have a predictable, enforced structure. For example, an authoritative stance in parenting—which reflects firmness coupled with caring—has repeatedly been found to be the most effective parenting strategy. Continue to maintain school rules and expectations, even when an adolescent continues to break the rules.
- *Collaborate to solve problems.* Working with risk-taking adolescents can be demanding, taxing, and worrisome. Talk regularly with colleagues for support. Contact appropriate consultants when your concern grows. Teens who see teachers collaborate with other adults benefit from these healthy models of problem solving.

It's important for educators to keep in mind that up to 80 percent of adolescents have few or no major problems during this period (Dahl, 2004). Remembering that most adolescents do well can encourage the positive outlook that educators need to effectively work with youth during this exciting and challenging time in their lives.

References

Bourgeois, J-P., & Rakic, P. (1993). Changes of synaptic density in the primary visual cortex of the macaque monkey from fetal to adult stage. *Journal of Neuroscience, 13,* 2801–2820.

Buchanan, C. M., Eccles, J. S., & Becker, J. B. (1992). Are adolescents the victims of raging hormones? *Psychological Bulletin, 111,* 62–107.

Cauffman, E., Steinberg, L., & Woolard, J. (2002, April 13). *Age differences in capacities underlying competence to stand trial.* Presentation at the Biennial Meeting of the Society for Research for Adolescence, New Orleans, Louisiana.

Dahl, R. E. (2004). Adolescent brain development: A period of vulnerabilities and opportunities. *Annals of the New York Academy of Science, 1021,* 1–22.

Herman-Giddens, M. E., Slora, E. J., Wasserman, R. C., Bourdony, C.J., Bhapkar, M. V., Koch, G. G., et al. (1997). Secondary sexual characteristics and menses in young girls seen in office practice. *Pediatrics, 99,* 505–512.

Kaplowitz, P. B., & Oberfield, S. E. (1999). Reexamination of the age limit for defining when puberty is precocious in girls in the United States. *Pediatrics, 104,* 936–941.

King, R. A. (2002). Adolescence. In M. Lewis (Ed.), *Child and adolescent psychiatry* (pp. 332–342). Philadelphia: Lippincott Williams & Wilkins.

Luna, B., & Sweeney, J. A. (2004). The emergence of collaborative brain function: fMRI studies of the development of response inhibition. *Annals of the New York Academy of Science, 1021,* 296–309.

Martin, C. A., Kelly, T. H., Rayens, M. K., Brogli, B. R., Brenzel, A., Smith, W. J., et al. (2002). Sensation seeking, puberty, and nicotine, alcohol, and marijuana use in adolescence. *Journal of the American Academy of Child and Adolescent Psychiatry, 41,* 1495–1502.

Masten, A. S. (2004). Regulatory processes, risk, and resilience in adolescent development. *Annals of the New York Academy of Science, 1021,* 310–319.

Rakic, P., Bourgeois, J-P., & Goldman-Rakic, P. S. (1994). Synaptic development of the cerebral cortex. *Progress in Brain Research, 102,* 227–243.

Spear, P. (2000). The adolescent brain and age-related behavioral manifestations. *Neuroscience and Biobehavioral Reviews, 24,* 417–463.

Steinberg, L. (2004). Risk taking in adolescence: What changes, and why? *Annals of the New York Academy of Science, 1021,* 51–58.

Steinberg, L., & Cauffman, E. (1996). Maturity of judgment in adolescence. *Law and Human Behavior, 20,* 249–272.

Steinberg, L., & Morris, A. S. (2001). Adolescent development. *Annual Review of Psychology, 52,* 83–110.

Tanner, J. M. (1968). Early maturation in man. *Scientific American, 218,* 21–27.

Lisa F. Price, *M.D., is the Assistant Director of the School Psychiatry Program in the Department of Psychiatry at Massachusetts General Hospital, 55 Fruit St., YAW 6900, Boston, MA 02114. She is also an Instructor in Psychiatry at Harvard Medical School.*

Differing Perspectives, Common Ground: The Middle School and Gifted Education Relationship

What Research Says

Middle school educators and advocates for the gifted share much common ground for addressing the needs of a wide variety of learners: flexible pacing, independent study, and teaching thinking skills.

By Hilda C. Rosselli & Judith L. Irvin

A curious relationship has evolved over the years between the fields of gifted education and middle grades education. On an initial glance, beliefs important to each field indicate an amazing overlap in philosophy and practices. However, when middle grades philosophy positioned heterogeneous grouping as one of the preeminent guideposts for policies and practices endorsed by the field, the common ground between the two fields lessened. Leaders in gifted education, unable to embrace a total abandonment of grouping, responded vehemently and expressed reservations regarding the ability of the middle school movement to meet the needs of high ability students (Gallagher, Coleman, & Nelson, 1995; Plucker & McIntire, 1996; Sicola, 1990; Tomlinson, 1992; 1994). The resulting differences reframed the relationship between experts from gifted education and middle grades education and fueled lively debates on the moral and efficacious nature of ability grouping. Others sought to re-examine the goodness of fit between the two movements by moving beyond the rhetoric of differences towards a healthier focus on programs and practices (Coleman, Gallagher, & Howard, 1993; Coleman & Gallagher, 1995; Mills & Durden, 1992; Rosselli, 1995). At the same time, with the advent of the National Research Center on the Gifted and Talented and federally funded Javits grants, a more defined research focus in gifted education provided a rich source for examining implications for middle level education. This article provides an overview of the literature that has historically framed the

debates between gifted education and middle grades education followed by discussion of research that seeks common ground between the two fields and implications relative to middle school education policies and practices that hold promise for considering the unique needs of high ability students.

Nature and definition of giftedness and intelligence

Although the field of gifted education has traditionally been grounded in the use of IQ scores for identification and definition purposes, the last twenty years has seen a growing interest in other views of intelligence and giftedness. On the heels of Howard Gardner's work (1983) has followed a redefining of gifted education by well-renowned experts (Gagne, 1995; Feldhusen, 1992; Renzulli, 1994; Treffinger, 1992) who are not convinced that traditional IQ measures are sufficient for identifying the unique and individual talents of capable youth. With the publication of National Excellence: A Case for Developing America's Talent (U.S. Department of Education, 1993), the term "talent" appeared liberally throughout the report and served as a cornerstone for encouraging more overlap between education reform and the development of individual gifts and talents. Furthermore, the 1990s saw growth in a researchable knowledge base regarding the diversity rather than the homogeneity within the gifted population (Betts & Neihart, 1988; Ford, 1993; Maker, 1996; Nielsen, Higgins, Hammond, & Williams, 1993). This work specifically focuses attention on the historically under-represented presence of students from culturally diverse backgrounds, from low socioeconomic environments, with limited English proficiency, and with two exceptionalities.

Characteristics and needs of gifted students

A number of developmental characteristics that apply to middle level adolescents apply to gifted adolescents as well, particularly: rapid physical growth, varying levels of cognitive operations, sporadic brain growth, affective ambivalence, and capacity of introspection. Like all adolescents, teens who are gifted must also cope with the achievement of independence, discovery of identity as a person, exploration and acceptance of sexuality, development of meaningful interpersonal relationships, and establishment of personal values and philosophy (Clark, 1988). Clearly, being gifted places some additional twists on the already difficult tasks of adolescent maturation. Wallace (1985) described the gifted adolescent as a doubly marginal individual. The obvious move is away from the family, which is part of the adolescent experience, as well as a move away from the system that perhaps supported and nurtured a specific gift or talent. This new autonomy may cause an additional burden or responsibility for the gifted adolescent, just at a time when he/she has few appropriate peer role models to emulate. Manaster and Powell (1983) reported that gifted adolescents may feel "out of stage" due to their perfectionism and focus on success, causing them to be out of touch with their immediate environment. In addition, alienation from their age-peer group may be influenced by gifted students' awareness of their unusual abilities or interests, causing them to feel "out of phase." Lastly, these students may feel "out of sync" as though they do not, should not, or cannot fit in. Buescher (1985) also found that ownership, or the simultaneous owning and questioning of the abilities of these youngsters, may compete with the beliefs that a debt is owed towards parents, teachers, and society.

To be gifted and to be under-challenged in school creates another undesirable combination. High ability students have reported school work being too easy (Tomlinson, 1995), spending little or no time studying, and group work leading to gifted students doing all the work (Clinkenbeard, 1991). In one study of high ability middle level students, Plucker and McIntire (1996) found that students exhibited a variety of nonconstructive behaviors such as interacting with peers, selected attention, and reduced effort when the level of stimulation or challenge was inappropriate. In addition, teachers in the study did not always recognize when high ability students were trying to stimulate themselves intellectually and sometimes even allowed the students to pursue nonconstructive behaviors rather than adapt or modify instruction.

Instructional implications

Middle school instruction is intended to respond to the recognized developmental needs of young adolescent students. Earlier research on brain periodicity fueled support for a movement away from abstract types of thinking. The resulting de-emphasis on academics also acknowledged that young adolescent students do not always prize school achievement and that over-challenging students at the middle school level could contribute to poor self-concept (National Association of Secondary School Principals, 1989). Tomlinson (1992) has questioned the implications of accepting findings that only 20% of 14 year-olds use even early formal operations. In her view, this finding still creates a need to explore viable options for these 20 percenters, many of whom might be identified as gifted students. In their study of talented teenagers, Csikszentmihalyi, Rathunde, & Whalen (1993) found that students seem to benefit more from a differentiated (more complex and even competitive) learning environment than an integrated (supportive and comfortable) environment. Beane and Lipka's (1986) finding that only 25% of an individual's academic school achievement is linked to IQ while 50% is related to self-concept has posed another dilemma. For gifted students, academic success plays an important role in maintaining self-esteem. This aspect of self-concept is supported by students' intellectual peers who act as "mental catalysts and who provide realistic perspective of their abilities" (Sicola, 1990). Furthermore, Bloom (1985) found in his study that "… exceptional levels of talent development require certain types of environmental support, special experiences, excellent teaching, and appropriate motivational encouragement at each stage of development" (p. 543).

To allow any student to underachieve continually can result in a negative impact on self-concept which, in turn, can impact future performance. Ironically, it was the middle school movement that reminded educators that lockstep-graded practices "force[s] many students to compromise the integrity of their individual readiness" (NASSP, 1989, p. 7). In 1988, Chapman and McAlpine conducted a study to examine the academic self-concepts of mainstreamed intellectually gifted and average students over a two-year period. They measured perceptions of ability in the areas of math, reading, spelling, general ability, penmanship, neatness, and confidence/satisfaction at the beginning and the end of the sixth grade year and then again at the end of the seventh year. These researchers found that, with the exception of penmanship, the students identified as gifted had overall higher perceptions of general ability as well as specific academic areas. However, the gifted students showed lower perceptions of school satisfaction than the average students. Chapman and McAlpine felt that lack of challenge in a mainstreamed environment may cause boredom which could explain the lower scores.

In a qualitative study conducted in a sixth grade gifted class, Clinkenbeard (1991) found that students who were identified gifted felt that their general classroom teachers and peers held sometimes unrealistic expectations of them. Teachers expected them to achieve and behave at a gifted level consistently, some days failing to acknowledge that the students' achievements were linked to effort as well as ability. Students who participated in the study also felt that they were graded harder than were other students and their age peers were sometimes jealous and insulting. Gifted adolescents appear to develop a variety of coping strategies to deal with these types of pressures, including the use of one's abilities to help others in classes, making friends with other bright students, selecting programs and classes designed for gifted/talented students, and achieving in areas outside of academics/school. In their study of gifted adolescents' adjustment, Buescher and Higharn (1989) found gender differences indicating girls to be more at risk for avoiding or walking away from their talents during early adolescence whereas boys more often select friends that provide support for their talent areas.

Equity and excellence

The greatest philosophical difference that separates advocates of gifted education and those of the middle school concept does not lend itself to traditional research methodology. As Plowman (1988) stated, "Education of the gifted and talented is consistent with the philosophical principles and basic tenets of our educational and political systems which include: concern for individuals, individualized instruction, equal opportunity, and equal access" (p. 60). Yet, services that address the needs of high ability learners are sometimes suspect and equated with social discrimination (Johnston & Markle, 1986; McKay, 1995). Helpful to this discussion is a closer look at what Salkind (1988) addressed as two other types of equity. Horizontal equity involves the equal treatment of individuals who have similar needs while vertical equity exists when children who have different needs are treated differently; otherwise referred to as the "unequal treatment of unequals." Both types of equity must guide policy and practices involving services for high ability adolescents.

Ability grouping

As mentioned previously, the main point of disagreement between the two fields often centers around the issue of ability grouping. Kulik and Kulik's

(1987) second meta-analysis coded 82 studies of between-class and 19 within-class programs and described the outcomes on a common scale. For inclusion in their analysis, the studies had to be quantitative, include both a control group and an experimental group with a similar aptitude, and involve a classroom rather than a lab setting. In 49 studies of comprehensive between-class grouping, the effect sizes were .12 for high, .04 for middle, and .00 for low groups with the difference between the high and low groups statistically significant at $p < .05$. In 25 studies dealing with special classrooms only for talented students, variation of effect size from -.27 to 1.25 led the Kuliks to believe that factors other than grouping played a role in the outcome. Two features showing significant relationships in an analysis of total class grouping within the classroom were instructor effects and flexibility/permanence of assignment. The Kuliks concluded that the strongest and clearest effects of grouping were in programs designed especially for talented students. They also concluded that programs designed for all students in a grade, rather than only for talented students, had significantly lower effects. The Kuliks noted that their results are, in some regards, similar to those of Slavin, particularly their findings that comprehensive grouping between classes has little or no effect, either positive or negative.

As the debates have ensued, Slavin (1990) has led a discussion on the practice of "regrouping" for select subject areas as an alternative to ability grouping. To be instructionally effective, Slavin believes that regrouping plans must meet two conditions: 1) instructional level and pace must be completely adapted to student performance level, and 2) regrouping should only be done for one or two subjects so that students remain in a heterogeneous setting most of the day. The National Association for Gifted Children believes that this type of flexible use of grouping will help match students' advanced abilities and knowledge while still maintaining the important social goals of the middle school movement (National Association for Gifted Children, 1994). However, many still question the practice of keeping high ability students in a heterogeneous setting for the majority of the day if their cognitive needs require more challenge.

Revisiting program organization

Over the years a wide variety of programs have been developed to meet the needs of gifted adolescents. Gifted education has rallied around options that move beyond the traditional pull-out and self-contained programs, such as early admission or acceleration options, special schools, mentorships, continuous progress, dual enrollment, and within-class individualization. As an alternative to formal grouping, Renzulli (1994) researched the use of Talent Pools which are composed of the top 15–20 percent of the general population using either general ability or one or more specific areas of ability. Students in these talent pools are then offered opportunities to learn subjects at a faster pace using "curriculum compacting"; thus, freeing up time for enrichment within the general education class. In addition, thousands of students now participate each year in Talent Searches during which seventh and eighth grade students take the SAT. The results of these talent searches can help districts identify able students who may be in need of more academic challenge. Allowing students to take Algebra as early as seventh grade permits them to be able to take more advanced math electives during high school such as: Differential Equations, Real Analysis, Linear Algebra, or Theory of Numbers.

Regardless of the delivery model employed, certain assumptions undergirding the philosophy of gifted services must be supported at the middle school level.

All children progress through challenging material at their own pace. Gifted students often reach mastery in significantly less time than other learners.

- Achieving success for all students is not equated with achieving the same results for all students.
- Most students gain self-esteem and self-confidence from mastering work that initially seems slightly beyond their grasp.
- In addition to sometimes serving as peer role models, high ability students also need to spend time learning new material and stretching to their full potential.
- Flexible grouping of gifted learners should be offered based on students' abilities and talents in these areas.
- Professionals working with gifted students require ongoing specialized training to support their ability to work with this population of students.
- Program strategies used with gifted students should address academic as well as social and personal needs.

In 1995, Coleman and Gallagher conducted a study to identify schools where the middle school movement was blended with quality program services for students who are gifted. Successful sites used instructional grouping to offer challenges to students as well as some form of enrichment. A variety of differentiation approaches were utilized, including mentoring, flexible pacing, independent studies, interdisciplinary units, and thinking skills. In addition, each site also had at least one person on staff who was knowledgeable about the needs of gifted students.

The call for more collaboration between the gifted and the middle school movements will be enhanced if schools first explore the common ground existing between the two fields (Coleman & Gallagher, 1992), namely, that both are committed to meeting the unique developmental needs of students during early adolescence. As programs for the middle school gifted student continue to evolve, the following touchstones can be useful in guiding program decisions:

1. Do the program services support excellence over mediocrity?
2. Will the program offerings help students see in themselves a strength, passion, or capability that can become a highly developed talent?
3. Do the program offerings support students' varying learning needs, e.g., pace, and style?
4. Do the program offerings eliminate an artificial ceiling for learning?
5. Do the program offerings promote depth of understanding rather than just access to quantity?
6. Do the program offerings promote the gifted student's capacities for creative and critical thinking skills?
7. Do the program offerings provide a balance of curricular and co-curricular offerings including appropriate exploratory activities?
8. Do the program offerings offer opportunities to develop an understanding for relationships within and between disciples?

References

Beane, J., & Lipka, R. (1986). *Self-concept, self-esteem, and the curriculum.* New York: Teachers College Press.

Betts, G., & Neihart, M. (1988). Profiles of the gifted. *Gifted Child Quarterly, 32*(2), 248–253.

Bloom, B. (1985). Generalizations about talent development. In B. Bloom (Ed.), *Developing talent in young people* (pp. 507–549). New York: Ballantine Books.

Buescher, T. M. (1985). A framework for understanding the social and emotional development of gifted and talented adolescents. *Roeper Review, 8*, 10–15.

Buescher, T. M., & Higham, S. J. (1989). A developmental study of adjustment among gifted adolescents. In J. Van Tassel-Baska & P. Olszcwski-Kubilius (Eds.), *Patterns of influence on gifted learners: The home, the self, and the school* (pp. 102–124). New York: Teachers College Press.

Chapman, J., & McAlpine, D. (1988). Students' perceptions of ability. *Gifted Child Quarterly, 32*(1), 222–225.

Clark, B. (1988). *Growing up gifted: Developing the potential of children at home and school* (3rd ed.). Columbus, OH: Charles E. Merrill.

Clinkenbeard, P. R. (1991). Unfair expectations: A pilot study of middle school students' comparisons of gifted and regular classes. *Journal for the Education of the Gifted, 15*(1), 56–63.

Coleman, M., & Gallagher, J. (1992). *Middle school survey report: Impact on gifted students.* Chapel Hill, NC: Gifted Education Policy Studies Program, University of North Carolina at Chapel Hill.

Coleman, M. R., & Gallagher, J. (1995). The successful blending of gifted education with middle schools and cooperative learning: Two studies. *Journal for the Education of the Gifted, 18*(4), 362–384.

Coleman, M. R., Gallagher, J., & Howard, J. (1993). *Middle school site visit report: Five schools in profile.* Chapel Hill, NC: Gifted Education Policy Studies Program, University of North Carolina at Chapel Hill.

Csikszentmihalyi, M., Rathunde, K., & Whalen, S. (1993). *Talented teenagers: The roots of success and failure*. Cambridge, UK: Cambridge University Press.

Feldhusen, J. (1992). *TIDE: Talent identification and development in education*. Sarasota, FL: Center for Creative Learning.

Ford, D. (1993). An investigation of the paradox of underachievement among gifted black students. *Roeper Review, 16*(2), 78–84.

Gagne, F. (1995). From giftedness to talent: A developmental model and its impact on the language of the field. *Roeper Review, 18*(2), 103–111.

Gallagher, J., Coleman, M. R., & Nelson, S. (1995). Perceptions of educational reform by educators representing middle schools, cooperative learning, and gifted education. *Gifted Child Quarterly, 39*(2), 66–76.

Gardner, H. (1983). *Frames of mind*. New York: Basic Books.

Johnston, J. H., & Markle, G. (1986). *What research says to the middle level practitioner*. Columbus, OH: National Middle School Association.

Kulik, J. A., & Kulik, C. L. C. (1987). Effects of ability grouping on student achievement. *Equity and excellence, 23* (1&2) 22–30.

Maker, C. L. (1996). Identification of gifted minority students: A national problem, needed changes, and a promising solution. *Gifted Child Quarterly, 40*(1), 41–50.

Manaster, G. J., & Powell, P. M. (1983). A framework for understanding gifted adolescents' psychological maladjustment. *Roeper Review, 6*(2), 70–73.

McKay, J. (1995). *Schools in the middle: Developing a middle-level orientation*. Thousand Oaks, CA: Corwin Press.

Mills, C. I., & Durden, W. G. (1992). Cooperative learning and ability grouping: An issue of choice. *Gifted Child Quarterly, 36*(1), 11–16.

National Association of Secondary School Principals. (1989). *Middle level education's responsibility for intellectual development*. Reston, VA: Author.

National Association for Gifted Children. (1994). *Position paper: Middle schools*. Washington, DC: Author.

Nielsen, E., Higgins, D., Harmmond, A., & Williams, R. (1993). Gifted children with disabilities. *Gifted Child Today, 15*(5), 9–12.

Plowman, P. (1988). Elitism. *Gifted Child Today, 56*(3), 60.

Plucker, J. A., & McIntire, J. (1996). Academic survivability in high-potential middle school students. *Gifted Child Quarterly, 40*(1), 7–14.

Renzulli, J. (1994). *Schools for talent development: A practical plan for total school improvement*. Mansfield Center, CT: Creative Learning Press.

Rosselli, H. (1995). Meeting gifted students halfway in the middle school. *Schools in the Middle, 5*(3), 12–17.

Salkind, N. (1988). *Equity and excellence: The case of mandating services for the gifted child*. Unpublished document. University of Kansas.

Sicola, P. K. (1990). Where do gifted students fit? An examination of middle school philosophy as it relates to ability grouping and the gifted learner. *Journal for the Education of the Gifted, 14*(1), 37–49.

Slavin, R. E. (1990). Achievement effects of ability grouping in secondary schools: A best evidence synthesis. *Review of Educational Research, 60*(3), 471–499.

Tomlinson, C. A. (1992). Gifted education and the middle school movement: Two voices on teaching the academically talented. *Journal for the Education of the Gifted, 15*(3), 206–238.

Tomlinson, C. A. (1994). Gifted learners: The boomerang kids of middle school? *Roeper Review, 16*(3), 177–182.

Tomlinson, C. A. (1995). Deciding to differentiate instruction in middle school: One school's journey. *Gifted Child Quarterly, 39*(2), 77–87.

Treffinger, D. (1992). Programming for giftedness: Needed directions. *INNOTECH Journal, 16*(1), 54–61.

U.S. Department of Education. (1993). *National excellence: A case for developing America's talent*. Washington, DC: Author.

Wallace, D. (1985). Giftedness and the construction of a creative life. In F. Horowitz (Ed.), *The gifted and talented: Development perspectives* (pp. 361–386). Washington, DC: American Psychological Association.

Hilda C. Rosselli is the Associate Dean for Undergraduate Programs in the College of Education at the University of South Florida, Tampa. E-mail: rosselli@tempest.coedu.usf.edu

Judith L. Irvin is a professor at Florida State University, Tallahassee. E-mail: irvin@coe.fsu.edu

Originally appeared in the January 2001 issue of *Middle School Journal,* pp. 57-62. Used with permission from National Middle School Association.

UNIT 3
Exceptional and Culturally Diverse Children

Unit Selections

Key Points to Consider

- What are some of the issues and concerns of including children in regular classrooms?

- Who are the gifted and talented? How can knowledge of their characteristics and learning needs help to provide them with an appropriate education?

- How will understanding the needs of culturally diverse and language minority students help them achieve success in school?

Student Website

www.mhcls.com/online

Internet References

Further information regarding these websites may be found in this book's preface or online.

The Council for Exceptional Children
http://www.cec.sped.org/index.html

Global SchoolNet Foundation
http://www.gsn.org

International Project: Multicultural Pavilion
http://curry.edschool.virginia.edu/curry/centers/multicultural/papers.html

Let 1000 Flowers Bloom/Kristen Nicholson-Nelson
http://teacher.scholastic.com/professional/assessment/100flowers.htm

National Association for Multicultural Education
http://www.nameorg.org

National Attention Deficit Disorder Association
http://www.add.org

National MultiCultural Institute (NMCI)
http://www.nmci.org

Teaching Tolerance
http://www.tolerance.org

The Equal Educational Opportunity Act for All Handicapped Children (Public Law 94-142) gives disabled children the right to an education in the least-restrictive environment, due process, and an individualized educational program that is specifically designed to meet their needs. Professionals and parents of exceptional children are responsible for developing and implementing an appropriate educational program for each child. The application of these ideas to classrooms across the nation at first caused great concern among educators and parents. Classroom teachers whose training did not prepare them for working with the exceptional child expressed negative attitudes about mainstreaming. Special resource teachers also expressed concern that mainstreaming would mitigate the effectiveness of special programs for the disabled and would force cuts in services. Parents feared that their children would not receive the special services they required because of governmental red tape and delays in proper diagnosis and placement.

It has been more than two decades since the implementation of P.L. 94-142, which was amended by the Individuals with Disabilities Education Act (IDEA) in 1991 and introduced the term "inclusion." Inclusion tries to assure that disabled children will be fully integrated within the classroom. Many of the above concerns have been studied by psychologists and educators, and their findings have often influenced policy. For example, research has indicated that inclusion is more effective when regular classroom teachers and special resource teachers collaborate and work cooperatively with disabled children.

The articles concerning the educationally disabled confront some of these issues. The first article by Susan Baglieri and Janice Knopf emphasizes differentiated instruction as a way to meet the needs of all students in an inclusive classroom. Brent Hardin and Marie Hardin present "Into the Mainstream: Practical Strategies for Teaching in Inclusive Environments" which identifies additional strategies to help teachers cope with demands of inclusion.

Other exceptional children are the gifted and talented. These children are rapid learners who can absorb, organize, and apply concepts more effectively than the average child. They often have IQs of 140 or more and are convergent thinkers (i.e., they give the correct answer to teacher or test questions). Convergent thinkers are usually models of good behavior and academic performance, and they respond to instruction easily; teachers generally value such children and often nominate them for gifted programs. There are other children, however, who do not score well on standardized tests of intelligence because their thinking is more divergent (i.e., they can imagine more than one answer to teacher or test questions). These gifted divergent thinkers may not respond to traditional instruction. They may become bored, respond to questions in unique and disturbing ways, and appear uncooperative and disruptive. Many teachers do not understand these unconventional thinkers and fail to identify them as gifted. In fact, such children are sometimes labeled as emotionally disturbed or mentally retarded because of the negative impressions they make on their teachers. Because of the differences between these types of students, a great deal of controversy surrounds programs for the gifted. Such programs should

enhance the self-esteem of all gifted and talented children, motivate and challenge them, and help them realize their creative potential. The two articles in the subsection on gifted children consider the characteristics of giftedness, and they explain how to identify gifted students and provide them with an appropriate education.

The third subsection of this unit concerns student diversity. Just as labeling may adversely affect the disabled child, it may also affect the child who comes from a minority ethnic background where the language and values are quite different from those of the mainstream culture. The term "disadvantaged" is often used to describe these children, but it is negative, stereotypical, and apt to result in a self-fulfilling prophecy whereby teachers perceive such children as incapable of learning. Teachers should provide academically and culturally diverse children with experiences that they might have missed in the restricted environment of their homes and neighborhoods. The articles in this section suggest ways to create culturally compatible classrooms. The first article suggests that assessments ought to identify a student's strengths as well as weaknesses, so he or she can be encouraged to use their strengths to show what has been learned. The last two articles in this section discuss strategies identified in the research for effectively teaching diverse students, including students for whom English is a second language.

Normalizing Difference in Inclusive Teaching

Abstract

Inclusion practices and special education can be transformed by using a disability studies perspective, which constructs differences as natural, acceptable, and ordinary. Although inclusion is a moral imperative in promoting social justice, some inclusive practices continue to marginalize students with disabilities. A truly inclusive school reflects a democratic philosophy whereby all students are valued, educators normalize difference through differentiated instruction, and the school culture reflects an ethic of caring and community.

Susan Baglieri and Janice H. Knopf

The discursive communities in which we live structure our knowledge of the world and the ways that we interact with each other. By *discourse*, we refer not only to ideas or ideology but also to the "working attitudes, modes of address, terms of reference, and courses of action suffused into social practice" (Gubrium & Hol- stein, 2000). One such discourse, scientific determinism, or what is often referred to in special education jargon as "the medical model," typically relies on binaries as a means of defining and identifying human characteristics. The medical model has informed the discourses surrounding dis/ability (see Note) and education in Western society during the modern era.

Such Cartesian binary thinking both informs and is informed by the construction of the biological ideal of the "normal," which privileges the normal body and mind in relation to those characteristics associated with "abnormality." Disability studies, particularly as applied in Disability Studies in Education (DSE), provide the foundation for us to problematize the simplistic binaries undergirding educational decision making. The DSE perspective frames difference as ordinary human variation and, thereby, enables us to rethink the normal–abnormal binary. The question is not whether we perceive differences among people but, rather, what meaning is brought to bear on those perceived differences (D. J. Gallagher, 2001). Rather than conceptualizing variations as *only* medical conditions of the body and mind, DSE foregrounds the power-laden social constructions that result from the social and political discourses in which special education operates (e.g., see Davis & Linton, 1995; Linton, 1998; Thomson, 2000).

Theorizing Learning Dis/Ability

Reid and Valle address the debates surrounding the construction of dis/ability within the field of learning dis/abilities (LD) and, by extension, (special) education. We agree that by using a DSE perspective to inform our practices, we may begin to acknowledge that change is possible and to suggest a vision of what such change could (and perhaps should) be like. The goal of DSE scholars is to uncover and eliminate social, cultural, and political barriers that prevent access to employment, academic, recreational, and residential opportunities afforded to those without the variations that society labels as impairments. Furthermore, DSE scholars problematize and challenge the accepted educational practices related to normalizing, labeling, and categorizing individuals as having a learning dis/ability. In so doing, they promote "a politics of difference that refuses to pathologize or exoticize the Other" (Kincheloe & McLaren, 2000, p. 275).

Our position is best theorized in Stiker's (1997) historical analysis: "Difference is not an exception … but something that happens in the natural course of things" (p. 12). Be-

cause so many in our society buy into difference as impairment (i.e., they construct difference as negative), the normalizing discourse and resulting social structures create barriers to access for individuals with differences and frequently prohibit them from active participation in the communities in which they reside. Dis/ability, then, is the inflexible, unyielding, and inaccessible nature of the social and political community, and not only individual physical or mental characteristics.

Our goal in discussing Dis/ability and identifying people as "dis/abled" is no longer to pathologize individuals but, rather, to politicize the term and identify the site of oppression (Freire, 1970). There are various ways that people with dis/abilities are using terms such as "dis/abled," "freak," and "crip" to reclaim personal identities (Linton, 1998).

Inclusion as a Moral Imperative

The philosophy undergirding the "agegraded, factory model of education common in most of our schools" (Dudley-Marling & Dippo, 1995, p. 410) assumes that children generally learn the same way and should strive to attain the same goals. The lockstep educational system privileges those students who are prepared to manage the specified type of academic structure, who possess the cultural capital that schools assume, and who can, therefore, operate within the range of expected behavior. Unspoken is the fact that schools clearly favor "certain ways of knowing, doing, thinking, and interacting" (Dudley-Marling & Dippo, 1995, p. 409). Reid and Valle point out that those students who do not fit the model are identified by teachers and selected for educational testing, which generally confirms an "abnormality." When such students are then segregated into remedial or special education classes, they are often subject to subpar educational preparation and teaching methodology (Heshusius, 1989).

If we understand the creation of dis/ability to be a discursive and so-

cial process, we see that we can take steps to disrupt dis/abling practices and attitudes that emerge from legitimating dis/ability as only a biological reality. Stiker (1997) adopted a social justice position for those with differences in his book *A History of Disability* and called for support of what has sometimes been referred to as a *moral imperative*—that society must work to deconstruct ableism and create a community that recognizes and embraces all differences. Stiker (1997) stated, "We must then inscribe in our cultural models a view of difference as the law of the real. It is a matter of stating and restating, first of all to children throughout their education, that it is inscribed in the human universe to value the differences it engenders and of which it is also a product" (p. 12). Differences are pervasive, ordinary, and acceptable. Inclusion of all students in general education is critically important for creating societies that recognize and embrace human variation (Thomas & Loxley, 2001; Wang & Reynolds, 1996).

The DSE perspective can inform inclusion practices that, in turn, have the potential to transform the structures of classrooms and the manner in which children with differences are treated in these classrooms. DSE scholars argue for embracing, honoring, and respecting differential characteristics. Although advocates for full inclusion acknowledge that there are some extraordinary circumstances that make inclusion difficult, they continue to promote the "fundamental right to self-determination" (D. J. Gallagher, 2001, p. 638) for individuals constructed as "impaired." Active and continual effort toward the acceptance and improvement of inclusive educational practices is a possible first move toward social justice.

The discussions that circulate around students who have not been successful in school constitute a major barrier to inclusion. Labeling, teacher attitudes, and current practices marginalize students labeled as having dis/abilities. As long as we continue to position students with the pejorative label of dis/ability, teachers

(Miller, 2001) and students (Shapiro, 2000) will continue to view difference as negative. The school and societal discourses that legitimate learning dis/ability as a physical and mental reality justify labeling and segregated educational settings and result in continued differential treatment (Shapiro, 2000).

Teachers often express a variety of concerns about inclusive education: their ability to meet simultaneously the needs of both "normal" children and those labeled as having dis/abilities in their general education classrooms; the lack of adequate supportive resources; and the pressures to meet academic performance standards enforced through standardized testing (D. J. Gallagher, 2001). Even when we include students in the general education setting, they frequently do not escape marginalization. Often, instruction in special education and inclusive settings attends only to the remediation of the individual with a dis/ability, rather than, as is mandated by law, access to the general education curriculum.

In addressing these concerns, it is helpful to acknowledge that many educators assume that only students labeled with a dis/ability (and not other students) require adaptation, accommodations, and modifications to the general education curriculum (Ellis, 1997; Fuchs & Fuchs, 1998; Jubala, Bishop, & Falvey, 1995). Although accommodating students with a dis/ability is clearly desirable, the term suggests that accommodations are different and separate from the "normal" curriculum. This understanding often results in wholesale reductionism (Heshusius, 1989) and simplification of both curriculum and expectations (Ellis, 1997). Such ineffective instructional practices confirm the understanding of students with learning dis/abilities as less able. As such, even "included" students labeled as having LD continue to be excluded, not by classroom location but by the instructional discourses that circulate in the school. Creating an environment in which the discourse of difference (Stiker, 1997) positions all students and their myriad differences as positive, "normal," and even enriching is a critical step toward reconceptualizing and restructuring schools.

In attending to the creation of a positive discourse that centers rather than marginalizes difference, Reid and Valle argue that the practice of referring to student "readiness" for inclusion (Biklen, 1992; Gantwerk, 1995; Garrick-Duhaney & Saland, 2000; Waldron & McLeskey, 1998) must give way to the conviction that access to general education classrooms is not an earned privilege, but a *right*: "Grounded in a civil rights discourse that focuses on interactions among difference, impairment, and disability . . . we assume that everybody belongs and ask how educators can make general education classrooms welcoming, productive . . . environments for *all* students." (p. 8).

We do not deny the existence of variation among students in school performance, nor are we suggesting that accommodation is undesirable. Rather, we suggest that the use of accommodations *only* in terms of students with LD is problematic. A truly inclusive classroom strives to bring "difference back to the norm" (Stiker, 1997, p. 192) and acknowledges the right of every individual to have access to all of the experiences and benefits available in schools. Our work, then, becomes that of creating a discourse of difference in which all students are allowed access, valued for their unique characteristics, and provided with opportunities to learn and perform in myriad ways that address individual needs and personal goals. Incorporating a DSE perspective assists educators in creating a discourse in schools that decenters the normal as the focus for curricular decisions, recognizes every student as an equal member of the community, and allows the needs and interests of each student to drive the choices made about instructional practices.

Using a Model of Differentiated Instruction

As members of a diverse society who interact within a democratic system, students are well served by a curriculum that is designed to disrupt discriminatory discourses. Teaching students to care about themselves and each other begins with providing the environments and the language they need to interact, both with students who are labeled and with those who are not.

Furthermore, to provide access and opportunity for all students, we urge educators to rethink separate assignments and activities, classroom seating positions, and lowered expectations that apply only to labeled students. In contrast, differentiated instruction can be designed for the education of *all* students. In the differentiated classroom (Tomlinson, 1999), three principles structure the educational philosophy. First, teachers create curricula based on where the students are, as opposed to where a graded, or standardized, curriculum assumes students should be. Second, teachers select methods through which each individual may learn as deeply and quickly as possible. This strategy is antithetical to the reductionist view of learning (Heshusius, 1989) in which teachers' task analyses reduce learning to its ordered component parts—a logical rather than psychological approach. Third, teachers understand that cultivation of teacher-student learning relationships is essential and takes time to develop.

Creating a curriculum that caters to where individual students are is a daunting process when considering a classroom of 25 (and often more) students. We agree with Reid and Valle and with Mariage, Paxton-Buursma, and Bouck that research demonstrates that a Vygotskian framework effectively guides and supports the learning of students with LD. By using instructional arrangements that provide opportunities to form cooperative relationships in which students support each other and serve as learning models, students have multiple models and guides to practice and encourage the development of new and emerging abilities (Gindis, 1999). Care should be taken to ensure that these relationships rely on collaboration, not helping, and that peers share equal status in the groupings (Shapiro, 2000). A way to encourage this type of cooperative learning is to provide activities that require multiple ways of interacting and accessing the curriculum.

An example that attends to the three principles of differentiated instruction in a secondary-level English class requires reading and responding to a text. Participation in and completion of the assignment can be made to fit each individual student's particular needs and strengths, which may be determined through individual teacher–student discussions and student choice and combined with specific individual, pair, or group curricular goals; in cooperative groupings, students support one another in meeting their goals. They may choose to read aloud to each other, for example, or listen to a recording so that even students who do not read proficiently can gain access to the text and engage in discussion and reflective activities. Student responses may also be enacted in varied ways, such as illustration, discussion, performance, and writing. By providing multiple opportunities to participate in the learning community, student learning is both social and individualized and is reinforced through interaction with knowledge in several ways—a favored method in current learning theory (Gardner & Hatch, 1989). The use of this model allows and encourages multiple ways to participate and also reinforces the value of difference in the classroom and society. In this way, difference is reconstructed as "normal" in the classroom community.

Noddings (1994) focused her work on the importance of human relationships in learning. Through providing instructional arrangements where students support and interact with each other in continual, meaningful ways, teachers promote relationships that lead to mutual caring. When teachers model positive language and attitudes toward difference, students also are affirmed in the development of their peer relationships. A classroom discourse that dialogically and pedagogically explores and embraces differences nurtures relationships within the classroom community and leads students toward a broader appreciation of difference.

Shapiro (2000) suggested that teachers confront students' negative attitudes toward dis/ability by implementing a dis/ability awareness program, incorporating images and stories of dis/ability into the curriculum. One goal is to disrupt the stereotypical tropes of people with dis/abilities as overcoming obstacles and seeking cures or as being pitiable, lesser, and supernatural (Davis, 1997a, 1997b; Linton, 1998; Longmore, 1997; Shakespeare, 1994). Classroom dialogue centered on discussing issues of dis/ability in positive ways disempowers the surrounding negative societal discourse. Inviting dis/abled members of the community with dis/abilities to talk with the students about their lives, families, careers, and aspirations, as well as the physical and social obstacles that stem from community responses to their differences, also works to replace typical assumptions with more real and positive counternarratives. Personal interaction has the potential to affect and change the negative attitudes that support the continued marginalization of those with difference.

A Call for Reflective Practice

DSE scholars call for self-reflection and critique of the manner in which we include, educate, and address students with differences. There is an urgent need to confront the inequities that are so evident in schools and to work toward creating equal status relationships for every student. "To really help, then, is to work daily to remove the stigma of differ-ence, to create classrooms in which relationship and dialogue, as opposed to treatment and training, are central, to create a conception of community based not on normalcy, competitiveness, and 'just desserts,' but rather on diversity, mutuality, and social justice" (Dudley-Marling & Dippo, 1995, p. 411). Teacher preparation programs that challenge commonly accepted values and structures of schooling support such goals.

The No Child Left Behind Act (NCLB) of 2001 presents a significant challenge to the implementation of inclusion and differentiated learning environments. Because NCLB supports scientific "research-based" instructional programs and methods, schools are increasingly using "proven" standardized programs and methods to boost test scores, which subsequently discourages teachers from using the type of critical pedagogy (Wink, 2000) that can engage and capitalize on the strengths of all learners. Bejoian and Reid (2004), for example, critiqued NCLB as dangerous in its focus on accountability testing that may serve to further segregate the already marginalized students with LD and English language learners. Although the requirement of nearly all students to meet achievement standards increases the accountability of schools and could push schools toward inclusion, the type of standards-driven testing employed to measure progress does little to discourage remedial grouping. A discourse of difference supports truly inclusive instructional arrangements and disrupts the normalizing power structures (S. Gallagher, 1999) at work in a standards-driven curriculum.

Differentiated instruction, on the other hand, drives the spirit of the classroom and school community toward critical reflection and disrupts the inequalities currently prevalent in our schools and our society. Such differentiated teaching practices reflect a democratic philosophy, wherein each student's voice is heard and valued. Inclusive environments that support equal status among students center curriculum on constructivist, student-centered principles that encourage the exploration and construction of ideas and questions. Finally, differentiated instruction supports a school culture that reflects an ethic of caring and a genuine community spirit wherein difference is valued, not considered an aberration, and is welcomed as a natural part of the school's landscape. When we create arrangements and expectations that cater to the individuality of students and not to their potential to conform, we take small but important steps toward constructing inclusive communities in our greater society.

ABOUT THE AUTHORS

Susan Baglieri, MA, is a special educator in Bergen County, New Jersey. Ms. Baglieri is also an instructor for the William Paterson University of New Jersey's ProjectGRAD summer program. A social justice perspective informs her teaching practices. **Janice H. Knopf, MA,** *is an instructor at Teachers College, Columbia University, where she is also pursuing a doctorate in learning dis/abilities. Her experience as a mother of four children and as a teacher in both elementary and secondary school settings has informed her appreciation for differences among all learners. Address: Janice H. Knopf, Teachers College, Columbia University Department of Curriculum & Teaching, Box 31, 525 West 120th Street, New York, NY 10027.*

AUTHORS' NOTE

Our names appear in alphabetical order. We contributed equally to the writing of this article.

NOTE

Our visual representation of the term disability as dis/ability is our effort to use the word as an indicator of an active process of disabling rather than as a descriptor for the wide variety of physical and mental characteristics to which it is often applied.

REFERENCES

Bejoian, L. M., & Reid, D. K. (in press). A disability studies perspective on the Bush education agenda: The No Child Left Behind act of 2001. *Equity and Excellence in Education.*

Biklen, D. (1992). The inclusion philosophy. In *Schooling without labels* (pp. 20–37). Philadelphia: Temple University Press.

Davis, L. J. (1997a). Constructing normalcy: The bell curve, the novel, and the invention of the disabled body in the nineteenth century. In L. J. Davis (Ed.), *The disability studies reader* (pp. 9–28). New York: Routledge.

Davis, L. J. (1997b). Nude Venuses, Medusa's body, and phantom limbs: Disability and visuality. In D. T. Mitchell & S. L. Snyder (Eds.), *The body and physical difference: Discourses of disability* (pp. 51–70). Ann Arbor: University of Michigan Press.

Davis, L. J., & Linton, S. (1995). Introduction. *Radical Teacher, 47,* 2–3.

Dudley-Marling, C., & Dippo, D. (1995). What learning disability does: Sustaining the ideology of schooling. *Journal of Learning Disabilities, 28,* 406–414.

Ellis, E. S. (1997). Watering up the curriculum for adolescents with learning disabilities: Goals of the knowledge dimension. *Remedial and Special Education, 18,* 326–346.

Freire, P. (1970). Pedagogy of the oppressed. In D. J. Flinders & S. J. Thornton (Eds.), *The curriculum studies reader* (pp. 150–158). New York: Routledge.

Fuchs, L., & Fuchs, D. (1998). General educators' instructional adaptation for students with learning disabilities. *Learning Disability Quarterly, 21,* 23–33.

Gallagher, D. J. (2001). Neutrality as a moral standpoint, conceptual confusion and the full inclusion debate. *Disability and Society, 16,* 637–654.

Gallagher, S. (1999). An exchange of gazes. In J. Kincheloe, S. Steinberg, & L. Villarverde (Eds.), *Rethinking intelligence* (pp. 69–83). New York: Routledge.

Gantwerk, B. (1995). *Placement decisions and least restrictive environment.* Trenton: New Jersey Department of Education.

Gardner, H., & Hatch, T. (1989). Multiple intelligences go to school: Educational implications of the theory of multiple intelligences. *Educational Researcher, 18*(8), 4–9.

Garrick-Duhaney, L. M., & Saland, S. J. (2000). Parental perceptions of inclusive educational practices. *Remedial and Special Education, 21,* 121–128.

Gindis, B. (1999). Vygotsky's vision: Reshaping the practice of special education for the 21st century. *Remedial and Special Education, 20,* 333–340.

Gubrium, J. F., & Holstein, J. A. (2000). Analyzing interpretive practice. In N. K. Denzin & Y. S. Lincoln (Eds.), *Handbook of qualitative research* (pp. 487–508). Thousand Oaks, CA: Sage.

Heshusius, L. (1989). The Newtonian mechanistic paradigm, special education, and the contours of alternatives: An overview. *Journal of Learning Disabilities, 22,* 402–415.

Jubala, K. A., Bishop, K. D., & Falvey, M. A. (1995). Creating a supportive classroom environment. In M. A. Falvey (Ed.), *Inclusive and heterogenous schooling: Assessment, curriculum, and instruction* (pp. 111–129). Baltimore: Brookes.

Kincheloe, J. L., & McLaren, P. (2000). Rethinking critical theory and qualitative research. In N. K. Denzin & Y. S. Lincoln (Eds.), *Handbook of qualitative research* (pp. 279–313). Thousand Oaks, CA: Sage.

Linton, S. (1998). *Claiming disability: Knowledge and identity.* New York: New York University Press.

Longmore, P. K. (1997). Conspicuous contribution and American cultural dilemmas: Telethon rituals of cleansing and renewal. In D. T. Mitchell & S. L. Snyder (Eds.), *The body and physical difference: Discourses of disability* (pp. 137–160). Ann Arbor: University of Michigan Press.

Miller, H. M. (2001). Including "the included." *The Reading Teacher, 54,* 820–822.

No Child Left Behind Act of 2001, 20 U. S. C. § 6301 *et seq.*

Noddings, N. (1994). An ethic of caring and its implications for instructional arrangements. In *The education feminism reader* (pp. 171–183). New York: Routledge

Shakespeare, T. (1994). Cultural representation of disabled people: Dustbins for disavowal. *Disability and Society, 9,* 283–299.

Shapiro, A. (2000). *Everybody belongs: Changing negative attitudes toward classmates with disabilities* (Vol. 14). New York: Routledge.

Stiker, H. J. (1997). *A history of disability.* Ann Arbor: University of Michigan Press.

Thomas, G., & Loxley, A. (2001). *Deconstructing special education and constructing inclusion.* Philadelphia: Open University Press.

Thomson, R. G. (2000). The new disability studies: Inclusion or tolerance? *ADE Bulletin, 124,* 18–22.

Tomlinson, C. A. (1999). *The differentiated classroom: Responding to the needs of all learners.* Alexandria, VA: ASCD.

Waldron, N. L., & McLeskey, J. (1998). The effects of an inclusive school program on students with mild and severe learning disabilities. *Exceptional Children, 64,* 395–405.

Wang, M. C., & Reynolds, M. C. (1996). Progressive inclusions: Meeting new challenges in special education. *Theory Into Practice, 35*(1), 20–25.

Wink, J. (2000). *Critical pedagogy: Notes from the real world* (2nd ed.). New York: Addison Wesley Longman.

Into the Mainstream: Practical Strategies for Teaching in Inclusive Environments

Brent Hardin and Marie Hardin

Christopher, thirty-two, teaches ninth-grade English at a high school on the outskirts of Atlanta, Georgia. Although he has been a teacher for eight years and has clearly moved beyond the induction phase of his career, some classroom challenges still seem overwhelming to him.

Christopher's average day begins before 7 a.m. After he arrives at his portable classroom behind the high school, he begins his first class at 7:30. He teaches six classes throughout the day—a mix of "Technical English" and college-preparatory courses. On top of his regular teaching load, Christopher often has to substitute teach during his one planning period during the day.

Christopher's job, however, involves far more than teaching about punctuation, active voice, and sentence structure to the 115 students who visit his trailer each day. He spends much of his energy on classroom management and administrative tasks, while he struggles to work with the many special-needs students who have been integrated into his courses. During first period, for instance, an aide joins Christopher to teach a group nearly half of whom have diagnosed emotional, behavioral, or learning problems. In another class later in the day, nine of fifteen students have some type of disability. Besides making accommodations for students during his lessons, Christopher is also required to remember other details, such as the times to send some students to the office to take medication. "I can put my kids into two different categories" he says, "They're completely bouncing off the walls or they're catatonic. It's a struggle. I try to keep my energy level up."

Christopher's situation is certainly not unique. Inclusion of students with a wide range of disabilities into regular classrooms can be a daunting prospect for teachers at any career stage. However, teachers at the induction or competency-building phases can find the task of teaching students with disabilities especially challenging because they lack sufficient training and support to work with these students (Werts et al. 1996).

Teachers can, however, use a number of strategies to cope with these demands and increase their effectiveness in an inclusive environment. Using peer tutors, implementing cooperative learning, and applying reverse-inclusion techniques in the classroom can be powerful strategies to provide successful learning for all students.

Changing Demographics

The need for teachers to cope with the demands of inclusive classrooms has increased during the past several years, as the numbers of students with disabilities in public education has climbed dramatically. The Nineteenth Annual Report to Congress on the Implementation of the Individuals with Disabilities Education Act revealed that during the 1994–1995 school year there were approximately 4.7 million schoolchildren with disabilities, or almost 10 percent of the student population. At least 48 percent of students requiring special education services attend inclusive classes for most or all of the school day, a 60 percent escalation from 1994 (McLeskey, Henry, and Hodges 1998). This trend is predicted to continue. All teachers, not just special educators, should be prepared to teach students with disabilities.

Teachers' Perceptions of Competence

Thousands of teachers, at all career stages, teach students with disabilities in inclusive classrooms every day, but many do not feel competent or confident in that role. Kelly, a third-year elementary teacher in north Florida, speaks of her confidence in teaching students with disabilities in an integrated classroom:

> Conceptually, I think inclusion is a great idea. But, at the same time, I don't think teachers are prepared. I know I am not. I really didn't get any experience or training teaching kids with disabilities mixed in with my regular classes. It's hard enough just handling a

regular class, but throw in students with special needs and it is really overwhelming if you don't have the training or the help.

Surveys of countless teachers echo Kelly's concerns. A recent synthesis of research (Scruggs and Mastropieri 1996), based on studies dating back to 1958, indicates that approximately two-thirds of the 10,560 general educators surveyed across the years agreed with the concept of inclusion, but their degree of enthusiasm decreased when asked, "Are you prepared to teach with disabilities in your classroom?" Confidence decreased even further when questions addressed teacher readiness to make curricular or instructional modifications for identified students. When Schultz (1982) surveyed teachers to determine what specific issues were of concern, teachers said that they felt a lack of expertise in accounting for individual differences when they designed and implemented their instructional strategies.

Research indicates that educators do not feel that they have been adequately trained for inclusive environments. Lyon, Vaasen, and Toomey (1989) surveyed 440 teachers concerning their perceptions of their undergraduate and graduate training programs, questioning how such programs prepared them to address individual differences within the classroom. Sadly, the majority of the respondents reported that the training programs that they completed did not prepare them to provide effective instruction for a diverse student population. Over 93 percent of the regular educators indicated that they did not receive any hands-on experience teaching students with disabilities in their training programs.

Gallagher, Malone, Cleghorne, and Helms (1997) interviewed 115 teachers concerning their perceived training needs related to children with disabilities. Although 64 percent of the respondents reported six or more years' experience teaching students with disabilities in inclusive classrooms, they reported low confidence in several areas of basic competency. Such challenges can be daunting for inexperienced teachers trying to learn basic classroom management skills, deal with failing students, and keep track of grades and paperwork.

Practical Classroom Strategies

Educators at any career stage can, however, implement a number of simple strategies to increase their effectiveness and grow more confident in inclusive environments. Subtle changes can accommodate students with special needs without obtrusively changing the class for other students.

Peer Tutoring

Students who serve as peer tutors have been trained to assist other students in the classroom. These tutors can work with special-needs students to provide the extra attention and feedback they need in order to learn, allowing the teacher to divide his or her attention more equally among the students. Also, students with and without disabilities can work together in tutoring pairs to positively affect each other.

Greenwood, Delquadri, and Garta (1997) maintain that teachers find peer tutoring valuable because it is adaptable to any teaching style and curriculum; easy to implement; cost effective; time efficient; and effective with all ability levels. Although students can learn from each other, the teacher should carefully select the peer tutors who will work with disabled students. Not all students will be ready or able to work in a partnership with special needs students. Ellery (1995) recommends that peer tutors be (*a*) slightly older than their disabled counterparts, (*b*) emotionally mature, (*c*) good communicators, (*d*) highly skilled, and (*e*) volunteers.

Peer tutors may need ongoing training to become skillful helpers. The teacher should allow time to make sure that tutors understand their responsibilities for the lesson. Also, the teacher should not overlook opportunities to offer students with disabilities the chance to tutor nondisabled students. For example, a student with spina bifida who is confined to a wheelchair is perfectly capable of providing instruction, encouragement, and feedback to another student. This arrangement extends the potential for a fully inclusive learning environment.

Cooperative Learning

This strategy brings students together in groups to accomplish shared goals. The goal of cooperative learning is to ensure that all members of the group master the information at their own levels. Oftentimes individuals in the group are given specific jobs or tasks that contribute to goal attainment. Students help each other and evaluate each member's progress toward individual and group goals. For cooperative learning to be effective, students must perceive that they are positively linked to other students in their group and that each member can and must contribute. In addition, each member must understand his or her role in the cooperative group. Less-skilled students, including students with disabilities, could be perceived to be the weak links if all members perceive that they must perform the same task. This will not happen if the group understands that each member has a unique task that maximizes his or her skills and contribution to the group goal.

One example of a cooperative learning activity is a literature circle (Zemelman, Daniels, and Hyde 1993). In a literature circle, groups of four or five students choose and read the same article or book. Each student then comes to the literature circle with an assigned discussion role that accommodates skill differences, allowing for different versions of the text, including tape, film, or Braille.

Kagan (1985) recommends a cooperative learning strategy called "numbered heads," designed to actively engage all students during teacher-led instruction and discussion. Students are organized into four-member heterogeneous learning teams. After the teacher directs a question to the entire class, students are asked to put their heads together to come up with their best answer. The teacher then calls for answers from one numbered member of a group, asking, for example, "Which number 1 can answer this question?"

A substantial body of research confirms the academic and social benefits of cooperative learning approaches to instruction for students of diverse abilities. Benefits have been noted in measures of student achievement (Slavin 1990), self-esteem (Johnson and Johnson 1989), and peer relationships and interactions (Johnson, Johnson, Warring, and Maruyama 1986).

Reverse Inclusion

One way to implement reverse inclusion is to integrate several students without disabilities into a class that has several students with disabilities (Block 1994). The students without disabilities participate in the class alongside students with disabilities. Another way is to have students without disabilities role-play the disabilities of their peers during certain lessons. Examples might include having students participate in a listening exercise while blindfolded or present a poem or speech using sign language. A teacher might also invite a guest speaker to teach the students about how to use and maneuver a wheelchair. The entire class may take part in a wheelchair basketball game as a culminating event for this instructional unit. This type of instruction promotes classwide understanding and respect for all students.

Planning to Mainstream

Although awareness of these strategies is advantageous, it is important that teachers focus on the particular needs of their individual students when designing classroom lessons. The goal is to allow all students the opportunity to participate and learn in a class that is challenging and that provides opportunities for success. Thus, it is important to evaluate the effect that any lesson strategy will have on the entire class. The following criteria, adapted from suggestions by Block (1994), can be used to evaluate classroom strategies:

1. Does the plan allow students with disabilities to participate successfully, yet still be challenged? For example, a teenage student with Down's syndrome should not be given reading material at a kindergarten level to present in a cooperative learning project. The student will probably be more challenged and comfortable working with age-related material that is developmentally appropriate.

2. Does the plan adversely affect students without disabilities? It might be wise from time to time to try alternative projects or activities that allow students without disabilities to experience what it is like to be in a wheelchair or have a visual impairment. However, such changes implemented on a regular basis might negatively affect the class for students without disabilities and promote resentment toward their disabled peers.

3. Does the application cause undue burden on the teacher? For example, a student with autism may need special assistance to complete many classroom tasks. It may not be feasible for the teacher to provide the individual attention needed while also teaching the other students in the class. A better adaptation might be assisting this student for part of the class and allowing a peer tutor or classroom aide to assist at other times.

Working with students in an inclusive classroom environment is a formidable prospect for teachers at all career stages; studies indicate that teachers feel neither confident nor competent about their training or ability to work with disabled students. For new teachers this challenge can be especially troublesome. Peer tutoring, cooperative learning, and reverse inclusion are three relatively simple techniques that inexperienced teachers can implement. Although no teaching strategy works in all situations and individual learner needs must be considered, such techniques have been demonstrated as effective in inclusive environments. The merits of such applications are clear. Teacher efficacy is enhanced and confidence is ensured while students' inclusive experiences are maximized.

Key words: special education, disabilities, inclusive classrooms, teacher competence, cooperative learning

REFERENCES

Block, M. E. 1994. A teacher's guide to including students with disabilities in regular physical education. Baltimore: Brookes.

Ellery, P. J. 1995. Peer tutors work. Strategies 5:12–14.

Gallagher P., M. Malone, M. Cleghorne, and A. Helms. 1997. Perceived in-service training needs for early intervention personnel. Exceptional Children 64:19–30.

Greenwood, C. R. J. G. Delquadri, and I. J. Carta. 1997. Together we can: Class-wide peer tutoring to improve basic academic skills. Longmont, GO: Sopris West.

Johnson, D. W., and R. T. Johnson. 1989. Cooperation and competition: Theory and research. Edina, MN: Interaction Books.

Johnson, D. W., R. T. Johnson, D. Warring, and G. Maruyama. 1986. Different cooperative learning procedures and cross-handicap relationships. Exceptional Children 53(3): 247–52.

Kagan, S. 1985. Cooperative learning. Mission Viejo, CA: Resources for Teachers.

Lyon, G., M. Vaasen, and F. Toomey. 1989. Teacher's perceptions of their undergraduate and graduate preparation. Teacher Education and Special Education 12(4): 164–69.

McLeskey, J., D. Henry, and D. Hodges. 1998. Inclusion: Where is it happening? Teaching Exceptional Children 31(1): 4–10.

Office of Special Education Programs. 1997. To assure the free appropriate public education of all children with disabilities. Nineteenth annual report to Congress on the implementation of the Individuals with Disabilities Education Act. Washington, DC: Office of Special Exceptional Children.

Schultz, L. 1982. Educating the special needs student in the regular classroom. Exceptional Children 48:366–67.

Scruggs, T. E., and M. A. Mastropieri. 1996. Teacher perceptions of mainstreaming/inclusion, 1958–1995: A research synthesis. Exceptional Children 63(1): 59–74.

Werts, M. G., M. Wolery, E. D. Snyder, N. K. Caldwell, and C. L. Salisbury. 1996. Supports and resources associated with inclusive schooling: Perceptions of elementary school teachers about need and availability. Journal of Special Education 30(2): 187–203.

Zemelman, S., H. Daniels, and A. Hyde. 1993. Best practice: New standards for teaching and learning in America's schools. Portsmouth, NH: Heinemann.

Brent Hardin is an assistant professor of physical education and Marie Hardin is an assistant professor of communications, both at State University of West Georgia, in Carollton.

From *The Clearing House,* March/April 2002. Reprinted with permission of the Helen Dwight Reid Educational Foundation. Published by Heldref Publications, 1319 Eighteenth St., NW, Washington, DC 20036-1802. © 2002.

Challenges of Identifying and Serving Gifted Children with ADHD

Lori J. Flint

How often have we, as parents and educators, watched a story about students labeled as one thing or another on the evening news and felt it was oversimplified? Those of us who regularly work with children know that we can't oversimplify like that because, like adults, children are not always what they appear to be. Children are complicated, with a variety of factors, both positive and negative, simultaneously affecting them. Many children are labeled as gifted or learning disabled or having attention-deficit hyperactivity disorder (ADHD) as though that label explains the child, when what it really does is provide appropriate educational services to that child. But what about children who bear one label and also display other tendencies?

Take, for example, the idea of gifted children. Many people probably think of children as being identified as gifted according to a single intelligence test and don't realize that giftedness today often is measured in other ways: high motivation, exceptional creativity, outstanding achievement, and fantastic products.

Whoever these children with exceptional gifts and talents are, and however their gifts are measured, they're all really good in school, and have it made in life, right? Not necessarily. Some students identified as being gifted have other exceptionalities, as well; some have exceptionalities that preclude them from ever being identified as gifted.

This article describes the special situations and needs of three children—Tony, Mikey, and Gina. As you read the first part of the article, think about your own suggestions for interventions—how you might help them in your home or classroom. Then read the rest of the article to see what others have to say about working with children who have both giftedness and attentional difficulties.

Three Children

Tony

Nine-year-old Tony is a charmer. He has an engaging smile and knows how to turn it on and off. Tony is also a challenge to have in the classroom. He blurts out answers constantly, never stops moving, and argues with the teacher and with his peers incessantly. He is of average intelligence, displays little creativity, earns low grades on both objective and project-based work,

does not like school, and typically achieves at a below-average level. Tony is disorganized and distractible and is always either talking or making other noise. He is usually missing either his work or some vital component needed to do his work. He visits the office on a regular basis because he is removed from the classroom when he is so disruptive the teacher cannot continue teaching. Tony's teacher will be happy when this school year is over, but worries about where Tony will go next year and whether his new teacher will be able to handle him—he needs a teacher who is neither too permissive nor too authoritarian. Tony carries with him two labels: He has been diagnosed with ADHD and oppositional defiant disorder (ODD). Tony is one of four children in a family headed by a single parent.

Mikey

Six-year-old Mikey was referred to the schools' student support team (SST) by his classroom teacher. Why was he referred? Mikey was distractible, inattentive, fast-moving, and talkative, to the point of not functioning well in his first-grade classroom. He also displayed some aggressive behavior and poor social skills. One member of the SST was a perceptive administrator whose experience included a 14-year stint teaching gifted children. The recommendation from the team included referring the boy for testing for the gifted program.

Exercise caution in both the identification and treatment of ADHD in children identified as being gifted.

The gifted intervention specialist in the school began evaluating Mikey, first by observing him in his classroom on several occasions, then by administering a variety of mental ability, achievement, creativity, and motivation instruments; all designed to ascertain whether Mikey was gifted according to his state's multiple criteria identification law. As he sat to take a mental ability test in a one-on-one testing situation with his school's gifted specialist, the differences this child exhibited were quickly noted. Mikey was, indeed, exceptionally active; hanging off the chair, even standing, at times, during the testing. He vocalized and was impulsive in answering nearly all questions on the tests. During the administration of a mental ability test, he rushed through the verbal and quantitative sections, performing only at the 48th percentile, and slowing only when he came to something entirely new: the matrix section of the test. He barely listened to the instructions, then dove in. As soon as he was allowed to begin, he started solving the problems rapidly and accurately; thriving on the challenge. He missed none. Unfortunately, his score on this single subtest was not adequate to place him in the gifted program, so he required additional testing. Mikey's performance on the other evaluation measures was inconsistent, ranging from the 99th percentile on some instruments designed to evaluate creativity and mental ability to the 48th on others that measured achievement and motivation. The gifted intervention specialist worked with him, using movement to set the stage for optimal performance.

After several weeks of evaluation, Mikey qualified for the gifted program, identified as creatively and cognitively gifted. Why did the gifted specialist work so hard to help this child qualify? Because she saw a child with immense potential, but who needed a great deal of help channeling that potential into constructive avenues. He was also identified, soon after this, by his family doctor as having ADHD, of both the inattentive and hyperactive types. Mikey comes from a blended family with economic difficulties. He was born when his mother was 14 years of age; his mother never finished high school, and is herself identified as having ADHD, like her mother before her.

Gina

Gina is a highly gifted fifth grader whose performance on mental ability, creativity, and achievement tests regularly place her in the 99th percentile, with scores at the ceiling of the tests. She is an award-winning artist and poet, and an academically high-achieving student who has been in gifted programs since kindergarten. Gina is easily frustrated by new tasks, cries with little or no provocation, and gloats when she figures out things the others have not. She takes great delight, outwardly at least, in all of her differences. She always wants to be first and best. Gina is in nearly constant motion: swooping into a room to announce her arrival; sitting like a frog on her chair, head hanging down and hair swinging around her face; always drawing, writing, or otherwise creating with her hands.

Most foods go untasted by her because she dislikes all but a few for various reasons: too strong, too slimy, wrong color, too disgusting. Gina will only wear clothing made of soft knits and whose tags have been removed, because everything else is either too constricting, or stiff, or makes her itch. She often has her nose turned up in distaste at environmental odors, whether they are caused by someone's lunch or the remnants of some cleaning solution.

Gina's social skills are not those of a typical fifth grader, either. Because of her emotional disability, she stands out in both her gifted and general classrooms. Her propensity toward arguing with adults amazes other students and frustrates the teachers, because she is not engaging in intellectual discourse, but rather, the sort of irrationality that comes of being opinionated and not listening to instructions, as well as an unwillingness to take academic risks. Gina comes from a family of highly gifted, highly educated people.

Attention Deficit or Overexcitability?

Though these three students display many similar behaviors, in each case the behaviors are attributable to different causes. In Tony's case, ADHD is considered the underlying problem; in Mikey's case, ADHD with psychological overintensities associated with giftedness; and in Gina's case, the psychological overintensities concomitant with giftedness alone. How can such similar behaviors be assigned such different attributions, and how can they be distinguished from one another so the correct diagnosis is made in each case?

Making a correct diagnosis is not simple; it requires that educators and other professionals make thorough evaluations for both giftedness and ADHD (Cramond, 1995; Lovecky, 1994; Ramirez-Smith, 1997). According to Webb and Latimer (1993), in recent years educators have increasingly referred gifted children for ADHD evaluation. Because characteristics and behaviors are the foundation of a diagnosis of ADHD, and they can be misleading in the case of gifted people, educators and other professionals must exercise great care when conducting such evaluation (Baum, Olenchak, & Owen, 1998), with parents and teachers working closely with the diagnosing physician.

Children with ADHD can't stop moving, whereas children with high psychomotor behavior love to move.

In children with average creative and cognitive intelligence, this diagnosis can be made by a physician well versed in the characteristics of children with attention-deficit disorder (ADD) or ADHD (see box, "What is Attention-Deficit Hyperactivity Disorder?") in a fairly straightforward manner by means of thorough psychological and physical examinations. In gifted children, however, the diagnosis may be complicated by other issues, such as psychological overexcitabilities (Dabrowski, 1972; Piechowski, 1986; Piechowski & Colangelo, 1984).

Dabrowski saw these "forms of psychic overexcitability" (OEs) as contributing to

What Is Attention-Deficit Hyperactivity Disorder?

Attention-deficit hyperactivity disorder is characterized by a particular set of behaviors that prevent a person from performing to his or her potential. These behaviors may include the following:

- Susceptibility to distraction with little provocation.
- Difficulty following instructions.
- Difficulty sustaining situation-appropriate attention (except when watching television or playing video games).
- Problems starting tasks.
- Constantly beginning new projects without finishing the existing ones.
- Hyperactivity.
- Impulsivity.
- Poor social skills.
- Rapid satiation to stimuli.
- Low frustration tolerance.
- Academic underachievement (American Psychiatric Association, 1994).

For professionals to make a diagnosis of ADHD, the behaviors must be pervasive and long lasting and interfere significantly with the discharge of daily responsibilities.

individuals' psychological development, so they were a measure of developmental potential. Overexcitabilities are so often present in creatively, academically, intellectually, or otherwise gifted people that some educators are searching for ways to measure overexcitabilities as a tool for identification of gifted people. Psychological intensities are such a part of people who are considered gifted that, for the purpose of this article, the behaviors should be considered to be present when giftedness is mentioned. Researchers have categorized *overexcitabilities* into five main areas: psychomotor, emotional, intellectual, imaginational, and sensual, as follows:

- Those with *psychomotor overexcitabilities* are easy to spot: They are nearly always moving. Their behavior has been characterized as feeling driven to move, a love of movement, restlessness, superenergy, and a need for a high level of activity. Rapid speech, impulsiveness, and a need to

act are also characteristic of those who possess this overintensity. All this sounds remarkably like the hyperactivity of ADHD (Barkley, 1990; Hallowell & Ratey, 1995), though the difference appears to be that children with ADHD *can't* stop moving, whereas children with high psychomotor behavior *love* to move.

- *Imaginational overexcitabilities* are characterized by a facility for invention and fantasy, an ability to engage in detailed visualization, a well-developed sense of humor, animistic and magical thinking, and elaborate application of truth and fiction. Children who possess imaginational OEs can have rich and fulfilling inner experiences during the pedestrian activities of a typical school day. What looks like inattention could be, instead, a rich imaginational scenario unfolding within the child's mind. A creatively gifted 4th-grade student described it like this: "Social studies can be really boring when we just read it aloud and take notes, so I like to pretend I'm in whatever situation we're learning about."

- *Emotional overintensity* is one of the more outwardly visible of the overexcitabilities. Characterized by an intensity of feeling, a marked ability to empathize with others, and somatic expression of feelings, these children are the ones who can see all sides of a situation, who can find it painfully difficult to make new friends, who cry at the smallest frustration. What appears to be the emotional overreactivity of ADHD could, instead, be the expression of emotional overintensity.

- *Sensual overexcitabilities* manifest themselves as extreme sensitivity to touch; delight with the aesthetic things in life, such as art, music, fabric, surroundings, or words; extreme dislike or love for certain foods due to specific textures or tastes; sensitivity to odors or chemicals in the environment; or any other sensory-related experiences. People who experience heightened pleasure when indulging in favorite foods or drinks are displaying this sort of sensual overexcitability. Stopping to feel the fabric of every item passed in a department store, noticing the particular blue of the sky, or admiring the shape of a flower could easily be con-

strued as distractibility, but it could also be illustrative of being tuned in to the beauty of one's surroundings.

Researchers have categorized *overexcitabilities* into five main areas: psychomotor, emotional, intellectual, imaginational, and sensual.

Look at a classroom full of students of any age. Some are simply there, doing as they are told, whereas others display an absolute thirst for learning. These individuals possess a drive to learn that knows no boundaries—**an intellectual overintensity.** What they learn does not seem to matter as long as it is new and interesting. These are the people who think and wonder, who ask the questions instead of knowing the answers, who exhibit sustained concentration, who have excessive curiosity, and who integrate intuition and concept. They are naturally metacognitive thinkers, are detailed planners, and express early concerns about values and morality. Many of these characteristics appear only in the child's mind, so may look, again, like inattention to the outside observer. At times, this overexcitability also may be seen as similar to the hyperfocusing in people with ADHD. Intellectual OEs may also be expressed as a hyperactivity seen by outsiders as distractibility, but which may be heightened mental arousal that never stops, even during sleep.

Who Are They?

With all these similarities, how can we tell the difference between a gifted child with overexcitabilities and one with ADHD? Both children possess exceptional mental faculties, but one has greater availability of resources, while the other founders in a quagmire of disorganization and distractibility. In such cases, parents and teachers find it difficult to distinguish between the child who *won't* do his or her work and the one who *can't*. Gifted children with ADHD are usually labeled as underachieving or lazy long before they are ever labeled as ADHD.

Studies have shown that gifted children identified as having ADHD are, generally, more gifted than their non-ADHD peers (Dorry, 1994; Zentall, 1997). Because the negative behavioral manifestations of ADHD may keep these children from performing well on group tests, many educators believe diagnostic tests uncover only the children who have extremely superlative talents or gifts. Though high intelligence can help the child overcome some of the challenges of ADHD over his or her lifetime (Barkley, 1990; Phelan, 1996), it does so only to the extent that it allows the child to compensate to the point of seeming average.

These children also tend not to be nominated for gifted testing or programs. Wolfle & French, in a presentation to the National Association for Gifted Children (1990), reported the following characteristics of a typical gifted child with ADHD excluded from gifted programs:

- Makes jokes or puns at inappropriate times.
- Is bored with routine tasks and refuses to do them.
- Is self-critical, impatient with failures.
- Tends to dominate others.
- Would rather stay by oneself.
- Has difficulty moving into another topic when engrossed.
- Often disagrees vocally with others in a loud, bossy manner.
- Is emotionally sensitive—may overreact.
- Is not interested in details, often hands in messy work.
- Refuses to accept authority, nonconforming, stubborn.

This is the portrait of a child who refuses to play the school game, has his or her own ideas about how to live, and will not compromise. Teachers do not particularly tend to like these children, thus they do not generally refer them for gifted programming because, in the teacher's mind, these students do not deserve to be there. Parents find them difficult to live with, and peers reject them, so life becomes a series of negative interactions with few opportunities for self-fulfillment. The worst part is that such children are intelligent enough to realize they are different, but may be helpless to change their behaviors at their own volition.

In his work with gifted children with ADHD, Mendaglio (1995) found that these children are painfully aware of their academic failures and misbehaviors. This awareness often manifests itself outwardly as nonspecific anger. On the positive side, he reported, when such children do qualify for and are placed into programs for gifted and talented children, they and their parents report immediate, lasting, positive increases in self-esteem and attitude.

The Creativity Link

Creativity and ADHD share many, many characteristics. Indeed, both creativity and ADHD are so difficult to define precisely and can look so much alike, one might be hard pressed to define certain characteristics as one or the other. In her study of 70 gifted children, Lovecky (1994) found that almost all of these children, even those with additional learning disabilities and exceptional hyperactivity, displayed creativity. The differences between them and their gifted/non-ADHD peers was, "organizing their creative ideas into products, and sustaining enough interest and motivation to finish a project once they had gotten past the novelty of the initial idea" (p. 3).

Hallowell and Ratey (1995) found certain characteristics of the ADHD mind beneficial to the development of creativity. These included a higher tolerance for chaos and ambiguity and no firm belief that there is one proper place for ideas or images. This can lead to unusual combinations of imagery and ideas and to new ways of seeing things.

Hyper-reactivity in the minds of people with ADHD is amazing to behold. The ideas come and come, changing from one topic to another with an awesome rapidity and proliferation. With this many ideas, new ones pop up with regularity, leading to people with creative/ADHD characteristics to think of themselves as "idea people."

Educators should place the child in classrooms where expectations are high and teaching is holistic, relevant, challenging, and meaningful.

The impulsivity of ADHD can lead to a need to create—anything. This impulse is an urge that demands satisfaction. Combined with the hyperfocusing of ADHD, this impulsivity can produce impressive results in a brief period of time. Of course, there will also be many times of distractibility to balance these periods of intense concentration and productivity.

Creative production also occurs when people spontaneously bring unlike items together in unusual ways. Creative people with ADHD do this often. They see and find amusing combinations others may never have thought of. This is a strategy others have to be taught to use, usually in expensive creativity-training workshops.

Cramond (1994), in a review paper, and Piirto (1992), in her book *Understanding Those Who Create*, noted that the defining characteristics of ADHD are also key descriptors in the biographies of highly creative people. Inattention, hyperactivity, and impulsivity were frequently mentioned as characteristic of many writers, artists, authors, inventors, and composers. These characteristics transferred across disciplines and were found in every area of creativity.

How Can You Tell Whether It Is Truly ADHD?

When we see ADHD-type behaviors, in combination with giftedness of either intellect or creativity, how can we tell if we need to take action to label and treat the ADHD? This is a question asked in nearly every article on the topic. The overwhelming primary response is this: Exercise caution in both the identification and treatment of ADHD in children identified as being gifted. Beyond that, research has identified several characteristics of gifted children with ADHD—characteristics that are not generally present in the child who is gifted but not identified as having ADHD.

The first is inconsistency in performance. Non-gifted ADHD children are known for inconsistency in school performance that occurs at any time in any subject (Barkley, 1990). Being gifted does not exempt children from these sorts of academic inconsistencies (Webb & Latimer, 1993). If children are functioning at a high level in a subject one day, then failing in the same subject days later, there may be reason to suspect a problem. A thorough history of the child's performance will reveal a pattern of variability of task performance over time. These children's performance may also be linked to the teacher's characteristics and teaching style; these students will not produce quality work for a teacher they do not like or respect.

There is a movement in the field now to find a means of measuring overexcitabilities as a tool for identification of gifted people.

A visit to a gifted resource classroom, otherwise known as a gifted "pullout" program, will generally reveal a higher than normal activity level, a great deal of talkativeness, and a high level of enthusiasm and task commitment for challenging, interesting tasks. The enthusiasm, movement, talkativeness, and high activity levels are desirable, though can be exhausting for the teachers involved, because these behaviors correspond to the ways gifted children are identified today. Gifted resource classrooms generally exist to serve gifted students in elementary schools, but sometimes can be found at higher grade levels. Wherever they are found, they are often the high point of a gifted students' day or week—time away from their general education classrooms to be spent with intellectual peers. While children with ADHD tend toward inattention, and distraction in nearly every situation, gifted children with ADHD will retain the hyperactivity and problems with sustained attention, except during certain highly stimulating, novel, motivating tasks, such as those to be found in the gifted resource classroom. Those gifted children who are unresponsive to even those tasks stand out among their peers and should be investigated.

Gifted children with ADHD, like all children, not only deserve, but *require* highly stimulating and mentally and psychologically challenging environments to be successful, something few schools provide. Many gifted children have problems with school environments that provide few opportunities for creativity, provide only concrete, linear-sequential instruction, teach only at the lower levels of the taxonomy, require excessively rote and repeti-

tive work, and do not allow learners to progress at their own rate (Baum et al., 1998; Cramond, 1995; Lovecky, 1994; Zentall & Zentall, 1983). This type of learning environment can be a disaster for any child, but you can virtually guarantee it will be for the child who has characteristics of both giftedness and ADHD. These children will frequently shut down when given repetitive tasks, even knowing that unfavorable consequences are certain to follow. When one 11-year-old gifted child with ADHD was asked about this, he responded, "It actually makes me feel sick to my stomach when they make me do the same thing over and over."

When the ADHD has gone undiagnosed for many years, the student may have developed problems with self-esteem and depression.

Whereas children with ADHD tend toward not liking school and gifted children usually do, gifted children with ADHD usually have a few subjects (particularly science) they really love and may not care about the rest (Zentall, 1997). This can lead to incredible power struggles in the home and school when parents and teachers see that the child can attend in some situations but won't (or can't) in others. In children like this, underachievement begins early, with the ADHD not generally identified until at least 6th grade (Lovecky, 1994). By then the child has set up a pattern of inconsistent performance and failure to complete work, leading to frequent negative feedback, leading in turn to diminished academic self-esteem and anger. This pattern of underachievement and the negative response it generates create a cycle within the school and the family that is difficult to break.

Though gifted children frequently display mental ages and social functioning well above those of their chronological peers, they still may exhibit some discrepancies within themselves between these developmental strands, while the gifted child with ADHD may exhibit a much wider and debilitating discrepancy between intellectual age and social and emotional ages. This can cause the child to be

out of sync with everyone (Lovecky, 1993). Social skills are usually underdeveloped in these children; as a result, they may have few friends, with those few generally being younger. Again, these children are aware of their differences and lack of friends, so may become depressed or oppositional in response.

How Do We Help These Paradoxical Children Become Achievers?

Research on underachievement in general, and in gifted people with ADHD specifically, has given us ideas on how to help these children become achievers. As far back as 1959, Passow and Goldberg provided insight in their landmark study on how to reverse underachievement. Their studies revealed that if teachers wish to reverse underachievement, they should place students in a stimulating, rich environment with a teacher who is kind and accepting, who values each of them as individuals, and who maintains high expectations. In addition, the researchers found that students needed further, intensive instruction in study and organizational skills; a characteristic shared by many underachievers, and nearly all children diagnosed with ADHD (Dorry, 1994; Maxwell, 1989). In today's world, gifted children with ADHD can be taught word processing and computer skills that will allow them to compensate for their inability to write quickly or neatly, or to keep their thoughts while writing (Ramirez-Smith, 1997).

Medication works most effectively when coupled with stable parental support at home.

Teachers who have successfully worked with gifted children with ADHD recognize that cognitive therapy is helpful. It is beneficial to talk openly with students about expectations and problems and include them in developing plans of action (Mendaglio, 1995). Contracts, with student-chosen rewards, are helpful in some cases. Because gifted children tend to be primarily intrinsically motivated, external rewards and punishments have little effect unless they are selected by the children themselves. Students need to be convinced that failure is not an option, that today's work will pay off in the future, and that hard work will benefit them personally. Goal setting is another useful strategy in this area, because it helps remove the child from the impulsivity of the moment and develop focus on the future.

What About Parents?

Parenting gifted children with ADHD can be an extremely frustrating experience. There is an awareness of the child's precocity and talents that leads to higher expectations, but that, when coupled with the ADHD behaviors, leads to frustration with the child's self-destructive behaviors. Parents need to deliberately educate themselves about how to deal appropriately with these children (see box, "Tried and True Strategies for Parents") and be advocates for them, while not being rescuers available to bail the children out of every jam (Zentall, 1997). Negativity and power struggles are common in families with gifted children with ADHD. On a more positive note, a child with ADHD who is gifted, who has a supportive family, and who is taught specific ways to compensate for his or her deficits has a much greater chance of becoming a productive adult (Phelan, 1996). Though the gifted child with ADHD may for many years demand an inordinate amount of the family's re-

sources, it appears that early intervention and long-term support eventually pay off.

Home-school communication is essential for the success of gifted children with ADHD (Baum et al., 1998; Ramirez-Smith, 1997; Wolfle & French, 1990). Teachers need to be informed about these children's specific needs, and most are not. How could they be? In teacher education programs, there has traditionally been little room for teaching about gifted children at all, let alone those with additional exceptionalities. Parents can be useful in providing materials that inform educators about the characteristics and needs of a gifted child with ADHD. There should be ongoing, open communication between parent and teacher, with the child included as needed.

Tried & True Strategies for Parents of Gifted Children with ADHD or Overexcitability

- **Love your children for who they are**, not for what they do or don't do; obvious, but not always easy with these extremely challenging children.
- **Set standards and *insist* they be met**. Do what it takes to communicate that failure is *not* an option, and that every action has its consequences. If there are no natural consequences, design some specific to the situation.
- **Use humor to defuse stress and anger**. An advanced sense of humor is a characteristic many gifted children share. Take advantage of it.
- **There are no quick fixes**. Know that gifted children with ADHD require intensive, long-term, interventions. Be consistent over time.
- **Communicate regularly with your child's teachers** in a positive fashion, no matter what grade your child is in, and do so *before* problems surface. Remember, your mutual goal is to help the child be successful.
- **Impose organization on your children until they prove they can do it themselves**. Find a good system and teach and reteach it. Expect backsliding from time to time, all the way through school.
- **Provide opportunities for your child to express his or her creativity**. When things get really bad, this may be his or her lifesaver.
- **Nothing breeds success like success**. Find some way to show your child that he or she can be successful at something meaningful, if only he or she tries. Provide a choice of opportunities and insist he or she chooses one and sticks with it until successful completion.
- **Make sure your child is provided with appropriate curriculum and teachers from the start**. Positively but honestly present your child and his or her needs to school administrators *before* the end of this school year for next year's placement, then trust the school personnel to do the work of placing the child appropriately.

Because of the myriad needs generated by having a gifted child with ADHD in the classroom, administrators and teachers must hold discussions about classroom placements and include both current and former teachers, administrators, and parents. Educators should place the child in classrooms where expectations are high and teaching is holistic, relevant, challenging, and meaningful (DeLisle, 1995), and where teachers are willing to teach to the child's strengths while remediating the weaknesses. Multi-modal approaches allow the gifted child with ADHD to play to his or her strengths and express creativity (Lovecky, 1994). Several successful research projects have employed talent development and attention to students' specific intelligences, talents, or gifts as means to promote academic success for at-risk students (Baum, Owen, & Oreck, 1996; Baum, Renzulli, & Hebert, 1994; Olenchak, 1994). It is clear that proper curriculums, instruction, and pacing can make a great deal of difference in the school lives of gifted children with ADHD.

In some cases, physicians may prescribe medication for students to help control the ADD/ADHD symptoms, allowing the giftedness to emerge more fully. According to many researchers, doctors should not prescribe medication unless educators, parents, and other professionals have explored all other possible avenues because medication may have some detrimental effects on creativity, imagination, and intellectual curiosity (Baum et al., 1998; Cramond, 1995). That, of course, is a question to be decided by the doctors, parents, and children; and they should make such decisions on an individual basis. Wolfle & French (1990) stated that medication works most effectively when coupled with stable parental support at home. A review of literature on the effects of stimulant medication and children with ADHD has reinforced that medication alone provides only short-term effects; people should not expect it to improve long-term adjustment in either social or academic areas (Swanson et al., 1993).

Finally, researchers have suggested counseling for some of these children, especially when the ADHD has gone undiagnosed for many years, because the child may have developed problems with self-esteem and depression. When counseling is undertaken, however, educators, parents, and others must be careful to select counselors familiar with both the social and emotional needs of gifted children and children with ADD/ADHD (Webb & Latimer, 1993).

Now What?

The literature has little to say about children doubly blessed with giftedness and ADHD, even less of the literature is research based. In a search for materials on the subject, I found no information on this topic in traditional educational literature; I found some in the social sciences literature; and the rest in the gifted literature. Because most teachers have a hard enough time keeping up with information in their own area of expertise and seldom have the opportunity to examine the gifted literature, it seems logical that this information must be disseminated into mainstream education.

Educators need to do more to improve the quality of identification of these high-potential, though terribly at-risk children and to reduce the likelihood of misdiagnosis of children who are gifted and creative and overexcitable as having ADHD. On the other hand, writers and researchers can heighten our awareness of the existence of this segment of the population so that gifted children who actually *do* have ADHD are not missed in diagnosis. Misdiagnoses can cut some students off from services that they may need. Teachers who are educated on this topic can be of immense help when it comes time to work with doctors in diagnosing possible medical conditions such as ADHD.

Finally, we must learn to value these children; they have much to offer. Though the learning environments and teaching practices discussed earlier are desirable for all children, gifted or not, these doubly-blessed students possess the creative potential to produce great ideas and make wonderful contributions to our society. With appropriate curriculums; informed teachers and administrators; and educated, involved parents working together, we can reclaim a segment of our population who currently underachieve at a high rate. Most of all, we can teach these young people that in working to show their strengths and overcome their deficits, they make themselves even better. As educators, we need to help them learn who they are, what they are capable of, and how to reach their potential.

References

American Psychiatric Association (1994). *Diagnostic and statistical manual of mental disorders* (4th ed.: DSM IV). Washington, DC: Author.

Barkley, R. (1990). *Attention deficit hyperactivity disorder: A handbook for diagnosis and treatment.* New York: Guilford Press.

Baum, S., Olenchak, F., & Owen, S. (1998). Gifted students with attention deficits: Fact or fiction? Or, can we see the forest for the trees? *Gifted Child Quarterly, 42*(2), 96–104.

Baum, S., Owen, S., & Oreck, B. (1996). Talent beyond words: Identification of potential talent in dance and music in elementary students. *Gifted Child Quarterly, 40*(2), 93–102.

Baum, S., Renzulli, J., & Hebert, T. (1994). Reversing underachievement: Stories of success. *Educational Leadership, 52*(3), 48–53.

Cramond, B. (1994). Creativity and ADHD: What is the connection? *Journal of Creative Behavior, 28*(3), 193–210.

Cramond, B. (1995). The coincidence of attention deficit hyperactivity disorder and creativity. *Monograph of the National Research Center on the Gifted and Talented, RBDM 9508, United States Government: Connecticut.* (ERIC Document Reproduction Service No. 388 016)

Dabrowski, K. (1972). *Psychoneurosis is not an illness.* London: Gryf.

DeLisle, J. (1995). ADD gifted: How many labels can one child take? *Gifted Child Today, 18*(2), 42–43.

Dorry, G. (1994). The perplexed perfectionist. *Understanding Our Gifted, 6*(5), 3, 10–12.

Hallowell, E., & Ratey, J. (1995). *Driven to distraction.* New York: Simon & Schuster.

Lovecky, D. (1993). Out of sync with everyone. *Understanding Our Gifted, 5*(5A), 3.

Lovecky, D. (1994, July/August). The hidden gifted learner. *Understanding Our Gifted, 3 & 18.*

Maxwell, V. (1989). Diagnosis and treatment of the gifted student with attention deficit disorder: A structure of intellect approach. *Reading, Writing & Learning Disabilities, 5,* 247–252.

Mendaglio, S. (1995, July/August). Children who are Gifted/ADHD., *Gifted Child Today, 18,* 37–38.

Olenchak, F. (1994). Talent development: Accommodating the social and emotional needs of secondary gifted/learning disabled students. *Journal of Secondary Gifted Education, 5*(3), 40–52.

Passow, H., & Goldberg, M. (1959). Study of underachieving gifted. *Educational Leadership, 16,* 121–125.

Phelan, T. (1996). *All about attention deficit disorder.* Minneapolis, MN: Child Management Press.

Piechowski, M. (1986). The concept of developmental potential. *Roeper Review, 8*(3), 190–197.

Piechowski, M., & Colangelo, N. (1984). Developmental potential of the gifted. *Gifted Child Quarterly, 28,* 80–88.

Piirto, J. (1992). *Understanding those who create.* Dayton: Ohio Psychology Press.

Ramirez-Smith, C. (1997). *Mistaken identity: Gifted and ADHD.* Reston, VA: The Council for Exceptional Children. (ERIC Document Reproduction No. ED413690)

Swanson, J., McBurnett, K., Wigal, T., Pfiffner, L., Lerner, M., Williams, L., Christian, D., Tamm, L., Willcutt, E., Crowley, K., Clevenger, W., Khouzam, N., Woo, C., Crinella, F., & Fisher, T. (1993). Effect of stimulant medication on children with attention deficit disorder. A "review of reviews." *Exceptional Children, 60,* 154–162.

Webb, J., & Latimer, D. (1993). *ADHD and children who are gifted (ERIC Digest No. 522).* Reston, VA: The Council for Exceptional Children.

Wolfle, J., & French, M. (1990). *Surviving gifted attention deficit disorder children in the classroom.* Paper presented at the meeting of the National Association for Gifted Children, Little Rock, AR.

Zentall, S. (1997, March). *Learning characteristics of boys with attention deficit hyperactivity disorder and/or giftedness.* Paper presented at the annual meeting of the American Educational Research Association, Chicago, IL. (ERIC Document Reproduction No. 407791)

Zentall, S., & Zentall, T. (1983). Optimal stimulation: A model of disordered activity and performance in normal and deviant children. *Psychological Bulletin, 94,* 446–471.

Lori J. Flint, *Doctoral Candidate, Department of Educational Psychology, The University of Georgia, Athens.*

Address correspondence to the author at Department of Educational Psychology, The University of Georgia, 325 Aderhold Hall, Athens, GA 30602-7143, (e-mail: LJFSTAT@AOL.COM)

Raising Expectations for the Gifted

*Five teaching strategies allow flexibility in meeting the needs of
gifted students in inclusive classrooms.*

By Colleen Willard-Holt

Most gifted students study in regular classrooms for most of their school careers and are taught using the same state standards intended for all students. Most state standards, however, do not provide sufficient intellectual challenge for gifted students.

Neuroscientific research has found that rats in unstimulating environments had thinner cortexes, the part of the brain where higher mental functions reside (Diamond & Hopson, 1998). This effect appeared after just four days!

Education research has shown that gifted students' motivation and performance also declined in the absence of mental stimulation, even leading to underachievement (Purcell, 1993; Whitmore, 1980), but that gifted students exposed to intellectually stimulating content at an accelerated pace outperformed gifted peers not in such programs (Cornell & Delcourt, 1990; Kulik, 1992). It is too great a risk to subject gifted students to a steady diet of unchallenging work.

Standards need not imply standardization of learning activities or expectations. Gifted students may need less time to master a given standard, or they may address the standard in greater depth. Classroom teachers might follow the principle of teaching all students at their optimal level of instruction—what Vygotsky would call their "zone of proximal development" (1978).

How can regular classroom teachers address the needs of their gifted students? The first step in differentiating a standards-based lesson or unit for gifted students is to identify the standards that the lesson will address. An efficient way to accomplish several tasks within one lesson is to combine content, skills, and arts standards. For example, making a poster for National Arbor Day can address science standards in environmental health, language arts standards in research and communication, and standards regarding the elements and principles of visual art.

Teachers can then assess students' grasp of content and skills. They might pretest the students, using an end-of-chapter test that integrates skills with content, or review students' achievement on content and skills that they have previously studied. Perusing student portfolios or assessing interests and multiple intelligences profiles can also provide insight into skills and content knowledge.

Once teachers have determined students' readiness levels, they can execute differentiation strategies. Curriculum compacting, flexible grouping, product choices, tiered assignments, and multilevel learning stations are excellent strategies for differentiating instruction for gifted students in regular classrooms (see Gregory & Chapman, 2002; Maker & Nielson, 1996; Reis, Burns, & Renzulli, 1992; Tomlinson, 1999; Willard-Holt, 1994). Some of these strategies also lend themselves well to meeting the needs of gifted students with disabilities.

Curriculum Compacting

Curriculum compacting is a powerful strategy for ensuring accountability for standards while acknowledging what students already know. Curriculum compacting means streamlining what is taught to students by first assessing their prior knowledge and then modifying or eliminating work that has been partially or fully mastered. After teachers assess student mastery of a particular standard, three groups often emerge: students with poor mastery, students with partial mastery, and students with full mastery who are ready for more advanced work.[1] The first group, usually the largest, proceeds with the planned sequence of instruction; the second group may accomplish the planned sequence more quickly and then proceed to a greater challenge; the third group may begin an independent project immediately.

Consider this math standard for grade 3: "Count, compare, and make change using a collection of coins and one-dollar bills" (PA Std. 2.1.3E).[2] The first group is ready to make several combinations of pennies, nickels, and dimes for given amounts. The second group is confident of these steps and can make change, but they need help using quarters. They will join the rest of the class when the teacher provides information and practice with quarters; the rest of the time they work together on a coin-related project that they will present to the class. The project might entail making a poster of U.S. coinage from colonial times to the present, using drawings, replicas, or actual coins when available. The third group's students, who tested 85 percent or above on the pretest, are making a chart that compares currency systems for different countries. They will defend their choice of the most efficient system at the end of the unit. Such higher-order thinking projects may also satisfy language arts standards, using a similar process for compacting skill standards in reading or writing.

In middle and high school grades, gifted students may not have the technical knowledge to meet a particular content standard and therefore may not show mastery on a pretest. They may be able to learn the content quickly by reading the text and completing application exercises on their own, however, and then successfully complete a criterion-referenced posttest. For example, a life sciences course might focus on the 10th grade standard, "Identify and characterize major life forms by kingdom, phylum, class, and order" (PA Std. 3.3.10A). The teacher invites students who have performed well in previous science units to read the text and work through a packet of exercises at their own pace. This packet consists of activities crucial to understanding the topic and differs from the step-by-step exercises given to the rest of the class. When ready, students take the posttest and, if they demonstrate mastery, undertake an in-depth project, such as creating a three-dimensional clay model of a dissected starfish (Miller & Willard-Holt, 2000). This project addresses skill and arts standards simultaneously.

Teachers can also use compacting with gifted students who have disabilities. If the goal is to master content quickly while circumventing the disability, the teacher can compact in areas of weakness as well as strength. For the standard, "Identify planets in our solar system and their general characteristics" (PA Std. 3.4.4D), the class assignment might be a written report on a planet. A gifted student with a writing disability who demonstrates mastery of the characteristics of the planets on a pretest might instead research current theories about the birth of galaxies and create a PowerPoint presentation.

It is not always necessary to focus on remediation. If the goal is to develop coping strategies for the disability, compacting can focus on the area of strength.

Flexible Grouping

Flexible grouping is particularly effective when students' achievement levels in content and skills differ, as is often the case for gifted students with disabilities. The teacher groups students according to strength, need, or interest, and groups change frequently, sometimes in the course of a single class session. As an illustration, an 11th grade English class might address the standards, "Analyze the relationships, uses, and effectiveness of literary elements used by one or more authors, including characterization, setting, plot, theme, point of view, tone, and style" (PA Std. 1.3.11B) and "Write short stories, poems, and plays" (PA Std. 1.4.11A). The class has read a scene from *Romeo and Juliet*, viewed the corresponding scene from *West Side Story*, and discussed similarities and differences. In groups, students write a contemporary scene in which young people are in love despite their families' differences. Drawing on their knowledge of current events, students research the conflict between the groups that the families represent, such as Israelis versus Palestinians, big business versus environmentalists, or Shiite versus Sunni Muslims. Students could also choose groups that are at odds in their immediate community.

Students initially come together around the specific conflict that most interests them, with groups changing later as needed. Each group has students with mixed levels of ability. The teacher provides mini-lessons to address specific skills—for example, how to research the conflict using print resources, Internet, and interviews of community leaders; write authentic dialogue; punctuate dialogue correctly; or write stage directions. Later, gifted students might meet together to choose a multi-layered conflict, the threads of which they must logically incorporate into the scene.

Product Choices

Another way to plan for gifted students is to allow them choices of what kind of product they will produce. In the *Romeo and Juliet* example, one group might complete a written script (verbal/linguistic intelligence); another, a videotaped dramatization of the scene (bodily/kinesthetic intelligence); and a third, a comic strip (visual/spatial intelligence). In this way, each group addresses the same content standard but uses a different skill or arts standard.

For the 6th grade standard, "Describe the human characteristics of places and regions by their cultural characteristics" (PA Std. 7.3.6B), students studying a unit on Central and South America might choose to create an authentic traditional costume, dance, food, artwork, or model of a home—developing a three-dimensional model, drawing, or verbal description. The projects appeal to different intelligences and address different skills and arts standards.

Product choices are important for gifted students with disabilities, allowing them to demonstrate their understanding of the content without their disability interfering. For example, a student with a learning disability in written expression may conduct research, make the necessary cognitive connections, and demonstrate understanding through art and oral expression, thereby circumventing writing. A blind student may conduct research by using text-to-speech interfaces on the Internet and create a three-dimensional model. In each case, the focus is on content mastery. Assignments in other areas would remediate or develop coping strategies for the disability.

Tiered Assignments

The advantage of this strategy is that the entire class studies the same content, but individual students choose assignments at different levels of complexity, with the teacher's assistance. For example, coupling a 4th grade science standard, "Know basic weather elements" (PA Std. 3.4.4C), with a math standard, "Organize and display data using pictures, tallies, tables, charts, bar graphs, and circle graphs" (PA Std. 2.6.5A), allows students to learn how to gather weather data from various sources and graph the data. Assignment choices might include

• Making a bar graph that shows the average monthly temperatures in two cities (basic level).

• Choosing two appropriate types of graphs to show the proportion of rainy days to sunny days, and the average rainfall by months in a city of your choice (average level).

• Generating two appropriate graphs on the computer to show the ratio of rain to snow, and monthly temperature and precipitation in a city of your choice (advanced level).

Students choose the assignment that sounds most interesting and best stimulates their learning. Gentle nudging might encourage students to accept the appropriate level of challenge.

Multilevel Learning Stations

Multilevel learning stations provide meaningful independent work that extends and enriches class discussions. For example, a learning station can assist 3rd grade students studying ancient civilizations by addressing history, geography, arts, and language arts standards, including the following:

• Compare similarities and differences between the earliest civilizations and life today (PA Std. 8.4.3C).

• Explain the historical, cultural, and social context of an individual work in the arts (PA Std. 9.2.3A).

• Relate works in the arts chronologically to historical events (PA Std. 9.2.3B) or geographic regions (PA Std. 9.2.3G).

Activity cards address such topics as leaders/famous people, arts, structures, ways of life, and location. In addition, the teacher codes the activity cards according to Bloom's thinking levels: red for knowledge/comprehension, blue for application, green for analysis, yellow for synthesis, and white for evaluation. On the basis of assessment data, each student receives an assignment sheet detailing the number of activities that he or she is to complete at each level. For example, Juan will do one of each color; Sarah will select five activities, all at green, yellow, or white levels; and Randy will choose five red or blue activities.

Product choices allow gifted students with disabilities to demonstrate their understanding of the content.

Teachers often assume that learning stations are appropriate only for the elementary grades, yet secondary students also seem to enjoy them. For example, U.S. history students addressing the Civil War might explore in depth topics relating to battles, leaders, military technology, camp life, civilian life, or the roles of women or African Americans in the war, according to their interests.

Inspiring Extraordinary Achievement

Some gifted students' capabilities and rates of learning are so far beyond their chronological ages that they would spend almost all of their time reviewing what they already knew if they followed the curriculum offered in a regular classroom. These students need a highly individualized program at an advanced level, perhaps through acceleration or mentoring. Other gifted students may be highly advanced in one subject and could benefit from acceleration or mentoring in that subject while remaining in the inclusive classroom for the remainder of the day.

Providing gifted students with instruction at the appropriate level also removes pressure that they might feel in cooperative learning situations within inclusive classrooms. It may be tempting to ask advanced students to tutor others—a strategy that is permissible on occasion, but inappropriate as a regular activity. Gifted students, like all students, come to school to encounter new learning challenges. Depending on gifted students as peer tutors also places them at risk for social isolation if other students come to view them as teacher's pets or know-it-alls (Robinson, 1990).

Teaching to standards need not mean standardization of learning activities or expectations. Simply meeting standards is not an adequate challenge for most gifted students, although that is all the law may require of them. As Tomlinson states in reference to the No Child Left Behind Act of 2001,

> There is no incentive for schools to attend to the growth of students once they attain proficiency…and certainly not to inspire those who far exceed proficiency. (2002, p. 36)

Don't we want more than minimal proficiency from our gifted students? By using strategies to challenge all students at their optimal levels of instruction, teachers can meet their responsibilities for accountability while inspiring extraordinary achievement.

Notes

1. A fourth group—those not yet ready to attempt the standard—is beyond the scope of this article.
2. I refer to Pennsylvania standards. The standards are available at www.pde.state.pa.us/stateboard_fed; click Academic Standards.

References

Cornell, D. G., & Delcourt, M. A. B. (1990). Achievement, attitudes, and adjustment. *Communicator, 20*(5), 28.

Diamond, M., & Hopson, J. (1998). *Magic trees of the mind.* New York: Plume Books.

Gregory, G. H., & Chapman, C. (2002). *Differentiated instructional strategies: One size doesn't fit all.* Thousand Oaks, CA: Corwin Press.

Kulik, J. A. (1992). *An analysis of the research on ability grouping* (RBDM 9204). Storrs, CT: University of Connecticut, The National Research Center on the Gifted and Talented.

Maker, C. J., & Nielson, A. B. (1996). *Curriculum development and teaching strategies for gifted learners* (2nd ed.). Austin, TX: Pro-Ed.

Miller, B., & Willard-Holt, C. (2000). *Dare to differentiate: Strategies for enrichment in middle school science.* Manassas, VA: Gifted Education Press.

Purcell, J. H. (1993). The effects of the elimination of gifted and talented programs on participating students and their parents. *Gifted Child Quarterly, 37*(4), 177-187.

Reis, S. M., Burns, D. E., & Renzulli, J. S. (1992). *Curriculum compacting.* Mansfield Center, CT: Creative Learning Press.

Robinson, A. (1990). Cooperation or exploitation? The argument against cooperative learning for talented students. *Journal for the Education of the Gifted*, 14(3), 9-27, 31-36.

Tomlinson, C. A. (1999). *The differentiated classroom: Responding to the needs of all learners*. Alexandria, VA: ASCD.

Tomlinson, C. A. (2002, Nov. 6). Proficiency is not enough. *Education Week*, 22(10), 36, 38.

Vygotsky, L. S. (1978). *Mind in society: The development of higher psychological processes*. Cambridge, MA: Harvard University Press.

Whitmore, J. R. (1980). *Giftedness, conflict, and underachievement*. Boston: Allyn and Bacon.

Willard-Holt, C. (1994). Strategies for individualizing instruction in regular classrooms. *Roeper Review*, 17(1), 43-45.

Colleen Willard-Holt is an associate professor of education in the School of Behavioral Sciences and Education at Penn State—Capital College; cxw20@psu.edu.

Celebrating Diverse Minds

*Many faltering students have specialized minds—brains exquisitely
wired to perform certain kinds of tasks masterfully.*

Mel Levine

A distraught mother recently sent me this e-mail: *Every morning when I send Michael off to school, I feel as if I'm sending him to jail. He can't spell, he forgets his math facts even after we study them together, his handwriting is hard to decipher, and he is hopelessly absent-minded. The other kids see his papers and say that he "writes like a mental case." All day, he faces nonstop criticism from his teacher. She scolds him in front of his classmates for not trying. And you know, his teacher's right. He's not trying—he's scared to try. He's decided that if you're going to fail, it's better to fail without trying.*

He can fix absolutely anything that's broken and he is brilliant when he plays with his Legos. I can't believe the complicated things he makes. He is convinced that he is hopelessly dumb, and he worries about school all the time. A lot of nights, Michael cries himself to sleep. We are losing this darling boy and he is such a beautiful child, such a decent kid. Please help us.

We have all heard the success stories of Albert Einstein, Thomas Edison, Steve Jobs, and Charles Schwab—accomplished adults whose minds failed to fit in school. But what becomes of those whom we never hear about—students like Michael, who give up on themselves because they lack the kinds of minds needed to satisfy existing criteria for school success?

For more than 30 years, my work as a pediatrician has been dedicated to such out-of-step children and adolescents. Although some of them have officially acknowledged collisions with word decoding or attention, many contend with more elusive differences in learning. These students may have trouble organizing time and prioritizing activities, communicating effectively, grasping verbal or nonverbal concepts, retrieving data precisely and quickly from long-term memory, recognizing and responding to recurring patterns, or assimilating fine detail.

Such insidious dysfunctions can constitute daunting barriers, especially when they are not recognized and managed. Most important, these breakdowns can mislead us into undervaluing, unfairly accusing, and even undereducating students, thereby stifling their chances for success in school and life.

The Challenge of Disappointing School Performance

Many faltering students have specialized minds—brains exquisitely wired to perform certain kinds of tasks masterfully, but decidedly miswired when it comes to meeting other expectations. A student may be brilliant at visualizing, but embarrassingly inept at verbalizing. Her classmate may reveal a remarkable understanding of people, but exhibit no insight about sentence structure.

Within every student contending with learning differences, an area invariably exists in which her or his mind has been amply equipped to thrive. In the e-mail from Michael's mother, the clue to his mind's early specialization practically jumps out at you: "He can fix absolutely anything that's broken." Michael's mechanical brilliance gets eclipsed by our focus on what he can't do.

I love to spend time explaining his strengths and their possibilities to a student like Michael who feels depleted and diminished (and perhaps even demolished) by the experience of school. I talk to him about the different careers in which he could readily succeed given the abilities he already possesses. I feel as if I have stepped inside a shadowy passageway suddenly illuminated, as revealed by a newly radiant facial expression. I can't help but conclude that the real challenge for schools rests more with identifying and fortifying individuals' strengths than with caulking academic crevices.

My long-term experience working at the interface between pediatrics and education has allowed me to synthesize the body of research on neurodevelopmental function and variation (Levine & Reed, 1999) and to construct a framework for understanding the enigma of disappointing school performance. Three factors play major roles:

• The traditional paradigms for understanding learning differences focus on exposing and fixing deficits, often neglecting the latent or blatant talents within struggling learners.

• Instructional practices and curricular choices fail to provide educational opportunities for diverse learners and to prepare them for a successful life.

• Because knowledge about learning emanating from the explosion of insights from brain research is not yet part of teacher preparation and professional development, most educators lack the expertise to understand and support their students' diverse minds.

To stem the tide of needless and wasteful failure facing thousands of kids, we need to take robust action on three fronts: broadened student assessment, curriculum reexamination, and professional development for educators.

Broadened Student Assessment

The methods that schools typically deploy to assess students with learning problems are not up to the task. The discrepancy formulas used to determine eligibility for specialized assistance have been shown repeatedly to have serious flaws (Kavale & Forness, 2000).

Moreover, testing that merely generates a label, such as LD or ADD, accomplishes little. These vague labels do not suggest specific approaches to remediation; instead, they pessimistically imply a relatively permanent pathological condition. What a colossal self-fulfilling prophecy! Most important, diagnosis spawned from a deficit model fails to take into account the most important feature of a student—his strengths.

Smokescreen Labels

Phillip's parents reported that he seemed to generate about two highly original and unorthodox ideas per minute. His teacher described this irrepressible 4th grader as a brilliant conceptualizer, always coming up with creative analogies. When the class studied terrorism, Phillip compared suicide bombers to strep germs that make you sick and then die in your throat.

But Phillip's day-to-day performance in school was disappointing. When he listened or read, Phillip missed or forgot much of the information he was expected to absorb. He would tune out and become fidgety during extended explanations or directions. His parents sought help from their son's pediatrician, who diagnosed ADD and prescribed a stimulant medication. This treatment helped, but not much.

It turns out that Phillip owned the kind of mind that becomes enthralled with the big picture and rejects fine detail. Consequently, in math he mastered the concepts readily but couldn't be bothered to notice the difference between a plus sign and a minus sign (a mere detail). His writing was creative and amusing but sparse on specific information. In subject after subject, Phillip's overall understanding far exceeded his handling of the details.

Like Phillip, many kids with problems don't ooze easily into categories. Students with his kind of detail intolerance often get diagnosed with ADD or accused of not really trying. In Phillip's case, the label ADD was a smokescreen that obscured people's view of his remarkable strengths and stopped them short of managing his specific weakness in detail assimilation. Phillip improved markedly after his teacher began encouraging him to make detail thinking a separate step in any activity he undertook—scan first, get the big picture, have some great ideas, and then revisit the material to vacuum up the important details.

Incidentally, society desperately needs big-picture people who can collaborate meaningfully with administrators who thrive on detail. So let's take care not to disparage or discourage the flourishing of Phillip's kind of mind.

Assessment for Diverse Minds

In addition to rethinking the assessments used to diagnose learning problems, schools need to design regular tests and quizzes so that different kinds of minds can show what they know in different ways. Teachers should be careful not to tap exclusively rote memory or straight regurgitation of skills and knowledge. They should often allow students to use notes and encourage them to take as much time as they need to respond to questions. It makes more sense to limit space than time—for instance, telling students, "You can't write more than two pages, but you can take as long as you want to do so."

High-stakes testing can pulverize many mismatched students. How commonly does end-of-grade testing discriminate against certain kinds of minds? Frequently. As a clinician, I encounter many students who have difficulty performing on multiple-choice tests or operating under timed conditions. These students' dysfunctions in certain skill areas are more than out-weighed by their assets in other domains, but standardized testing never gives them the opportunity to exhibit their strengths.

> I look forward to the day when our schools offer every student the opportunity to become a leading expert on a chosen topic.

On entering the medical profession, we take an oath that in our practice we will first of all "do no harm." I offer five suggestions (see "Do No Harm" Testing Practices, p. 17) to my professional colleagues in education so that they may strive for testing practices that do no harm to students with different kinds of minds. We need to advocate for the elimination of testing practices that inflict needless damage and unfair humiliation on so many students.

Curriculum Reexamination

It's ironic that at the same time that neuroscience is telling us so much about differences in learning, we are imposing curriculum standards that offer our students fewer learning alternatives than ever before. If we aspire to meet the challenge of leaving no child behind, we must provide diverse learners with diverging pathways that lead to their success. Such roads should maintain rigorous performance standards, while permitting innovation and creativity in curricular choices and allowing early, highly specialized minds to envision and prepare for productive adulthood.

For example, children like Michael, with his impressive mechanical aptitude, should not be sentenced to wait until adulthood to experience success. We should encourage, not constrain, the development of magnet schools and vocational education opportunities. I look forward to the day when thousands of students pursue a vocationally oriented curriculum that does not put a ceiling on their aspirations.

> ## If we aspire to meet the challenge of leaving no child behind, we must provide diverse learners with diverging pathways that lead to their success.

While studying auto mechanics (and the physics that is a part of it), a teenager should learn the ins and outs of various related careers. She or he should see the possibility of someday climbing the corporate ladder at Ford Motor Company, owning a repair business franchise, designing solar-powered engines, or managing the service department of a dealership. In this way, no one gets written off or limited because of the nature of his passions or the specialized apparatus of her mind.

Many schools have worked against odds to provide educational experiences that involve all students in conducting independent study projects in their area of personal affinity and ability. One school, for example, asked all 3rd grade students to pick a country and become the school's leading expert on that nation. The projects carried over from 3rd through 5th grade, and the students traversed content areas as they studied their country's culture, history, language, animal life, government, and music. They did art projects and wrote reports on their country.

Students learned how it feels to know more about something than anyone around, including their teachers and parents. They became valued consultants on particular countries; when the newspaper reported a current event in their country, they were asked to provide some commentary in class—a great vitamin for intellectual self-esteem!

Another school pursued a similar strategy during students' three years in middle school. Students selected any topic from a list for long-term pursuit across disciplines. They found experts in the community to assist them with their topics. Any student who did not want to claim one of the listed topics could submit one of his or her own choosing.

I look forward to the day when our schools offer every student the opportunity to become a leading expert on a chosen topic—one that harmonizes with his or her kind of mind—and to share that expertise with the community through Web sites, community-based projects, and other venues. Such a practice would give students a powerful experience of success, as well as cultivate their appetite for systematic research and focused, in-depth knowledge.

While advocating ardently for flexibility in achieving the educational aims of schooling, we can still preserve student accountability. No student should be permitted to work, study, or produce less than his or her peers. But we should never insist that everyone put forth identical output.

Professional Development for Educators

In medical practice, highly specific knowledge of the individual needs of a patient is indispensable when selecting the best treatment. This holds true in all "helping" professions—especially in education.

Teachers are in an excellent position to observe, interpret, and celebrate all kinds of minds on a daily basis. Newly acquired knowledge emanating from neuroscientific and education research can empower educators to observe and understand students' minds. Most of the phenomena that determine a student's individual strengths, shortcomings, and preferred ways of learning and producing cannot be found on any test that a clinician gives. Classroom teachers enjoy exclusive screenings—if they pay attention and know what to look for.

Becky

Eight-year-old Becky is an accomplished origami creator, a deft modern dancer, and a gifted mathematician. She thrives on science and computers. Yet in school, this girl appears shy, passive, and eternally anguished. Becky has accurate spelling, but she dislikes writing and avoids it. Becky's teacher, Mrs. Sorenson, having been educated to observe neurodevelopmental phenomena, has noticed that Becky seems to struggle and falter when called on in class. Recently, the teacher led a discussion on whether animals have feelings as people do. She called on Becky and the following dialogue ensued:

Becky: My puppy feels, uh, things like happy and, um, sad.

Mrs. Sorenson: Becky, what makes her happy or sad?

Becky (after a long pause): Different things.

Mrs. Sorenson: Such as?

Becky: Like a dog, uh, basket.

Mrs. Sorenson: Do you mean a dog biscuit?

Becky: Yeah, like that.

Becky's reading comprehension is more than a year above grade level. Yet she has trouble with word finding, shows pronounced verbal hesitancy, puts forth only simple or incomplete sentences, and fails to use verbal elaboration. The same phenomena are conspicuous in her

"Do No Harm" Testing Practices

1. Testing can help elevate education standards, but not if it creates larger numbers of students who are written off as unsuccessful. When a student does poorly, determine which link in the learning chain is uncoupled. Always have constructive, nonpunitive contingency plans for students who perform poorly on a test. Testing should not be an end in itself, but rather a call to action.

2. Not all students can demonstrate their strengths in the same manner. Allow different students to demonstrate their learning differently, using the means of their choice (portfolios, expert papers, oral presentations, and projects, as well as multiple-choice tests).

3. Never use testing as justification for retaining a student in a grade. Retention is ineffective and seriously damaging to students. How can you retain a child while claiming you are not leaving anyone behind?

4. Some students who excel on tests might develop a false sense of security and confidence, failing to realize that adult careers tap many abilities that no test can elicit. Take care to nurture vital capacities that are not testable.

5. Avoid the hazard of teachers' teaching to the tests because your work or school is being judged solely on the basis of examination scores. Teachers should never have their students rehearse or explicitly prepare for tests. Testing should be unannounced. Good results on such tests should be the product of the regular, undisturbed curriculum.

—Mel Levine

writing. Becky has strong receptive language but markedly weak expressive language—she understands better than she talks. No wonder she's so shy, self-conscious, and passive! Language output plays a vital role in school success. Verbal communication affects writing, class participation, social success, and the control of emotions and behavior.

Becky could fall through the cracks because we do not have valid tests of language production. For example, the WISC (the commonly used IQ test in her age group) does little to capture expressive language fluency. In fact, by far the best test of expressive language is a classroom teacher who knows what to listen for in gauging the adequacy of a student's verbal output, and who understands the everyday classroom phenomena associated with breakdowns in language production.

Bruce

Here's another example of the role that teachers can play in detecting learning differences. Bruce was disruptive in most of his 7th grade classes. He fashioned himself as an entertainer and often disengaged from classroom activities. Mr. Jackson, a social studies teacher knowledgeable about early adolescent development and learning, made the astute observation that Bruce often appeared confused about dates and about the sequences of events in the various historical periods that they studied. Mr. Jackson also noted that Bruce often looked distressed when given directions.

On one occasion, Mr. Jackson told the class:

> This morning I want you all to open your books to page 47, read the first three paragraphs, and study the diagram at the top of the page. And when you're finished doing that, read and think about the first two questions at the end of the chapter. I'm going to give you 10 minutes, and then I'll be calling on you to discuss the questions.

Bruce seemed to hear only something about page 47 (or was it 57?). His teacher suspected rightly that this boy was having problems processing sequences—sequential directions, chains of events in history, and multi-step explanations. His weak temporal-sequential ordering accounted for his problems in social studies and in math. This insight enabled teachers to give Bruce strategies to manage his sequencing problems: taking notes, whispering sequences under his breath, and picturing sequences in his mind. His behavior and demeanor in class improved dramatically.

Although continuing education programs abound to help teachers stay abreast of their content, we have found few comprehensive programs devoted to helping educators deepen their expertise in the science of learning. Our not-for-profit institute, All Kinds of Minds, has developed a professional development and school service model called Schools Attuned to help experienced classroom educators become knowledgeable about neurodevelopmental function and variation.[1] Participating teachers learn to analyze how their own instructional delivery and content taps specific aspects of memory, attention, motor function, language, and other areas of brain function. They are guided to observe everyday classroom phenomena that open windows on relevant learning processes (Levine, 1994).

Equipped with their Schools Attuned training, teachers lead a coalition involving the student, parents, and other adults in the school to unmask the specific learning profile of a struggling student. With help from professionals trained as neurodevelopmental consultants, whom we call profile advisors (usually school psychologists or special educators), teachers become the primary detectors of student strengths, weaknesses, and content affinities. The teachers then infuse their insights into their daily group instructional strategies and lesson designs. Frequently, a strategy that they develop to help a particular struggling student benefits the entire class. It's called excellent pedagogy.

Testing that merely generates a label, such as LD or ADD, accomplishes little.

Schools Attuned teachers are also committed to making sure that all of their students learn about learning while they are learning. Through a process called demystification, they help students whose neurodevelopmental profiles do not currently mesh with expectations to learn about their own strengths and weaknesses and acquire the terms for the specific processes that they need to work on. With profile advisors as their consultants, regular classroom teachers take the lead in formulating management plans for these students.

Where We Need to Go

The core theme of K-12 education in this century should be straightforward: high standards with an unwavering commitment to individuality. In proposing that educators reexamine assessment, curriculum, and the role of teachers, I am advocating neurodevelopmental pluralism in our schools—the celebration of all kinds of minds. Such an ethos will be the most effective and humane way of realizing our commitment to leave no child behind.

Note

1. More information about the Schools Attuned program and All Kinds of Minds is available online at www.allkindsofminds.org.

References

Kavale, K. A., & Forness, S. R. (2000). What definitions of learning disability say and don't say: A critical analysis. *Journal of Learning Disabilities, 33,* 239-256.

Levine, M. (1994). *Educational care* (2nd ed.). Cambridge, MA: Educators Publishing Service.

Levine, M., & Reed, M. (1999). *Developmental variation and learning disorders* (2nd ed.). Cambridge, MA: Educators Publishing Service.

Author's note: Mary Dean Barringer, Stacy Parker-Fisher, Chris Osmond, and Tamara Nimkoff contributed to this article.

Mel Levine, M.D., is a professor of pediatrics at the University of North Carolina Medical School in Chapel Hill, North Carolina; Director of the University's Clinical Center for the Study of Development and Learning; and the founder of All Kinds of Minds. His most recent books are *A Mind at a Time* (Simon and Schuster, 2002) and *The Myth of Laziness* (Simon and Schuster, 2003).

Article 16

Creating Culturally Responsive Schools

Barbara Bazron, David Osher, Steve Fleischman

During the last 10 years, U.S. schools have experienced a rapid growth in ethnic and racial diversity. In the near future, the young people now filling classrooms will be paying taxes, working in the public and private sectors, and consuming the goods and services that fuel our economy. Given the increased diversity of the student population, how can schools ensure that all students master the social, emotional, intellectual, and technical competencies necessary to fulfill these essential roles?

What We Know

An increasing body of research demonstrates the importance of addressing the needs of culturally and linguistically diverse students and their families. Unfortunately, the cultural underpinning of schools in the United States is largely congruent with middle-class, European values (Boykin, 1994), leading many schools to ignore or downplay the strengths of diverse students and their families. Valenzuela (1999), after studying Mexican American high school students, defined this approach as *subtractive schooling*. For example, schools ignored students' knowledge of Spanish or even treated it as a deficit.

> **Culturally responsive education can strengthen student connectedness with schools.**

This cultural disconnect often leads to poor self-concepts, discipline problems, and poor academic outcomes for ethnic minorities. Part of the problem is that teachers unfamiliar with students' diverse backgrounds sometimes misinterpret cultural difference as misbehavior (Osher, Cartledge, Oswald, Artiles,

& Coutinho, 2004). Several statistical studies have established that compared with their Caucasian peers, minority students are suspended from school more frequently and for longer durations (Skiba, Michael, Nardo, & Peterson, 2000), punished more severely (Office for Civil Rights, 1992), and disproportionately referred for restrictive special education services (Losen & Orfield, 2002).

But research has also identified ways in which schools can serve students of color effectively. For example, studies of the AVID program in San Diego, California, show that rather than tracking ethnic and language-minority students into low-level classes, setting high expectations and providing a "scaffold" of support helps students of color succeed (Mehan, Villanueva, Hubbard, & Lintz, 1996). AVID gives students direct instruction in the "bidden curriculum" of the school—which courses to take, which teachers to seek out, the importance of tests, how to study, and so on.

Another approach, supported by both experimental and quasi-experimental research, is creating an environment that enables teachers and students to connect with one another. For example, the Project STAR experiment in Tennessee found that students of color disproportionately benefited from reduced class size in 1st grade; these advantages persisted over time (Finn, Gerber, Achilles, & Boyd-Zaharias, 2001). Similarly, a six-district, quasi-experimental study of the Child Development Project found that building classroom community produced even more benefits for students of color than for Caucasian students (Solomon, Battistich, Watson, Schaps, & Lewis, 2000).

Perhaps the most powerful approach is making classroom instruction more congruent with the cultural value systems of a diverse student population. Ethnographic studies have demonstrated that *culturally responsive* education—defined by Gay (2002) as "using the cultural knowledge, prior experiences, frames of reference, and performance styles of ethnically diverse students to make learning more relevant and effective for them"—can strengthen student connectedness with schools, reduce behavior problems, and enhance learning (Kalyanpur, 2003).

What You Can Do

Educators should consider the following approaches supported by the research to promote culturally responsive education.

• Match classroom instruction to cultural norms for social interaction to enhance students' social skills development and problem-solving ability. For example, many African American youths thrive on intense and sensitive peer relations (Tharp, 1989). Teachers can make positive instructional use of these skills and behaviors by creating assignments that require group interaction.

• When asking questions or giving directions, adjust wait time for students from different cultures to enhance classroom participation and the development of critical thinking skills. Rowe (1987) found that Pueblo Indian students took twice as much time to respond spontaneously to instruction as Native Hawaiians did. A teacher who moves on too quickly might falsely assume that Pueblo Indian students are unresponsive or do not understand the concepts being presented. In contrast, a teacher might inappropriately consider Native Hawaiian students' preference for short wait times and overlapping speech as "acting out."

• Be sensitive to the cultural shifts that immigrant students, or other students with minority family and community cultures, must make as they move between school and home. This transition may be most difficult at the beginning of the school week, after students have been immersed in their home culture over the weekend. Teachers need to be sensitive to transition challenges and collaborate with families to develop mechanisms to ease the stress caused by them.

• Help parents gain *cultural capital*—the skills to negotiate the education system and knowledge of the norms of behavior that govern schools (Briscoe, Smith, & McClain, 2003). Without this information, many minority parents, especially new immigrants, may not feel competent to negotiate the system on behalf of their child or knowledgeable enough to support their child's efforts. Teachers can help by talking with parents directly rather than using more formal written communications, such as letters or notes. This is particularly valuable for families from relational cultures, in which personal connections and conversational language are the preferred ways of gathering information (Kalyanpur, 2003).

• Use culturally responsive and respectful approaches in character education, social skill instruction, and discipline. For example, a school district located in the Navajo Nation built on tradition and created a Sweat Lodge Program that helped students with behavioral problems reflect on their behavior while they reconnected to a communal spiritual perspective. This enhanced both the students' self-esteem and their willingness to become responsible community members (Osher, Dwyer, & Jackson, 2004).

Educators Take Note

Embracing the strengths and addressing the diverse learning needs of our increasingly multicultural, multilingual student population requires major transformation of our current school practices. The culturally responsive education practices outlined here can help establish a learning environment that promotes success for all students.

References

Boykin, A. W. (1994). Afrocultural expression and its implications for schooling. In E. R. Hollins, J. E. King, & W. C. Haymen (Eds.), *Teaching diverse populations* (pp. 243–256). Albany, NY: State University of New York Press.

Briscoe, R. V., Smith, A., & McClain, G. (2003). Implementing culturally competent research practices. *Focal Point, 17*(1), 10–16.

Finn, J. D., Gerber, S. B., Achilles, C. M., & Boyd-Zaharias, J. (2001). The enduring effects of small classes. *Teachers College Record, 103*, 145–183.

Gay, G. (2002). *Culturally responsive teaching*. New York: Teachers College Press.

Kalyanpur, M. (2003). A challenge to professionals: Developing cultural reciprocity with culturally diverse families. *Focal Point, 17*(1), 1–6.

Losen, D., & Orfield, G. (Eds.). (2002). *Minority issues in special education*. Cambridge, MA: The Civil Rights Project, Harvard University & The Harvard Education Publishing Group.

Mehan, H., Villanueva, I., Hubbard, L., & Lintz, A. (1996). *Constructing school success: The consequences of untracking low-achieving students*. Cambridge, UK: Cambridge University Press.

Office for Civil Rights. (1992). *Elementary and secondary civil rights survey, 1990*. Arlington, VA: DBS.

Osher, D., Cartledge, G., Oswald, D., Artiles, A. J., & Coutinho, M. (2004). Issues of cultural and linguistic competency and disproportionate representation. In R. Rutherford, M. Quinn, & S. Mather (Eds.), *Handbook of research in behavioral disorders* (pp. 54–77). New York: Guilford Publications.

Osher, D., Dwyer, K., & Jackson, S. (2004), *Safe, supportive and successful schools: Step by step*. Longmont, CO: Sopris West Educational Services.

Rowe, M. B. (1987). Wait time: Slowing down may be a way of speeding up. *American Educator, 11*(1), 38–47.

Skiba, R. J., Michael, R., Nardo, A., & Peterson, R. (2000). *The color of discipline*. Bloomington, IN: Indiana Education Policy Center.

Solomon, D., Battistich, V., Watson, M., Schaps, E., & Lewis, C. (2000). A six-district study of educational change: Direct and mediated effects of the Child Development Project. *Social Psychology of Education, 4*, 3–51.

Tharp, R. (1989). Psychocultral variables and constants: Effects on teaching and learning in schools. *American Psychologist, 44*(2), 249–359.

Valenzuela, A. (1999). *Subtractive schooling: U.S.-Mexican youth and the politics of caring*. Albany, NY: State University of New York Press.

Barbara Bazron *is a Managing Director and* ***David Osher*** *is a Managing Research Scientist the American Institutes for Research (AIR).* ***Steve Fleischman***, *series editor of this column, is a Principal Research Scientist at AIR; editorair@air.org.*

UNIT 4
Learning and Instruction

Unit Selections

Key Points to Consider

- Compare and contrast the different approaches to learning. What approach do you think is best, and why? What factors are important to your answer (for example, objectives, types of students, setting, personality of the teacher)?
- What are some principles for effective teaching that derive directly from brain research and different conceptualizations of intelligence?
- What teaching strategies could you use to promote greater student retention of material? What are good ways to attract and keep students' attention? Must a teacher be an "entertainer"? Why or why not?
- How can a teacher promote positive self-esteem, values, character, caring, and attitudes? How are they related to cognitive learning? How much emphasis should be put on cultivating character or positive student interactions? How would you create a "caring" classroom? Discuss whether or not this would interfere with achievement of cognitive learning targets.
- If you wanted to create a constructivist classroom in the subject area and/or grade in which you want to teach, what would the classroom look like? What would you emphasize, and how would your actions reflect constructivist principles and research on intelligence? How would technology be used in an effective manner with constructivist approaches?
- What are some of the advantages and disadvantages to differentiated instruction? What skills should the teacher have to be able to organize learning experiences that are matched to student abilities, achievement, and interests?

Student Website

www.mhcls.com/online

Internet References

Further information regarding these websites may be found in this book's preface or online.

The Critical Thinking Community
http://criticalthinking.org

Education Week on the Web
http://www.edweek.org

Online Internet Institute
http://www.oii.org

Teachers Helping Teachers
http://www.pacificnet.net/~mandel/

The Teachers' Network
http://www.teachers.net/

Learning can be broadly defined as a relatively permanent change in behavior or thinking due to experience. Learning is not a result of change due to maturation or temporary influences. Changes in behavior and thinking of students result from complex interactions between their individual characteristics and environmental factors. A continuing challenge in education is understanding these interactions so that learning can be enhanced. This unit focuses on approaches within educational psychology that represent different ways of viewing the learning process and related instructional strategies. Each approach to learning emphasizes a different set of personal and environmental factors that influence certain behaviors. While no one approach can fully explain learning, each is a valuable contribution to our knowledge about the process and the improvement of student performance.

The discussion of each learning approach includes suggestions for specific techniques and methods of teaching to guide teachers in understanding student behavior and in making decisions about how to teach. The articles in this section reflect a recent emphasis on applied research conducted in schools, research on the brain, on intelligence, and on constructivist theories.

Researchers have recently made significant advances in understanding the way our brain works. Information processing refers to the way that the mind receives sensory information, stores it as memory, and recalls it for later use. This procedure is basic to all learning, no matter what teaching approach is taken, and we know that the method used in processing information determines to some extent how much and what we remember. The first two articles in this subsection present some of the fundamental principles of brain functioning, information processing, and cognition. The third, fourth, and fifth articles focus on human intelligence and metacognition processes that form the foundation of student learning and understanding.

Until relatively recently, behaviorism was the best-known theory of learning. Most practicing and prospective teachers are familiar with concepts such as classical conditioning, reinforcement, and punishment, and there is no question that behaviorism has made significant contributions to understanding learning. But behaviorism has also been subject to much misinterpretation, in part because it seems so simple. In fact, the effective use of behavioristic principles is complex and demanding, as the fifth article points out.

Constructivist learning theory is currently the predominant theory of learning that is recognized by educational psychologists. According to constructivists, it is important for students to actively create and reorganize knowledge. There is a need for students to interpret within meaningful contexts so that what is learned is well connected with existing knowledge. Constructivism is highlighted in the sixth article in this section and is also emphasized in two articles in the section on Instructional Strategies.

Social psychological learning emphasizes the affective, social, moral, and personal learning of students. Social psychology is the study of the nature of interpersonal relationships in social situations. In education, this approach looks at teacher/pupil relationships and group processes to derive principles of interaction that affect learning. Three articles in this section examine the application of social psychological principles to learning. In the first, the importance of recognizing and developing a positive school culture is stressed. The second article argues for the importance of social and emotional learning. In the third article, the authors argue for the importance of cooperative learning.

Instructional strategies are the teacher behaviors and methods of conveying information that affect learning. Teaching methods or techniques can vary greatly, depending on objectives, group size, types of students, and personality of the teacher. For example, discussion classes are generally more effective for enhancing thinking skills than are individualized sessions or lectures. For the final subsection, articles have been selected that show how teachers can use principles of cognitive psychology and intelligence in their teaching within the current standards-based environment. The first article provides implications of using a constructivist approach, with an emphasis on collaboration and cooperative inquiry. In the second article the principles of constructivism are used as a foundation for using block scheduling to promote deep understanding. Differentiated instruction is addressed in the last article as a teaching method that can accommodate learning for all students.

Successful Strategies for English Language Learners

Tracy Gray and Steve Fleischman

Cut through the fog of competing claims made by researchers and policymakers about effective approaches for meeting the needs of English language learners (ELLs) and one fact remains: Educators daily face the challenge of teaching this large and growing student population. More immigrants arrived in the United States during the 1990s than during any other decade on record. This fall, in response to this trend toward linguistic and cultural diversity, the New York City school district created an office to translate information for parents into eight languages. The Los Angeles Unified School District already spends more than $6 million yearly to translate its materials (Zehr, 2004).

Today, students in our schools speak more than 450 languages (Kindler, 2002). About 12 percent of all preK–12 students are considered English language learners. Projections indicate that by 2015, more than 50 percent of all students in K–12 public schools across the United States will not speak English as their first language (Pearlman, 2002).

The accountability requirements of the No Child Left Behind Act of 2001 add a new dimension to this challenge because ELLs are included in the law's testing requirements. Their test scores may be factored into the determination of whether a school is making adequate yearly progress (AYP).

Although ideology often trumps evidence in this area, amid the conflicting claims research has established a number of straightforward strategies that educators can use to meet the academic, linguistic, and cultural needs of English language learners.

What We Know

A review of effective instructional strategies for linguistically and culturally diverse students reveals that many of these strategies are simply extensions of approaches that work well with all students. For example, sound principles and practices of classroom organization and management—such as small instructional groups—seem to work well for ELLs (Garcia, 1991).

One key to successfully working with ELLs is to view them as a resource in the classroom. According to Zehler (1994), these students can offer information about other countries and cultures; new perspectives about the world, different societies, and belief systems; and opportunities for exposing native English speakers to other languages.

In addition, many researchers support the use of scaffolding strategies to help ELLs organize their thoughts in English, develop study skills, and follow classroom procedures. To provide meaning, scaffolding uses contextual supports— simplified language, teacher modeling, visuals and graphics, and cooperative and hands-on learning. According to Diaz-Rico and Weed (2002) and Ovando, Collier, and Combs (2003), English language learners show progress when their content-area teachers consistently use these supports as they deliver instruction. These researchers identify the following scaffolding approaches as effective.

Keep the language simple. Speak simply and clearly. Use short, complete sentences in a normal tone of voice. Avoid using slang, idioms, or figures of speech.

Use actions and illustrations to reinforce oral statements. Appropriate prompts and facial expressions help convey meaning. Pointing to the chalkboard while asking, "Please come up and complete the math problem" is more effective than repeating commands or directions.

Ask for completion, not generation. Ask students to choose answers from a list or to complete a partially finished outline or paragraph. Encourage students to use language as much as possible to gain confidence over time.

Model correct usage and judiciously correct errors. Use corrections to positively reinforce students' use of English. When ELLs make a mistake or use awkward language, they are often attempting to apply what they know about their first language to English. For example, a Spanish-speaking student may say, "It fell from me"—a direct translation from Spanish—instead of "I dropped it."

Use visual aids. Present classroom content and information whenever possible in a way that engages students—by using graphic organizers, tables, charts, outlines, and graphs, for example. Encourage students to use these tools to present information.

Educators Take Note

A final key component of serving the needs of English language learners is establishing strong relationships with families. Educators sometimes view low levels of parental involvement as a lack of parental interest in the education process. However, non-English-speaking families often have no means for communicating with the school. They may also have different cultural expectations regarding the appropriate relationship with their children's school. Therefore, schools need to make additional efforts to engage these families.

Boothe (2000) emphasizes the importance of inviting immigrant families to participate in meaningful activities in school, such as classroom demonstrations of their culture (food or clothing, for example) or awards ceremonies acknowledging their children's accomplishments. Schools also need to clearly state their expectations for both parents and students, especially to families newly arrived in the United States. Whenever possible, schools should translate all written communications to families into these families' native languages.

Smaller school districts may not have the resources to translate their written communications into numer-ous languages. However, many translation resources are available on the Internet at no cost, including `http://babelfish.altavista.com` and `www.itools.com`.

In addition, schools should identify bilingual contacts in the school and community as well as foreign language instructors in local colleges and universities who might be willing to provide translation support. Research indicates that establishing partnerships between bilingual families and non-English-speaking families encourages family involvement in school (Epstein, 1998; Moll, Amanti, Neff, & González, 1992). Additional translation and interpreter resources are available through local organizations such as intercultural institutes, social service agencies, and state bar associations.

Although none of these communication solutions is perfect, schools that adopt them demonstrate their willingness to communicate with the families of all their students. Using these tools to reach out to families is an important step in including ELLs in the school community and promoting their achievement.

References

Boothe, D. (2000). Looking beyond the ESL label. *Principal Leadership, 1*(4), 30–35.

Diaz-Rico, L. T., & Weed, K. Z. (2002). *The cross cultural, language, and academic development handbook* (2nd ed.). Boston: Allyn and Bacon.

Epstein, J. (1998). *School and family partnerships: Preparing educators and improving schools.* Boulder, CO: Westview Press.

Garcia, E. (1991). *The education of linguistically and culturally diverse students: Effective instructional practices (Educa-tional Practice Report 1).* Santa Cruz, CA: National Center for Research on Cultural Diversity and Second Language Learning. Available: www.ncela.gwu.edu/pubs/ncrcdsll/eprl/index.htm

Kindler, A. L. (2002). *Survey of the states' limited English proficient students and available educational programs and services, 2000–2001 Summary Report.* Washington, DC: National Clearinghouse for English Language Acquisition and Language Instruction Educational Programs.

Moll, L. C., Amanti, C., Neff, D., & González, N. (1992). Funds of knowledge for teaching: Using a qualitative approach to connect home and classrooms. *Theory into Practice, 31*(2), 131–141.

Ovando, C., Collier, V., & Combs, M. (2003). *Bilingual and ESL classrooms: Teaching multicultural contexts* (3rd ed.). Boston: McGraw–Hill.

Pearlman, M. (2002). *Measuring and supporting English language learning in schools: Challenges for test makers.* Presentation at CRESST Conference, Los Angeles, California.

Zehler, A. (1994). *Working with English language learners: Strategies for elementary and middle school teachers.* (Program Information Guide Series, Number 19). Washington, DC: National Clearinghouse for English Language Acquisition and Language Instruction Educational Programs.

Zehr, M. A. (2004, Oct. 6). Translation efforts a growing priority for urban schools. *Education Week,* pp. 1, 15.

Tracy Gray is a Principal Research Scientist at the American Institutes for Research (AIR), specializing in technical innovation for students with disabilities, education for English language learners, and online learning tools for teachers and students. She is the Director of the National Center for Technology. Steve Fleischman, series editor of this column, is a Principal Research Scientist at AIR.

Article 18

ASK THE COGNITIVE SCIENTIST

Students Remember... What They Think About

How does the mind work—and especially how does it learn? Teachers make assumptions all day long about how students best comprehend, remember, and create. These assumptions—and the teaching decisions that result—are based on a mix of theories learned in teacher education, trial and error, craft knowledge, and gut instinct. Such gut knowledge often serves us well. But is there anything sturdier to rely on?

Cognitive science is an interdisciplinary field of researchers from psychology, neuroscience, linguistics, philosophy, computer science, and anthropology who seek to understand the mind. In this regular American Educator *column, we will consider findings from this field that are strong and clear enough to merit classroom application.*

By Daniel T. Willingham

Issue: The teacher presents a strong, coherent lesson in which a set of significant facts is clearly connected to a reasonable conclusion. But, at test time, the students show no understanding of the connections. Some students parrot back the conclusion, but no facts. Others spit back memorized facts, but don't see how they fit together. Though the lesson wasn't taught in a rote way, it seems like rote knowledge is what the students took in. Why do well-integrated, coherent lessons often come back to us in a less meaningful, fragmented form? Can cognitive science help explain why this result is so common—and offer ideas about how to avoid it?

Response: Rote knowledge is devoid of all meaning (as discussed in my last column, Winter 2002). The knowledge that these students appear to be regurgitating is probably not rote knowledge. It is probably "shallow" knowledge: The students' knowledge has meaning (unlike rote knowledge), in that the students understand each isolated part, but their knowledge lacks the deeper meaning that comes from understanding the relationship among the parts. For reasons noted below, this is a common problem in the early stages of learning about a new topic. But it also has another remediable source, which is the focus of this column.

Cognitive science has shown that what ends up in a learner's memory is not simply the material presented—it is the product of what the learner thought about when he or she encountered the material. This principle illuminates one important origin of shallow knowledge and also suggests how to help students develop deep and interconnected knowledge.

Let's start with an example of shallow knowledge. Suppose that you are teaching a high school class unit on World War II and

develop a lesson on the Japanese attack on Pearl Harbor. Many facts might be included in such a lesson: (a) Japan had aspirations to be a regional power; (b) Japan was engaged in a protracted war with China; (c) because they were at war, European countries could not protect their colonies in the South Pacific; and (d) the attack on Pearl Harbor resulted in a declaration of war on Japan by the United States. The overarching point of this lesson might be to show that the attack on Pearl Harbor was a strategic mistake for the Japanese, given their war aims. (See Figure 1 for a diagram of the lesson.)

We can see two ways that this meaningful lesson might end up as shallow knowledge in the student's mind. The student might commit to memory some or all of these four facts. But knowing these facts without understanding how they relate to one another and can be integrated to support the conclusion leaves the facts isolated; they are not without meaning, but neither are they as rich as they might be. The student has the trees, but no view of the forest.

Alternatively, the student might commit to memory the conclusion, "The attack on Pearl Harbor, although militarily a successful battle for Japan, was ultimately detrimental to its long-range war plans." But memorizing this conclusion without understanding the reasoning behind it and knowing the supporting facts is empty. It isn't rote—the student knows Japan initiated and won a battle at the place called Pearl Harbor. But the knowledge certainly is "shallow"—it has no connections.*

We have all had students memorize phrases from class or a textbook more or less word-for-word, and although what the student says is accurate, we can't help but wonder whether he or she really understands the ideas those words represent. Let's dig deeper.

78

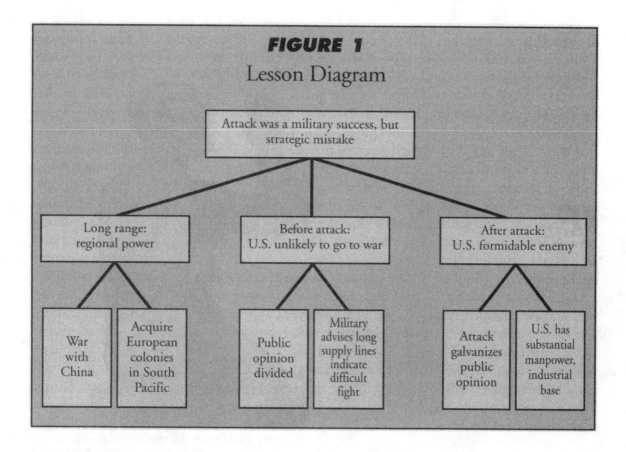

FIGURE 1

Lesson Diagram

Memory Is as Thinking Does

When students parrot back a teacher's or the textbook's words, they are, of course, drawing on memory. Thus, the question of why students end up with shallow knowledge is really a question about the workings of memory. Needless to say, determining what ends up in memory and in what form is a complex question, but *there is one factor that trumps most others in determining what is remembered: what you think about when you encounter the material*. The fact that the material you are dealing with has meaning does not guarantee that the meaning *will* be remembered. If you think about that meaning, the meaning will reside in memory. If you don't, it won't. For example, if I teach about Pearl Harbor, some sailing enthusiasts may start thinking about the ships of the era and pay minimal attention to the rest of the class—just a few minutes after the bell rings they won't remember much about the causes and consequences of Pearl Harbor. Memory is as thinking does.

A classic experiment illustrating this principle was conducted by Thomas Hyde and James Jenkins in 1969. It examined how one thinks about material and the effect of that thinking on memory. Subjects in their experiment listened to a list of words at a rate of one word every two seconds. Different groups of subjects were to perform different tasks upon hearing each word. Some were to rate each word as to whether it made them think of pleasant or unpleasant things, whereas others were asked to count the number of times the letter E appeared in the word. Rating the pleasantness forces the subject to think about the word's meaning; the word *garbage* is unpleasant because of what it means—what it is associated with in one's memory. Counting Es, on the other hand, forces one to think about the spelling of the word, but not its meaning. Thus, the experimenters manipulated what subjects thought about when they encountered each word. Subjects were not told that their memory for the words would later be tested; they thought they were merely to make the pleasantness or the E-counting judgment.

One other detail of the experiment is especially important. The word list actually consisted of 12 pairs of very highly associated words, such as *doctor–nurse*, although this fact was not pointed out to any of the subjects. The order in which the words were read was random (except that related words were not allowed to be next to one another in the list).

The results are shown in Figure 2. First look at the left side of the chart, which shows the mean number of words recalled. Memory was much better when subjects made the pleasantness ratings. Thinking about the meaning of material is especially helpful to memory. This finding is consistent across hundreds of other experiments.

The right side of the figure shows a measure of clustering—the extent to which subjects paired the associated words as they tried to remember them. When a subject recalled a word (e.g., *doctor*), what percentage of the time was the next word recalled the highly associated one (*nurse*)? As the figure shows, subjects who thought about the word's meaning (i.e., rated pleasantness) not only remembered more words, they tended to remember the related words together, even though the related words did not appear together in the list. The subjects who counted Es did not tend to remember related words together.

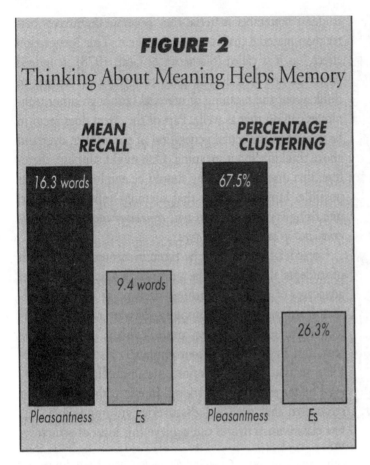

FIGURE 2

Thinking About Meaning Helps Memory

MEAN RECALL

16.3 words

9.4 words

Pleasantness   Es

PERCENTAGE CLUSTERING

67.5%

26.3%

Pleasantness   Es

These results forcefully make the point that meaningful structure that is in the environment may or may not end up being stored in memory. In the Hyde and Jenkins experiment, the fact that some of the words were related in meaning was largely lost on the subjects who counted Es because thinking about Es did not encourage the subjects to process meaning. Subjects who made the pleasantness ratings tended to group the words together by meaning as they recalled them. Whatever subjects thought about when they heard the words (which, teachers will note, depends on what they were *asked* to think about) was what ended up in memory.

In the Hyde and Jenkins experiment, the "what they think about" principle is divided into thinking about meaning versus not thinking about meaning. Other experiments show that even if one thinks about meaning, the particular *aspect* of the meaning that one considers will be stored in memory, and other aspects of meaning will not. For example, in one experiment (Barclay et al., 1974), subjects were presented with words to remember in the context of a sentence. The sentence biased subjects to think of one or another feature of the to-be-remembered word: For example, some subjects read "The man lifted the *piano*," which encouraged thinking about the fact that pianos are heavy. Other subjects read "The man tuned the *piano*," which encouraged considering that pianos produce music. In the next phase of the experiment subjects were told that their memory for some of the nouns in the sentences would be tested and that for each sentence they would get a hint. For *piano,*

some subjects were given the hint, "something heavy." If they had read the sentence about lifting the piano, this hint matched the feature they had thought about, but if they read the sentence about tuning the piano, the hint didn't match. (Other subjects saw a hint that matched the piano tuning sentence; that hint was "something with a nice sound.")

The results showed that subjects remembered about three times as many words when the hint for the test matched what subjects had thought about when they first read the word. Again, the point is that what is stored in memory is quite specific to what you think about when you encounter the material. It is not the case that if you think about *piano*, then *piano* and all of its features are stored in memory. You might think about its music-producing qualities, its weight, its cost, and so on. Or you might not focus on the referent at all, but rather on the physical properties of the word itself, as when Hyde and Jenkins asked subjects to count *E*s. In each case, what you think about is what you remember.

So what does this have to do with shallow knowledge? It shows where shallow knowledge might come from. Meaning that is in the environment won't end up in memory if students don't think about it. Students with shallow knowledge have apparently thought about the material in a shallow way. This conclusion reframes the question we might ask: Why would students think about the material in a shallow way, given that we didn't present it to them that way? Obviously, a student would learn only isolated facts or unsupported conclusions if that is what the teacher taught, but I find it difficult to believe that this is a common practice. The notion that education should emphasize meaning is deeply ingrained in our system and has been for a generation or more. There cannot be many teachers who ask their students to learn facts without concern for a larger picture. So how do students end up with shallow knowledge? There are several possible answers.

1. As noted at the beginning of this article, in one form, shallow knowledge is simply a step on the way to deep knowledge. Consider again the hierarchical diagram shown in Figure 1. I argued that shallow knowledge could either be memorization of the conclusion (top of the hierarchy) without knowing the facts that back it up (bottom of the hierarchy), or memorization of the facts without integrating them into a conclusion. Clearly the sort of deep knowledge we want our students to have is objectively harder to obtain than shallow knowledge, because knowledge of the facts *and* knowledge of the conclusion *and* knowledge of their interrelationships are prerequisite to it. We want students to know how the different levels of hierarchy relate to one another; it's not enough to have memorized each level in isolation of the others. That connected knowledge will inevitably be the last thing that the student acquires. Thus, some students' knowledge will be shallow simply because they are not far enough along yet.

2. Other students may effectively quit learning before they reach the deep understanding that is our goal for them. A student may learn the facts about Pearl Harbor and think

"All right, I've learned a lot about this stuff." The student is correct (so far as it goes) and simply doesn't realize that there is yet more to do.

3. Students' perception of what they are supposed to learn—and what it means to learn—may contribute to shallow knowledge. A student may seek to memorize definitions and pat phrases word-for-word from the book because the student *knows* that this information is correct and cannot be contested. When I was in eighth grade, we were given a list of vocabulary terms that we were to define and then study in preparation for a weekly test. A friend defined "cherub" as "an angel of the second order." My friends and I teased him because his definition missed what we thought was the key aspect of the word—that a cherub is small, chubby, and rosy-cheeked. He was unmoved and kept repeating "that's what the dictionary said." He liked the fact that his answer was uncontestable. Students may memorize exactly what the teacher or textbook says in order to be certain that they are *correct*, and worry less about the extent to which they understand.

4. Despite what was offered to students in the teacher's lesson, the students attended to (thought about) something different—and that's what they remembered.

What Does This Mean for Teachers?

This fundamental principle of memory—memory is as thinking does—yields a clear strategy to encourage deep, meaningful knowledge. If students think about the meaning of material, meaning will end up in memory. How can teachers be sure that students are thinking about meaning?

Obviously there is no one way to ensure that students think about the meaning of material. A compelling story may be appropriate for one lesson, whereas a carefully designed laboratory project works for a second, and a well-structured group discussion for a third. One possible common misconception is that learners can only understand meaning if they themselves construct the meaning in a physically active way. A moment's reflection should tell us that "listening" does not imply passivity or shallowness. We have all been to "active, participatory" workshops that felt like a waste of time, and we have been to lectures where we "just listened" that were gripping and informative. Constructing meaning is a matter of being *mentally* engaged; being physically engaged might help at times, but it is not necessary.

How can we ensure that students are mentally engaged? While there is still more to learn about applying this research on thinking and memory to teaching, several key principles have emerged to guide teachers in developing assignments, classroom activities, and assessments.

• **Anticipate what your lesson will lead students to think about**. The direct relationship between thought and memory is so important that it could be used as a self-check for a teacher preparing virtually any assignment: *Always try to anticipate what students will be thinking when they are doing the assignment*. Doing so may make it clear that some assignments de-

signed with one purpose in mind will achieve another. For example, a teacher once told me that, as part of a unit on the Underground Railroad, he had his students bake biscuits so that they would appreciate what escaped slaves ate most nights. He asked what I thought of the assignment and my reply was that his students will remember baking biscuits. In other words, his students probably thought for 30 seconds about the relation of the baking to the course material, and then spent 30 minutes thinking about measuring flour, mixing dough, and so on.

Another example comes from my recent observation of my nephew as he completed a book report. The teacher asked the students to draw a poster that depicted all of the events of the book. The purpose of the assignment was to have students think of the book as a whole, and to consider how the separate events related to one another. This purpose got lost in the execution. My nephew spent a lot more time thinking about how to draw a good castle than he did about the plot of the book.

• **Use discovery learning carefully**. The principle above—anticipate the students' thoughts—also illuminates the use and misuse of discovery learning. There is little doubt that students remember material they generate themselves better than material that is handed to them. This "generation effect," as it is called (Slamecka & Graf, 1978), is indeed powerful, and it is due, in part, to forcing the learner to think about the meaning of material (although other techniques can do that as well). Part of the effect does seem to be unique to the actual generation of the answer, over and above thinking about meaning. One might suppose, therefore, that discovery learning should be employed whenever possible. However, given that memory follows thought, one thing is clear: *Students will remember incorrect "discoveries" just as well as correct ones*.

Considerable care must be taken to ensure that the path of students' thoughts will be a profitable one. For example, advocates of discovery learning often point out that children learn to use some computer software rapidly and effectively merely by "playing around with it." That may be true, but that learning environment is also quite structured in that profitless actions are immediately discouraged by the system not working. In effect, the system is so structured that profitless discoveries are impossible; but few classroom activities can achieve this kind of structure. How much anatomy will students learn by "playing around" with frog dissection? Can one anticipate the thoughts of students who dissect frogs with little direction? Although discovery learning may be powerful in highly structured contexts that make the correct discovery virtually inevitable, in others it is likely to prove unproductive.

Constructing meaning is a matter of being mentally engaged.

• **Design reading assignments that require students to actively process the text**. Many concrete strategies have been suggested for helping students to get more out of reading that likely have some or all of their effect by making readers think about the meaning of what they are reading. *Techniques such as writing outlines, self-examination during learning, review* *questions, and previews can encourage or require students to integrate the material and to thereby process (i.e., think about) the meaning.* These different techniques are more or less effective in different situations, perhaps due to the specific materials being studied (e.g., McDaniel & Einstein, 1989); general principles guiding when each technique should be used have not been forthcoming. Nevertheless, although one technique or another may be more effective for a given lesson or group of students, using any strategy that encourages the processing of meaning is almost always better than not using one.

• **Design lessons so that students can't avoid thinking about the lesson's goal.** On a more positive note, the "memory is as thinking does" principle can yield steps teachers can take to help students develop deep, interconnected knowledge: *Lessons should be directed so that students are very likely to think (or can't help but think) about the goal of the lesson.* The goal of the Underground Railroad lesson was not really about biscuits—it was to encourage students to consider the experience of escaped slaves. Therefore, a more effective starting point for that lesson would be to ask students leading questions that encourage consideration of what escaped slaves' experiences would be like, which might include questions of how they would obtain food, and what the constraints were on the food they could get (inexpensive, cooked rapidly, etc.). My nephew would have gotten more out of his book report project if it had emphasized what the teacher was really interested in (the connection among the book's events), perhaps by having the students label the events and connections among them (e.g., this event moves the character towards his goal; this event causes that event) and de-emphasizing the students' artistic contribution by having them use clip art or simply writing the events in words.

• **Design tests that lead students to think about and integrate the most important material.** The "memory is as thinking does" principle may also be applied to methods of assessing student knowledge: *Like lessons, study guides for texts should be developed that force students to think about the goals of the lessons being assessed.* For better or worse, some students expend their greatest effort to understand material as they prepare for an examination. Even if you would rather see such students motivated by a passion to learn, you can use the students' motivation to earn a good grade to ensure that they are getting the most out of your lessons. Announcing the general topics to be covered on an exam leaves the specifics of what to learn up to the student. Even if the teacher emphasizes that deep understanding will be tested, the student may misconstrue what is deep or, as noted earlier, the student may quit once some facts have been memorized, believing that he or she has already done quite a bit of studying. Suppose, however, that the teacher provides a list of integrative questions for the students to study from, such as "Describe why the attack on Pearl Harbor was a strategic mistake by Japan, given its war aims." Suppose further that the students know that the examination will consist of five questions from the 30-question list that they have been given, with an essay to be written on each of

the five questions. Students will very likely restrict their studying to the 30 question list, but that might be just fine with the teacher if he or she feels that any student who can answer those 30 questions has mastered the material. This method of testing has the advantage of ensuring that while students are highly motivated, they think about the deepest meaning of the material that the teacher intended.

In summary, in the early stages of learning, students may display "shallow" learning. These students have acquired bits of knowledge that aren't well-integrated into a larger picture. Research tells us that deep, connected knowledge can be encouraged by getting students to think about the interrelation of the various pieces of knowledge that they have acquired. Cognitive science has not progressed to the point that it can issue prescriptions of exactly how that can be achieved—that job is very much in the hands of experienced teachers. But in considering how to encourage students to acquire meaningful knowledge, teachers will do well to keep the "memory is as thinking does" principle in mind.

References

Barclay, J. R., Bransford, J. D., Franks, J. J., McCarrel, N. S., & Nitsch, K. (1974). Comprehension and semantic flexibility. *Journal of Verbal Learning & Verbal Behavior, 13*, 471–481.

Hyde, T. S. & Jenkins, J. J. (1969). Differential effects of incidental tasks on the organization of recall of a list of highly associated words. *Journal of Experimental Psychology, 82*, 472–481.

McDaniel, M. A. & Einstein, G. O. (1989). Material-appropriate processing: A contextualist approach to reading and studying strategies. *Educational Psychology Review, 1*, 113–145.

Slamecka, N. J. & Graf, P. (1978). The generation effect: Delineation of a phenomenon. *Journal of Experimental Psychology: Human Learning & Memory, 4*, 592–604.

Readers can pose specific questions to "Ask the Cognitive Scientist," American Educator, *555 New Jersey Ave. N.W., Washington, DC 20001 or to* **amerend@aft.org**

*My last column (Winter 2002, available at **www.aft.org/ american_educator/winter2002/CogSci.html**) discussed another common problem for students: inflexible knowledge. Like shallow knowledge, inflexible knowledge is meaningful—the catch is that it doesn't translate well to other relevant situations. To extend our World War II example, a student with inflexible knowledge may learn the conclusion and an adequate number of supporting facts, developing a real understanding of Japan's mistake. But, when the history class moved on to study another war, the student may not recognize an analogous strategic mistake. Developing flexible knowledge, such as being able to track strategic mistakes as a theme throughout military history (or to generalize, for example, to corporate history) requires much further study.

Daniel T. Willingham is associate professor of cognitive psychology and neuroscience at the University of Virginia and author of Cognition: The Thinking Animal. *His research focuses on the role of consciousness in learning.*

Beyond Learning By Doing: The Brain Compatible Approach

The current position of the field of experiential education within mainstream education places at a premium attempts to significantly broaden and deepen experiential pedagogy beyond mere "learning by doing." This article will explore one such attempt—the Brain Compatible Approach—and its potential linkages with experiential education. An overview of the Brain Compatible Approach will be outlined, followed by a discussion of several key principles. Linkages between these principles and experiential education will be discussed, as well as several "Quick Tips" on possible practical applications of the research. Finally, the benefits of aligning experiential education with the Brain Compatible Approach will be explored.

Keywords: Education, Brain Compatible, Pedagogy

Jay W. Roberts

Over the last ten years, experiential education has made many in-roads with the mainstream educational establishment. The success of programs such as Project Adventure and Outward Bound working within schools has been well documented. Additionally, ropes course, environmental, and outdoor education programs have become prevalent in many school districts across the country. Yet, with all these advances, there are still many barriers between our pedagogy and traditional schooling. We remain literally, and figuratively, "outside" the educational establishment. Recent initiatives toward accountability and standards have placed experiential education in the crosshairs of reform-minded politicians and school consultants. "Learning by doing" is often described as "process heavy," devoid of content, and a hold-out from 1960s progressivists' approaches. One researcher has gone so far as to say "recent history of American education and controlled observations have shown that learning by doing and its adaptations are among the least effective pedagogies available to the teacher" (Hirsch, 1996, p. 257).

The current position of the field within mainstream education places at a premium attempts to significantly broaden and deepen experiential pedagogy beyond mere "learning by doing." This paper will explore one such attempt—the Brain Compatible Approach—and its potential linkages with experiential education. An overview of the Brain Compatible Approach will be outlined, followed by a discussion of several key principles. Linkages between these principles and experiential education will be discussed as well as several "Quick Tips" on possible practical applications of the research. Finally, the benefits of aligning experiential education with the Brain Compatible Approach will be explored.

The Brain Compatible Approach

In July of 1989, President George Bush declared the 1990s the "Decade of the Brain." What followed was a revolution in research, articles, books, and television specials on what we know about how the brain functions and learns. The medical advances in particular have been many and remarkable. We have learned more about the brain in the past five years than the previous one hundred. Additionally, nearly 90 percent of all neuroscientists who have ever lived are alive today (Brandt & Wolfe, 1998).

While still relatively new as a field of inquiry, the Brain Compatible Approach has yielded several intriguing findings:

- *Neuroplasticity:* The brain changes physiologically as a result of experience and it happens much quicker than originally thought. The environment in which the brain operates determines to a large degree the functioning ability of the brain (Brandt & Wolfe, 1998).

- *The brain is complex and interconnected:* Just as a city or jazz quartet has many levels of interaction and connectedness, the brain has an infinite number of possible interconnections. In essence, there are no isolated, specialized areas but rather the brain is simultaneously processing a wide variety of information all at once (Caine & Caine, 1994).

- *Every brain is unique:* Our brains are far more individualized in terms of physiology, neural wiring, bio-chemical balance, and developmental stage than previously thought (Jensen, 2000).

Each of these findings suggests re-consideration of the way we currently educate. Caution must also be practiced. Much of the current research is new, and steps from research to application are inherently complex and difficult. Already, several researchers have questioned the validity of educational applications of brain research (Bruer, 1997). If nothing else, the sheer volume of new information about how the brain functions and learns forces us to question what we truly "know" about learning and educational practice.

Principles of Brain Based Learning

Drawing from the findings above, several intriguing principles and practical implications have emerged. The following principles are of particular interest to experiential educators as they support some long-standing practices within experiential education and also push the envelope of what may be possible in the future.

Principle #1: Pattern and Meaning Making

Research supports the claim that the search for meaning is innate and occurs through patterning (Caine & Caine, 1994). Patterning refers to the meaningful organization and categorization of information (Nummela & Rosengren, 1986). The brain is designed to search for and integrate new information into existing structures and actively resists "meaningless" patterns (Caine & Caine). The process is constant and does not stop—regardless of whether or not we have stopped teaching! This principle reinforces many of the practices we attribute to experiential learning including emphasis on context and framing, learner involvement in the teaching of the material, alternating between details and big picture (whole/part), reflection components, and relevancy (i.e., relating information to students' previous experience and learning).

Quick Tip #1: Chunking can be an effective tool for presenting the learner with information in an organized, meaningful way. Look at the following list of letters: IBFVTNOJBLKFJ. Try to memorize them as presented. Now look at the next list of letters: JFK, LBJ, ON, TV, FBI. The second list is much easier to memorize even though they are the same letters. They have simply been chunked and arranged in a meaningful way that draws on previous experience and information. Consider how you might chunk small activities (lessons or even directions) and large, multi-day experiences. How can you arrange the information in a more meaningful, patterned way?

Quick Tip #2: Use a "Big Picture." Remember that your students do not have the same view of the course, lesson, or program that you do. Provide them with a big picture as soon as possible at the beginning of the experience. Rather than an exhaustive outline or itinerary, the big picture gives your students a taste of what's coming and allows them to begin making pat-

terns, connections, and frames for the experience. Revisit the big picture a few times throughout the experience to further solidify the link. In this regard, it is helpful to have it on a flip chart or other visual aid. Try using a "you are here" map with a movable arrow.

Principle #2: The Brain as a Parallel Processor

The human brain is the ultimate, multi-tasking machine, constantly doing many things at once. This is because the brain is geared toward survival and is, in actuality, poorly designed for linear, lock-step instruction (Jensen, 2000). Consider how you learned to ride a bicycle. Did you learn through reading a book or hearing a lecture on the separate topics of bike parts, safety, and operation? No. It is more likely you learned through a more dynamic and complex series of experiences. Current research supports the notion that the brain learns best through rich, complex, and multi-sensory environments (Jensen). In this sense, the teacher is seen more as an *orchestrator* of learning environments rather than an instructor of linear lesson plans or even a facilitator of experiences (Deporter, Reardon, & Singer-Nourie, 1999). Practical applications for parallel processing include the use of multi-modal instructional techniques (visual, auditory, kinesthetic) and multiple intelligence activities (Gardner, 1985). Simulations and role-plays mimic our natural learning environment and encourage complex processing. Lastly, enriched learning environments can be orchestrated through the components of challenge, novelty, choice, high feedback, social interaction, and active participation (Diamond & Hopson, 1998). If the benefits of enriched, multi-sensory, complex learning environments continue to be supported by the research, experiential theory and practice can and must play a larger role in the classroom of the future.

Quick Tip #3: Use the EELDRC (Enroll, Experience, Label, Demonstrate, Review, Celebrate) design frame (Deporter et al., 1999) to create a dynamic, complex, multi-sensory lesson plan. In the *Enroll* segment, seek to engage students in the material through intrigue and answering the learner question "What's In It For Me?" Give them a brief *Experience* to immerse students in the new information. Use the *Label* segment to punctuate the most salient points with a "lecturette" or debrief. Provide an opportunity for the participants to *Demonstrate* with the new information to encourage connections and personalization of the material. *Review* the material to cement the big picture and, finally, find a way to *Celebrate* the experience to reinforce positive associations with the learning.

Principle #3: Stress and Threat

Learning is enhanced by challenge and inhibited by threat (Jensen, 2000). Paul MacLean offers a model for considering this principle through his Triune Brain theory (1978). MacLean categorizes the brain into three main regions or separate brains—the Reptilian (or R-complex), the Mammalian (or Limbic), and the Neo-Mammalian (or Neo-Cortex). The reptilian brain controls physical survival and basic needs (flight or fight responses). This is our most primitive "brain." The second brain—the Mammalian—houses both the hippocampus and amygdala—the primary centers for emotion and memory. Lastly, the most advanced part of our brains, according to MacLean, is our Neo-Cortex. It is here where we use higher order thinking skills—synthesizing, logical and operational thinking, speech, and planning for the future (Caine & Caine, 1994).

In this model, the brain has the capacity to "shift" up or down depending on perception of the immediate environment. Perceived threat an force the brain to "downshift" to lower order thinking (Hart, 1983). Yet, heightened challenge and stress, referred to as eustress, can invite an up-shift response into higher order thinking skills in the neo-cortex. Recent research has suggested that the chemical and physiological responses to stress and threat are radically different (Caine & Caine, 1994). Psychological models also support a difference between perceived challenge and threat (Csikszentmihalyi, 1991). This idea is expressed in experiential pedagogy through the concepts of adaptive dissonance and the "comfort zone." In both cases, the felicitator or teacher intentionally places the learner in stressful situations to encourage and invite new adaptive behaviors and mental models that may be more successful or effective for the learner.

Caine and Caine (1994), suggest that specific learning conditions can create situations of up-shifting or downshifting. Downshifting can occur when "pre-specified 'correct' outcomes have been established by an external agent; personal meaning is limited; rewards and punishments are externally controlled; restrictive time lines are given; and the work to be done is relatively unfamiliar with little support available" (Caine & Caine, p. 84). By contrast, to create up-shifting conditions "outcomes should be relatively open ended; personal meaning should be maximized; emphasis should be on intrinsic motivation; tasks should have relatively open-ended time lines; and should be manageable and supported" (Caine & Caine, p. 85). Emotions also play a critical role in both memory encoding and threat perception (LeDoux, 1996). Too little emotion and the brain has a difficult time "tagging" the material for long term memory. Too much emotion and the situation may be perceived as threatening, causing a downshift in mental functions (Brandt & Wolfe, 1998).

Practical applications of the stress/threat principle are numerous and exciting for the experiential field. Experiential pedagogy, with its emphasis on novelty, interpersonal interaction, challenge by choice, and the use of emotions such as play, fear, and humor, is uniquely suited to address stress/threat balances. Understanding how these brain compatible principles can be strengthened by experiential learning opens the possibility for meaningful dialogue with mainstream education.

Quick Tip #4: To lower threat levels early in your program, make a strong emphasis on relationship building both peer-peer and teacher-student. Work the group from the "inside-out" by making a conscious effort to spend personal time with as many students as possible, either on the trail or at water breaks. Work the group "outside-in" by facilitating highly interactive experiences like paired shares, new games, or trust activities.

Quick Tip #5: Use the 60/40 rule for planning your lesson plans. Sixty percent of your experiences should be ritual based activities that are repetitive (like morning check-ins, skill progressions, warm-ups, or post-activity debriefs) to allow your participants to experience known activities in an unknown environment. But be sure to make approximately 40 percent of activities novel. The introduction of elements of suspense, surprise, and disorder keep learners engaged and can be an effective way to manage attention spans. Instead of circling up every time, "rhombus-up" with your group every so often. Mix-up de-briefs by using paired shares, group reports, or silent journaling instead of large group discussion. Introduce skill sections playfully with characters and costumes (knots with Ivana Climbalot, or baking with Chef Boyarentyouhungry).

Conclusion

Evidence and theories from the Brain Compatible Approach support much of what we do. Understanding the human brain's tendency toward pattern and "meaning-making" reinforces the intentional use of reflection and synthesis in experiential education. Viewing the brain as a parallel processor encourages the creation of enriched environments for learners. Experiential methodology facilitates such enriched environments through challenge, social interaction, feedback, and active participation. Finally, the differences between stress and threat responses support our pedagogical approach including the effective use of emotion and the importance of novelty and choice. Recent developments in brain research should also push us toward new questions and research queries. What is the role of emotion in experiential education? How do we define, operationally, the differences between stressful and threatening experiences and responses? How is the mind-body connection supported in current brain research? What part can experiential methodology play in the creation of enriched classroom environments?

We must move beyond mere "learning by doing" for our fields' philosophical underpinnings and practical approaches to become more influential in mainstream education. Using only the learning by doing definition, experiential education becomes nothing more than activities and events with little to no significance beyond the initial experience. One educator recently told me she calls this the "Inoculation Effect" (shoot 'em up; hope it takes). This was not John Dewey's vision and it cannot be our lasting legacy. Many of us entered this field after becoming disenchanted or burned-out on mainstream educational practice. We have also seen the remarkable changes and results that can occur through experiential learning. We believe very strongly that it works. Yet, as a field, we remain long on practice and short on theory and research. The Brain Compatible Approach is one avenue for helping experiential educators articulate how and why the methodology is effective.

How can we achieve more legitimacy while holding fast to our principles? Moves toward identifying the philosophical approaches of experiential education should be encouraged (Itin, 1999). Efforts must be made to increase both qualitative and quantitative research that cross into mainstream education. As educators, we also have a responsibility to learn about our field. At a recent AEE conference, I was surprised to learn how few experiential education practitioners knew of E.D. Hirsch—one of the strongest critics of progressive approaches and a major figure in the standards-based movement. Hirsch defines learning by doing as "a phrase once used to characterize the progressivist movement but little used today, possibly because the formulation has been the object of much criticism and even ridicule" (Hirsch, 1996, p. 256). With critics like this and few legitimate platforms from which to respond, it is not surprising that experiential education remains largely locked out of our schools. Knowing some of the latest trends and movements within the fields of education, psychology, and sociology will strengthen our voice and message.

While there is value in experiential education's subversive, outside-the-mainstream persona, we must also seek ways to come in from the "outside," invite dialogue, and encourage interaction across disciplines. The Brain Compatible Approach, as a promising new area of research and study, offers an excellent opportunity to do just that. In the next 20 years, will experiential education be a program (like field trips, ropes courses, and character education) to be implemented in schools or, will it be a broader, pedagogical foundation from which to work? The future depends on how we live that question.

References

Brandt, R., & Wolfe, P. (1998). What do we know from brain research? *Educational Leadership, 56*(3), 8–13.

Bruer, J. T. (1997). Education and the brain: A bridge too far. *Educational Researcher, 26*(8), 4–16.

Caine, G., & Caine, R. (1994). *Making connections: Teaching and the human brain.* New York: Addison Wesley.

Csikszentmihalyi, M. (1991). *Flow: The psychology of optimal experience.* New York: Harper Perrenial.

Deporter, B., Reardon, M., & Singer-Nourie, S. (1999). *Quantum teaching.* Needham Heights, MA: Allyn & Bacon.

Diamond, M., & Hopson, J. (1998). *Magic trees of the mind.* New York: Penguin Putnum.

Gardner, H. (1985). *Frames of mind: The theory of multiple intelligences.* New York: Basic Books.

Hart, L. (1983). *Human brain, human learning.* New York: Longman.

Hirsch, E. G. (1996). *The schools we need and why we don't have them.* New York: Doubleday.

Itin, C. (1999). Reasserting the philosophy of experiential education as a vehicle for change in the 21st century. *Journal of Experiential Education, 229*(2), 91–98.

Jensen, E. (2000). *Brain-based learning.* San Diego, CA: The Brain Store.

LeDoux, J. (1996). *The emotional brain: The mysterious underpinnings of emotional life.* New York: Simon & Schuster.

MacLean, P. D. (1978). A mind of three Minds: Educating the triune brain. In J. Chall, & A. Mirsky (Eds.), *Education and the brain* (pp. 308–342). Chicago: University of Chicago Press.

Nummela, R., & Rosengren, T. (1986). What's happening in students' brains may redefine teaching. *Educational Leadership 43*(8), 49–53.

Jay Roberts, M.Ed., is the Director of Wilderness Programs at Earlham College in Richmond, Indiana and teaches in the Education program. He also spent seven years working as a facilitator for Learning Forum Supercamp, an internationally recognized brain compatible learning program. He can be reached at roberja@earlham.edu

Metacognition: A Bridge Between Cognitive Psychology and Educational Practice

Although they have their differences, educational practitioners and academic researchers largely agree on a broad goal: to develop in students the kinds of thinking skills that will prepare them to contribute to a democratic society. But the two groups largely speak different languages. While educators frequently talk about critical thinking as an objective, researchers have largely avoided the term, preferring constructs that can be more precisely defined and measured. How do we connect critical thinking to modern research on cognition and learning? The authors propose the construct of metacognition as having the potential to bridge the concerns of educators and researchers whose work is addressed to the development of skilled thinking. Given its growing importance in studies of cognition and learning, teachers would benefit from an understanding of the mechanisms involved in metacognition and how best to foster it.

Deanna Kuhn
David Dean Jr.

THEY HAVE THEIR DIFFERENCES to be sure, but today's educational practitioners and the academic theorists and researchers who concern themselves with education would likely agree on a broad goal: to develop in students the conceptual skills that will prepare them to contribute to a democratic society. Academics are inclined to decry the growing emphasis on "objective" standardized tests and to endorse "education for understanding" (Gardner, 1999) and development of the learning and thinking skills that will equip students to thrive in tomorrow's society (Bereiter, 2002; Kuhn, in press). Practitioners have long appeared to be of the same mind. The mission statement of the school district in which one of us was recently a teacher reads, "... our students will graduate with the knowledge, skills, and values necessary to be successful contributors to our democratic society." These educational goals can be traced back at least as far as Thomas Jefferson, who proclaimed (in a personal communication to W. Jarvis in 1820),

> I know no safe depository of the ultimate powers of the society but the people themselves; and if we think them not enlightened enough to exercise their control with a wholesome discretion, the remedy is not to take it from them, but to inform their discretion by education.

The Great Divide

The challenge comes, of course, in trying to implement these lofty goals, and here we find academics and practitioners navigating largely unconnected paths. Academics pursue their agendas isolated from the demands of the classroom, while practitioners are pressed to find methods that work, and quickly. Even if they had the time and energy to seek them out, research findings are not disseminated in a way that facilitates practitioners' consumption of them. And practitioners are unlikely to do so, having acquired the attitude, conveyed from their preservice training onward, that research studies are not going to be of any direct help—findings are inconsistent and far removed from classroom realities. Scant attention in the preservice curriculum to educational research, and to the tools needed to evaluate it, is perhaps the strongest meta-level message to practitioners as to its value.

Bereiter (2002) argues that this state of affairs needs to change dramatically. Teachers must become collaborators in the research enterprise, in close contact with knowledge building in their field, seeing themselves and being accepted as part of the endeavor. Educational reformers, Bereiter says, "are likely to fail in even their immediate objectives if they do not become more deeply engaged with the unsolved problems of pedagogy" (p. 421).

A major "unsolved problem of pedagogy," we would add, is exactly what are the higher order thinking skills that will equip students to participate in modern democratic society? Practitioners traditionally have ignored the question. "We all know good thinking when we see it," their attitude has been, "so let's focus on finding effective techniques to foster it." Increasingly, it is becoming clear that this stance will not suffice. We cannot effectively teach cognitive skills in the absence of very clear and precise understandings of what those skills are (Kuhn, 1999, in press). Given the prevalence of the "we'll know good thinking when we see it" stance, educators today are more likely to agree on promising educational activities and settings for fostering thinking than on what the thinking skills are that they seek to induce in these settings.

Educators must collaborate with researchers in achieving these understandings, creating the need for a different kind of collaborative role for the academic researcher. In the past, when educators have turned to academics for assistance, the role the academic has been asked to play is that of technician: Here is what we want students to know; can you advise us of the most efficient means for them to acquire it? Instead, both practitioners and academics need to collaborate not just with respect to devising means but also in better defining ends—the nature of the intellectual skills that need to develop.

The kinds of cognitive skills that educators think about as coming under the heading of critical thinking are amenable to empirical investigation. It is possible to learn something about their nature and about how they develop. In our research we have examined two major families of skills—inquiry and argument (Kuhn, in press). The case we make is the same with respect to both. Teachers need a roadmap of what is developing and what needs to develop. In contrast to elementary skills such as classification or number that emerge in all normal children during the early years, skills of inquiry and argument do not necessarily develop, or at least do not develop to the degree we would like. Here the efforts of educators and researchers studying cognitive development truly intersect. Researchers need to be examining forms of development that are unlikely to occur in the absence of appropriate educational environments. At the same time, educators need the developmental knowledge that will inform their efforts.

What, then, needs to develop? A cornerstone of inquiry is the idea of a thesis, or question, and potential evidence that bears on it. There must be something to find out. Entertaining a thesis that is understood as capable of being disconfirmed by evidence reflects rudimentary skill in coordinating theory and evidence. Without this understanding and intention, there can be little point to inquiry. At worst, in the student's eyes inquiry becomes nothing more than demonstration of what one already accepts as true. Skills of argument have received much less attention than those of inquiry, but they are just as important. Children are not natural-born arguers. There are skills that need to develop. Our argument research indicates that young adolescents do not have great difficulty learning how to provide support for a claim. In debating someone who holds an opposing view, however, they find it much harder than do adults to attend to and address their opponent's claim and supporting argument (Felton & Kuhn, 2001). In analyses of their argumentive discourse with a peer, we found they engaged in exposition regarding their own argument almost four times as frequently as they sought clarification of the opponent's argument and four times as frequently as they undertook to critique the opponent's argument. Adults' utterances, in contrast, more often addressed the partner's argument, usually through counterargument. Adolescents appear to interpret the goal of argumentive discourse as prevailing over an opponent by superior presentation of one's own position. This objective, if successfully met, undermines the opponent's position but without addressing the opponent's argument. Deep-level processing of the opponent's argument, in addition to exposition of one's own argument and negotiating the mechanics of discourse, may represent cognitive overload for the novice arguer.

Metacognition and Critical Thinking

Definitions of critical thinking are numerous and wide-ranging. However, one non-controversial claim we can make about critical thinking is that it entails awareness of one's own thinking and reflection on the thinking of self and others as an object of cognition. Metacognition, a construct that is assuming an increasingly central place in cognitive development research, is defined in similar terms as awareness and management of one's own thought, or "thinking about thinking." Metacognition originates early in life, when children first become aware of their own and others' minds. But like many other intellectual skills, metacognitive skills typically do not develop to the level we would like.

In cognitive psychology, metacognitive functions are most often examined under the heading of "executive control." Whatever its exact label, the management of one's own cognition is crucial, as both researchers and practitioners are likely to have observed. It is usually not difficult to teach a child to perform a particular procedure in a particular context. But it is the meta-level of operations that determines whether the child will continue to exercise this skill in other settings once instruction is withdrawn and the child resumes meta-level control of his or her own behavior.

One way of supporting metacognitive development is to encourage students to reflect on and evaluate their activities. Doing so should heighten interest in the purpose of these activities. Why are we doing this? What was gained from having done it? Questions such as these are less likely to arise when activity is imposed by authority figures without negotiation, uating students' standing relative to one another—a function that so often steals attention away from any other objective.

Another source of metacognitive development is the interiorization that both Vygotksy and Piaget talked about, which occurs when forms that are originally social become covert within the individual. If students participate in discourse where they are frequently asked, "How do you know?" or "What makes you say that?" they become more likely to pose such questions to themselves. Eventually, we hope, they will interiorize the structure of argument as a framework for much of their own individual thinking. They will think in terms of issues or claims, with facts summoned in their service, rather than the reverse—storing up facts with the idea that some conclusion may emerge from them.

Metacognitive functions can be procedural or declarative. The former invokes awareness and management of one's own thinking. The latter involves one's broader understanding of thinking and knowing in general. It has been studied under the heading of epistemological understanding. Like thinking itself, the understanding of thinking undergoes development. The study of students' developing epistemological understanding has blossomed in the last decade. As a result, we now have a fairly convergent picture of a series of steps that mark development toward more mature epistemological understanding in the years from early childhood to adulthood.

Epistemological Understanding as a Metacognitive Development

Preschool age children are realists. They regard what one knows as an immediate reading of what's out there. Beliefs are faithful copies of reality. They are received directly from the external world, rather than constructed by the knower. Hence, there are no inaccurate renderings of events, nor any possibility of conflicting beliefs, since everyone is perceiving the same external reality. Minds provide everyone the very same pictures of reality.

Not until about age 4 does a knower begin to emerge in children's conceptions of knowing. Children become aware that mental representations, as products of the human mind, do not necessarily duplicate external reality. Before children achieve a concept of false belief, they are unwilling to attribute to another person a belief that they themselves know to be false. Once they attain this understanding, the knower, and knowledge as mental representations produced by knowers, come to life. The products of knowing, however, are still more firmly attached to the known object than to the knower. Hence, while inadequate or incorrect information can produce false beliefs, these are easily correctable by reference to an external reality—the known object. If you and I disagree, one of us is right and one is wrong and resolving the matter is simply a matter of finding out which is which. At this absolutist level of epistemological understanding, knowledge is an accumulating body of certain facts.

Further progress in epistemological understanding can be characterized as an extended task of coordinating the subjective with the objective elements of knowing. At the realist and absolutist levels, the objective dominates. By adolescence typically comes the likelihood of a radical change in epistemological understanding. In a word, everyone now becomes right. The discovery that reasonable people—even experts—disagree is the most likely source of recognizing the uncertain, subjective aspect of knowing. This recognition initially assumes such proportions, however, that it eclipses recognition of any objective standard that could serve as a basis for evaluating conflicting claims. Adolescents typically fall into what Chandler has called "a poisoned well of doubt," and they fall hard and deep. At this multiplist (sometimes called relativist) level of epistemological understanding, knowledge consists not of facts but of opinions, freely chosen by their holders as personal possessions and accordingly not open to challenge. Knowledge is now clearly seen as emanating from knowers, rather than the known, but at the significant cost of any discriminability among competing knowledge claims. Indeed, this lack of discriminability is equated with tolerance: Because everyone has a right to their opinion, all opinions are equally right. That ubiquitous slogan of adolescence—"whatever"—holds sway.

Evidence suggests that hoisting oneself out of the "whatever" well of multiplicity and indiscriminability is achieved at much greater effort than the quick and easy fall into its depths. Many adults remain absolutists or multiplists for life. Yet, by adulthood, many adolescents will have reintegrated the objective dimension of knowing to achieve the understanding that while everyone has a right to their opinion, some opinions are in fact more right than others, to the extent they are better supported by argument and evidence. Justification for a belief becomes more than personal preference. "Whatever" is no longer the automatic response to any assertion—there are now legitimate discriminations and choices to be made. Rather than facts or opinions, knowledge at this evaluativist level of epistemological understanding consists of judgments, which require support in a framework of alternatives, evidence, and argument. An evaluativist epistemology provides the intellectual basis for judging one idea as better than another, a basis more powerful than mere personal preference.

Intellectual Values

The evolution just described is a necessary condition for the development of intellectual values. Adolescents who never progress beyond the absolutist belief in certain knowledge, or the multiplist's equation of knowledge with personal preference, lack a reason to engage in sustained intellectual inquiry. If facts can be ascertained with certainty and are readily available to anyone who seeks them, as the absolutist understands, or if any claim is as valid as

Table 1
Levels of Epistemological Understanding

Level	Assertions	Knowledge	Critical Thinking
Realist	Assertions are COPIES of an external reality.	Knowledge comes from an external source and is certain.	Critical thinking is unnecessary.
Absolutist	Assertions are FACTS that are correct or incorrect in their representation of reality.	Knowledge comes from an external source and is certain but not directly accessible, producing false beliefs.	Critical thinking is a vehicle for comparing assertions to reality and determining their truth or falsehood.
Multiplist	Assertions are OPINIONS freely chosen by and accountable only to their owners.	Knowledge is generated by human minds and therefore uncertain.	Critical thinking is irrelevant.
Evaluativist	Assertions are JUDGMENTS that can be evaluated and compared according to criteria of argument and evidence.	Knowledge is generated by human minds and is uncertain but susceptible to evaluation.	Critical thinking is valued as a vehicle that promotes sound assertions and enhances understanding.

any other, as the multiplist understands, there is little point to expending the mental effort that the evaluation of claims entails. Only at the evaluativist level are thinking and reason recognized as essential support for beliefs and actions. Thinking is the process that enables us to make informed choices between conflicting claims. Understanding this leads one to value thinking and to be willing to expend the effort that it entails (Table 1).

Our research has found striking differences across cultural groups and subcultural groups within the United States in the responses of parents and children to several questions like this one:

> Many social issues, like the death penalty, gun control, or medical care, are pretty much matters of personal opinion, and there is no basis for saying that one person's opinion is any better than another's. So there's not much point in people having discussions about these kinds of issues. Do you strongly agree, sort of agree, or disagree?

Reasons respondents offer for disagreement are similar and refer to values of discussion in enhancing individual and/or collective understanding, solving problems, and resolving conflicts. Reasons offered for agreement, however, tend to be of two distinct types. Some participants respond along these lines, suggestive of the multiplist level of epistemological understanding: "It's not worth it to discuss it because you're not going to get anywhere; everyone has a right to think what they want to." Others take this position, suggestive of the absolutist's equation of knowledge with right answers: "It's not worth it to discuss it because it's not something you can get a definite answer to."

Parents and children within the cultures and subcultures we have studied respond similarly to one another. Middle school and high school students in American ethnic subcultures, however, show some movement away from their parents' response patterns in the direction of those of their American peers. These results suggest that parents do matter in transmitting intellectual values to their children. At the same time, children to a significant degree construct these values anew in a context of their peer culture, especially when the values of the culture outside the home deviate from those within the home.

The transitions from realist to absolutist to multiplist epistemological understanding don't seem to require a great deal of tending by those wishing to scaffold children's development. Unless the child's experience is unusually restricted, children become aware that people's beliefs vary and they must figure out a way of understanding this state of affairs. The vast majority take at least a brief dip, and more often a prolonged one, into the well of multiplicity. The last major transition, however, from multiplist to evaluativist, is another story. It is helping young people climb out of the multiplist well that requires the concerned attention of parents and educators, especially if it is this progression that provides the necessary foundation for intellectual values.

The goal will not be achieved by exhortation—by telling students that a particular activity is valuable, or even how or why it's valuable. A more promising adult role involves introducing young people to activities that have a value that becomes self-evident in the course of engaging them and developing the skills the activities entail. By serving as a guide, or coach, as students engage in such activities, the adult models his or her own commitment to the activity and belief in its worth. As students' skill and commitment and self-direction increase, the coach's role diminishes.

Much of what we ask students to do in school simply does not have these characteristics. We have been experimenting with involving middle school students in activities that we believe have this crucial characteristic of revealing their intrinsic value as they are engaged in them. These activities fall under the broad headings of inquiry and argument and entail the skills that have been described previously. We are able to follow students' progress microgenetically as they develop these two families of skills. Through their involvement in such activities, we hope students will discover for themselves that there is something to find out and a point to arguing, sufficient to make the effort worthwhile. It is only their own experiences that will lead them to the conviction that inquiry and reasoned argument offer the most promising path to deciding between competing claims, resolving conflicts, solving problems, and achieving goals.

Conclusion

The growing reliance on standardized testing of basic skills, with higher and higher stakes, poses a grave danger to the quality of education. We need better definitions of what it means to be an educated person (Bereiter, 2002; Kuhn, in press). The skills of inquiry and argument, we believe, should be central to such definitions. If so, it is essential to understand more about these skills. But these skills need to be understood not just as performance tools; it is essential that the broader meta-level structure develop that reflects understanding of how, when, and why to use them. This is the critical thinking ability that educators and researchers want to see students acquire.

We suggest that cognitive development researchers and educators can and must collaborate in constructing these more adequate definitions of the ends toward which the educational enterprise is directed. Fewer and fewer cognitive development researchers remain content to preoccupy themselves with narrow agendas while ignoring the larger, more difficult questions that the education of children poses. At the same time, educators for the most part are discouraged by the professional challenges facing them, would like to be part of the knowledge-seeking process, and appreciate the importance of evidence as a basis for policy (Feuer, Towne, & Shavelson, 2002). Without being naïve about the obstacles involved, we would conclude that both groups seem poised for meaningful collaboration.

References

Bereiter, C. (2002). *Education and mind in the knowledge age*. Mahwah, NJ: Erlbaum.

Feuer, M.J., Towne, L., & Shavelson, R.J. (2002). Scientific culture and educational research. *Educational Researcher, 31*, 4–14.

Felton, M., & Kuhn, D. (2001). The development of argumentive discourse skills. *Discourse Processes, 32*, 135–153.

Gardner, H. (1999). *The disciplined mind: What all students should understand*. New York: Simon and Schuster.

Kuhn, D. (1999). A developmental model of critical thinking. *Educational Researcher, 28*, 16–25, 46.

Kuhn, D. (in press). *Education for thinking*. Cambridge MA: Harvard University Press.

Deanna Kuhn *is a professor and* **David Dean Jr.** *is a graduate research fellow, both at Teachers College, Columbia University.*

From *Theory Into Practice,* vol. 43, no. 4, Autumn 2004. Copyright © 2004 by Lawrence Erlbaum Associates. Reprinted by permission.

Successful Intelligence in the Classroom

Many students could learn more effectively than they do now if they were taught in a way that better matched their patterns of abilities. Teaching for successful intelligence provides a way to create such a match. It involves helping all students capitalize on their strengths and compensate for or correct their weaknesses. It does so by teaching in a way that balances learning for memory, analytical, creative, and practical thinking. This article describes how such teaching is done and provides data supporting the efficacy of the approach.

Robert J. Sternberg
Elena L. Grigorenko

MANY CHILDREN FAIL TO LEARN at a level that matches their ability to learn. There can be a number of reasons for this failure. One reason is that the way students are taught and often assessed in school does not enable them to learn and perform in an optimal way. We have developed the theory of successful intelligence in order to understand these children (Sternberg, 1997a, 1999), and a set of methods of teaching for successful intelligence to help these students reach their full potential (Sternberg & Grigorenko, 2000).

The Theory of Successful Intelligence: A Capsule Description

According to the proposed theory, *successful intelligence* is the use of an integrated set of abilities needed to attain success in life, however an individual defines it, within his or her socio-cultural context. Thus, there is no one definition of intelligence. People are successfully intelligent by virtue of recognizing their strengths and making the most of them at the same time they recognize their weaknesses and find ways to correct or compensate for them. Both are important. On one hand, students need to learn to correct aspects of their performance in which they are underperforming. On the other hand, they have to recognize that they probably will never be superb at all kinds of performance. It helps to find ways around weaknesses, such as seeking help from others and giving it in return. In other words, people find their own unique path to being intelligent. Successfully intelligent people adapt to, shape, and select environments. In adaptation, they change themselves to fit the environment. For example, a teacher may adapt to the expectations of her principal by teaching in a way she believes the principal will endorse. In shaping, people change the environment to fit them. The teacher may try to persuade the principal to support a new way of teaching different from what the principal has been ac-

customed to in the past. And in selection, they find a new environment. For example, the teacher may decide to seek a placement in another school if she is unable to convince the principal that her way of teaching is valid and will result in benefits for the students. They accomplish these ends by finding a balance in their use of analytical, creative, and practical abilities (Sternberg, 1997a, 1999).

This definition of successful intelligence contains within it several implications for teaching.

Classroom Applications

Teaching for successful intelligence attempts to help teachers reach a larger cross-section of students than more traditional teaching methods that emphasize memory and analytical instruction. In teaching for successful intelligence, a teacher follows a number of fundamental ideas.

There is no one right way of teaching and learning. Moreover, there is no one right way of assessing students' achievement. Teaching and assessment should balance use of analytical, creative, and practical thinking. Fundamentally, teachers need to help students capitalize on individual patterns of strengths and, at the same time, help them correct or compensate for weaknesses. Students, like teachers, need to develop flexibility, giving students multiple and diverse options in assessment.

Because students have different life goals, student success needs to be defined in terms that are meaningful to them as well as to the institution. Students are more likely to see meaning if teachers provide numerous examples of concepts that cover a wide range of applications. Grade student work in a way that preserves the integrity of the course as well as the integrity of the students' varied life goals.

Sometimes teachers are reluctant to teach for successful intelligence because they believe that these techniques may apply

Table 1
Assignments for Applying Triarchic Intelligence

Analytical	Creative	Practical
Analyze	Create	Apply
Critique	Invent	Use
Judge	Discover	Put into practice
Compare/contrast	Imagine if…	Implement
Evaluate	Suppose that…	Employ
Assess	Predict	Render practical

to other teachers' students, but not to their own. We would say in response that our research, some of which is described below, has not turned up any groups of students who cannot profit from this form of instruction. The students whose performance improves the most tend to be those who do not profit optimally from conventional instruction. For example, children from out-of-the way areas, such as rural Alaska, have tremendous stores of practical knowledge that can help them learn if only teachers give them the chance to use their knowledge to succeed (Sternberg, Lipka, Newman, Wildfeuer, & Grigorenko, 2003).

We encourage teachers to teach and assess achievement in ways that enable students to analyze, create with, and apply their knowledge. When students think to learn, they also learn to think. And there is an added benefit: Students who are taught analytically, creatively, and practically perform better on assessments, apparently without regard to the form the assessments take. That is, they outperform students instructed in conventional ways, even if the assessments are for straight factual memory (Sternberg, Torff, & Grigorenko, 1998a, 1998b). Moreover, our research shows that these techniques succeed, regardless of subject-matter area. But what, exactly, are the techniques used to teach analytically, creatively, and practically (see Table 1 for a summary)?

Each of the methods of teaching is described below. For many more examples of each method at grade levels ranging from primary to college, see Sternberg and Grigorenko (2000).

Teaching analytically

Teaching analytically means encouraging students to (a) analyze, (b) critique, (c) judge, (d) compare and contrast, (e) evaluate, and (f) assess. When teachers refer to teaching for "critical thinking," they typically mean teaching for analytical thinking. How does such teaching translate into instructional and assessment activities? Consider various examples across the school curriculum:

(a) *Analyze* the development of the character of Heathcliff in *Wuthering Heights*. (Literature)

(b) *Critique* the design of the experiment (just gone over in class or in a reading) showing that certain plants grew better in dim light than in bright sunlight. (Biology)

(c) *Judge* the artistic merits of Roy Lichtenstein's comic-book art, discussing its strengths as well as its weaknesses as fine art. (Art)

(d) *Compare and contrast* the respective natures of the American Revolution and the French Revolution, pointing out ways they were similar and ways they were different. (History)

(e) *Evaluate* the validity of the following solution to a mathematical problem, and discuss weaknesses in the solution, if there are any. (Mathematics)

(f) *Assess* the strategy used by the winning player in the tennis match you just observed, stating what techniques she used in order to defeat her opponent. (Physical Education)

Teaching creatively

Teaching creatively means encouraging students to (a) create, (b) invent, (c) discover, (d) imagine if . . . , (e) suppose that . . . , and (f) predict. Teaching for creativity requires teachers not only to support and encourage creativity, but also to role-model it and reward it when it is displayed (Sternberg & Lubart, 1995; Sternberg & Williams, 1996). In other words, teachers need not only to talk the talk, but also to walk the walk. The following examples of instructional or assessment activities encourage students to think creatively:

(a) *Create* an alternative ending to the short story you just read that represents a different way things might have gone for the main characters in the story. (Literature)

(b) *Invent* a dialogue between an American tourist in Paris and a French man he encounters on the street from whom he is asking directions on how to get to the Rue Pigalle. (French)

(c) *Discover* the fundamental physical principle that underlies all of the following problems, each of which differs from the others in the "surface structure" of the problem but not in its "deep structure." (Physics)

(d) *Imagine if* the government of China keeps evolving over the course of the next 20 years in much the same way it has been evolving. What do you believe the government of China will be like in 20 years? (Government/Political Science)

(e) *Suppose that* you were to design one additional instrument to be played in a symphony orchestra for future compositions. What might that instrument be like, and why? (Music)

(f) *Predict* changes that are likely to occur in the vocabulary or grammar of spoken Spanish in the border areas of the Rio Grande over the next 100 years as a result of continuous interactions between Spanish and English speakers. (Linguistics)

Teaching practically

Teaching practically means encouraging students to (a) apply, (b) use, (c) put into practice, (d) implement, (e) employ, and (f) render practical what they know. Such teaching must relate to the real practical needs of the students, not just to what would be practical for other individuals (Sternberg et al., 2000). Consider some examples:

(a) *Apply* the formula for computing compound interest to a problem people are likely to face when planning for retirement. (Economics, Math)

(b) *Use* your knowledge of German to greet a new acquaintance in Berlin. (German)

(c) *Put into practice* what you have learned from teamwork in football to make a classroom team project succeed. (Athletics)

(d) *Implement* a business plan you have written in a simulated business environment. (Business)

(e) *Employ* the formula for distance, rate, and time to compute a distance. (Math)

(f) *Render practical* a proposed design for a new building that will not work in the aesthetic context of the surrounding buildings, all of which are at least 100 years old. (Architecture)

It might seem as though teaching for successful intelligence would require much more classroom time per topic than would teaching in more conventional ways. This is not the case, however. The idea is not to teach each topic three times in three ways. Rather, it is to alternate teaching styles so that some of the time one teaches in a way more geared toward analytical thinking, other times in a way more geared to creative thinking, and still other times in a way more geared to practical thinking. The total time spent in teaching given material is the same as in any other way of teaching the material.

Because teaching for successful intelligence reaches more students' patterns of abilities, the students are more likely to be intrinsically motivated to succeed in their work. Some teachers may be reluctant to do this kind of balanced teaching, because they see their own strengths as being primarily in one of the ways of thinking, such as analytical. But teaching only to one's own strengths deprives students with different patterns of abilities valuable opportunities to learn.

Clearly, it is possible to implement teaching for successful intelligence in a wide variety of academic contexts. But there are potential problems with any new methodology. How do these methods work in practice?

Some Supporting Research

We have sought to test the theory of successful intelligence in the classroom. Our studies extend down to grade 4, and although we believe the methods would apply with younger children, we have not systematically tested their efficacy for them. In a first set of studies, we explored the question of whether conventional education in school systematically discriminates against children with creative and practical strengths (Sternberg & Clinkenbeard, 1995; Sternberg, Ferrari, Clinkenbeard, & Grigorenko, 1996; Sternberg, Grigorenko, Ferrari, & Clinkenbeard, 1999). Motivating this work was the belief that the systems in most schools strongly tend to favor children with strengths in memory and analytical abilities. However, schools can be unbalanced in other areas as well. One school we visited in Russia in 2000 placed a heavy emphasis on the development of creative abilities—much more so than on the development of analytical and practical abilities. While on this trip, we were told of another school—catering to the children of Russian businessman—that strongly emphasized practical abilities. The children who were not practically oriented were told that, eventually, they would be working for their classmates who were.

We used the Sternberg Triarchic Abilities Test, measuring analytical, creative, and practical abilities, in some of our instructional work. The test was administered to 326 children around the United States and in other countries who were identified by their schools as gifted by any standard whatsoever. Children were selected for a summer program in college-level psychology if they fell into one of five ability groupings: high analytical, high creative, high practical, high balanced (high in all three abilities), or low balanced (low in all three abilities). The students were gifted, but in a broader sense than the term is traditionally used. They were not necessarily in the top few percent, and their gifts were not necessarily analytical in nature. Students who came to Yale were divided into four instructional groups. All four instructional groups used the same introductory psychology textbook and listened to the same psychology lectures. What differed was the type of afternoon discussion section to which they were assigned. They were randomly assigned to an instructional condition that emphasized either memory, analytical, creative, or practical instruction. For example, in the memory condition, they might be asked to describe the main tenets of a major theory of depression. In the analytical condition, they might be asked to compare and contrast two theories of depression. In the creative condition, they might be asked to formulate their own theory of depression. In the practical condition, they might be asked how they could use what they had learned about depression to help a friend who was depressed.

Students in all four instructional conditions were evaluated in terms of their performance on homework, a midterm exam, a final exam, and an independent project. Each type of work was evaluated for memory, analytical, creative, and practical quality. Thus, all students were evaluated in exactly the same way.

Our results suggested the utility of the theory of successful intelligence. This utility showed itself in several ways.

First, we observed that the students in the high creative and high practical groups were much more diverse in terms of racial, ethnic, socioeconomic, and educational backgrounds than were the students in the high analytical group. This suggests that correlations of measured intelligence with status variables such as these may be reduced by using a broader conception of intelligence. Thus, the kinds of students identified as strong differed in terms of populations from which they were drawn in comparison with students identified as strong solely by analytical measures. More importantly, just by expanding the range of abilities measured, we discovered intellectual strengths that might not have been apparent through a conventional test.

Second, we found that all three ability tests—analytical, creative, and practical—significantly predicted course performance. When multiple-regression analysis was used, at least two of these ability measures contributed significantly to the prediction of each of the measures of achievement. Perhaps as a reflection of the difficulty of de-emphasizing the analytical way of teaching, one of the significant predictors was always the analytical score. However, in a replication of our study with low-income African-American students from New York, Deborah Coates of the City University of New York found a different pattern of results. Her data indicated that the practical tests were better predictors of course performance than were the analytical measures, suggesting that what ability test predicts what criterion depends on population as well as mode of teaching.

Third, and most importantly, there was an aptitude-treatment interaction where students placed in instructional conditions that better matched their pattern of abilities outperformed students who were mismatched. In other words, when students are taught in a way that fits how they think, they do better in school. Children with creative and practical abilities, who are almost never taught or assessed in a way that matches their pattern of abilities, may be at a disadvantage in course after course, year after year.

A follow-up study (Sternberg, Torff, & Grigorenko, 1998a, 1998b) examined learning of social studies and science by third graders and eighth graders. The 225 third graders were students in a low-income neighborhood in Raleigh, North Carolina. The 142 eighth graders were students who were largely middle- to upper middle-class in Baltimore, Maryland, and Fresno, California. In this study, students were assigned to one of three instructional conditions. In the first condition, they were taught the course that basically they would have learned had there been no intervention. The emphasis in the course was on memory. In a second condition, students were taught in a way that emphasized critical (analytical) thinking. In the third condition, they were taught in a way that emphasized analytical, creative, and practical thinking. All students' performance was assessed for memory learning (through multiple-choice assessments) as well as for analytical, creative, and practical learning (through performance assessments).

As expected, students in the successful-intelligence (analytical, creative, practical) condition outperformed the other students in terms of the performance assessments. One could argue that this result merely reflected the way they were taught. Nevertheless, the result suggested that teaching for these kinds of thinking succeeded. More important, however, was the result that children in the successful-intelligence condition outperformed the other children even on the multiple-choice memory tests. In other words, if the goal is just to maximize children's memory for information, teaching for successful intelligence is still superior. It enables children to capitalize on their strengths and to correct or to compensate for their weaknesses, and it allows children to encode material in a variety of interesting ways.

We have now extended these results to reading curricula at the middle school and the high school level. In a study of 871 middle school students and 432 high school students, we taught reading either triarchically (analytically, creatively, practically) or through the regular curriculum. At the middle school level, reading was taught explicitly. At the high school level, reading was infused into instruction in mathematics, physical sciences, social sciences, English, history, foreign languages, and the arts. In all settings, students who were taught triarchically substantially outperformed students who were taught in standard ways (Grigorenko, Jarvin, & Sternberg, 2002).

Thus the results of three sets of studies suggest that the theory of successful intelligence is valid as a whole. Further, the results suggest that the theory can make a difference not only in laboratory tests, but in school classrooms and even the everyday life of adults as well.

Why Teaching for Successful Intelligence Works

Why should teaching for successful intelligence improve performance relative to standard (or critical-thinking) instruction, even when performance is assessed for straightforward memory-based recall? There are at least four reasons. First, teaching for successful intelligence encourages deeper and more elaborated encoding of material than does traditional teaching, so students learn the material in a way that enhances probability of retrieval at test time. Second, teaching for successful intelligence encourages more diverse forms of encoding material, so there are more retrieval paths to the material and greater likelihood of recall at test time. Third, teaching for successful intelligence enables students to capitalize on strengths and to correct or compensate for weaknesses. Fourth, teaching for successful intelligence is more motivating to both teachers and students, so teachers are likely to teach more effectively and students are likely to learn more. Ideally, of course, exams should *not* assess only static memory learning.

Conclusion

Teachers may wish to consider the option of teaching for successful intelligence. In doing so, they will improve their teaching, improve student learning, and most importantly, modify in a constructive way the entire teaching-learning process. Data collected with thousands of students shows that teaching for successful intelligence works for many students, in many subject-matter areas, at many grade levels. Of course, this form of teaching is not a panacea for the problems of schools, and it most likely will not work for everyone—whether student or teacher. But in our research we have found that the majority of students and teachers benefit from the methods described in this article.

Teaching for successful intelligence obviously relates to other kinds of teaching that emphasize thinking. One example is Bloom's taxonomy, which specifies a set of skills that are arrayed from those at the lowest level of cognition to the highest level of cognition. There are probably three key differences between the present theory and the taxonomy. The first is that the theory of successful intelligence does not array thinking skills hierarchically, but rather, interactively. The second is that there is a more nearly equal balance among analytical, creative, and practical skills than in Bloom's taxonomy. And the third is that the methods of teaching described here are based on a psychological theory rather than a descriptive list of thinking skills.

A second example is Gardner's (1983) theory of multiple intelligences. This theory specifies a number of distinct intelligences, such as linguistic and musical, that can serve as bases for teaching thinking. The present theory is complementary to Gardner's in the sense that any of Gardner's domains, such as the linguistic, can employ analytical, creative, or practical processes (e.g., analyzing a story, writing a story, writing a persuasive essay). But there are differences. One is that the theory of successful intelligence has been subject to many controlled studies seeking empirically to validate it, while Gardner's theory has not. A second difference is that the theory of successful intelligence is more process-oriented: Gardner's theory is more content-oriented. And a third difference is that not all of Gardner's theories fall under the purview of the theory of successful intelligence, such as the candidate "existential intelligence."

A third example is Vygotksy's (1978). Vygotsky suggested that basic to intelligence is *internalization*, which is the internal reconstruction of an external operation. The basic notion is that we observe those in the social environment around us acting in certain ways and we internalize their actions so that they become a part of ourselves.

Vygotsky also proposed the important notion of a *zone of proximal development*, which refers to functions that have not yet matured but are in the process of maturation. The basic idea is to look not only at developed abilities, but also at abilities that are developing. This zone is often measured as the difference between performance before and after instruction. Thus, instruction is given at the time of testing to measure the individual's ability to learn in the testing environment. The research suggests that tests of the zone of proximal development tap abilities not measured by conventional tests. Our conception is wholly consistent with this notion.

The similarities among the various proposed methods of teaching are more salient than the differences, however. All of the methods are designed to help students develop thinking skills that they will be able to use to enhance their academic performance and their lives.

Note

Preparation of this article was supported by Grant REC-9979843 from the National Science Foundation and by a government grant under the Javits Act Program (Grant R206R00001) as administered by the Institute of Educational Sciences, U.S. Department of Education. Grantees undertaking such projects are encouraged to express freely their professional judgment. This article, therefore, does not necessarily represent the positions or the policies of the U.S. government, and no official endorsement should be inferred.

References

Gardner, H. (1983). *Frames of mind: The theory of multiple intelligences.* New York: Basic.

Grigorenko, E.L., Jarvin, L., & Sternberg, R.J. (2002). School-based tests of the triarchic theory of intelligence: Three settings, three samples, three syllabi. *Contemporary Educational Psychology, 27,* 167–208.

Sternberg, R.J. (1997). *Successful intelligence.* New York: Plume.

Sternberg, R.J. (1999). The theory of successful intelligence. *Review of General Psychology, 3,* 292–316.

Sternberg, R.J., & Clinkenbeard, P.R. (1995). The triarchic model applied to identifying, teaching, and assessing gifted children. *Roeper Review, 17*(4), 255–260.

Sternberg, R.J., Ferrari, M., Clinkenbeard, P.R., & Grigorenko, E.L. (1996). Identification, instruction, and assessment of gifted children: A construct validation of a triarchic model. *Gifted Child Quarterly, 40,* 129–137.

Sternberg, R.J., Forsythe, G.B., Hedlund, J., Horvath, J., Snook, S., Williams, W.M., et al. (2000). *Practical intelligence in everyday life.* New York: Cambridge University Press.

Sternberg, R.J., & Grigorenko, E.L. (2000). *Teaching for successful intelligence.* Arlington Heights, IL: Skylight.

Sternberg, R.J., Grigorenko, E.L., Ferrari, M., & Clinkenbeard, P. (1999). A triarchic analysis of an aptitude-treatment interaction. *European Journal of Psychological Assessment, 15*(1), 1–11.

Sternberg, R.J., Lipka, J., Newman, T., Wildfeuer, S., & Grigorenko, E.L. (2003). *Triarchically-based instruction and assessment of sixth-grade mathematics in a Yup'ik cultural setting in Alaska.* Manuscript submitted for publication.

Sternberg, R.J., & Lubart, T.I. (1995). *Defying the crowd: Cultivating creativity in a culture of conformity.* New York: Free Press.

Sternberg, R.J., Torff, B., & Grigorenko, E.L. (1998a). Teaching for successful intelligence raises school achievement. *Phi Delta Kappan, 79*(9), 667–669.

Sternberg, R.J., Torff, B., & Grigorenko, E.L. (1998b). Teaching triarchically improves school achievement. *Journal of Educational Psychology, 90,* 1–11.

Sternberg, R.J., & Williams, W.M. (1996). *How to develop student creativity.* Alexandria, VA: Association for Supervision and Curriculum Development.

Vygotsky, L.S. (1978). *Mind in society: The development of higher psychological processes.* Cambridge, MA: Harvard University Press.

Robert J. Sternberg *is the IBM Professor of Psychology and Education at Yale University,* ***Elena L. Grigorenko*** *is an associate professor at Yale University and Moscow State University.*

It's No Fad: Fifteen Years of Implementing Multiple Intelligences

by Thomas R. Hoerr

Educators do a great job of identifying winners and losers in the classroom. Regardless of how sensitively academic hierarchies are designed, everyone recognizes the pecking order they create. Is it any wonder, then, that students who aren't considered smart often lose interest in school? How many of us, after all, continue to engage in activities at which we repeatedly fail?

Granted, not all children are equally smart, and failure can sometimes be even more enlightening than the smooth road of success. What makes the theory of multiple intelligences (MI) significant is its acknowledgment that children demonstrate intelligence in many different ways. The job of an educator, then, becomes identifying the ways in which children exhibit intelligence and using their particular strengths to help them learn.

In *Frames of Mind* (1983), Howard Gardner challenged the general perception of intelligence by suggesting that there are eight different ways to learn (see Table 1). Gardner was speaking mainly to an audience of psychologists, but the realization that there are many ways to demonstrate intelligence resonated with educators. MI revealed a way to help more students learn and to help students learn more.

Table 1
THE THEORY OF MULTIPLE INTELLIGENCES

Intelligence	Definition	Examples of persons who evidence this intelligence
LINGUISTIC	sensitivity to the meaning and order of words	Winston Churchill Mario Cuomo Barbara Jordan
LOGICAL-MATHEMATICAL	the ability to handle chains of reasoning and to recognize patterns and order	Benjamin Banneker Bill Gates Stephen Jay Gould
MUSICAL	sensitivity to pitch, melody, rhythm, and tone	Louis Armstrong George Gershwin Yo Yo Ma
BODILY-KINESTHETIC	ability to use the body skillfully and handle objects adroitly	Mia Hamm Harry Houdini Michael Jordan
SPATIAL	ability to perceive the world accurately and to re-create or transform aspects of that world	Maya Lin Peter Max Frank Lloyd Wright
NATURALIST	ability to recognize and classify numerous flora and fauna of an environment	Charles Darwin Jane Goodall John Muir
INTERPERSONAL	ability to understand people and relationships	Martin Luther King, Jr. Ronald Reagan Oprah Winfrey
INTRAPERSONAL	access to one's emotional life for understanding oneself and others	Bill Cosby Anne Frank Eleanor Roosevelt

The faculty of New City School has been implementing MI since 1988. Before 1988, New City was considered a creative and diverse school, but there was no organizing framework, no intellectual or pedagogical model that guided our efforts. *Frames of Mind* seemed to support our faculty's extant beliefs: All children have strengths; the arts are important; and who you are is more important than what you know. I convened a voluntary faculty committee at New City, and we spent several months discussing the practicalities of implementing MI.

MI gave us a model and a vocabulary to talk about how curriculum, instruction, and assessment could be designed to enable more students to succeed. Not only did MI expand our conception of academics; it changed how we communicate with parents. For us, MI has become a philosophy of education that affects our relationships with students, administrators, parents, and each other.

Despite our grounding in MI, New City still administers standardized tests each spring (Hoerr 2000). Our students' scores on these tests, consistently several years above grade level, illustrate that high test scores can be achieved through non-traditional teaching techniques.

MI has made our curriculum and instruction far more inclusive of varied learning styles. Rather than simply relying on the linguistic approach to teaching, we have found ways to incorporate other intelligences into our instruction. One first-grade teacher introduces the *th* sound by having her students *th*read yarn into a piece of fabric. A third-grade teacher at New City demonstrates ratios by having her students lie on the floor inside a full-size shape of a buffalo made with masking tape so they can compare the length of their limbs to the buffalo's. A fifth-grade teacher has his students explore the American Civil War period through visual art. Students learn that through clothing, facial expressions, jewelry, and even calluses on hands, they can make inferences about how people lived and what they believed.

At New City, solid assessment is intertwined with curriculum and instruction; here, too, MI provides the foundation. In one class, kindergartners demonstrate how the systems of the human body function using everyday objects to create a model. The children then explain the life-size bodies they have created: a juice box serves as the heart and, as it contracts, forces air into plastic bags that serve as lungs. There is a spine of popsicle sticks and a brain of pasta. Veins and arteries, made of yarn, are respectively red and blue. Second-graders show their understanding of the challenges that faced Lewis and Clark by creating frontier stores to sell the provisions needed for the journey across the uncharted West. Fourth-graders dress as famous figures they have studied to demonstrate an understanding of the concept of biography. As Rosa Parks or Albert Einstein, the students are encouraged to embrace the characteristics that made the individual famous. Sixth-graders reflect on identity and the future by creating multi-volume biographies that include writings, drawings, family photos, survey results, charts, graphs, and information obtained from interviews with relatives.

These examples capture only part of what happens at New City School each day. Rather than fitting kids to curriculum, predetermining scholastic winners and losers, MI allows educators to help develop kids' strengths. Some of the core differences between traditional teaching and teaching in an MI school are shown in Table 2.

Educators at New City believe that who you are is more important than what you know. Success in most of life's endeavors is dependent upon knowing oneself, capitalizing on personal strengths, and working well with others. As a result, we explicitly teach the interpersonal and intrapersonal intelligences. Our report card, for example, begins with *Intrapersonal Intelligence* and addresses areas such as motivation, confidence, problem-solving, responsibility, effort, and work habits. *Interpersonal Intelligence* follows and focuses on appreciation for diversity and teamwork. At each parent-teacher conference, we begin by talking about the qualities—the intelligences—that we feel are most important.

Table 2

DIFFERENCES BETWEEN TRADITIONAL AND MI CLASSROOMS

In a traditional classroom	In an MI classroom
The kids with strong scholastic intelligences are smart and the other kids are not.	Everyone has a different profile of intelligences; we are all smart in different ways.
Teachers create a hierarchy of intellect.	Teachers use all students' intelligences to help them learn.
The classroom is curriculum-centered.	The classroom is child centered.
Teachers help students acquire information and facts.	Teachers help students create meaning in a constructivist way.
The focus is on the scholastic intelligences, the 3 R's.	The Personal Intelligences are valued: Who you are is more important than what you know.
Teachers work from texts.	Teachers create curriculum—lessons, units, themes.
Teachers assess students by paper and pencil "objective" measures.	Teachers create assessment tools—Projects, Exhibitions, Portfolios (PEPs)—which incorporate MI.
Teachers close the door and work in isolation.	Teachers work with colleagues in using MI, developing collegiality.

Our pursuit of MI has transformed our faculty relations as well. Roland Barth's notion of "collegiality" (1990)—adults learning with and from one another—has become the norm. Our faculty committees, framed around our professional growth, examine various aspects of MI implementation, from the garden committee for exploring the naturalist intelligence, to the assessment committee incorporating MI in determining what students know, to the diversity committee for helping us better appreciate one another. Our frequent educator visitors and our MI conferences have helped us become reflective practitioners, aware of what we are doing and why we are doing it.

Implementing MI requires a creative and energetic faculty willing to work together to find strategies that help kids grow. Rather than just presenting information in a test-retest format, teachers develop curriculum and design assessment tools. Both students and teachers flourish in this kind of setting. Clearly, based on the fifteen-year experiment with multiple intelligences at New City School, MI is no fad, but a proven approach to education for the twenty-first century.

References

Barth, R. 1990. *Improving Schools from Within.* Jossey-Bass: San Francisco.

Gardner, H. 1983. *Frames of Mind: The Theory of Multiple Intelligences.* New York: Basic Books.

Hoerr, T. 2002. *Becoming a Multiple Intelligences School.* Alexandria, Va.: ASCD Press.

Thomas R. Hoerr is the head of the New City School in St. Louis

CAUTION— PRAISE CAN BE DANGEROUS

By Carol S. Dweck

THE SELF-ESTEEM movement, which was flourishing just a few years ago, is in a state of decline. Although many educators believed that boosting students' self-esteem would boost their academic achievement, this did not happen. But the failure of the self-esteem movement does not mean that we should stop being concerned with what students think of themselves and just concentrate on improving their achievement. Every time teachers give feedback to students, they convey messages that affect students' opinion of themselves, their motivation, and their achievement. And I believe that teachers can and should help students become high achievers who also feel good about themselves. But how, exactly, should teachers go about doing this?

In fact, the self-esteem people were on to something extremely important. Praise, the chief weapon in their armory, is a powerful tool. Used correctly it can help students become adults who delight in intellectual challenge, understand the value of effort, and are able to deal with setbacks. Praise can help students make the most of the gifts they have. But if praise is not handled properly, it can become a negative force, a kind of drug that, rather than strengthening students, makes them passive and dependent on the opinion of others. What teachers—and parents—need is a framework that enables them to use praise wisely and well.

Where Did Things Go Wrong?

I believe the self-esteem movement faltered because of the way in which educators tried to instill self-esteem. Many people held an intuitively appealing theory of self-esteem, which went something like this: Giving students many opportunities to experience success and then praising them for their successes will indicate to them that they are intelligent. If they feel good about their intelligence, they will achieve. They will love learning and be confident and successful learners.

Much research now shows that this idea is wrong. Giving students easy tasks and praising their success tells students that you think they're dumb.[1] It's not hard to see why. Imagine being lavishly praised for something you think is pretty Mickey Mouse. Wouldn't you feel that the person thought you weren't capable of more and was trying to make you feel good about your limited ability?

But what about praising students' ability when they perform well on challenging tasks? In such cases, there would be no question of students' thinking you were just trying to make them feel good. Melissa Kamins, Claudia Mueller, and I decided to put this idea to the test.

Mueller and I had already found, in a study of the relationship between parents' beliefs and their children's expectations, that 85 percent of parents thought they needed to praise their children's intelligence in order to assure them that they were smart.[2] We also knew that many educators and psychologists thought that praising children for being intelligent was of great benefit. Yet in almost 30 years of research, I had seen over and over that children who had maladaptive achievement patterns were already obsessed with their intelligence—and with proving it to others. The children worried about how smart they looked and feared that failing at some task— even a relatively unimportant one—meant they were dumb. They also worried that having to work hard in order to succeed at a task showed they were dumb. Intelligence seemed to be a label to these kids, a feather in their caps, rather than a tool that, with effort, they could become more skillful in using.

In contrast, the more adaptive students focused on the process of learning and achieving. They weren't worried about their intelligence and didn't consider every task a measure of it. Instead, these students were more likely to concern themselves with the effort and strategies they needed in order to master the task. We wondered if praising children for being intelligent, though it seemed like a positive thing to do, could hook them into becoming dependent on praise.

Praise for Intelligence

Claudia Mueller and I conducted six studies, with more than 400 fifth-grade students, to examine the effects of praising children for being intelligent.[3] The students were from different parts of the country (a Midwestern town and a large Eastern city) and came from varied ethnic, racial, and socioeconomic backgrounds. Each of the studies involved several tasks, and all began with the students working, one at a time, on a puzzle task that was challenging but easy enough for all of them to do quite well. After this first set, we praised one-third of the children for their *intelligence*. They were told: "Wow, you got x number correct. That's a really good score. You must be smart at this." One-third of the children were also told that they got a very good score, but they were praised for their *effort*: "You must have worked really hard." The final third were simply praised for their *performance*, with no comment on why they were successful. Then, we looked to see the effects of these different types of praise across all six studies.

We found that after the first trial (in which all of the students were successful) the three groups responded similarly to questions we asked them. They enjoyed the task equally, were equally eager to take the problems home to practice, and were equally confident about their future performance.

In several of the studies, as a followup to the first trial, we gave students a choice of different tasks to work on next. We asked whether they wanted to try a challenging task from which they could learn a lot (but at which they might not succeed) or an easier task (on which they were sure to do well and look smart).

The majority of the students who had received praise for being intelligent the first time around went for the task that would allow them to keep on looking smart. Most of the students who had received praise for their effort (in some studies, as many as 90 percent) wanted the challenging learning task. (The third group, the students who had not been praised for intelligence or effort, were right in the middle and I will not focus on them.)

These findings suggest that when we praise children for their intelligence, we are telling them that this is the name of the game: Look smart; don't risk making mistakes. On the other hand, when we praise children for the effort and hard work that leads to achievement, they want to keep engaging in that process. They are not di-

verted from the task of learning by a concern with how smart they might—or might not—look.

The Impact of Difficulty

Next, we gave students a set of problems that were harder and on which they didn't do as well. Afterwards, we repeated the questions we had asked after the first task: How much had they enjoyed the task? Did they want to take the problems home to practice? And how smart did they feel? We found that the students who had been praised for being intelligent did not like this second task and were no longer interested in taking the problems home to practice. What's more, their difficulties led them to question their intelligence. In other words, the same students who had been told they were smart when they succeeded now felt dumb because they had encountered a setback. They had learned to measure themselves from what people said about their performance, and they were dependent on continuing praise in order to maintain their confidence.

In contrast, the students who had received praise for their effort on the easier task liked the more difficult task just as much even though they missed some of the problems. In fact, many of them said they liked the harder problems even more than the easier ones, and they were even more eager to take them home to practice. It was wonderful to see.

Moreover, these youngsters did not think that the difficulty of the task (and their relative lack of success) reflected on their intelligence. They thought, simply, that they had to make a greater effort in order to succeed. Their interest in taking problems home with them to practice on presumably reflected one way they planned to do this.

Thus, the students praised for effort were able to keep their intellectual self-esteem in the face of setbacks. They still thought they were smart; they still enjoyed the challenge; and they planned to work toward future success. The students who had been praised for their intelligence received an initial boost to their egos, but their view of themselves was quickly shaken when the going got rough. As a final test, we gave students a third set of problems that were equal in difficulty to the first set—the one on which all the students had been successful. The results were striking. Although all three groups had performed equally well on the first trial, the students who had received praise for their intelligence (and who had been discouraged by their poor showing on the second trial) now registered the worst performance of the three groups. Indeed, they did significantly worse than they had on the first trial. In contrast, students who were praised for working hard performed the best of the three groups and significantly better than they had originally. So the different kinds of praise apparently affected not just what students thought and felt, but also how well they were able to perform.

Given what we had already seen, we reasoned that when students see their performance as a measure of their intelligence, they are likely to feel stigmatized when they perform poorly and may even try to hide the fact. If, however, students consider a poor performance a temporary setback, which merely reflects how much effort they have put in or their current level of skill, then it will not be a stigma. To test this idea, we gave students the opportunity to tell a student at another school about the task they had just completed by writing a brief description on a prepared form. The form also asked them to report their score on the second, more difficult trial.

More than 40 percent of the students who had been praised for their intelligence lied about their score (to improve it, of course). They did this even though they were reporting their performance to an anonymous peer whom they would never meet. Very few of the students in the other groups exaggerated their performance. This suggests that when we praise students for their intelligence, failure becomes more personal and therefore more of a disgrace. As a result, students become less able to face and therefore deal with their setbacks.

The Messages We Send

Finally, we found that following their experiences with the different kinds of praise, the students believed different things about their intelligence. Students who had received praise for being intelligent told us they thought of intelligence as something innate—a capacity that you just had or didn't have. Students who had been praised for effort told us they thought of intelligence more in terms of their skills, knowledge, and motivation—things over which they had some control and might be able to enhance.

And these negative effects of praising for intelligence were just as strong (and sometimes stronger) for the high-achieving students as for their less successful peers. Perhaps it is even easier to get these youngsters invested in looking smart to others. Maybe they are even more attuned to messages from us that tell them we value them for their intellects.

How can one sentence of praise have such powerful and pervasive effects? In my research, I have been amazed over and over again at how quickly students of all ages pick up on messages about themselves—at how sensitive they are to suggestions about their personal qualities or about the meaning of their actions and experiences. The kinds of praise (and criticism) students receive from their teachers and parents tell them how to think about what they do—and what they are.

This is why we cannot simply forget about students' feelings, their ideas about themselves and their motivation, and just teach them the "facts." No matter how objective we try to be, our feedback conveys messages about what we think is important, what we think of them, and how they should think of themselves. These messages, as

we have seen, can have powerful effects on many things including performance. And it should surprise no one that this susceptibility starts very early.

Melissa Kamins and I found it in kindergarten children.[4] Praise or criticism that focused on children's personal traits (like being smart or good) created a real vulnerability when children hit setbacks. They saw setbacks as showing that they were bad or incompetent—and they were unable to respond constructively. In contrast, praise or criticism that focused on children's strategies or the efforts they made to succeed left them hardy, confident, and in control when they confronted setbacks. A setback did not mean anything bad about them or their personal qualities. It simply meant that something needed to be done, and they set about doing it. Again, a focus on process allowed these young children to maintain their self-esteem and to respond constructively when things went wrong.

Ways of Praising

There are many groups whose achievement is of particular interest to us: minorities, females, the gifted, the underachieving, to name a few. The findings of these studies will tell you why I am so concerned that we not try to encourage the achievement of our students by praising their intelligence. When we worry about low-achieving or vulnerable students, we may want to reassure them they're smart. When we want to motivate high-achieving students, we may want to spur them on by telling them they're gifted. Our research says: Don't do that. Don't get students so invested in these labels that they care more about keeping the label than about learning. Instead of empowering students, praise is likely to render students passive and dependent on something they believe they can't control. And it can hook them into a system in which setbacks signify incompetence and effort is recognized as a sign of weakness rather than a key to success.

This is not to say that we shouldn't praise students. We can praise as much as we please when they learn or do well, but should wax enthusiastic about their strategies, not about how their performance reveals an attribute they are likely to view as innate and beyond their control. We can rave about their effort, their concentration, the effectiveness of their study strategies, the interesting ideas they came up with, the way they followed through. We can ask them questions that show an intelligent appreciation of their work and what they put into it. We can enthusiastically discuss with them what they learned. This, of course, requires more from us than simply telling them that they are smart, but it is much more appreciative of their work, much more constructive, and it does not carry with it the dangers I've been describing.

What about the times a student really impresses us by doing something quickly, easily—and perfectly? Isn't it appropriate to show our admiration for the child's ability? My honest opinion is that we should not. We should not be giving students the impression that we place a high value on their doing perfect work on tasks that are easy for them. A better approach would be to apologize for wasting their time with something that was too easy, and move them to something that is more challenging. When students make progress in or master that more challenging work, that's when our admiration—for their efforts—should come through.

A Challenging Academic Transition

The studies I have been talking about were carried out in a research setting. Two other studies[5] tracked students with these different viewpoints in a real-life situation, as they were making the transition to junior high school and during their first two years of junior high. This is a point at which academic work generally becomes more demanding than it was in elementary school, and many students stumble. The studies compared the attitudes and achievement of students who believed that intelligence is a fixed quantity with students who believed that they could develop their intellectual potential. We were especially interested in any changes in the degree of success students experienced in junior high school and how they dealt with these changes. For the sake of simplicity, I will combine the results from the two studies, for they showed basically the same thing.

First, the students who believed that intelligence is fixed did indeed feel that poor performance meant they were dumb. Furthermore, they reported, in significantly greater numbers than their peers, that if they did badly on a test, they would seriously consider cheating the next time. This was true even for students who were highly skilled and who had a past record of high achievement.

Perhaps even worse, these students believed that having to make an effort meant they were dumb—hardly an attitude to foster good work habits. In fact, these students reported that even though school achievement was very important to them, one of their prime goals in school was to exert as little effort as possible.

In contrast to the hopelessly counterproductive attitude of the first group, the second group of students, those who believed that intellectual potential can be developed, felt that poor performance was often due to a lack of effort, and it called for more studying. They saw effort as worthwhile and important—something necessary even for geniuses if they are to realize their potential.

So once again, for those who are focused on their fixed intelligence and its adequacy, setbacks and even effort bring a loss of face and self-esteem. But challenges, setbacks, and effort are not threatening to the self-esteem of those who are concerned with developing their potential; they represent opportunities to learn. In fact, many of these students told us that they felt smartest when things were difficult; they gained self-esteem when they applied themselves to meeting challenges.

What about the academic achievement of the two groups making the transition to junior high school? In both studies, we saw that students who believed that intelligence was fixed and was manifest in their performance did more poorly than they had in elementary school. Even many who had been high achievers did much less well. Included among them were many students who entered junior high with high intellectual self-esteem. On the other hand, the students who believed that intellectual potential could be developed showed, as a group, clear gains in their class standing, and many blossomed intellectually. The demands of their new environment, instead of causing them to wilt because they doubted themselves, encouraged them to roll up their sleeves and get to work.

These patterns seem to continue with students entering college. Research with students at highly selective universities found that, although they may enter a situation with equal self-esteem, optimism, and past achievement, students respond to the challenge of college differently: Students in one group by measuring themselves and losing confidence; the others by figuring out what it takes and doing it.[6]

Believing and Achieving

Some of the research my colleagues and I have carried out suggests that it is relatively easy to modify the views of young children in regard to intelligence and effort in a research setting. But is it possible to influence student attitudes in a real-life setting? And do students become set in their beliefs as they grow older? Some exciting new research shows that even college students' views about intelligence and effort can be modified—and that these changes will affect their level of academic achievement.[7] In their study, Aronson and Fried taught minority students at a prestigious university to view their intelligence as a potentiality that could be developed through hard work. For example, they created and showed a film that explained the neural changes that took place in the brain every time students confronted difficulty by exerting effort. The students who were instructed about the relationship between intelligence and effort went on to earn significantly higher grades than their peers who were not. This study, like our intelligence praise studies, shows that (1) students' ideas about their intelligence can be influenced by the messages they receive, and (2) when these ideas change, changes in performance can follow.

But simply getting back to basics and enforcing rigorous standards—which some students will meet and some will not—won't eliminate the pitfalls I have been describing. This approach may convey, even more forcefully, the idea that intelligence is a gift only certain students possess. And it will not, in itself, teach students to value learning and focus on the *process* of achievement or how to deal with obstacles. These students may, more than ever, fear failure because it takes the measure of their intelligence.

A Different Framework

Our research suggests another approach. Instead of trying to convince our students that they are smart or simply enforcing rigorous standards in the hopes that doing so will create high motivation and achievement, teachers should take the following steps: first, get students to focus on their potential to learn; second, teach them to value challenge and learning over looking smart; and third, teach them to concentrate on effort and learning processes in the face of obstacles.

This can be done while holding students to rigorous standards. Within the framework I have outlined, tasks are challenging and effort is highly valued, required, and rewarded. Moreover, we can (and must) give students frank evaluations of their work and their level of skill, but we must make clear that these are evaluations of their current level of performance and skill, not an assessment of their intelligence or their innate ability. In this framework, we do not arrange easy work or constant successes, thinking that we are doing students a favor. We do not lie to students who are doing poorly so they will feel smart: That would rob them of the information they need to work harder and improve. Nor do we just give students hard work that many can't do, thus making them into casualties of the system.

I am not encouraging high-effort situations in which students stay up studying until all hours every night, fearing they will displease their parents or disgrace themselves if they don't get the top test scores. Pushing students to do that is not about valuing learning or about orienting students toward developing their potential. It is about pressuring students to prove their worth through their test scores.

It is also not sufficient to give students piles of homework and say we are teaching them about the importance of effort. We are not talking about quantity here but about teaching students to seek challenging tasks and to engage in an active learning process.

However, we as educators must then be prepared to do our share. We must help students acquire the skills they need for learning, and we must be available as constant resources for learning. It is not enough to keep harping on and praising effort, for this may soon wear thin. And it will not be effective if students don't know *how* to apply their effort appropriately. It is necessary that we as educators understand and teach students how to engage in processes that foster learning, things like task analysis and study skills.[8]

When we focus students on their potential to learn and give them the message that effort is the key to learning, we give them responsibility for and control over their achievement—and over their self-esteem. We acknowledge that learning is not something that someone gives students; nor can they expect to feel good about themselves because teachers tell them they are smart. Both learning and self-esteem are things that students achieve as they tackle challenges and work to master new material.

Students who value learning and effort know how to make and sustain a commitment to valued goals. Unlike some of their peers, they are not afraid to work hard; they know that meaningful tasks involve setbacks; and they know how to bounce back from failure. These are lessons that cannot help but serve them well in life as well as in school.

These are lessons I have learned from my research on students' motivation and achievement, and they are things I wish I had known as a student. There is no reason that every student can't know them now.

Endnotes

1. Meyer, W. U. (1982). Indirect communications about perceived ability estimates. *Journal of Educational Psychology, 74*, 888–897.
2. Mueller, C. M., & Dweck, C. S. (1996). Implicit theories of intelligence: Relation of parental beliefs to children's expectations. Paper presented at the Third National Research Convention of Head Start, Washington, D.C.
3. Mueller, C. M., & Dweck, C. S. (1998). Intelligence praise can undermine motivation and performance. *Journal of Personality and Social Psychology; 75*, 33–52.
4. Kamins, M., & Dweck, C. S. (1999). Person vs. process praise and criticism: Implications for contingent self-worth and coping. *Developmental Psychology*.
5. Henderson, V., & Dweck, C. S. (1990). Achievement and motivation in adolescence: A new model and data. In S. Feldman and G. Elliott (Eds.), *At the threshold: The developing adolescent*. Cambridge, MA: Harvard University Press; *and* Dweck, C. S., & Sorich, L. (1999). Mastery-oriented thinking. In C. R. Snyder (Ed.). *Coping*. New York: Oxford University Press.
6. Robins, R. W. & Pals, J. (1998). Implicit self-theories of ability in the academic domain: A test of Dweck's model. Unpublished manuscript, University of California at Davis; *and* Zhao, W., Dweck, C. S., & Mueller, C. (1998). Implicit theories and depression-like responses to failure. Unpublished manuscript, Columbia University.
7. Aronson, J., & Fried, C. (1998). Reducing stereotype threat and boosting academic achievement of African Americans: The role of conceptions of intelligence. Unpublished manuscript, University of Texas.
8. Brown, A. L. (1997). Transforming schools into communities of thinking and learning about serious matters. *American Psychologist, 52*, 399–413.

Carol S. Dweck is a professor of psychology at Columbia University, who has carried out research on self-esteem, motivation, and academic achievement for thirty years. Her new book, Self-Theories: Their Role in Motivation, Personality, and Development, *was just published by The Psychology Press.*

Constructing Learning

Using Technology to Support Teaching for Understanding

Thomas M. Sherman and Barbara L. Kurshan

A frequent criticism of technology applications in classrooms is that they are little more than extraneous bells and whistles pointlessly tacked onto routine instruction. The flash and splash of a PowerPoint presentation may look good, but many question the value added to student learning. This leads to the question, how can technologies genuinely contribute to enhanced learning? We need to show explicitly how a constructivist perspective can be helpful in planning and delivering instruction and how technologies can significantly support effective and theoretically sound teaching.

We discussed contructivism in depth in our article last month (December–January). Briefly, constructivism is based on the conception that we learn by relating new experiences to our prior knowledge; we construct new understandings based on what we already know. This theory has emerged from research across a broad range of disciplines, but the challenge has been to understand how to promote deeper, more substantive learning. Three principles capture the essence of the challenge. Understanding is:

- the product of actively relating new and prior experiences
- a function of learning facts and core principles of a discipline
- a consequence of using and managing intellectual abilities well

As educators, our challenge is to identify, invent, adopt, and use classroom practices that are consistent with these principles. However, this is no easy quest. For example, one common concern relates to the central role of individual prior knowledge. How can we measure and tailor instruction to each individual's unique experiences? Our response is to identify key characteristics of effective teaching consistent with constructivist theory. Then, for each characteristic we identify ways you can use technology to make these characteristics regular features of your classroom.

Consistency between theoretical conceptions of learning and teaching practice has been shown to support effective applications of technologies to increase achievement. We explore eight teaching characteristics that are consistent with constructivist principles:

- Learner centered
- Interesting
- Real life
- Social
- Active
- Time
- Feedback
- Supportive

Learner Centered

Learner-centered classrooms focus instruction on the intellectual strategies, experiences, culture, and knowledge that students bring into classrooms. The instruction you create uses these experiences as learning paths for students to follow as they examine and transform the new ideas into their own understanding. You can use technology to support this transformation in two important ways.

First, you can use access to extensive libraries of teaching examples and suggestions to tune your instruction to student needs, experiences, and unique situations. For example, Edgate and ProQuestK-12 provide large repertoires of Web-based teaching resources. (**Editor's note:** Find these URLs and other information in the Resources section on p. 39.) Using online resources such as these, you can search for activities that are consistent with students' learning needs. For example, consider teaching a geography lesson in a classroom where students have limited and extensive experiences with local conditions such as a central business district. You could also use the Edgate site to design language lessons that are related to student cultural experiences from home, such as recipes from Mexico. You can personalize study by using local information resources (e.g., GIS databases, museum records and images online, property records, census data), as a focus for study in science (investigating pollution issues), literature (reading local stories), and social studies (examining the politics of local decisions). Students can use geographic principles to study data about their own neighborhoods as well as examine other features of interest specifically to them.

Interested students challenge their existing knowledge and are more likely to develop conceptual frameworks that integrate prior knowledge and new information into understanding.

Second, you can teach students to organize their knowledge using computer-based tools and software simulations that model forming and expressing alternate conceptions of concepts and strategies. For example, CSILE (Computer-Supported Intentional Learning Environments) offers several projects and many application examples in which the technology is integrated into curricula so that students' thinking is revealed. With sites such as these, you can help students focus on their thinking as well as look for information. As students develop understandings, you guide them to examine their conclusions based on interactions between their peers, their writing, the information they collect, and their prior knowledge. By trying to explain their ideas to other students and interacting with their peers around academic content, students improve their thinking skills and gain new knowledge. In addition, by reviewing students' CSILE entries, you can find evidence of the kinds of help students provide for each others' thinking and communication skills.

Interesting

Interested students challenge their existing knowledge and are more likely to develop conceptual frameworks that integrate prior knowledge and new information into understanding. Lack of interest is generally the number one reason that students give for not learning to mastery. By focusing on students' current beliefs, you increase the probabilities that students will be intrigued and explore their understandings. Technologies can be an effective tool to promote this interested and active exploration.

Technology-based demonstrations and illustrations such as the math and science animations at ExploreLearning, the Day in the Life Series, and MathMagic stimulate discussions in which students' current beliefs are expressed and tested. By creating classroom environments that encourage manipulating and discussing new ideas, you build opportunities for students to engage their interests and examine the perceptions of others. Although these opportunities can be very rich, it is also important to ensure that students have the skills to interact with each other. Sites such as these usually are open to teacher-led and whole class discussion as well as small and independent group work. Technology enables students to propose an effect and then to test that proposal with a virtual manipulative.

Manipulatives are concrete or symbolic artifacts that students interact with while learning new topics. They are powerful instructional aids because they provide active, hands-on exploration of abstract concepts. Research supports the premise that computer-based manipulatives are often more effective than ones involving physical objects, in part because they can dynamically link multiple representations together.

In addition, because there is a wide range of technology-based materials available on many topics, you can provide opportunities for students to self-select learning activities that are developmentally and topic appropriate as well as capture their personal interests. Thus, rather than a single demonstration of a reaction of chemicals or one perspective on a war battlefield, you can open a broad range of options for students to select those that are most interesting to them.

Real Life

Constructivist teaching incorporates students' communities as the context for learning. Consider the Schools For Thought (SFT) project of the Learning Sciences Institute at Vanderbilt University. In the SFT Jasper Woodbury series, students are presented with computer-based scenarios that involve complex information and sophisticated decisions. You contribute to successful learning by guiding students' inquiry through focused questions and directing students to consider how these principles affect their community-generated questions. As students work through the SFT dilemmas, you can help them recognize the many ways they have used information they learned in math, science, social studies, and literature to address the issues raised.

You can also facilitate depth of understanding by integrating technologies into the fabric of teaching as intellectual tools that students use to study, learn, and communicate with others in their classes as well as others in different locations. Students can respond by using organizing tools, making complex calculations, and employing search engines to mirror the strategies they will use outside of school to seek answers. In this way, real life in school becomes as much a second nature response as real life outside of school. The result should be a much higher potential for transfer in addition to deeper and more meaningful learning.

Social

Constructing meaning comes from interacting with others to explain, defend, discuss, and assess our ideas and challenge, question, and comprehend the ideas of others. Social activities allow students to express and develop their understandings with peers as they pursue projects through conversations that stimulate examining and expanding their understandings.

One increasingly common technology-based strategy is to create online communities of students and adults who collaborate on specific problems. For example, Global Lab and CoVis link students from as many other sites as you choose to monitor, collect, and share scientific data. The Global Lab project was tested in more than 300 schools in 30 countries. These technologies provide opportunities for students to join a large community and analyze data in a very diverse social environment.

Understanding grows from studying difficult concepts several times and in different ways.

As students analyze and share conclusions across different cultures and perspectives, you have the opportunity to help them evaluate the quality and quantity of the evidence on which they build their conceptions. One outcome is that you can demonstrate the effects of cultural and geographical perspectives by discussing the reasons for differences. These technology-based collaborative social classrooms create learning environments in which students can openly express their conclusions, challenge the conclusions of others, and build extensive information resources. Your role is to help students develop standards to judge evidence, lead students as they reflect on and discuss issues, and encourage students to form conceptual frameworks based on social considerations of the ideas they are studying.

Active

The visible learning actions students use to gather and consider information include writing, discussing, and searching. The covert actions that result in monitoring and choosing how to learn are reading, listening, monitoring, reflecting, considering, evaluating, and checking.

Technology-based interactivity can be a tool to facilitate active learning with dialogue between students as well as to evaluate and revise their propositions. WebPals is a collaborative interaction between teacher education students and middle school students in which they jointly read and discuss their interpretations of novels and review implications for their communities and lives. You would moderate these discussions by posing stimulating questions to your students about the novels they read and also about the observations that their Web pals make. By emphasizing thoughtful interpretation of their questions and observations, you show students that how they think is as important as mastering details.

Time

Time and carefully planned experiences are necessary for broad and deep understanding. Two overarching outcomes from in-depth study are essential. First, understanding is the result of well-organized and widely linked concepts. This allows learners to recall and use their knowledge quickly and appropriately in unfamiliar situations. Second, understanding consists of knowing the important questions and cognitive strategies that characterize the disciplines they are studying.

You can employ technology to increase the efficiency and personalization of the time to learn new ideas as well as to rethink and revise existing ideas. Technologies can facilitate these recursive processes in several ways. Word processors and databases can be used to record thoughts and observations so that students can review them regularly and revise as needed. You can embed this individual review in student self-directed routines guided by metacognitive questions such as: Why are you learning this? What do you already know that relates to this information? How interested are you in learning this? How difficult will it be for you to learn? Are you checking your understanding as you study? How should you correct errors? Are there other ways you can study that may be better? These questions focus students to use their time well and to maximize success by selecting and applying the most effective learning strategies.

Supportive scaffolding shows students that you understand their needs and "walk" with them as they work to meet learning goals.

Understanding grows from studying difficult concepts several times and in different ways. You can use technologies to foster these recursive learning processes by providing the same information in different formats and for different situations. For example, presenting math from sites such as Global Grocery List and MathMagic provides variety and maintains students' interest.

Technology can help teachers and students use time more efficiently. Students are empowered to control and organize their learning in programs that respond to their specific needs. Some examples of tutoring programs that use time efficiently are Get A Clue, which provides vocabulary development through stories, and HomeworkSpot, which provides homework help through access to subject-specific links. With sites such as these, you can link students to many help and reference sites. For structured practice, students can be directed to use many available drill and practice programs tailored to independent use. These resources offer students multiple presentations of classroom lessons that use time efficiently and promote greater understanding.

Feedback

Feedback is essential to the process of acquiring and reflecting on the relation between existing knowledge and new information. The feedback you provide is most effective as a continual stream of performance-based observations from which students can revise their thinking as they work on projects. When teachers successfully integrate feedback authentically into projects to support and guide students, learning becomes a journey that is constantly being adjusted as students individually and collectively pursue solving problems or explaining observed phenomena.

Software such as Logal Simulations in Science and Math and Decisions, Decisions in Social Studies and others in nearly all disciplines offer students the opportunity to plug in data or observations and model the results of their efforts. Technology-based feedback is immediate and focused on the learning at hand. Feedback can be presented in graphs that illustrate the effects of the students' propositions and by indicating if a test question has been answered correctly. Test questions can also be put into databases from which practice questions can be generated for students to test their own knowledge. Computer simulations can give students realistic problems to solve for evaluating their use of their knowledge and understanding.

This kind of feedback lets students know what they have and have not learned; students then have the ability to manage their own learning, use their metacognitive skills, and establish personal goals. You can promote this sense of efficacy when students make data-based judgments about what they know and how well they know it. Your models of how to think about using feedback are an important ingredient in students learning to make the most of the feedback they receive.

Supportive

Instructional support provides the right assistance at the right time for learners. You can support or scaffold learning by doing things such as reducing the complexity of a task, limiting the steps needed to solve a problem, providing cues, identifying critical errors, and demonstrating how tasks can be completed.

This kind of supportive scaffolding shows students that you understand their needs and enables you to "walk" with them as they work to meet learning goals. A key part of this support is to determine when students are ready for a nudge and then to provide the scaffold that will support them as they make progress. As learners develop new concepts, the scaffolds are removed.

> You can provide opportunities for students to self-select learning activities that are developmentally and topic appropriate as well as capture their personal interests.

When you use technologies such as calculators, spreadsheets, and graphing and modeling programs, you help students as they develop their understandings. In addition, you can use computer programs that serve as mentors to students as they develop their skills and knowledge. Programs with access to experts and tutoring also offer scaffolding for students to question their knowledge and find support for exploring questions with multiple correct answers. For example, the site Smarthinking is designed to increase academic retention and achievement for individual students with interactive mentors and tutors. The Electronic Emissary Project is another site that connects online mentors with K–12 students in collaborative and team projects that are curriculum based.

Conclusion

We have described eight characteristics of effective learning environments consistent with modern constructivist theory. As we see research becoming more interdisciplinary—including not only education but also the physiology of the brain, neurology, psychology, and medicine—the constructivist explanation of how to influence learning and learners appears more and more consistent with the emerging evidence. This research has direct and important implications for what we do in classrooms. Classrooms that are active, interesting, learner centered, focused on real life, and social and provide time to learn, frequent and facilitative feedback, and support both learning to be good learners as well as learning content have consistently been shown to be more effective with all learners.

Creating these environments is a daunting challenge and requires considerable restructuring of classroom routines and teaching practices. Nobody denies the challenge is great, and we do not claim that technologies will make the task easy. But, as we have illustrated, technologies can provide teaching tools that you can genuinely integrate into the instructional fabric of classrooms. In addition, we can teach our students to use technologies to meet their own responsibility to become good learners and also use these technologies as effective tools to teach content. The goal of constructivism—teaching students so they know how and what to learn—is the path to fuller and more relevant understanding of life's important lessons.

Resources

CoVis: http://www.covis.nwu.edu
CSILE: http://www.ed.gov/pubs/EdReform-Studies/EdTech/csile.html
Day in the Life Series: http://www.colonial-williamsburg.com/History/teaching/Day-series/ditl_index.cfm
Decisions, Decisions in Social Studies: http://www.scholastic.com/products/tomsnyder.htm
Edgate: http://www.edgate.com
Electronic Emissary Project: http://emissary.wm.edu
ExploreLearning: http://www.explorelearning.com
Get A Clue: http://www.getaclue.com
Global Grocery List: http://landmark-project.com/ggl/
Global Lab: http://globallab.terc.edu
HomeworkSpot: http://homeworkspot.com
Logal Simulations in Science and Math: http://www.riverdeep.com/products/logal
MathMagic: http://mathforum.org/mathmagic/
ProQuestK-12: http://www.proquestk12.com

Schools For Thought: http://peabody.vanderbilt.edu/projects/funded/sft/general/sfthome.html

Smarthinking: http://www.smarthinking.com

WebPals: http://teacherbridge.cs.vt.edu/public/projects/Web+Pals/Home

---

Thomas M. Sherman is a professor of education in the College of Liberal Arts and Human Sciences at Virginia Tech. He teaches courses in educational psychology, evaluation, and instructional design and has written more than 100 articles for professional publications. Tom works regularly with practicing teachers and students in the areas of learning improvement and teaching strategies. He is also active in civic affairs, serving on local and state committees.

Dr. Barbara Kurshan is the president of Educorp Consulting Corporation. She has a doctorate in education with an emphasis on computer-based applications. She has written numerous articles and texts and has designed software and networks to meet the needs of learners. She works with investment banking firms and venture groups on companies related to educational technology. She serves on the boards of Fablevision, Headsprout, and Medalis, and on the advisory boards of Pixel, WorldSage, and Tegrity.

On Balance

Creating a Culture for Learning

Sidney Trubowitz

Everywhere we read about efforts to revitalize schools. Such initiatives include restructuring governance by centralizing the power to make decisions, introducing a mandated curriculum for all teachers to follow, and reinforcing an accountability process with a strong focus on test scores. All these school-improvement proposals rely on a belief that change can be imposed from the outside without the participation of teachers, administrators, students, and parents. The likely results of such proposals are the development of learning environments that devote little time to reflection on what constitutes good practice; teachers who function in a mechanical fashion; and, after a momentary flurry of activity, a return to the status quo.

To achieve growth that will be lasting and more than superficial, what is needed are opportunities for public school staffs, parents, students, college faculty, and professional organizations to work together. Their aim must be to build a different kind of school culture, one that develops an exemplary curriculum, identifies effective teaching approaches, and establishes an atmosphere of mutual respect.

Having worked for more than twenty years with the Queens College-Louis Armstrong Middle School collaboration in New York City, I have seen firsthand what helps to establish a different kind of educational tone and what gets in the way of creating a culture promoting learning. Here is what I have learned.

The Elements of a New School Culture

A Thinking Atmosphere

The usual school organization finds the elementary schoolteacher with children all day long and the secondary school instructor seeing 150 students five times a week for a daily forty-five-minute period. The teacher begins each morning by signing in or by punching a time clock. From there it's a walk to a room, a door closed, and a day without peer dialogue. Professional development is restricted to the occasional guru-led workshop. No time is provided for teachers to reflect on the day's happenings with others or by themselves. In other countries "alone time" as part of the teacher's day is considered essential. It is not unusual in the corporate world to provide weekly brainstorming sessions for employees. Recent trends toward extending the school day and year will leave teachers with even less time for reflection.

In our public school-college collaboration, no single event or procedure made up the emotional and intellectual scaffolding that supported a thinking atmosphere. Rather, a day-to-day series of happenings contributed to a climate that encouraged reflection before moving into action. School administrators gave ready approval for teachers to attend professional conferences or visit other schools. A well-publicized professional library to which teachers and parents had easy access was established. Administrators, teachers, and professors who worked in the school recommended articles to each other. Faculty conferences were planned with teachers to demonstrate and discuss what colleagues were doing. At brown-bag luncheons and breakfast meetings with coffee provided, such topics as a favorite children's book or how best to use student teachers were explored. Teacher schedules were organized so that small numbers could meet regularly to discuss topics of mutual interest.

Open Communication

A school culture promoting learning bespeaks an openness of communication in which ideas and feelings are freely expressed and acknowledged. But if that is to occur, there is a need to move through and beyond times of distrust and suspicion. The origin of these negative attitudes is grounded in past experience. There are the years of criticism leveled at public school teachers and administrators by the press, college faculty, the public at large, and even the educational bureaucracy itself. Newspaper headlines highlight the sins of individual instructors and the inadequacies of public education and its personnel. External agencies and professors issue reports describing low levels of student achievement. Central office administrators talk blithely of inferior principals and teachers. It's little wonder that public school personnel experiencing the never-ending onslaught of reprimand view outsiders and often their own school administrators with skepticism and defensiveness. The messages they hear say "This is what you're doing wrong." They never see "This is what you're doing right." In our collaboration we found that only after extensive shared experience did staff feel comfortable enough to express its views without fearing retaliation.

Barriers between people eroded as college faculty and school administrators worked with teachers in their classrooms, as parent-teacher retreats took place at the college environmental center, as parents were invited to shadow their children through a typical day, and as parent-teacher-professor committees explored school concerns. When administrators, teachers, professors, and parents met to discuss educational matters, they interacted not as figures occupying particular roles but as individuals with views to offer. This is not to say that the participants all brought similar levels of expertise and experience to the discussions: only that everyone's contributions received respect. The aim always was to develop an atmosphere of trust in which attitudes of superiority and critical judgments were absent and where opposing stances provided leeway for empathic understanding.

We also recognized the value of social interaction to professional growth. School parties, student-faculty athletic events, theater groups, and book clubs all assisted in getting to the real person, moving past the outer layers of personality, and facilitating authentic communication.

The Value of an Outside Observer

One of the assets school staffs bring to their work is extensive experience within their own institutions. Even the most introspective educators, however, face the dangers of allowing familiarity to influence objectivity and of failing to profit from what others have learned elsewhere. Perceptive observers can ask questions and make comments that broaden understanding and supply insights that may escape those who are immersed in a project.

In our public school-college collaboration, we worked with people of broad backgrounds whose lack of knowledge of bureaucratic strictures proved a boon as they made suggestions free from traditional thinking. For example, at one session dealing with the problem of acclimating students and parents from throughout Queens to a new middle school, Seymour Sarason, a professor emeritus of Yale University and a periodic visitor to the school, recommended conducting a week-long orientation for newcomers and their families before the beginning of the school year. We were able to persuade the board of education of the value of such an activity despite its departure from usual practice. It has since become a fixture in how the school operates.

In another instance, Clarence Bunch, a professor of art education, proposed installing a school museum. After consultation with the principal, teachers, and colleagues, it too has become an integral part of how the Louis Arm-

strong Middle School functions. It is now the scene of displays of student work, shows by neighborhood artists, and exhibitions of artifacts produced by children from other countries.

The Need to Develop a Common Language

A healthy educational community needs to avoid jargon and to use words and phrases that have shared meaning. The list of terms bandied about in discussions of education without clear definition is long. For example, there is much support for the idea of parental involvement, but there is little talk about how parents are to participate in a school. Are they to help set goals? To be used only as resource people? To evaluate teachers? To establish budgetary priorities? To select texts?

Other ideas needing clarification include accountability, curriculum, staff development, and leadership. To create a culture in which the participants communicate with clarity, there is a need to reach common understanding of these terms and others.

In our collaboration, the effort to ensure that people used mutually understood terms was supported by weekly preschool meetings attended by the principal, teachers, parents, and college faculty. Teachers and professors joining with parents at the monthly Parent-Teachers Association (PTA) meetings also helped to bridge language barriers.

Respecting Teacher Autonomy

In many schools, teachers are besieged by external impositions on instructional time. Public-address announcements interrupt the day. Directives from the district office insist on participation in citywide contests. A steady stream of messages emanating from the school's main office, administrators, colleagues, and others fragments the flow of teacher-student interaction. Test scores become the single measure of teacher effectiveness, with the result that teaching to the test becomes the norm and occupies much of the school day. Teachers are mandated to teach in a prescribed manner. A one-size-fits-all approach views teaching as a robotic endeavor rather than one demanding thoughtful analysis of student needs.

At the Louis Armstrong Middle School, curriculum exploration and experimentation are the norm, undergirded by a belief that a rich educational program will result in good student test scores. That has been the case over the years. It has also become a cardinal rule that the public-address system is used only for the direst of emergencies; that for the first hour at least, messages to classrooms are forbidden; and that demands for written reports are to be kept to a minimum. If time for instruction is to be valued, then the teacher's domain, the classroom, needs respect and not indiscriminate intrusion.

Obstacles to Building a Positive School Culture

The task of building a school culture that promotes learning is ongoing with the constant struggle to overcome obstacles. For example, the traditional way in which schools function inhibits an easy exchange of ideas among professionals. Schools have a hierarchical organization headed by a principal aided by assistant principals, chairpeople, and deans. The teacher group alone is seen as the target for improvement. A common method for achieving instructional growth is the supervisory observation, with classroom visits followed by a discussion in which the principal, after an initial listing of strengths, outlines areas in need of improvement. Rarely is this process viewed as a conversation in which ideas are shared. Rarely are questions asked that might encourage reflection. Rarely are plans made to pursue issues in greater depth. The subordinate position of the teacher is reinforced by requiring that planbooks gain administrative approval and letters sent home are first screened by the principal.

If thinking is to become part of the school culture, there should be a different conception of how people in different roles are to operate. The hierarchical nature of schools, with communication flowing only one way, leaves little opportunity for groups to dialogue about instructional issues.

The limitations of professional preparation present another problem. Cooperation and collegiality are characteristics of a school culture promoting group exploration of ideas. When educators have had little experience in working together, the attempt to collaborate is likely to meet strong obstacles. The education of teachers, administrators, and such specialists as reading instructors, school psychologists, and special education staff takes place in separate courses. With other faculty I arranged to bring graduate classes of special education teachers, prospective school psychologists, and potential administrators together for a few sessions. The initial inability of the participants to listen to the point of view of the others was startling. It is clear that if school professionals are to work effectively with one another, teacher-preparation programs must help future educators become aware of how roles shape behavior and learn ways of dealing with conflict.

The culture prevailing in the society outside schools also impacts the task of creating a thoughtful school community. We live in an environment filled with demands for immediate solutions to complex problems. Profound political issues are presented in sound bites. Popular television programs appeal to instincts removed from any need to think. The speed of e-mail and fax machines obliterates the opportunity for considered contemplation before making a response. To build a culture supportive of learning, schools must resist external pressures pushing for precipitous action unsupported by prior thinking.

Another obstacle to establishing a culture for learning is the inevitability of resistance to new ideas. The teaching profession draws people who are hard workers, who are committed to service, and who place a high value on stability. Attempts to alter customary work patterns will encounter resistance. The desire for the security of the status quo will serve to reinforce customary modes of behavior and to block out ideas that are different. The challenge for those trying to create a new school culture is to empathize with the reluctance to change and, at the same time, to support those ready to explore new approaches to education.

To develop schools that are not simply institutions responding to the external pressures prevailing at a particular time but rather are centers of ongoing exploration, learning, thinking, and adapting to the needs of students, we need to look more closely at how schools are organized, how people interact with one another, how change occurs, and how we view the role of the teacher.

Sidney Trubowitz is a professor emeritus at Queens College of the City University of New York.

Promoting Academic Achievement through Social and Emotional Learning

by Katharine Ragozzino, Hank Resnik, Mary Utne-O'Brien, and Roger P Weissberg

In this day of high-stakes testing, educators are eager and even anxious to find new policies, instructional methods, and educational practices to improve academic performance. In their search they have reexamined such policies as teacher certification, school choice, grade retention, summer school, and the latest pedagogies for teaching particular academic subjects. Increasingly, however, educators and policymakers are also discovering the importance of social and emotional variables for academic performance and achievement. Consequently, they are turning their attention to methods and practices that foster students' social and emotional development.

Acknowledging the importance of social and emotional variables is one thing. Really understanding their critical role and developing social and emotional skills among students are different matters. What teacher has not felt the frustration of working with a capable student who has neither the motivation nor the perseverance to perform to capacity? What teacher has not felt that he or she could teach better, and his or her students learn better, in caring, supportive school and classroom environments? Teachers have long recognized, and a body of research now corroborates, that facilitating student achievement means addressing barriers to learning. Many of these barriers are social and emotional.

Social and Emotional Learning (SEL) Defined

Social and emotional competence refers to the capacity to recognize and manage emotions, solve problems effectively, and establish and maintain positive relationships with others (see sidebar, next page). Social and emotional competence and the learning environments that support their development have been shown to enhance academic performance in various direct and indirect ways (Zins et al. in press). SEL programming in schools, when carried out systematically and comprehensively, supports caring classroom environments and helps develop positive relationships. SEL programming also provides students with varied skills that positively affect academic achievement. They include:

- managing emotions that interfere with learning and concentration
- developing motivation and the ability to persevere even in the face of academic setbacks and challenges
- working cooperatively and effectively in the classroom and in peer learning groups
- setting and working toward academic goals

For example, learning in a history class improves markedly when students are taught to use problem solving to understand and analyze a historic event. Teaching students social and emotional skills also makes them less likely to behave in ways that interfere with learning.

What the Research Says

A substantial body of research supports the notion that social and emotional variables are integral rather than incidental to learning (Wang, Haertel, and Walberg 1997). Wilson, Gottfredson, and Najaka's meta-analysis (2001) of 165 studies examined the effectiveness of various school-based prevention activities. Their study revealed that social and emotional learning programs increased attendance and decreased the dropout rate. Zins et al. (in press) found that SEL programs improved student attitudes, behaviors, and academic performance.

Rather than diverting schools from their primary academic mission, improving students' social and emotional competence advances the academic mission of schools, while also ensuring that they meet their broader mission to produce caring, responsible, and knowledgeable students. Social and emotional learning provides students with basic skills for success not just in school but ultimately in their personal, professional, and civic lives.

What teacher has not felt the frustration of working with a capable student who has neither the motivation nor the perseverance to perform to capacity?

Such findings should not be surprising. The nature of learning, certainly in school settings, is fundamentally social. In the classroom the most successful children are likely to be actively and prosocially engaged with their peers and teachers Feshbach and Feshbach 1987; Chen, Rubin, and Li 1997). Such students communicate ideas effectively; listen to, evaluate, and integrate the ideas of others; elicit ideas and input from others; and ask teachers and peers for help when necessary.

Students emotionally connected to peers and teachers who value learning and high academic performance often adopt similar values (Hawkins et al. 2001). Student perceptions of teacher warmth and supportiveness can accurately predict student engagement (Ryan and

Patrick 2001). Similarly, students who benefit from positive relationships and interactions tend to achieve above the average academically (Osterman 2000).

In short, educators who want children to care about learning must first ensure they feel supported and offer them frequent opportunities to use SEL skills in meaningful ways (Hawkins 1997).

From Research to Reality

The Collaborative for Academic, Social, and Emotional Learning (CASEL), an organization working to establish SEL as an essential part of P–12 education, has identified specific ways in which SEL, programs positively affect academic performance. These approaches are documented in more detail at <www.CASEL.org>, CASEL's Web site.

Encourage students to apply SEL skills to classroom behaviors that enhance learning. For instance, a teacher can encourage active listening by asking students to identify specific academic goals for themselves. Such goals could be grade-based ("to receive better than C's in all my courses") or related to academic behaviors ("to turn in all my assignments on time"). Students can then anticipate barriers to reaching their goals ("I hate math") and identify ways to overcome those barriers ("I can stay after school and receive tutoring").

Encourage students to apply SEL skills directly to subject matter. Students can apply SEL skills not just to situations in their own lives but to circumstances facing characters in novels or to actual events, past or present. For a class discussion of the Israeli-Palestinian conflict, students can analyze how each party would define the problem. Questions might include:

"What are the perspectives of each party?"

"What are some possible solutions that would reduce the tension between the parties?"

"What are the possible consequences of each proposed solution?"

Such activities both promote deeper understanding of academic material and help students gain familiarity and ease with SEL skills.

Use instructional practices that promote SEL and academic learning. Specific SEL-focused classroom-management techniques—cooperative learning groups, academic choice periods, peer tutoring, and service-learning—can improve students' social-emotional competence and academic performance. Such techniques help establish a respectful classroom environment and minimize disruptions. Instruction in interpersonal skills, followed by opportunities to use the skills in cooperative learning groups, teaches students to collaborate on group goals. Service-learning can enhance students' social awareness and commitment to others.

CORE SEL COMPETENCIES

Self-Awareness: Knowing what we are feeling in the moment; having a realistic assessment of our own abilities and a well-grounded sense of self-confidence

Social Awareness: Sensing what others are feeling; being able to take their perspective; appreciating and interacting positively with diverse groups

Self-Management: Handling our emotions so they facilitate rather than interfere with the task at hand; being conscientious and delaying gratification to pursue goals; persevering in the face of setbacks and frustrations

Relationship Skills: Handling emotions in relationships effectively; establishing and maintaining healthy and rewarding relationships based on cooperation; resistance to inappropriate social pressure; negotiating solutions to conflict; seeking help when needed

Responsible Decision-Making: Accurately assessing risks; making decisions based on a consideration of all relevant factors and the likely consequences of alternative courses of action; respecting others; taking personal responsibility for one's decisions

(From Safe and Sound: An Educational Leader's Guide to Social and Emotional Learning Programs, 2003.)

Remember that learning is relationship-centered. Teachers should make sure they know their students by name, take time to talk with students individually, show concern for their academic progress, and create a caring classroom environment.

Many teachers and administrators contend that effort devoted to SEL may harm academic performance. However, addressing SEL helps schools provide students with a learning context in which students are less likely to behave in ways that harm their health, academic performance, and ability to stay in school. All educators want to create knowledgeable, responsible, and caring

students. SEL is an approach to learning that helps students achieve success in school and life.

References

Chen, X., K. Rubin, and D. Li. 1997. "Relation between Academic Achievement and Social Adjustment: Evidence from Chinese Children." *Developmental Psychology* 33: 518-525.

Collaborative for Academic, Social, and Emotional Learning (CASEL). 2003. *Safe and Sound: An Educational Leader's Guide to Social and Emotional Learning Programs.* Available at <www.casel.org>.

Feshbach, N., and S. Feshbach. 1987. "Affective Processes and Academic Achievement." *Child Development* 51: 1149-1156.

Hawkins, J. D. 1997. "Academic Performance and School Success: Sources and Consequences." Pp. 278-305 in *Enhancing Children's Wellness,* eds. R. P Weissberg, T. R Gullotta, R. L. Hampton, B. A. Ryan, and G. R. Adams. Thousand Oaks, Calif.: Sage.

Hawkins, J. D., J. Guo, K. G. Hill, S. Batfin-Pearson, and R. D. Abbott. 2001. "Long-term Effects of the Seattle Social Development Intervention on School Bonding Trajectories." *Applied Developmental Science* 5(4): 225-236.

Osterman, K. E. 2000. "Students' Need for Belonging in the School Community." *Review of Educational Research* 70:323-367.

Ryan, A., and H. Patrick. 2001. "The Classroom Social Environment and Changes in Adolescents' Motivation and Engagement during Middle School." *American Educational Research Journal* 38(2): 437-60.

Stevahn, L., D. W. Johnson, R. T. Johnson, and D. Real. 1996. "The Impact of a Cooperative or Individualistic Context on the Effectiveness of Conflict Resolution Training." *American Educational Research Journal* 33(3): 801-823.

Wang, M. C., G. D. Haertel, and H. J. Walberg. 1997. "Learning Influences." Pp. 199-211 in *Psychology and Educational Practice,* eds. H. J. Walberg and G. D. Haertel. Berkeley, Calif.: McCutchan.

Wilson, D. B., D. C. Gottfredson, and S. S. Najaka. 2001. "School-based Prevention of Problem Behaviors: A Meta-analysis." *Journal of Quantitative Criminology* 17:247-272.

Zins, J. E., R. P. Weissberg, M. L. Wang, and H. J. Walberg, eds. In press. *Building School Success through Social and Emotional Learning: Implications for Practice and Research.* New York: Teachers College.

The authors acknowledge and appreciate the support of the Academic Development Institute, the Ford Foundation, the Mid-Atlantic Regional Educational Laboratory for Student Success at Temple University, the Surdna Foundation, the U.S. Department of Education, and the William T. Grant Foundation.

Katharine Ragozzino is a projects coordinator at the Collaborative for Academic, Social, and Emotional Learning (CASEL). Hank Resnik is the Director of Communications at CASEL. Mary Utne-O'Brien is the associate director of CASEL. Roger P Weissberg is Professor of Psychology and Education at the University of Illinois at Chicago and the executive director of CASEL.

Reprinted with permission of *educational HORIZONS,* quarterly journal of Pi Lambda Theta Inc., International Honor Society and Professional Association in Education, P O Box 6626, Bloomington, IN 47401, Summer 2003, pp. 169-171.

Implementing a Research-Based Model of Cooperative Learning

ABSTRACT   The author used qualitative research methods to explore an 8th-grade mathematics teacher's personal definition of cooperative learning and the enactment of cooperative learning in his classroom according to that definition. Data collection involved interviews and classroom observations. The author used coding schemes and descriptive statistics for data reduction and analysis. Constructivist psychology provided the theoretical groundwork for conclusions based on consistency across interview and observational data. Results revealed that while the teacher implemented a research-based model of cooperative-learning instruction, he adapted the model for use in his classroom. Results also identified the teacher's prior experience and teaching context as factors that influenced his implementation of cooperative-learning instruction.

Key words: cooperative learning, implementation, qualitative research

CHRISTINE SIEGEL
Georgia State University

Cooperative learning involves groups of students working to complete a common task. It is a rich educational strategy because it affords elaborate student interactions. That richness makes cooperative learning a complex construct to study. Given its complexity, researchers have attempted to specify its methods and to control its implementation.

The preponderance of research on the outcomes and processes associated with cooperative learning suggests that it can effectively promote academic achievement and social skills development (Elmore & Zenus, 1992; Johnson & Johnson, 1978, 1982, 1983; Johnson, Johnson, Buckman, & Richards, 1985; Johnson, Johnson, & Stane, 1989; Johnson, Maruyama, Johnson, Nelson, & Skoi, 1981; Madden & Slavin, 1983; Nastasi & Clements, 1991, 1993; O'Melia & Rosenburg, 1994; Qin, 1992; Qin, Johnson, & Johnson, 1995; Slavin, 1983a, 1983b, 1985, 1987; Stevens & Slavin, 1995a, 1995b). In those studies, however, cooperative learning differed from what might happen in actual classrooms and schools. The researchers decided (a) which instructional methods to use for fostering cooperative learning, (b) the frequency and duration of cooperative learning lessons, (c) which activities and materials to use, and (d) the composition of student groups. Whereas those researchers considered experimental rigor in their decision making, teachers are more likely to consider (a) curriculum content, (b) available time and materials, and (c) student factors when they make such decisions.

Because of its potential to increase student academic achievement and social skills development, researchers have advocated the implementation of cooperative learning for school reform (Carnegie Council on Adolescent Development, 1989; Johnson & Johnson, 1983; Stevens & Slavin, 1995b). To researchers, the implementation of cooperative learning in reform settings has been construed as an issue of treatment fidelity. That is, re-searchers define successful implementation as adherence to a research-based model (Hertz-Lazarowitz, Ivory, & Calderon, 1993; Hintz, 1993; McCarty, 1993; Sapon-Shevin, 1992; Stevens & Slavin, 1995a, 1995b; Talamage, Pascarella, & Ford, 1984). That conceptualization emphasizes the standards of fidelity, effectiveness, and longevity typically used by researchers to judge the effectiveness of education reform, but it ignores the adaptations of reform practices valued by teachers (Cuban, 1996). In contrast to researchers who view variations in practice as signs of poor implementation, teachers view variation as evidence of creative problem solving (Cuban). If teachers likely modify cooperative learning as they implement it, the results of quasi-experimental studies of cooperative learning will have limited "generalizability" to real-life classrooms.

Grossen (1996) cautioned against recommending educational innovations based on the results of quasi-experimental studies with limited generalizability. She argued that in order to understand how new practices are integrated into existing school structures, research of instructional innovations in full context is needed. Potentially negative (or positive) side effects may be visible only over time in uncontrolled settings. Grossen identified cooperative learning as one such instructional innovation that, despite its research base, may produce different effects when implemented by practitioners rather than researchers.

Theoretical Framework

In the present study, constructivist psychology provides the framework for investigating the implementation of cooperative learning by teachers in real classrooms. Traditional constructivist psychology is rooted in the beliefs that knowledge is constructed (i.e., built on prior knowledge) and that knowledge is acquired through interactions with the environment (Perret-Clermont, Perret, & Bell, 1991; Vygotsky, 1978). A constructivist approach suggests that in the process of implementation, teachers are engaged in the active construction of knowledge about cooperative learning. Newly developed concepts will be reflected when cooperative learning is used in the classroom.

When teachers are trained to use cooperative learning, their understanding should be influenced by their existing knowledge of teaching practices and instructional methods and by their previous knowledge of current teaching contexts, including school structure, curriculum, and student characteristics. Through the mechanism of assimilation, teachers should reorganize the information that they receive about cooperative learning to fit their existing schema of teaching. In addition, the teaching schema should include cooperative learning.

As a result of changes in their mental frameworks, teachers should use new methods in the classroom. Teachers should internalize the resulting classroom experiences so those experiences contribute to their further understanding of cooperative learning. In some cases, teachers' understanding and subsequent use of cooperative learning may need to be altered to accommodate new information obtained through their experiences. Thus, a constructivist approach suggests that teachers' understanding of cooperative learning and the enactment of cooperative learning in their classrooms are related. Constructivism suggests that when teachers implement cooperative learning, they will not adhere precisely to researcher-developed models of cooperative learning.

Researchers who were interested in the education reform movement have used the constructivist approach to examine teachers' understanding and use of instructional innovations (Alexander, Murphy, & Woods, 1996; Ball, 1996), changes in new teachers' concepts of effective teaching (Jones & Vesiland, 1996), systematic mathematics reform (Grant, Peterson, & Shojgreen-Downer, 1996), and effects of subject content on efforts to restructure high schools (Grossman & Stodolsky, 1995). I located only one study, however, that considered the ways in which teachers think about and use cooperative learning in their classrooms. Antil, Jenkins, and Wayne (1998) used surveys and interviews to examine the prevalence, conceptualization, and form of cooperative learning employed by elementary school teachers. As one would expect from a constructivist point of view, teachers described their use of cooperative learning as modifications or adaptations of "more formal" research-based models. Antil and colleagues concluded that a chasm between researchers' and practitioners' approaches to cooperative learning existed, noting that few teachers were using recognizable models of cooperative learning. However, the researchers noted that their method did not allow them to identify the source of such differences. A further limitation of the Antil et al. study is that it relied solely on interviews and surveys. Classroom observations are required for one to complete the examination of implementation in real-life classrooms.

To summarize, the goal of many researchers who investigated cooperative learning has been to document its effectiveness. To that end, researchers have attempted to standardize the methods for using cooperative learning and control its implementations. As a result, little is known about cooperative learning as it is used in real-life classrooms. Although evidence suggests that teachers adapt research-based models of cooperative learning for use in their classrooms, teacher concepts of cooperative learning by teachers without researcher input and control are not well understood. Finally, the relationships between concepts and enactment have not been considered.

Method

Purpose

My purpose was to explore the implementation of cooperative learning by an expert eighth-grade mathematics teacher. Rather than examine the extent to which the teacher adhered to a research-based model, I, along with members of a larger research team,[1] described how he conceptualized and enacted cooperative learning instruction in his classroom. Specifically, we examined the teacher's personal definition of cooperative learning and the enactment of cooperative learning in his classroom according to that definition.

This study was part of a large project titled The Model Project for the Reform of Special Education in the Iroquois School District. (Iroquois is a pseudonym.) In that larger project, researchers documented the reform efforts and instructional innovations designed to change the overall education system of a school district.

During the reform process, schools in the Iroquois district adopted various reform initiatives; middle school teachers adopted a cooperative-learning initiative. To provide the staff development needed for implementing reform initiatives, the district administration established the position of project leader. The role of the project leader was twofold. He or she received training in the initiative and then used various methods to educate other teachers. An eighth-grade mathematics teacher was appointed as the cooperative-learning project leader (also referred to as the "teacher" in this study) to facilitate the implementation of cooperative learning in the middle school. He was taught how to use the Johnson and Johnson (1983) model of cooperative learning. After his initial training, he was involved in providing training to and consulting with teachers who used cooperative learning in their classes. In the present study, we examined the implementation of cooperative learning by the project leader.

Design

The author chose qualitative methods for this study to address the limitations of the previous implementation research. According to Miles and Huberman (1994), qualitative research is conducted through an intense or prolonged contact with a real-life setting. A main task of qualitative research is an explication of the ways in which persons in a particular setting understand, account for, take action, and otherwise manage their day-to-day situations. The researcher attempts to identify themes to describe persons in their contexts. Finally, although many interpretations of qualitative data are possible, conclusions are made on the basis of theory and internal consistency.

Prolonged contact between the Iroquois school district and faculty and graduate students from the University at Albany provided the groundwork for this study. For 5 years, researchers from the university collected data in the school district. Data collection included participating in and observing project leader meetings, observing middle school classes, and interviewing project leaders, middle school teachers, and middle school students. Through conversations with school district administrators, we identified critical research questions. From a broad initial interest in school reform, cooperative learning became the focus of this study.

Our main task was to explicate the ways in which the cooperative-learning project leader understood and used the cooperative learning in his classroom. Data collection involved interviews and observations for soliciting the teacher's perspective. The goal of data analysis was the identification of themes that explained the teacher's conceptualization and enactment of cooperative learning. Constructivist theory provided the framework for conclusions on the basis of consistency across interview and observational data.

Participant

Administrators in the Iroquois school district appointed an eighth-grade mathematics teacher as the district's cooperative-learning project leader. After receiving initial training in cooperative learning, he used cooperative learning in his eighth-grade mathematics classes and provided training to and consulted with other teachers who were using cooperative learning. He was viewed as the "cooperative learning expert" in the district. Other teachers referred to him as their "guru." For those reasons, the author chose the project leader as the participant in this study.

In addition to being the district's cooperative-learning expert, the project leader possessed several other interesting professional and personal characteristics. He taught eighth-grade mathematics students at a variety of levels, including remedial, general, and accelerated. Special education students were included in his remedial and general mathematics classes. The project leader had an inquisitive nature and motivation for professional development, which together resulted in his being best described as a lifelong learner. Although the project leader was near the end of his teaching career, he eagerly embraced new methods. In addition to his involvement in the cooperative-learning initiative, he explored ways to incorporate authentic assessment into his curriculum.

Interviews

To obtain information about the project leader's personal definition of cooperative learning, we interviewed him several times. We conducted two formal interviews at the start and at the end of the data collection period and developed the protocol for this study. The initial interview protocol, which is contained in Appendix A, is a semi-structured instrument intended to engage the teacher in conversation about cooperative learning. We developed follow-up interview questions based on data that we collected during the study for clarification purposes. Follow-up interview protocol is contained in Appendix B of this study. Both interviews were tape-recorded for later transcription and analysis.

In addition to the two formal interviews, we engaged in conversation with the project leader throughout the data collection period. During the informal conversations, the project leader provided information about his understanding of cooperative learning and explained the use of cooperative learning in his classroom. We recorded information from those informal conversations and considered it as data for analysis.

Observations

To obtain information about the enactment of cooperative learning in the project leader's classes, we conducted classroom observations. The observations focused on students in cooperative-learning groups during 40-min class periods. We observed six student groups—three groups from one general mathematics class and three groups from one accelerated mathematics class. We observed each group three times, totaling 18 observations, over a period of 10 weeks during the third marking period of the 1995–1996 school year. We did not observe remedial mathematics classes because the project leader said that he used cooperative learning less frequently in those classes.

To ensure that key events were not overlooked, the author developed a preliminary coding scheme along with another researcher who was examining cooperative-learning instruction in a high school in the Iroquois school district. On the basis of the literature and previous observations in the district, we identified the following broad categories of interest: (a) basic elements of cooperative learning; (b) grouping patterns; (c) presentation of content, learning tasks, material, and activities; and (d) evaluations of learning, classroom management, and classroom environment. During classroom observations, we recorded narrative field notes in 5-min intervals. We then coded observations by recording observed events in each category and modified and elaborated categories to account for all observed events.

Interrater agreement for the preliminary coding scheme and observation procedure was established; the researcher and I simultaneously observed classes. Using that scheme, we recorded field notes independently. We examined results for congruent evidence of each category identified; interrater agreement was 92%.

Data Analysis

To analyze the data specific to the current study, the researcher and I developed a more focused coding scheme. From the data organized in broad categories identified in the preliminary coding schema, two major categories of phenomena emerged as relevant: cooperative-learning methods and lesson plan format. Cooperative-learning methods included those aspects of instruction that were specific to cooperative learning; lesson plan format included those aspects of instruction that represented the project leader's general teaching style. We developed several subcategory codes to classify different types of events under each category. In the process of classification, we identified 20 cooperative-learning variables and 6 lesson plan variables; Table 1 contains a list of those variables.

Following the development of the coding scheme, we used descriptive statistical methods to analyze and reduce the emergent variables. We used the 18 class periods, which served as the units of observation, as the primary units for data analysis. Although some cooperative-learning methods were used in nearly all class periods, many of them were evident in only some of the classes

TABLE 1. Emergent Variables

Variable	Item
Cooperative learning	
Group discussion	Academic
	Off task
	Taking turns
	Discussing solutions
	Disagreements
	Solutions to disagreements
	Discuss with group
	Consult teacher/book
Individual accountability	Tests and quizzes
techniques	Individual assignments
Group interdependence	Assigned roles
techniques	Group test
	Group worksheets
	Verbal reminders
Social skills instruction	Teacher demonstration
techniques	Verbal directions
	Written directions
Debriefing techniques	Walk around and give feedback
	Sit and discuss functioning with group
	Give feedback at end of class
Lesson plan	
Type of activity	Whole class
	Small group
Review previous material	Teacher-led review
	Group review
New material presentation	Teacher led
Practice new skills	Group practice

that were observed. For that reason, we used frequency counts by class period to summarize the cooperative-learning variables. To obtain frequency counts, we determined the presence or absence of each cooperative-learning variable in each class period. For example, we counted 13 of the classes as including evidence of round-robin discussion between student group members (i.e., face-to-face interaction via turn taking). Frequency counts for cooperative-learning variables are shown in Table 2.

In contrast to the use of cooperative-learning methods that varied, the project leader's lesson plan format appeared consistent across multiple classes. Therefore, we determined that calculations of the amount of class time engaged for each lesson plan variable would be the most descriptive method. For each class period, we identified the number of minutes that we observed each lesson plan variable. To summarize the data further, we calculated the average number of minutes for each variable by dividing the total number of minutes across observations by total number of observations. For example, we recorded engagement in cooperative-learning activities as occurring for 360 min, which we calculated was an average of 20 min for each of the 18 classes observed. Average amount of time engaged for each lesson plan variable is shown in Table 3.

In the process of computing frequency counts and determining amount of class time engaged, we detected differences between the general mathematics class and the accelerated mathematics class. Although differences between groups within the same class were considered, these comparisons did not demonstrate a consistent pattern. For purposes of further analysis and comparison between types of classes, we calculated percentages for each of the cooperative-learning frequency counts and for each of the lesson plan class time averages. We calculated cooperative-learning percentages by dividing the number of classes for which each variable was observed by the total number of classes observed. Returning to the previous example, round-robin discussion between group members was evident in 72% of the classes observed. We calculated lesson plan percentages by dividing the average amount of class time by the total number of minutes per class (i.e., 40). For example, I found that cooperative-learning activities accounted for 50% of class time. Cooperative-learning percentages and lesson plan percentages are shown in Tables 2 and 3, respectively.

We next applied the coding scheme to transcripts of the teacher interviews. We used teacher descriptions of observed events to elaborate major themes and subcategory codes. In addition, we used quotes from the transcripts to explain (a) the teacher's understanding and use of emergent cooperative-learning and lesson plan variables in general and (b) differences in these variables between the two types of classes. I based my conclusions on consistency between observation and interview data.

Results

Analysis of observation and interview data supported three major findings. First, the project leader's conceptualization of cooperative learning was consistent with a research-based model. Second, as would be expected given a constructivist approach, the project leader adapted the research-based model for use in his classroom. Finally, we identified three distinct types of adaptations: (a) the project leader used personal techniques to implement cooperative learning, (b) implementation involved the integration of cooperative learning with the project leader's previous basic lesson plan, and (c) implementation differed between accelerated and general mathematics classes.

Personal Definition of Cooperative Learning

As revealed in the interview transcripts, the project leader's concept of cooperative learning reflected the Johnson and Johnson (1983) model in which he was trained. He defined cooperative learning as instruction that contained the five essential elements identified by Johnson and Johnson: (a) face-to-face interaction, (b) individual accountability, (c) positive group interdependence, (d) social skills instruction, and (e) debriefing. The project leader described *face-to-face interaction* as "equal participation and discussion between all group members." He identified *individual accountability* as "the part that makes most kids work, and do the job … whether it is a test, a quiz, or verbal questions, something that makes them know they each have to understand what's being taught." Also, he defined *positive group*

TABLE 2. Cooperative Learning Variables (Occurrence by Type of Class)

Cooperative learning variable	General classes (n = 9)		Accelerated classes (n = 9)		All classes (N = 18)	
	f	%	f	%	f	%
Academic discussion	9	100	9	100	18	100
Off-task discussion	4	44	1	11	5	28
Face-to-face interaction via turn taking	6	67	7	78	13	72
Disagreement during face-to-face interaction	3	33	7	78	10	56
Solution to disagreement via group discussion	1	11	6	67	7	39
Solution to disagreement via asking the teacher	2	22	0	0	2	11
Individual accountability via test/quiz	1	11	3	33	4	22
Individual accountability via individual assignment	2	22	1	11	3	17
Individual accountability via activity structure	9	100	4	44	13	72
Group interdependence via roles	0	0	1	11	1	6
Group interdependence via group test/quiz	0	0	2	22	2	11
Group interdependence via group worksheet	6	67	0	0	6	33
Group interdependence via verbal reminders	0	0	2	22	2	11
Social skills instruction via written directions	5	56	5	56	10	56
Debriefing via teacher comments during group work	4	44	5	56	9	50
Debriefing via teacher discussion with group	1	11	1	11	2	11

Note. n = number of classes observed; *f* = number of classes in which each variable was evident; % = percentage of total classes for which each variable was evident.

TABLE 3. Lesson Plan Variables (Minutes of Class Time by Type of Class)

Lesson plan variable	General classes (n = 9)		Accelerated classes (n = 9)		All classes (N = 18)	
	x	%	x	%	x	%
Whole-class activity	22	55	16	40	19	48
Cooperative-learning activity	16	40	24	60	20	50
Teacher-led review	12	30	8	20	10	25
Group review	0	0	8	20	4	10
Teacher presentation of new material	9	23	8	20	8.5	22
Group practice	16	40	20	50	18	45

Note. n = number of classes observed; *x* = average amount of class time in minutes for each variable; % = average percentage of total class time for each variable.

interdependence as "the idea that we sink or swim together, everyone has to understand and do the work." He described *social skills instruction* as teaching students "how to listen, how to speak, and practice taking turns" at the beginning of the school year. The project leader explained that he emphasized the social skills of "politeness and courtesy, showing respect for other people and their ideas" throughout the school year. Finally, he described *debriefing* as "the time at the end of the class to reinforce what was good and discourage what was bad," including academic and social aspects of group functioning.

Implementation of a Research-Based Model With Personal Techniques

Analysis of classroom observation data revealed that the teacher used specific techniques to implement each of the five elements of cooperative learning. Examples of the techniques

and percentages of classes in which they were observed are presented in Table 2. I observed face-to-face interaction in most classes as students took turns explaining problem solutions to the group. The teacher fostered individual accountability through individual tests and quizzes and structured activities. He used group worksheets to promote positive interdependence. Because I conducted observations in the second half of the school year, verbal directions and reminders were the most commonly observed method of social skills instruction. Finally, we observed that debriefing most often entailed the teacher providing general comments during group work.

Review of classroom observation data further revealed that the enactment of cooperative learning in the project leader's class involved the integration of the five elements with his basic lesson plan. This lesson plan consisted of review of previously learned material, introduction of new material, and practice of newly acquired skills. Data on the lesson plan variables are shown in Table 3. The teacher used cooperative learning primarily for practicing newly acquired skills and occasionally for reviewing previously learned material.

A typical lesson in the project leader's classes began with students sitting in rows facing forward. The project leader began with review. He announced answers to the previous night's homework or a recently administered quiz. Students checked to see if their answers were correct. The teacher demonstrated solutions to difficult items. In the accelerated mathematics classes, students compared and discussed homework answers with their group members.

Following review, the teacher often introduced new material. He outlined definitions of concepts and sample problems on the blackboard. The teacher used a type of guided practice to model solutions to sample problems. During that process, he demonstrated initial steps to a solution and then called on students to answer questions or provide the next step in the solution. For example, when demonstrating how the students could determine the area of a triangle, the teacher drew a triangle on the blackboard and announced the length of the base and the height. He then asked, "What's the formula for the area of a triangle?" When a student replied, "One-half base times height," the teacher wrote the formula on the board and asked, "What should I do next?" As students supplied the answers to his questions, the teacher completed the steps on the chalkboard. He often used that method to model several examples before he assigned students to small groups for continued practice.

Following the whole-class introduction of new material, the students typically worked in groups of 2 or 4 students to practice new skills. The project leader presented the assignment and directions for group work by writing them on the chalkboard or distributing a typed list. The assignment often included real-life applications of the new skills. For example, group practice problems on percentages and decimals consisted of calculating restaurant bills and determining the appropriate tip.

The students moved their desks from facing forward to facing their group members. Each group worked with one textbook or worksheet. Typically, one student who was the discussion leader read the problem to the group and verbalized the solution. Other group members wrote down the solution as it was explained. If a calculator were necessary to complete the problem, a second student in the group entered numbers and computed the answer as the first student described the solution process. If the group were required to submit one page of written answers to the teacher, a third student in the group took the responsibility for writing the answer. Students switched roles at the beginning of each problem. The textbook, the calculator, and the answer page were passed to other group members.

Most often, the process was enacted in each group for each question. Variations to the typical process occurred, however, when students did not understand the problem or when members disagreed about the solution described. When misunderstandings did occur, students (a) asked for clarification, (b) gave more detailed explanations, (c) tried different methods of problem solving and comparing answers, (d) referred to the textbook, or (e) asked the teacher for help.

During group practice, the teacher observed the students, monitored group progress, and provided help where needed. Occasionally, the teacher called out reminders for the students to "stay together," "help each other," and "take turns." As he walked around the classroom, he also stopped to provide feedback to groups about their process of interaction. Sometimes that feedback consisted of a verbal summary of the group process as seen by the teacher. On other occasions, the teacher returned a group worksheet or quiz with an academic grade and a group-process score. He explained how he had arrived at the score and offered suggestions for improving group functioning.

At the conclusion of the group activity, the teacher typically collected one worksheet or answer page per group. Sometimes he randomly selected one student's paper. Other times, the group had completed one paper to be submitted. Following group practice, the teacher often assigned homework problems for individual practice. If time were remaining in the class period, students moved their desks back into rows facing the blackboard and began the practice problems. On a few occasions, the teacher made concluding comments about the new skills that were practiced or described positive aspects of group functioning that he observed.

Effects of Context

In terms of the emergent variables, we noted differences between the general and accelerated mathematics classes. Although differences in individual variables were not large, taken together they represented a pattern of difference between the classes. That pattern was evident in the cooperative-learning variables and the lesson plan variables (see Tables 2 and 3, respectively).

With regard to lesson plan format, we noted differences between the two types of classes in the amount of time and type of activity for which each variable was used. For example, in the general mathematics classes, cooperative learning accounted for 40% of class time; 55% of class time was designated for whole-class instruction. In contrast, in the accelerated classes, 60% of class time was spent in cooperative-learning activities, and 40% of class time was spent in whole-class instruction. In the general mathematics classes, cooperative-learning activities were limited to practice of new skills. In contrast, cooperative-learning activities were used for review of previously learned material as well as practice of newly acquired skills in accelerated classes. Teacher-led review of previously learned material accounted for a greater percentage of class time in general (30%) than in accelerated mathematics classes (20%).

With respect to cooperative-learning methods, we noted differences between the two classes regarding methods for promoting individual accountability and group interdependence. To promote individual accountability, the teacher used individual assignments and structured activities more often in general classes (22% and 100%, respectively) than he did in accelerated classes (11% and 44%, respectively). He used worksheets to promote group interdependence in 67% of the observed general mathematics classes; no instances of group worksheets were observed in the accelerated mathematics classes.

In addition to teacher behavior, differences in student behavior between the two types of classes also were noted among the cooperative-learning variables. Disagreements during group discussion were observed less often in the general mathematics classes (33%) than in the accelerated mathematics classes (78%). When disagreements did occur, students in general mathematics classes asked the teacher for a solution twice as often as they solved the disagreement through group discussion (22% vs. 11%). In contrast, group solutions to disagreements were observed in most of the accelerated classes (67%), with no instance of asking the teacher.

We reviewed narrative notes for further analysis of the differences between general mathematics and accelerated mathematics students' approaches to disagreements. In the general mathematics classes, the discussion leader's method for solving a problem, as well as providing the solution, was typically viewed as correct and adopted by the group. On the few occasions when general mathematics students disagreed about the solution process, they adopted another member's method and solution as correct, referred to the textbook, or asked the teacher for help. In contrast, in the accelerated mathematics class, students in groups often disagreed with the discussion leader's method for solving a problem. Accelerated students suggested alternative solutions and discussed different possible solutions within the group. Often, more than one solution yielded the correct answer. Individual group members adopted different methods, but all agreed on one answer.

Perspective of the Project Leader

Data from interview transcripts provided insight about the project leader's (a) perspective on his adaptation of the Johnson and Johnson (1983) model, (b) integration of the model with his previous lesson plan, and (c) differences between the general and accelerated mathematics classes.

According to the project leader, his approach to cooperative learning differed from the Johnson and Johnson (1983) model in two ways. First, the project leader explained that he did not assign students to specific jobs. Rather, he suggested that students take turns and switch roles throughout the lesson. He believed that his approach encouraged each student to practice a variety of different skills. Second, he limited group size to two to four students. Whereas Johnson and Johnson recommended up to six or eight students in a group, the project leader believed that smaller group size better facilitated equal participation.

In terms of the integration of cooperative learning with his basic lesson plan, the project leader explained that he used cooperative learning in this manner because he had been trained to use cooperative learning only after teaching for 20 years. He added that if he had been trained in cooperative learning as a new teacher, he probably would have used it differently.

When planning a cooperative-learning lesson, the project leader considered the content that he would cover, as well as student ability. Differences in those factors between his general and accelerated mathematics classes might have accounted for observed differences in implementation. The project leader explained that when planning for cooperative-learning lessons, he first determined the lesson objective and then considered "how to do it in a cooperative way." He reported that objectives in the accelerated classes often required multiple-step problem solving that fit with cooperative-learning activities. When planning for review of previously learned material, the project leader also considered student ability. He said he often used cooperative learning for review activities in the accelerated classes because he was "confident at least one student in the group would have an accurate understanding" of the procedure or content. He admitted that he had less confidence in the ability of students in the general mathematics classes and suggested that he subsequently felt a need to use teacher-led instruction methods for review in those classes.

Conclusions

Because of its potential to increase student achievement and social skills development, cooperative learning has been advocated for school reform. Prior to such broad-based recommendations, however, Grossen (1996) identified a need for research in real-life classrooms, as opposed to researcher-controlled classes. In response to Grossen's recommendation, the author undertook the research reported here to demonstrate that the implementation of cooperative learning in real-life classrooms is a complex process, a point that despite the extensive previous research in cooperative learning appeared to be lacking. The findings of this study are consistent with Cuban's (1996) conclusion that teachers will adapt research-based models for use in their classroom, but they contrast with results reported by Antil and colleagues (1998) in which research-based models of cooperative learning were unrecognizable among practitioner approaches. We expanded Cuban's conclusion by identifying sets of factors that influenced variations in teachers' implementation of cooperative learning. Interpreted within a constructivist framework, results support the conclusions that in real life, the project leader used personal techniques derived from prior knowledge and experience to implement research-based models of cooperative learning and that use of these personal techniques was influenced by his teaching context.

Consistent with Cuban's (1996) conclusion that, in practice, teachers' use of instructional innovations will vary, the project leader's approach to cooperative learning demonstrated that he adapted the Johnson and Johnson (1983) model for his classroom. A constructivist framework suggests that one set of factors influencing a teacher's use of cooperative learning will be his or her prior knowledge of teaching and experience as a teacher. The effect of the project leader's prior knowledge and experience was evident in his basic lesson plan. During his 20 years as a mathematics teacher, the project leader had developed a personal structure for executing his classes. For implementation purposes, the project leader used cooperative learning within his existing lesson plan format. A constructivist framework suggests that a second set of factors influencing a teacher's use of cooperative learning is his or her teaching context. The project leader's explanation of differences in implementation between his accelerated and general mathematics classes revealed that his use of cooperative learning was influenced by lesson content and perceived student ability.

The results have implications for educators who are interested in school reform. Rather than making broad-based recommendations to use cooperative learning, proponents of this instructional initiative should consider designing professional development programs based on a constructivist framework. Specifically, in-service training should include activities that encourage teachers to describe their knowledge of teaching and their daily teaching practices, strategies that help teachers incorporate cooperative learning (or other instructional innovations) into their daily practices, and opportunities for teachers to consider specific contextual variables that may influence their use of cooperative learning.

A unique contribution of this study was that the project leader implemented a research-based model of cooperative learning without researcher supervision. That finding contrasts with results reported by Antil and colleagues (1998) in which practitioner approaches differed significantly from research-based models. One possible explanation for the discrepancy is that the research methodology and theoretical orientation used in this study might have allowed for the detection and explanation of a research-based model, which was not evident through the methods used by Antil and colleagues. Those researchers used interview and survey methods to obtain information about teachers' use of cooperative-learning techniques. Although those methods yielded considerable information about implementation, the researchers reported that they were left to infer some things about their practice from illustrations of cooperative-learning lessons that were described in earlier studies. The use of observations and follow-up interviews in the current study left little to researcher inference. Furthermore, Antil and colleagues evaluated practitioner approaches by using a checklist of criteria derived from the research literature on cooperative learning. In this study, I used a theoretical framework that allowed for examination and explanation of the relationship between a research-based model and a practitioner's approach.

There are several alternative explanations for the discrepant findings between this study and the Antil et al. (1998) research, each of which has implications for practice. First, in the Antil et al. study, practitioners were trained in several different research-based models of cooperative learning. In contrast, the Iroquois School District adopted one model of cooperative learning—the Johnson and Johnson (1983) model. The use of other models was not encouraged. Antil and colleagues hypothesized that when teachers are exposed to multiple methods of cooperative learning, they are likely to conclude that there is great latitude in what is considered cooperative learning. The results of this study suggest that fidelity of implementation can be increased when teacher attention is focused on one model.

A second alternative explanation for the greater fidelity of implementation that I observed was the congruence between the project leader's belief system and the Johnson and Johnson (1983) model of cooperative learning. The project leader reported that the goals of education are to promote academic, as well as social, development of students. To the project leader, cooperative learning was one logical way to attain those goals. That finding has implications for educators who are interested in school reform, as well as

researchers who are studying cooperative-learning implementation. To facilitate use of cooperative learning (and other instruction innovations), one might need to consider the congruence between teacher philosophy and novel methods. Knowledge of teacher beliefs about education might allow researchers to predict which teachers will be more likely to implement cooperative learning.

Finally, the project leader's implementation of the Johnson and Johnson (1983) model could be related to the fact that he has taken ownership of the model. In the position of "project leader," he has been assigned a leadership role. He defined that role as modeling the implementation of the Johnson and Johnson approach to cooperative learning. To encourage the use of cooperative learning, the project leader invited newly trained teachers to observe how he used cooperative learning in his classroom. Thus, the present results suggest that in order to promote the use of cooperative learning for school reform, teachers need to share in the ownership of the instructional innovation.

Discussion and Future Directions

The major limitation of this study is that conclusions were drawn on the basis of data from 1 teacher. Considered an expert in cooperative learning, the project leader is not a typical teacher. Thus, the current findings may have limited generalizability to other teachers. Nonetheless, results of this study demonstrated that teacher implementation of cooperative learning is influenced by prior knowledge and experience and current teaching context. In addition, findings suggest that use of cooperative learning can be promoted by (a) teacher attention to one model, (b) congruence between teacher philosophy and instruction methods, and (c) teacher ownership of the innovation.

In contrast to previous implementation studies that emphasize the researcher's perspective, I provide a description of the practitioner's perspective of cooperative learning implementation. To obtain that perspective, I used (a) qualitative methods of prolonged engagement in a natural setting, (b) collaboration with the participants in defining the research agenda, (c) multiple data collection methods, and (d) data analysis based on consistency of findings within a theoretical framework. Those aspects of the current design are strengths of this study. The design provided methods for the exploration of expected variation in the teacher's use of cooperative learning, specifically differences between practitioner and researcher approaches. In addition, the design allowed for detection of unanticipated variations, most notably within-teacher differences in implementation.

Researchers need to use a constructivist framework and qualitative methods to examine cooperative learning. Data provided by other teachers would allow researchers to further explore the notion that variations in teacher implementation are related to differences in prior knowledge and experience and would confirm the conclusion that within-teacher differences in implementation are related to differences in teaching contexts. Further exploration also would reveal other factors that influence teacher implementation of cooperative learning.

NOTE

1. The pronoun "we" is used throughout the article to indicate that this research was conducted by the author and by members of a larger research team, including faculty and graduate research assistants, unless otherwise specified.

REFERENCES

Alexander, P. A., Murphy, P. K., & Woods, B. S. (1996). Of squalls and fathoms: Navigating the seas of educational innovation. *Educational Researcher, 25*, 31–36.

Antil, L. R., Jenkins, J. R., & Wayne, S. K. (1998). Cooperative learning: Prevalence, conceptualizations, and the relation between research and practice. *American Educational Research Journal, 25*, 419–454.

Ball, A. (1996). Envisioning new possibilities for the reform of urban schools. *Educational Researcher, 25*, 37–39.

Carnegie Council on Adolescent Development. (1989). *Turning points: Preparing American youth for the 21st century*. Washington, DC: Carnegie Corporation of America.

Cuban, L. (1996). Myths about changing schools and the case of special education. *Remedial and Special Education, 17*, 75–82.

Elmore, R. F., & Zenus, V. (1992). Enhancing social-emotional development of middle school gifted students. *Roeper Review, 24*, 5–11.

Grant, S. G., Peterson, P. L., & Shojgreen-Downer, A. (1996). Learning to teach mathematics in the context of systematic reform. *American Educational Research Journal, 33*, 509–541.

Grossen, B. (1996). Making research serve the profession. *American Educator, 20*(3), 7–27.

Grossman, P. L., & Stodolsky, S. S. (1995). Content as context: The role of subjects in secondary school teaching. *Educational Researcher, 24*, 5–11.

Hertz-Lazarowitz, R., Ivory, G., & Calderon, M. (1993). *The bilingual cooperative learning reading and composition (BCIRC) project in the Yselta independent school district: Standardized test outcomes*. Baltimore, MD: Johns Hopkins University, Center for the Effective Schooling of Disadvantaged Students.

Hintz, J. L. (1993, April). *Teacher implementation of change*. Paper presented at the annual meeting of the American Educational Research Association, Atlanta, GA.

Johnson, D. W., & Johnson, R. T. (1978). Cooperative, competitive, and individualistic learning. *Journal of Research and Development in Education, 12*, 3–15.

Johnson, D. W., & Johnson, R. T. (1982). Effects of cooperative and individualistic instruction on handicapped and non-handicapped students. *The Journal of Social Psychology, 118*, 257–268.

Johnson, D. W., & Johnson, R. T. (1983). The socialization and achievement crisis: Are cooperative learning experiences the answer? *Applied Social Psychology, 4*, 199–224.

Johnson, D. W., Johnson, R. T., Buckman, L. A., & Richards, P. S. (1985). The effect of prolonged implementation of cooperative learning on social support in the classroom. *The Journal of Social Psychology, 119*, 405–411.

Johnson, D. W., Johnson, R. T., & Stane, M. B. (1989). Impact of goal and resource on interdependence of problem-solving success. *The Journal of Social Psychology, 129*, 621–629.

Johnson, D. W., Maruyama, G., Johnson, R. T., Nelson, D., & Skoi, N. (1981). Effects of cooperative, competitive, and individualistic goal structures on achievement: A meta-analysis. *Psychology Bulletin, 89*, 47–62.

Jones, M. G., & Vesiland, E. M. (1996). Putting practice into theory: Changes in the organization of preservice teachers' pedagogical knowledge. *American Educational Research Journal, 33*, 91–117.

Madden, N. A., & Slavin, R. E. (1983). Cooperative learning and social acceptance of handicapped students. *Journal of Special Education, 17*, 171–182.

McCarty, T. L. (1993). *Creating conditions for positive change: Case studies in American Indian education*. Proceedings of the National Association for Bilingual Education Conferences.

Miles, M. B., & Huberman, A. M. (1994). *Qualitative data analysis: An expanded sourcebook* (2nd ed.). Thousand Oaks, CA: Sage.

Nastasi, B. K., & Clements, D. H. (1991). Research on cooperative learning: Implications for practice. *School Psychology Review, 20*, 110–131.

Nastasi, B. K., & Clements, D. H. (1993). Motivational and social outcomes of cooperative computer environments. *Journal of Computing in Childhood Education, 4*, 15–43.

O'Melia, M. C., & Rosenburg, M. S. (1994). Effects of cooperative homework teams on the acquisition of mathematics skills by secondary students with mild disabilities. *Exceptional Children, 60*, 538–548.

Perret-Clermont, A. N., Perret, J. F., & Bell, N. (1991). The social construction of meaning and cognitive activity in elementary school children. In L. B. Resnick, J. M. Levine, & S. D. Tesley (Eds.), *Perspectives on socially shared cognition* (pp. 41–62). Washington, DC: American Psychological Association.

Qin, Z. (1992). *A meta-analysis of the effectiveness of achieving higher order learning tasks in cooperative learning vs. competitive learning*. Unpublished doctoral dissertation, University of Minnesota.

Qin, Z., Johnson, D. W., & Johnson, R. T. (1995). Cooperative vs. competitive efforts and problem solving. *Review of Educational Research, 65*, 129–143.

Sapon-Shevin, M. (1992). Cooperative learning and middle schools: What would it take to really do it right? *Theory into Practice, 33*(3), 183–190.

Slavin, R. E. (1983a). When does cooperative learning increase student achievement? *Psychological Bulletin, 94*, 429–445.

Slavin, R. E. (1983b). *Cooperative learning*. New York: Longman.

Slavin, R. E. (1985). An introduction to cooperative learning research. In R. E. Slavin, S. Sharam, R. H. Lazarowitz, C. Webb, & R. Schmuck (Eds.), *Learning to cooperate, cooperating to learn* (pp. 5–15). New York: Plenum.

Slavin, R. E. (1987). Developmental and motivational perspectives on cooperative learning: A reconciliation. *Child Development, 58*, 1161–1167.

Stevens, R. J., & Slavin, R. E. (1995a). The cooperative elementary school: Effects on students' achievement, attitudes, and social relations. *American Educational Research Journal, 32*, 321–351.

Stevens, R. J., & Slavin, R. E. (1995b). Effects of a cooperative learning approach in reading and writing on academically handicapped and nonhandicapped students' achievement and attitudes. *Elementary School Journal, 3*, 121–134.

Talamage, H., Pascarella, E. T., & Ford, S. (1984). The influence of cooperative learning strategies on teacher practices, student perceptions of the learning environment, and academic achievement. *American Educational Research Journal, 21*, 163–179.

Vygotsky, L. S. (1978). *Mind in society*. Cambridge, MA: Harvard University Press.

---

*Address correspondence to **Christine Siegel**, Department of Counseling and Psychological Services, Georgia State University, MSC 6A0915, 33 Gilmer Street, SE Unit 6, Atlanta, GA 30303-3086. (E-mail: csiegel@gsu.edu)*

APPENDIX A
Initial Teacher Interview Protocol

1. What grade level and subject do you teach?
2. How many years have you been teaching?
3. How long have you been at (Iroquois) school district?
4. Describe your students in general.
5. Describe the cooperative learning training that you received.
6. What is your personal definition of cooperative learning?
7. How did you arrive at that definition?
8. What do you think are the essential elements of cooperative learning? Why?
9. What do you think are the goals of education?
10. What are the goals of (subject area) instruction?
11. How is your definition of cooperative learning consistent with those goals?
12. What do you believe is the teacher's role in cooperative-learning instruction?
13. What do you believe is the student's role during cooperative-learning instruction?
14. What are the advantages/disadvantages of cooperative learning?
15. Why do you use cooperative learning?
16. How does cooperative learning vary in your classes and why?
17. For what tasks do you think cooperative learning is the most appropriate? Why?
18. How do you plan for cooperative-learning lessons?
19. What factors influence your planning decisions?
20. How do you group your students for cooperative-learning lessons?
21. How do you arrange your classroom during cooperative-learning lessons?
22. What materials do you use during cooperative-learning lessons?
23. What do your students produce during cooperative-learning lessons?
24. When and how often do you use cooperative learning? Why?
25. For cooperative learning activities, what aspects of student functioning do you assess? How?

APPENDIX B
Follow-up Teacher Interview Protocol

1. What is your personal definition of cooperative learning?
2. What do you mean by positive group interdependence?
3. How do you establish individual accountability?
4. What does social skills instruction mean to you?
5. Describe face-to-face interaction.
6. What do you consider debriefing?
7. What do you think are the advantages of cooperative-learning instruction?
8. What are the disadvantages of cooperative-learning instruction?
9. How do you plan for cooperative-learning lessons?
10. What does a typical cooperative-learning lesson look like in your class?
11. Why do you use cooperative learning this way?

Teachers Bridge to Constructivism

Kathryn Alesandrini and Linda Larson

People learn while doing," says the constructivist update of an old adage. Teachers, however, often learn without doing when it comes to learning about constructivism and related teaching methods. Many teachers have not participated in a constructivist-type classroom or even seen it modeled, so they tend to teach as they were taught. Until teachers experience constructivism themselves, they may not be equipped to plan and facilitate constructivist activities by their students. In this article, we discuss and illustrate the value of using a constructivist bridge-building activity to help teachers make the transition to constructivist classrooms.

What Teachers Need to Know about Constructivism

Constructivism has become a popular term that can refer to many things, including the way teachers teach and the way students learn. Some have dubbed the constructivist approach that we describe "radical constructivism" (Spiro et al. 1991), but we refer to it simply as "constructivism." Indeed, the constructivist approach posits a radical departure from traditional teaching practices (Brooks and Brooks 1993; Jonassen, Peck, and Wilson 1999; Kafai and Resnick 1996; Lambert 1995) as the following basic tenets of constructivism illustrate:

Learning results from exploration and discovery. Constructivists see learning as a process of actively exploring new information and constructing meaning from the new information by linking it to previous knowledge and experience. Throughout the learning experience, meaning is constructed and reconstructed based on the previous experiences of the learner. In the constructivist paradigm, the teacher's role is not to lecture or provide structured activities that guide students, step by step, to mastery of some teacher-imposed goal. Instead, teachers in a con-

structivist classroom are called to function as facilitators who coach learners as they blaze their own paths toward personally meaningful goals.

Learning is a community activity facilitated by shared inquiry. Collaboration and cooperative inquiry have proved to be effective educational strategies, yet conventional methods often limit interactivity to cooperative discussion groups. Constructivism favors collaborative work groups that actually work together interactively to accomplish shared goals. Collaboration goes beyond cooperation, because it requires learners to reflect upon and share their insights with the group (cf. Henderson 1996; Driscoll 1994). Collaboration facilitates each member's ability to see problems from multiple perspectives or different points of view. Group members constantly "negotiate meaning" during the constructivist activity to adjust to the developing solution of the problem. The product evolves and changes as a result of the interaction between group members.

Learning occurs during the constructivist process. Rather than requiring an understanding *before* applying that understanding to the construction of something, students in a constructivist classroom learn concepts *while* exploring their application. During this application process, students explore various solutions and learn through discovery. Learners play an ongoing, active, and critical role in assessment. Teachers evaluate end products in traditional assessment, but the constructivist approach to evaluation emphasizes self-assessment. In constructivist classrooms, learners articulate what they have learned as it relates to their prior knowledge. In fact, it is through the self-assessment activities of reflection and verbalization that learners actually realize the meaning of what they have experienced.

Another major difference from the traditional approach is that assessment is done throughout the entire learning process, not just at the end. Formative evaluation (assessment that occurs throughout the learning process) therefore plays a key role in helping learners as they experiment during the constructivist activity. To the constructivist, the process of evaluation is as important, if not more important, than the outcomes of evaluation.

Learning results from participation in authentic activities. Constructivists believe that learning should be based on activities and problems that students might encounter in the "real world." In traditional classrooms, however, activities often are decontexualized to the point that they bear little resemblance to meaningful, authentic activities.

Outcomes of constructivist activities are unique and varied. A traditional hands-on activity that is teacher guided often results in student products that essentially "all look alike." In contrast, constructivism posits that learners create knowledge from new information in light of their previous experiences. Since each learner brings a distinct background of experience, results of constructivist projects will differ. Typically, no two products from a constructivist activity look anything alike.

Constructivism clearly represents a fundamental change in all aspects of the teaching and learning process. Teachers cannot be expected to embrace these changes without adequate preparation involving hands-on experience and modeling in the adoption of these new methods.

Why Bridge Building for Teachers?

Based on the premise that the best way to learn about constructivism is to experience it firsthand, we devised a simple constructivist activity—building a paper bridge—that teachers could experience to learn the basics about constructivism. A follow-up authentic activity allowed the teachers to take the next step and develop a constructivist activity for their own classrooms.

In the bridge-building activity, teachers work in small groups to plan, construct, and reflect on building a paper bridge (figures 1-3). The challenge is for each group to create, using only newspaper, tape, and rubber bands, a unique structure strong enough to hold at least a 16-ounce bottle of water. Prior to actually building the bridge, each group specifies several additional objectives and develops a scoring rubric.

The bridge-building activity consists of a 10-step "constructivist activity" process closely related to the design technology process (Dunn and Larson 1998). The constructivist activity process entails five major components: investigation, invention, implementation, evaluation, and celebration. Investigation includes the development of context, clarification of the task, and inquiry through questioning and research. Invention consists of planning and realizing or building a model. Implementation sometimes overlaps with invention and occurs through the process of realizing or building a model and later modifying it as needed. Evaluation refers to the activities of testing, interpreting, and reflecting on the experience. The last major component, celebration, is described below along with the preceding nine steps illustrated with comments from several teams of teachers.

1. *Contextualizing.* Working in small groups, teachers draw on their past experiences in deciding how the team will proceed. "Bridges are normally sturdy; they have support poles. We integrated multiculturalism in our design by designing human figures as the support base" (Team A).

2. *Clarifying.* Teams determine what they needed to know to build the bridge. "We need to know how bridges are structured, how weight is held by a bridge" (Team A).

3. *Inquiring.* Teachers conduct research by posing relevant questions and searching credible sources for answers. "One member of our group found a Web site that outlined all components and typical designs of bridges. From our research we have concluded that our bridge will consist of vertical and horizontal beams" (Team B).

4. *Planning.* Teachers sketch their plans on paper and may even build a test-case model. "Since we decided to create the bridge using beams, we used pencils, pens, and tape to create our premodel. Our premodel proved that our bridge would be easy to construct, functional, and sturdy" (Team B).

Team A

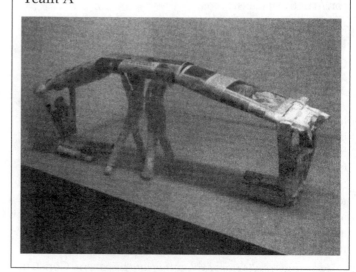

5. *Realizing.* Using only newspaper, tape, and rubber bands, teachers construct bridges to achieve their objectives. No two bridges look alike since groups are not following a cookbook-type recipe for the project. Each group produces a unique creation to achieve its own objectives. "Once we knew how to assemble the bridge from our premodel, we started the construction process" (Team B).

6. *Testing.* Teachers test the model bridge and record observations. "We tested our model by placing a 20-ounce water bottle on top, and it held up fine as long as the dolls' legs were in the right position. But there was not enough diagonal support" (Team A). "Our bridge did not hold the bottle of water. We decided to create a frame for our bridge" (Team C).

7. *Modifying.* Teachers make necessary modifications to achieve stated objectives. "We repositioned the two center supports to face a different direction and better support the bridge" (Team A). "We added the frame which worked" (Team C).

8. *Interpreting.* Teachers interpret the results of their tests. "This is a great model for building a bridge out of newspaper. This bridge was easy to construct, sturdy, and structurally sound, fast to construct, and looked very much like a bridge" (Team B).

9. *Reflecting.* Teachers evaluate their bridges by applying the rubrics they created earlier. "I felt our bridge represented our group, because we had a Latina, an Asian, a Caucasian, and an African American. We used newspapers in English, Spanish, Japanese, and Chinese. I really felt passionate and proud of our bridge. I felt that its main purpose, which was to represent different cultures coming together, was clear" (Team A).

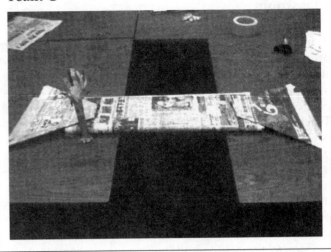

Team C

constructivism. Of the four teams cited here, 82 percent found the activity "very or extremely useful." Over 90 percent of the participants say they enjoyed the social interaction of the activity.

Assessment within a Constructivist Framework

Teachers actively engage in the assessment process from the beginning, when they specify objectives and write rubrics to score the results of the constructivist activity. As stated, the only imposed requirement is that the bridges be strong enough to hold at least a 16-ounce bottle of water. In addition to the strength criterion, each group specifies three other objectives and related criteria for their rubrics. Often the criteria reflect the values, experiences, and backgrounds of group members. For example, Team A selected multiculturalism as one of their criteria to reflect the cultural diversity of the group. Their bridge looked like a parade float, with an arch supported by human figures from different cultures. Other criteria have included design creativity, design simplicity, bridge span, conservation of resources, and a host of other factors. Each group of teachers uses the rubric they initially create to score their final product. Not surprisingly, each group generally achieves a perfect or near-perfect score. After scoring their own team's bridge, teams participate in a "gallery walk" in which each team uses both their own and the other teams' rubrics to score the bridges produced by others. Teachers realize that their "excellent" work would likely receive a poor or failing grade when held to a different standard. For example, Team B's more traditional bridge structure with beams did not adhere to the multicultural or creativity criteria of Team A and would therefore be graded down if Team A's rubric were used to score it. The experience helps teachers appreciate the limitations of traditional grading practices in a constructivist classroom.

Team B

10. *Celebration.* Teachers in the small groups share their accomplishments by presenting results to the larger group. "We shared our rubric with the group, explaining our criteria for a [top] score of 4. The group agreed that we earned a 4" (Team A). Another teacher wrote, "Celebration and sharing was the best! It gave us a sense of pride and accomplishment."

Most teachers who participate in this 10-step bridge-building activity report that it helps them learn about

Taking the Next Step: Constructivism in the Classroom

In the follow-up activity to bridge building, teachers prepare an authentic constructivist activity for their own students on any topic of their choosing. The only requirements are that the activity be authentic and that it address one or more skills in the subject matter frameworks. Teachers work individually to structure an activity according to the same 10-step process they used to build the paper bridge. They begin by setting objectives and creating a scoring rubric that both they and their students may use to assess the final products. They then plan the activity, create a model, and reflect upon their respective projects. Finally, they try out the activity with their own students.

Prior to the bridge-building activity, a common misconception among teachers is that a hands-on activity is synonymous with a constructivist activity. Many hands-on activities, of course, don't allow for multiple solutions and outcomes—students are expected to follow the teacher's directions and create a copy-cat product rather than generating their own unique productions. While less than one-third of teachers surveyed felt confident that they could create constructivist activities for their students prior to the bridge-building activity, over 90 percent successfully created a true constructivist activity on the first try after it. We believe that this success results from the modeling they experienced during the bridge-building activity.

The benefits of constructivism are reinforced as teachers observe the impact of their authentic constructivist projects on their students. A high school math teacher, for example, devised a geometry activity that requires students to construct 3-D scenes or objects from three-dimensional polygons. The teacher's model consisted of a small paper-flower garden. Students used paper pyramids, cubes, decahedrons, and more to construct a wide array of unique characters: a dinosaur, clown, rat, puppy, flower, turtle, and so forth. In another project, a sixth grade teacher created a phonogram chart to help students understand hieroglyphics used by the ancient Egyptians. Her students worked in teams to create unique charts, which they used to code their own names and common words. These teachers reported that their students enjoyed the constructivist project, just as they had, and gained a sense of accomplishment in what they created.

Most teachers find it difficult to create a truly constructivist activity for their students. As one participant explained, "The activity that we created was very difficult. It really makes you examine your subject thoroughly and understand how difficult these concepts are for students to master. The inclusion of constructivist activities greatly increases a student's involvement in the topic."

The bridge-building activity helps teachers literally see the unique productions that result when team members bring their own background and experience to bear on the creative process. They witness that constructivism goes beyond the typical hands-on activity. They also learn that assessment is relative—grades result from applying a rubric that relates to specified criteria or objectives. Perhaps most important, teachers appreciate the pure enjoyment joined with a sense of pride and accomplishment that result from constructivist activities.

Key words: constructivism, classroom activities, assessment, teaching process, facilitation

REFERENCES

Brooks, J. G., and M. C. Brooks. 1993. *The case for constructivist classrooms.* Alexandria, VA: Association for Supervision and Curriculum Development.

Driscoll, M. P. 1994. *Psychology of learning for instruction.* Boston, MA: Allyn & Bacon.

Dunn, S., and R. Larson. 1998. *Design technology: Children's engineering.* Philadelphia: The Palmer Press.

Henderson, J. G. 1996. *Reflective teaching.* 2nd ed. Englewood Cliffs, NJ: Merrill.

Jonassen, D. H., K. L. Peck, and B. G. Wilson. 1999. *Learning with technology: A constructivist approach.* Columbus, OH: Prentice Hall.

Kafai, Y. B., and M. Resnick. 1996. *Constructionism in practice: Designing, thinking and learning in a digital world.* Mahwah, NJ: Lawrence Erlbaum Associates.

Lambert, L. 1995. *The constructivist leader.* New York: Teachers College Press.

Spiro, R., P. Feltovich, M. Jacobson, and R. Coulson. 1991. Knowledge representation, content specification, and the development of skill in situation-specific knowledge assembly: Some constructivist issues as they relate to cognitive flexibility and hypertext. *Educational Technology* 31 (9): 22–25.

Kathryn Alesandrini is a professor of instructional design and technology at California State University, Los Angeles. Linda Larson is a full-time lecturer in the Department of Educational Psychology at California State University, in Long Beach.

From *The Clearing House,* January/February 2002, pp. 118-121. Reprinted with permission of the Helen Dwight Reid Educational Foundation. Published by Heldref Publications, 1319 Eighteenth St., NW, Washington, DC 20036-1802. © 2002.

Constructivism and Block Scheduling:

Making the Connection

The student-centered learning practices associated with constructivism could benefit from the increased class time that block scheduling offers. But, Mr. Hackmann observes, too often block scheduling is adopted as an end in itself, not as a tool to facilitate a specific pedagogical approach.

BY DONALD G. HACKMANN

THROUGHOUT much of the 20th century, classroom instructional practices tended to follow behaviorist learning theory, which regards teaching as a highly diagnostic and prescriptive process. The behaviorist approach typically advocates the presentation of curriculum content in small increments followed immediately by student practice. Behaviorism continues to play a significant role in today's classrooms, where many teachers rely primarily on direct instruction methods.[1]

In the past few decades, a growing body of research on cognitive processing has made inroads into classroom practices. Whereas behaviorism primarily focuses on the teacher's role as transmitter of knowledge, a different view of learning has emerged—constructivism—that emphasizes the student's role in the learning process. Building upon the work of Jean Piaget, Lev Vygotsky, and others, constructivist theory is based on the premise that individuals must be socially engaged in learning—actively creating knowledge from their existing knowledge base, beliefs, and personal experiences.[2] Constructivists advocate learners' participation in context-bound, real-world problem solving and call upon students to engage in meta-cognition.

Although constructivism appears to be attracting a growing following, it has not been readily embraced at the secondary school level. Arguably, constructivist practices may be implemented more easily in self-contained elementary classrooms or through the interdisciplinary teaming approach commonly used in middle schools. High schools tend to be departmentalized and more concerned with curriculum, and secondary teachers may be less willing to employ methods perceived as reducing the emphasis on content.

An additional factor limiting attention to the constructivist movement at the secondary level could be the involvement of many faculties in another restructuring initiative—block scheduling. Much of the recent literature on high school education has addressed alternative scheduling, which may have overshadowed other educational trends. In the 1980s and 1990s, national task forces denounced the excessive rigidity of the traditional high school schedule—uniform 45- to 55-minute periods—and its stifling effect on classroom practices.[3] In response, many faculties created block models that divide the instructional day into 80- to 110-minute class sessions, roughly double the length of traditional daily-period classes.

Block scheduling has become established practice in high schools, but many educators are unable to explain why it is superior to traditional daily-period formats and what results it is intended to produce. Currently, there is no solid theoretical foundation for block scheduling, and there also is limited research documenting its effectiveness in improving student achievement.[4] Many teachers have struggled to make effective use of the longer time blocks because they lack a conceptual understanding of the purpose for these extended time frames and of how they may facilitate learning.

Constructivism and block scheduling appear to have occurred in parallel, yet independent, movements. However, there are many points of convergence between these two concepts. Here I present the commonalities between the two movements and demonstrate that block scheduling should logically be considered as a vehicle to promote constructivist practices.

CONSTRUCTIVIST DIALOGUE AT THE SECONDARY SCHOOL LEVEL

In contrast to the well-developed teaching models based on behaviorism, constructivism is an emerging theory that is currently descriptive, not prescriptive, in nature.[5] To promote greater comprehension and mastery of content, constructivists emphasize depth of understanding rather than a superficial treatment of subject matter. Educators are encouraged to refashion their roles to become learning facilitators—acting as a "guide on the side" instead of a "sage on the stage." As teachers strive to create constructivist environments, they initially may find it difficult to grasp how specific instructional methods align with constructivist principles. However, as this theory evolves, it seems likely that more refined constructivist models will emerge.

When describing the shift from teaching to learning, educators sometimes revert to catch phrases—such as "hands-on learning," "active engagement of the learner," and "depth over breadth"—without explaining how these concepts can be applied in the classroom and without attributing them to constructivism. For example, two principles of the Coalition of Essential Schools—"less is more" and "student as worker,"[6]—promote constructivist beliefs, and the National Association of Secondary School Principals recommends that teachers act "as coaches and as facilitators of learning to promote more active involvement of students in their own learning."[7] Neither organization, however, suggests strategies that educators can use to implement these concepts or cites constructivist theory as the pedagogical foundation for these practices.

Some writers warn that constructivists are overzealous in promoting learner-centered practices, arguing that behaviorist models are necessary in certain instructional situations and that hands-on approaches are not easily developed in every discipline.[8] The key is to strike an appropriate balance so that teacher-directed and student-centered learning activities complement one another. However, secondary teachers may find it difficult to maintain this equilibrium, especially when addressing the content standards now mandated in 49 states. A complicating factor is the excessive number of standards identified by various professional organizations. Although the standards movement, ironically, was heavily influenced by constructivism,[9] teachers may fall back on direct instruction as an efficient means to effect at least a superficial treatment of an immense amount of subject content.

Although the topic of scheduling does not appear frequently in the constructivist literature, a few writers have expressed the desirability of increased time to facilitate constructivist practices. For example, observing that structure frequently drives practice, Richard Elmore notes that teachers find it difficult to implement constructivist strategies within rigid, discrete time frames.[10] Elmore and Mark Windschitl advocate for larger blocks to facilitate the use of constructivist instructional strategies.[11]

HISTORICAL OVERVIEW AND EMERGENCE OF BLOCK SCHEDULING

Prior to the 1900s, American high schools and academies were characterized by significant flexibility. Subjects were offered in varied formats—each course differing in the number of days each week in which instruction was delivered.[12] In 1909, in an effort to eliminate inconsistencies among institutions, the College Entrance Examination Board adopted the Carnegie unit, which mandated a total of 120 hours of classroom instruction to be delivered in 40- to 60- minute classes during an academic year of 36 to 40 weeks.[13] This drive toward standardization was influenced by the scientific management era, which emphasized efficiency, mass production, and work uniformity. The daily-period schedule was created during this time as an organizational solution to the problem of efficiently educating large numbers of students.

Much of the published literature on block scheduling tends to focus primarily on issues having to do with school climate or implementation—pedagogy typically receives only cursory treatment.

Scheduling models remained relatively unchanged until the introduction of modular scheduling in the late 1950s. Instructional responsiveness was the hallmark of this model, since class sessions could be structured according to the number of modules (10, 15, or 20 minutes in length) needed to teach a concept.[14] The model afforded varied course formats, with classes meeting daily or scattered throughout the week in differing lengths. Modular scheduling peaked in the early 1970s, when approximately 15% of the nation's high schools used this approach.[15] However, variations in class sessions meant that many students were unscheduled and unsupervised at various times throughout the school day, leading to potential disciplinary problems. Consequently, although it is still used in a small number of schools today, flexible modular scheduling faded from the secondary scene in the late 1970s, and most schools returned to daily-period scheduling.

In the late 1980s, critics began challenging the wisdom of daily-period models, arguing that they reinforce the use of lecturing, contribute to excessive fragmentation of the instructional day, discourage in-depth exploration, and inhibit curriculum integration. Block scheduling emerged partly in response to these criticisms, although charting the birth and development of the block-scheduling movement is a difficult task. Shared through such administrative venues as conference presentations, educational publications, and professional networking, block scheduling was rapidly proliferating by the mid-1990s. In Virginia, for example, the percentage of blocked high schools leaped from 2% to 33% in only two years' time.[16]

In the past 20 years, various block formats have been piloted in secondary schools, including hybrids that incorporate both block and daily-period features. Two approaches have emerged as the most common: the 4x4 semester plan, in which students complete four classes each semester for a total of eight courses per year, and the eight-block alternating-day model, in which students receive instruction in one-half of their courses on alternate days and continue in these courses throughout the year. The most recent estimates indicate that approximately 30% of the nation's high schools now use some form of block scheduling,[17] although implementation levels vary regionally.

Faculties implement block scheduling for numerous reasons, which include providing course flexibility, enhancing the quality of students' educational experiences, improving instructional strategies, providing enhanced time for learning, improving the school climate, stimulating curriculum reform, and addressing staffing needs.[18] Surveys indicate that blocks improve teacher morale, increase student satisfaction, and enhance the quality of teacher/student relationships.[19] Much of the published literature on block scheduling, however, tends to focus primarily on issues having to do with school climate or implementation—pedagogy typically receives only cursory treatment.

WHERE BLOCK SCHEDULING AND CONSTRUCTIVISM CONVERGE

In many schools, the decision to adopt a block schedule is made after extensive study and dialogue, from which the faculty develops a comprehensive understanding of the reasons for initiating the change. However, as they go about restructuring, many educators do not seem to have fully interconnected the dimensions of teaching, the process of learning, and the organization of the school day. For example, principals of blocked schools often express a desire to increase opportunities for hands-on learning, yet they do not cite constructivism to support this aim.[20] In fact, many secondary principals and teachers are unaware of constructivist theory, and they frequently are at a loss to explain how scheduling adjustments are intended to promote improved student learning.

In other schools, the change may result from a unilateral administrative decree, possibly because block scheduling appears to be the latest fad, or because it is intended

to spearhead a dramatic transformation in the school, or because principals "just want to shake things up."[21] There may have been relatively little discussion among the faculty and administration concerning why block scheduling may be desirable or what problem the change is intended to resolve.

The adoption of block scheduling has significant instructional implications, but some teachers may resist changing their classroom practices because they do not fully understand how longer time frames can facilitate learning. Furthermore, without adequate professional development, even supportive and well-intentioned teachers may incorporate ineffective methods. As Linda Wyatt warns, "block scheduling without fundamental changes in instruction is merely longer blocks of the same old stuff."[22] Even when faculties implement block scheduling simply to improve their school climate, they cannot ignore the instructional ramifications of their decision. Regardless of the factors prompting it, once the decision is made to adopt block scheduling, teachers are immediately confronted with the hard reality of figuring out how to use the blocks effectively.

> Absent a solid theoretical framework, secondary school faculties cannot fully grasp the purpose of these longer instructional units and are likely to view block scheduling as the end itself rather than a means to an end.

It is on this point of instructional practices that the block-scheduling literature begins to show striking similarities to constructivist principles, even though constructivist theory is rarely mentioned. Various reports related to changing instructional strategies in blocked classrooms discuss an increased emphasis on depth of understanding and a "less is more" approach to curriculum content.[23] Two leading block-scheduling proponents, Robert Lynn Canady and Michael Rettig, note that one of the goals of the high school scheduling reform movement—although it is far down on their list—is to "allow and encourage the use of active teaching strategies and greater student involvement."[24] Yet they fail to mention constructivist theory in any of their published works on the topic of scheduling, including their edited text devoted to instructional strategies in a block.

A variety of instructional approaches and models of teaching are mentioned in both the block-scheduling and constructivist literature, including cooperative learning, problem-based learning, curriculum integration, teaming, and performance assessments. These techniques, however, are presented in significantly different frameworks. In constructivist writings, instructional strategies are explained as vehicles for creating and sustaining a classroom culture that promotes "deep and elaborate understandings of subject matter."[25] In contrast, block-scheduling proponents typically use a very limited frame of reference, describing how blocks can be subdivided "for purposes of survival of both teachers and students."[26] In the block-scheduling dialogue, the emphasis is frequently placed on reducing reliance on the lecture method and eliminating boredom rather than on structuring a culture that promotes student learning.

WHICH COMES FIRST?

One segment of the block-scheduling debate focuses on a perennial "chicken or egg" issue: Should a scheduling change initiate new instructional practices, or should pedagogical beliefs dictate the scheduling model to be implemented? Canady and Rettig appear to support the former position, asserting, "We strongly believe that scheduling is an untapped resource which can serve as a catalyst for school improvement."[27] Michael Wronkovich argues the latter position:

> Often, schools start with the concept of changing to blocking, then try to assess what outcomes are being observed from the change. It would be preferable to ask first what changes the school is seeking to make collectively, then to assess if alternative scheduling is one means for accomplishing these goals.[28]

Kurt Lewin once said, "There is nothing so practical as good theory."[29] One also may argue a corollary to Lewin's statement: there is nothing so impractical as the absence of theory. In examining the block-scheduling phenomenon, it is apparent that this movement was conceived without a clear theoretical foundation. Absent a solid theoretical framework, secondary school faculties cannot fully grasp the purpose of these longer instructional units and are likely to view block scheduling as the end itself rather than a means to an end.

Lacking in theory, many blocked schools may fall victim to the same problem that has besieged schools using the traditional model: the schedule's rigid format does not provide the flexibility to promote varied teaching/learning activities. Uniform blocks force all disciplines into larger time frames, even though some subjects actually may benefit from shorter instructional times.[30] For some disciplines, several spaced and evenly distributed practices may be far more effective in facilitating student learning than a few massed practice sessions.[31] Time allocations are arbitrary, regardless of whether they are 50- or 100-minute intervals. When the schedule is chosen without a pedagogical foundation, teachers may continue to focus on the *act* of teaching—simply "filling up" the blocks—instead of concentrating on the *process* of learning, as promoted by constructivist principles.

In this era of school accountability, educators would be remiss if they adopted reforms without considering the potential effects on student performance. To date, the research base related to block scheduling and student achievement is relatively sparse and inconclusive. Ann Pliska, Matt Harmston, and I found no differences in mean composite ACT scores between students in eight-period, eight-block, alternating-day schools and 4x4 block schools.[32] In a study conducted by the College Board, students enrolled in semester-blocked schools generally scored lower on Advanced Placement (AP) examinations than did students in yearlong classes.[33] While blocked schools in Virginia demonstrated greater percentile gains in the subjects of reading and math than did traditionally scheduled schools,[34] students in blocked schools in Canada scored lower on the Third Provincial Assessment of Science than did their peers in traditional schools.[35]

One limitation of these studies is that they were unable to control for variations in teaching strategies in individual classrooms. The Texas Education Agency acknowledged this problem in its investigation of the impact of scheduling on student achievement, which used a variety of standardized metrics, including the SAT, ACT, AP examinations, and the Texas Assessment of Academic Skills. After controlling for numerous variables—including school size, student demographics, staff characteristics, and attendance—the report concluded that

> available data on high school schedules used in Texas public education do *not* systematically explain or account for variation in overall high school performance. When school context is taken into account, other factors, including *how effectively* students engage in the teaching-learning process, appear to matter more than the particular length of the class periods.[36]

Theoretical principles must drive practice, and, as Elmore strongly advocates, "principles of practice should drive structure."[37] It seems reasonable to conclude that faculties should first reach consensus on theories of the teaching/learning process and then create a scheduling structure that allows them to put their theories into practice.

MAPPING BLOCK SCHEDULING ONTO CONSTRUCTIVIST THEORY

Block-scheduling discussions are currently on the periphery of constructivist dialogue, but the two movements should become more closely aligned. The rationale is simple: when educators' pedagogical beliefs are too far removed from the primary theoretical source, the result is often the adoption of distorted tertiary-source practices that are not an adequate match for school purposes.[38] Such is the case with block scheduling. Secondary educators who lack a comprehensive theoretical foundation may mistakenly assume that the catch phrases and slogans, created as metaphors to illustrate the theory, are the actual theory. Consequently, teachers may implement a host of relatively minor and disconnected instructional strategies simply to fill time, without considering their appropriateness as learning tools or fully comprehending how they connect in the "big picture" to promote student learning.

Constructivism has been described as "a culture—a set of beliefs, norms, and practices that constitute the fabric of school life."[39] Once the connection between block scheduling and constructivism becomes firmly rooted in the consciousness of teachers and part of ongoing professional dialogue, block scheduling can be considered as part of a comprehensive model that is intended to help transform the classroom. The emphasis will shift from the *event* of implementing a block schedule to the *process* of creating a constructivist school culture.

In such a culture, teachers purposefully select strategies during lesson preparation, not because they are "hands-on" and use up time, but because they are designed to help students construct meaning from the curriculum. Instructional techniques—such as interdisciplinary teaming, curriculum integration, direct instruction, problem-based learning, cooperative learning, Socratic seminars, and inquiry learning—and assessment strategies are viewed collectively through a constructivist lens and are employed when they support learning in the constructivist culture that is being created within the school.

My aim here has not been to retrofit the block-scheduling movement to constructivist theory. Rather, my purpose has been to demonstrate that block scheduling, as a stand-alone initiative, has no theoretical foundation and does not constitute a school reform. It should simply be considered as one component of a comprehensive and concurrent package of reforms. Constructivist theory helps faculties to understand the interrelationships of teaching and learning and to recognize how the schedule can be an essential tool in creating a culture that promotes improved student achievement.

Practice should drive structure. Constructivist principles should be the driving force behind any decision to implement block scheduling.

Notes

1. Allan C. Ornstein and Francis P. Hunkins, *Curriculum: Foundations, Principles, and Issues*, 3rd ed. (Needham Heights, Mass.: Allyn and Bacon, 1998).

2. Jacqueline G. Brooks and Martin D. Rettig, *In Search of Understanding: The Case for Constructivist Classrooms* (Alexandria, Va.: Association for Supervision and Curriculum Development, 1993).

3. *Prisoners of Time: Report of the National Educational Commission on Time and Learning* (Washington, D.C.: National Educational Commission on Time and Learning, 1994).

4. Richard F. Bowman, "If Block Scheduling Is the Answer, What Is the Question?," *Clearing House*, vol. 71, 1998, pp. 242-44.

5. Peter W. Airasian and Mary E. Walsh, "Constructivist Cautions," *Phi Delta Kappan*, February 1997, pp. 444-49.

6. Coalition of Essential Schools, "Ten Common Principles," www.essentialschools.org/aboutus/phil/10cps/10cps.html.

7. *Breaking Ranks: Changing an American Institution* (Reston, Va.: National Association of Secondary School Principals, 1996), p. 21.

8. Airasian and Walsh, op. cit.; and Karen R. Harris and Steve S. Graham, "Memo to Constructivists: Skills Count, Too," *Educational Leadership*, February 1996, pp. 26-29.

9. William G. Cunningham and Paula A. Cordeiro, *Educational Administration: A Problem-Based Approach* (Needham Heights, Mass.: Allyn and Bacon, 2000).

10. Richard F. Elmore, "Teaching, Learning, and School Organization: Principles of Practice and the Regularities of Schooling," *Educational Administration Quarterly*, vol. 31, 1995, pp. 355-74.

11. Ibid.; and Mark Windschitl, "The Challenges of Sustaining a Constructivist Classroom Culture," *Phi Delta Kappan*, June 1999, pp. 751-55.

12. Burton W. Gorman, *Secondary Education: The High School America Needs* (New York: Random House, 1971).

13. John D. McNeil, *Curriculum: A Comprehensive Introduction*, 5th ed. (New York: Harper-Collins, 1996); and Ornstein and Hunkins, op. cit.

14. J. Lloyd Trump and Dorsey Baynham, *Focus on Change: Guide to Better Schools* (Chicago: Rand McNally, 1961).

15. Jeri Goldman, "Flexible Modular Scheduling: Results of Evaluations in Its Second Decade," *Urban Education*, vol. 18, 1983, pp. 191-228.

16. Robert L. Canady and Michael D. Rettig, *'Block Scheduling': A Catalyst for Change in High Schools* (Princeton, N.J.: Eye on Education, 1995).

17. Michael D. Rettig and Robert L. Canady, "The Effects of Block Scheduling," *School Administrator*, March 1999, pp. 14-16, 18-20.

18. Donald G. Hackmann, "The Status of High School Scheduling in Illinois," *Mid-Western Educational Researcher*, Spring 1999, pp. 25-31.

19. Daniel C. Buckman, B. B. King, and S. Ryan, "Block Scheduling: A Means to Improve School Climate," *NASSP Bulletin*, May 1995, pp. 9-18.

20. Hackmann, op. cit.

21. Tony Wagner, "Change as Collaborative Inquiry: A 'Constructivist' Methodology for Reinventing Schools," *Phi Delta Kappan*, March 1998, p. 515.

22. Linda D. Wyatt, "More Time, More Training: What Staff Development Do Teachers Need for Effective Instruction in Block Scheduling?," *School Administrator*, September 1996, pp. 16-18.

23. Jodi Benton-Kupper, "Can Less Be More? The Quantity Versus Quality Issue of Curriculum in a Block Schedule," *Journal of Research and Development in Education*, vol. 32, 1999, pp. 168-77; and Wyatt, op. cit.

24. Canady and Rettig, p. 12.

25. Windschitl, p. 754.

26. Canady and Rettig, p. 210.

27. Ibid., p. 29.

28. Michael Wronkovich, "Block Scheduling: Real Reform or Another Flawed Educational Fad?," *American Secondary Education*, June 1998, pp. 1-2.

29. Kurt Lewin, *Field Theory in Social Science: Selected Theoretical Papers* (New York: Harper and Row, 1951), p. 169.

30. Wronkovich, pp. 1-6.

31. Lorin W. Anderson and Herbert J. Walberg, *Timepiece: Extending and Enhancing Learning Time* (Reston, Va.: National Association of Secondary School Principals, 1993); and Wronkovich, op. cit.

32. Ann-Maureen Pliska, Matt T. Harmston, and Donald G. Hackmann, "The Relationship Between Secondary School Scheduling Models and ACT Assessment Scores," *NASSP Bulletin,* May 2001, pp. 42-55.

33. *Block Schedules and Student Performance on AP Examinations: Research Notes, RN-03* (New York: Office of Research and Development, The College Board, 1998).

34. Yvonne V. Thayer and Thomas L. Shortt, "Block Scheduling Can Enhance School Climate," *Educational Leadership,* December 1998-January 1999, pp. 76-81.

35. David J. Bateson, "Science Achievement in Semester and All-Year Courses," *Journal of Research and Science Teaching,* vol. 27, 1990, pp. 233-40.

36. *Block Scheduling in Texas Public High Schools* (Austin: Office of Policy Planning and Research , Division of Research and Evaluation, Texas Education Agency, 1999), p. 24.

37. Elmore, p. 370.

38. Thomas J. Sergiovanni, *Leadership for the Schoolhouse* (San Francisco: Jossey-Bass, 1996).

39. Windschitl, p. 752.

DONALD G. HACKMANN is an associate professor in the Department of Educational Leadership and Policy Studies, Iowa State University, Ames.

Using Data to Differentiate Instruction

In an age of standards, using assessment data to differentiate instruction is essential.

Kay Brimijoin, Ede Marquissee, and Carol Ann Tomlinson

At Redlands Elementary School, Ms. Martez's 5th graders are studying the math concept of greatest common factor.[1] Following an interactive lesson, students participate in a self-assessment procedure that Ms. Martez has created. Using a car windshield metaphor, she asks,

> How many [of you] are clear as glass about how greatest common factor works? How many have bugs on your windshield? How many have windshields covered with mud? (Brimijoin, 2002)

On the basis of their spontaneous self-assessment of "glass, bugs, and mud" and their earlier work on greatest common factor, Ms. Martez assigns students to three follow-up activities. With only a few exceptions, the students' self-assessment matches what Ms. Martez had determined from her pre-assessment.

Because the group of students who are as "clear as glass" understands and can apply greatest common factor at both the conceptual and skill levels, she has these students use a Euclidean algorithm to find the greatest common factor in a series of exercises. A group of "buggy" students—who understand the basic concept of greatest common factor, but still need to build their confidence through application—play a greatest common factor game that Ms. Martez has created. And she sends the "muddy" group to sort factors in a giant Venn diagram constructed of two hula-hoops. This oversized graphic organizer provides a kinesthetic and interpersonal learning experience for those who need additional practice to master the basic concept and skills.

During this time, Ms. Martez offers support and answers questions using a red-yellow-green cup system to prioritize student requests for assistance. A student sets a red cup on his or her desk to say "I can't go on without help." A yellow cup means that the student has questions but isn't completely blocked, and a green cup means that the student understands what he or she is doing. Two students tell Ms. Martez they are "really buggy *and* muddy," and she immediately announces the opening of a "math clinic" where she works on intensive, explicit instruction.

Because Ms. Martez had devoted time at the beginning of the year to talk with her students about the importance of gathering assessment data directly from them, students engage in their tasks smoothly and do not question groupings or complain about assignments. She had modeled the windshield strategy and together she and her class had created a generic rubric for each degree of understanding. Teaching students this self-assessment technique helped accustom them to instruction differentiated by readiness and structures that support student-centered learning (Tomlinson, 1999).

Three-Dimensional Data Collection

For Ms. Martez, informal and formal data about student learning not only shape instruction but also determine its effectiveness. She uses multiple methods of data collection and views the process as dynamic and continuous. She sees her role as data collector in three dimensions: to determine students' prior understanding and achievement, to track their responses to moderate challenges, and to measure their outcomes against expected performance goals (Brimijoin, 2002; Bruner, 1963; Tomlinson, 1995).

Pre-Assessment

Ms. Martez uses a wide array of pre-assessments when teaching new content. During a math lesson introducing basic algebra concepts, for instance, she asks students,

> What do you suppose it means to think algebraically? Take out your math logs and write, even if you write that you don't know.

Oral questioning, written journal prompts, objective tests, webbing, K-W-L (What do you *know*? What do you still *want* to know? What did you *learn*?) charts, group discussions, and brainstorming sessions provide rich data about students' existing schema, including critical misconceptions (Bransford, Brown, & Cocking, 2000).

Moderate Challenges

Ms. Martez believes that because students differ in their grasp of key concepts, she must modify her instruction to help them build knowledge, refine skills, and apply understandings on increasingly sophisticated tasks (Wiggins & McTighe, 1998). Assessment helps her modify instruction so that each student is appropriately challenged. She uses paper-and-pencil or performance-based formative assessments, including objective tests or quizzes, quickwrites, essays, and open-ended problems, varying the type according to the content being studied. She also develops a clear sense of what the culminating assessment will be when she first lays out the lesson or unit.

Rather than seeing assessment as an end-of-lesson or end-of-unit phenomenon, Ms. Martez incorporates it at the beginning, at the end, and everywhere in between.

Ms. Martez gives her students "task cards," which specify the steps in a learning process or experience. These cards include a set of directions for a task in order to facilitate independent learning and nurture autonomy. For example, each of Ms. Martez's learning groups had task cards with step-by-step directions to guide them through their assignments on greatest common factor. The task cards also frequently include rubrics that spell out performance expectations on assignments.

At the end of a lesson, students write in their journal a one-line description or an answer to a question about what they have learned in the lesson. Their responses are "exit tickets" for formative or ongoing assessment to help the teacher evaluate the effectiveness of a lesson design and keep instruction focused on key learning goals and individual needs.

Standards Testing

Teaching in a grade that requires state standardized assessments forces Ms. Martez to reconcile her "gotta get it covered and memorized by testing time" mentality and her belief in concept-centered differentiated instruction. She confesses to feeling conflicted about working wholeheartedly in two seemingly contradictory worlds of teaching and learning.

Three weeks before state standards testing, Ms. Martez asks students to go through their math books and select topics that they have mastered and those that need more work. She reflects on the results and decides to set up centers on such topics as

fractions, place value, geometry, and statistics, cycling students through centers related to their areas of need, and assigning "experts" to assist their peers.

Using Assessment to Target Learner Needs

Ms. Martez uses questioning and observing to differentiate instruction and ensure that her instruction is a good match for the varied needs of her students (Brimijoin, 2002). She adjusts questions or performance tasks to be more structured for those who are struggling with a concept and more abstract for those who have mastered the concept. Rather than seeing assessment as an end-of-lesson or end-of-unit phenomenon, Ms. Martez incorporates it at the beginning, at the end, and everywhere in between.

Ms. Martez invests much time and energy in mapping the "start and finish" by first constructing a big picture of assessment results that students bring with them. By the 5th grade at Redlands Elementary, students have one set of state standards test scores from 3rd grade and one set of nationally standardized scores from 4th grade. Ms. Martez enters all these scores on a spreadsheet. During individual conferences, Ms. Martez guides students in setting target goals for their progress and areas of emphasis for her instruction. At the end of the year, she enters all 5th grade scores from state standardized tests and calculates the percentage gains for each student and for the class overall.

Informal and formal data about student learning not only shape instruction but also determine its effectiveness.

At the end of this past year, 74 percent of her students passed the reading assessment, an overall gain of 27 percentage points over their 3rd grade test results; 58 percent passed math, a gain of 5 percentage points; 58 percent passed social studies, a gain of 24 percentage points; and 74 percent passed the science assessment, a gain of 32 percentage points (Brimijoin, 2002). Ms. Martez attributes the improvement in test score results chiefly to her use of pre-assessment, self-assessment, and ongoing assessment to differentiate instruction for individual learning needs:

The facts stuck because they were scaffolded into existing information, taught at the students' readiness levels, hooked in with interests, and nailed down with instruction targeted to the students' strongest learning styles.... Differentiation works in a standardized testing world.... We can't afford not to do it and expect to meet state standards, especially in low socioeconomic areas like Redlands. (Brimijoin, 2002, p. 263)

Ms. Martez uses the results of test score analysis to reflect on her teaching, comparing her curriculum design and instruction from one year to the next, noting strengths as well as weaknesses, and identifying questions that still need answering in order to refine her practice (Zeichner & Liston, 1996).

The students are also data collectors. They accept responsibility for monitoring their own progress and see that they have a role in shaping instruction. Ms. Martez weaves information gleaned from journal responses with formative quiz and test results. She sees assessment as a powerful tool to be used through the whole process of teaching and learning; one that demands the same kind of evaluation skills that good teachers use for effective management.

Ms. Martez advises other teachers that carefully articulated, continuous assessment that drives curriculum design "maximizes teaching time, streamlines instruction, and facilitates learning for all students." She insists that assessment is not "just another plate added to the 12-piece service," but a means of enhancing student and teacher performance.

Note

1. This article uses pseudonyms for the teacher and school.

References

Bransford, J., Brown, A., & Cocking, R. (Eds.). (2000). *How people learn: Brain, mind, experience, and school.* Washington, DC: National Academy Press.

Brimijoin, K. (2002). *A journey toward expertise in differentiation: A preservice and inservice teacher make their way.* Unpublished doctoral dissertation. University of Virginia, Charlottesville.

Bruner, J. (1963). *The process of education.* New York: Vintage Books.

Tomlinson, C. (1995). *Differentiating instruction for mixed-ability classrooms*. Alexandria, VA: ASCD.

Tomlinson, C. (1999). *The differentiated classroom: Responding to the needs of all learners*. Alexandria, VA: ASCD.

Wiggins, G., & McTighe, J. (1998). *Understanding by design*. Alexandria, VA: ASCD.

Zeichner, K., & Liston, D. (1996). *Reflective teaching: An introduction*. Mahwah, NJ: Lawrence Erlbaum Associates.

Kay Brimijoin is an assistant professor at Sweet Briar College, Sweet Briar, VA 24595; brimijoin@sbc.edu. **Ede Marquissee** teaches 6th grade at Summit Middle School, 4509 Homestead Road, Fort Wayne, IN 46814; emarquissee@sacs.k12.in.us. **Carol Ann Tomlinson** is a professor at the Curry School of Education, University of Virginia, Ruffner Hall, Charlottesville, VA 22904; cat3y@virginia.edu

UNIT 5
Motivation and Classroom Management

Unit Selections

Key Points to Consider

- Discuss several ways to motivate both at-risk and typical students. What difference is there?

- Why should motivational style be consistent with instructional techniques?

- How are motivation and classroom management related?

- Discuss several ways to discipline both typical students and those with exceptionalities.

- How are classroom management and discipline different? Discuss whether discipline can be developed within students, or whether it must be imposed by teachers, supporting your argument with data derived from your reading.

Student Website

www.mhcls.com/online

Internet References

Further information regarding these websites may be found in this book's preface or online.

Canada's Schoolnet Staff Room
http://www.schoolnet.ca/home/e/

I Love Teaching
http://www.iloveteaching.com

The Jigsaw Classroom
http://jigsaw.org

North Central Educational Regional Laboratory
http://www.ncrel.org/sdrs/

Teaching Helping Teachers
http://www.pacificnet.net/~mandel/

The term *motivation* is used by educators to describe the processes of initiating, directing, and sustaining goal-oriented behavior. Motivation is a complex phenomenon, involving many factors that affect an individual's choice of action and perseverance in completing tasks. Furthermore, the reasons why people engage in particular behaviors can only be inferred; motivation cannot be directly measured.

Several theories of motivation, each highlighting different reasons for sustained goal-oriented behavior, have been proposed. We will discuss two of them: humanistic and cognitive.

Humanistic approaches to motivation are concerned with the social and psychological needs of individuals. Humans are motivated to engage in behavior to meet these needs. Abraham Maslow, a founder of humanistic psychology, proposes that there is a hierarchy of needs that directs behavior, beginning with physiological and safety needs and progressing to self-actualization. Some other important needs that influence motivation are affiliation and belonging with others, love, self-esteem, influence with others, recognition, status, competence, achievement, and autonomy.

The dominant view of motivation in the educational psychology literature is the cognitive approach. This set of theories proposes that our beliefs about our successes and failures affect our expectations and goals concerning future performance. Students who believe that their success is due to their abilities and efforts are motivated toward mastery of skills. Students who blame their failures on inadequate abilities have low self-efficacy and tend to set ability and performance goals that protect their self-image.

In this unit's first selection, Marge Scherer focuses on how to encourage a love of learning. She reflects on a conversation with Mihaly Csikszentmihalyi and his concept of "flow" in which a high level of challenge is met with the skills to meet the challenge. In the second article, Howard Margolis and Patrick McCabe show the interconnection between motivation and self-efficacy. They suggest that teachers can improve self efficacy by "stacking the deck for success," if they teach needed learning strategies and facilitative attributions, reinforce effort and persistence, and help students create personal goals. In the final article about motivation, Denise Clark Pope and Richard Simon, explore the potential negative impacts on adolescents of increased focus and pressure for high academic achievement and success in school.

No matter how effectively students are motivated, successful teachers are those that also establish and maintain a classroom environment that supports successful teaching and learning. Classroom management is more than controlling the behavior of students or disciplining them following misbehavior. Instead, teachers need to develop skills which include effective preplanning of lessons, deliberate introduction of rules and procedures, appropriate assertiveness, ongoing monitoring of student behavior, providing consistent feedback to students, and a set of specific, consistently enforced consequences.

The next four articles address specific classroom management issues facing teachers today. The first article, "When Children Make Rules," shows how constructivism extends to classroom management. The next article by Robert and Jana Marzano emphasizes the importance of quality student-teacher relationships as a basis for classroom management. The third article presents proactive strategies for handling discipline problems that do occur, so that the situation is kept from escalating. The final article in this section speaks to the subject of corporal punishment in the classroom as a means of discipline, and how children's rights must be protected.

Do Students Care About Learning?

A Conversation with Mihaly Csikszentmihalyi

Learning to enjoy the intrinsic rewards of hard work is essential to successful human development, Mihaly Csikszentmihalyi, author of Becoming Adult: How Teenagers Prepare for the World of Work, *tells us. Here he talks with* Educational Leadership *about how to help students seek out the challenging and engaging activities that will propel them on their way toward becoming productive adults.*

Marge Scherer

In your study, you identified students who stood out from the crowd because they, more than their peers, could find enjoyment in both work and play. You also found students who were disengaged and passive about most of the activities they participated in. What was the context of your longitudinal study?

With the help from a grant from the Alfred P. Sloan Foundation, we identified 1,000 children who were in 6th, 8th, 10th, and 12th grades in 12 school districts from Orlando, Florida, to Long Beach, California, and everywhere in between. Nine years later, we are still following some of the participants as young adults, although a much smaller group of them.

We selected students randomly. We were not looking for children who enjoyed school or did not enjoy school. We just tried to get as much of a cross-section as possible. We developed questionnaires and interviewed these students, but we obtained most of our data through giving each student a programmable pager for a week. This pager would go off eight times a day, early morning to 11 P.M., at random moments. Whenever the pager signaled, the students would take out a little booklet and write where they were, what they were doing, what they were thinking about, their level of concentration, how happy they were, and how creative they felt when doing different activities.

They reported about 30 times during the week, so we received about 30,000 reports. And that allowed us to begin to see these children's experiences, the feelings and thoughts they had during the day, both at school and out of school. For instance, every time the pager went off, they had to say whether what they were doing was more like play, more like work, or like neither work nor play.

Was life more like work or play for these teenagers?

About 30 percent of the time they stated that it was like work; 30 percent of the time, they said that what they were doing was like play; 30 percent neither; and they reported that for 10 percent of their time, what they were doing was like both work and play.

In your follow-up studies, you concluded that students who often say that what they are doing is like both work and play are more likely to go on to college or make a successful transition to work.

Those students who say that whatever they do is more like work seem to do well in high school. Although they say that what they are doing is work and they don't enjoy it at the moment, they record on the response sheet that the activity is important to their future. So they understand that, "Okay. This is work. It's not pleasant. But it will profit me in the future."

It's when they are participating in extracurricular activities that students most often say that they are both working and playing.

Those kids who say that what they do is mostly play enjoy their activities, but they don't think of them as being important for the future. But the best situation is when a person sees a life activity as both work and play. Unfortunately, only about 10 percent of the time do students report this experience. Some kids never report that they have this experience. The worst thing is to frequently feel that what you do is neither enjoyable right now nor good preparation for the future.

You say affluent students are more likely to say they are enjoying their activities than poorer students. Did you see any differences in attitudes among other groups of students?

Males much more than females say that what they do is play. Caucasian students play more than Asians, Hispanics, or African Americans. The survey has a lot of markers in terms of ethnicity, class, and gender. We found that those who see what they do as play get into better colleges after they leave high school. College selection procedures favor kids who do well academically but who also are engaged in original or interesting extracurricular activities.

It's when they are participating in extracurricular activities that students most often say that they are both working and playing.

What is it about extracurricular activities that makes them engaging to students?

Students say that they are doing something that is important to them. The activity is voluntary to a large extent. Kids can choose to do things that match their own interests and skills. So they are doing something fun. But at the same time they are doing work to adult specifications. If you work on the high school newspaper, you have to observe the deadlines and you produce something that is real.

Our youngest son, for instance, was uninterested in school until he began to hang out with the theater group and started building sets, doing the lighting and sound effects, painting the scenery, doing carpentry, and so forth. Once he did that, he became more able to focus on everything. And now he's teaching at MIT.

Flow describes the spontaneous, effortless experience you achieve when you have a close match between a high level of challenge and the skills to meet the challenge.

His academic classes did not offer him an opportunity to meet serious adult standards, but the extracurricular activity did.

Explain what you mean by the flow experience, the title of your earlier book.

Flow describes the spontaneous, effortless experience you achieve when you have a close match between a high level of challenge and the skills you need to meet the challenge. Flow happens when a person is completely involved in the task, is concentrating very deeply, and knows moment by moment what the next steps should be. If you're playing music, you know what note will come next, and you know how to play that note. You have a goal and you are getting feedback. The experience is almost addictive and very rewarding.

Small children are in flow most of the time as they learn to walk and talk and other new things. They choose what to do and they match their skills with challenges. Unfortunately, they begin to lose this feeling once they go to school because they can't choose their goals and they can't choose the level at which they operate. They become increasingly passive. We find that in Europe and the United States, about 15 percent of adults really can't remember any experience that seems like flow. A similar proportion, about 15 percent, claim that they have the flow experience several times a day.

We've published many articles on multiple intelligences and learning styles. Do you think people of a certain kind of intelligence are more likely to have the flow experience?

It depends on whether there are opportunities for your particular skill or intelligence. If you are musically inclined, for instance, and there is no opportunity to play music at your school and no other place to get the experience of playing, then you are at a disadvantage. In some cultures, there will be opportunities for one kind of intelligence more than for another.

The learning disability that may be an obstacle to experiencing flow is the inability to concentrate. Concentration is one of the hallmarks of the flow experience. If you have, for instance, an attention deficit, it may be difficult to get focused enough.

Have you found that any curriculum subjects lend themselves to more engagement than others?

Yes. There have been quite a few dissertations on this topic. Typically, students rate history the worst subject for engagement, whereas they rate anything having to do with computers high. And vocational subjects seem to be better than academic subjects for encouraging engagement.

Students get flow from group work, from individual tasks, and from quizzes much more often than they do from listening to the teacher or from watching audiovisuals.

We're in a testing culture now, with much emphasis on standards and high-stakes assessments. Is this new priority deflating students' love of learning, or is it beneficial because it offers challenges?

To the extent that the results of the tests are taken seriously, testing worries me. If a test

is fair and not above the heads of most of the kids, then students can take the test as a game and a challenge. Flow is easiest to experience when you are challenged, have clear goals, and get clear feedback. Now, if you're listening to a teacher, all of those things are missing. There's nothing to keep your attention focused. Whereas in a test, you have to pay attention. There is a challenge. The goals are clear. You can lose yourself in the activity. Unless it's way too difficult or way too easy, you can enjoy taking a test. But that doesn't mean that one should take any test very seriously because test results don't correlate much with anything.

Not with higher achievement or success in life?

Not that I know of. I would be interested in seeing the evidence that scores on tests correlate with happiness or success in life.

What recommendations do you have for teachers who want to structure instructional activities to achieve more flow or more engagement for students?

The more they can show the relevance of what they're doing to the life of the student, the better. That's the first and most obvious requirement. You also have to make clear the goal of every lesson. The student must know what he or she is supposed to achieve at the end. And teachers need a way to find out how well the students are learning. Computer-assisted teaching can be quite useful because there you can see your progress and you can change and correct your work as you move along. The fact that students feel positive about group activities suggests the need for more group work. There's too little group activity in high school except in science labs where two or three kids have to solve a problem or learn something together. There are many things that adults could do to make learning more engaging to students.

On the other hand, sometimes it seems to me that the best thing would be to forbid children to go to school until they can demonstrate that they have a real interest in something. Of course, such a system would be fair only if we had preschools for all children, where they could be exposed to a stimulating environment in a playful setting.

Education should be available to everyone, obviously. But education should not be an obligation, but rather a privilege that you earn by showing that you're curious about some part of the world. You get your education through that curiosity. The role of the teacher would then be to find the material that would allow the student to explore his or her curiosity. Because no matter what you're curious about, if you are really curious, you will have to learn everything else.

Whether the topic is bugs or stars or singing, there are connections. There is mathematics behind the music and chemistry behind the animals. Once the students are hooked on their interest, the teacher should be the gatekeeper to the enormous richness of information in the world. The role of the teacher is not to convey the same content to a captive audience, which becomes almost immediately aversive to most children.

I'm interested in how you became interested in the idea of flow. Was it an experience of your own that led you to find out more about it?

Essentially, I was interested in psychology. At the time, you couldn't get a degree in psychology by studying happiness or well-being, but creativity was something you could study.

So I studied creativity in artists. And I was struck by how these artists would get completely lost in what they were doing for long periods of time. And yet, once they finished the canvas, they never looked at it again. Most of them weren't trying to sell their art. The finished painting was an excuse for them to paint. The process of painting was the reward that motivated them.

So I started wondering, Does this happen in other aspects of life? It turned out that people play music for the same reason. They play music to go on the journey, not to reach the destination. In sports, it is the same. I thought that the experience that made the activity so rewarding would be different in music or chess or rock climbing. Instead, what was so surprising was how similarly everyone described how they felt, even though what they were doing was so different.

And for yourself, what are the activities that give you the experience of flow?

When I was in high school, I played chess competitively. I used to paint. I did serious rock climbing. Later, I wrote fiction for *The New Yorker*. All of these are wonderful flow activities. Now I get creative enjoyment mostly from work and from hiking here in Montana with the family.

What family characteristics are most conducive to inspiring a love of learning?

Modeling is the best strategy. If the kid grows up seeing that his parents and other adults have no interest in anything except making money, it's unlikely that he or she will learn that it's fun to study or learn new things.

It boils down to the essentials: support and challenge. By challenge I mean high expectations, high standards, allowing the child a lot of independence, exposing students to new opportunities whenever possible. Support means simply that the child feels that the family as a whole is interested in every member's welfare. If the mother comes home tired, the kids will notice it and try to help her and so forth.

When their families give them both support and challenge, children are more likely to choose harder subjects in high school, get better grades, end up in better colleges, and have higher self-esteem in college or after college. If they receive support only, the kids tend to be happy and feel better about themselves, but they're not necessarily ambitious. They don't try to advance in school. They don't take harder classes.

If the family offers a lot of challenges but does not provide support, then the kids tend to do well in school, but they're not very happy. And if they have neither support nor challenge from the family, then it's bad all around. Support and challenge impart different strengths. Challenge gives children vision and direction, focus and perseverance. Support gives the serenity that allows them freedom from worry and fear.

I was struck by how these artists would get completely lost in what they were doing for long periods of time.

Teenagers often have a great deal of anxiety that gets in their way when they tackle a challenge. What's the antidote to anxiety?

Well, there are several. One is tutoring or help in the subjects that provide the most anxiety; another is building up students' strengths. It's often the case that once the students find something that they are really good at, then the anxiety disappears in the other situations. The parents should monitor what the child is interested in and give opportunities to excel at those subjects.

Going back to our youngest son, we weren't the ones who helped him. Once he found that he was as good as or better than others at something, it gave him the feeling that he could do other things, too.

We have an idea in education that we have to work on our weaknesses. To a certain extent, that makes sense. But it makes even more sense to work on the strengths. Because once someone has developed strengths, then everything else becomes easier. Second, if you feel miserable studying mathematics and you spend all your time learning mathematics, chances are you will never be very good at it anyway. If the child is good at photography, allow him or her to explore and develop those strengths.

So you wouldn't be a fan of the core curriculum that requires all students to master certain culturally important content?

No, I think that's kind of silly. Look at our presidents. President Bush was a low *C* student all his life, and so was Clinton until he got to be a Rhodes scholar. It's kind of hypocritical to expect that all children should be good across the board when most adults aren't successful at everything.

The important thing is to stimulate the curiosity, reinforce the curiosity, and build on the strengths of the child. And then you have a vibrant, lively community instead of people who have been stuffed with information that they don't care about.

Of all the students you interviewed, do any stand out as special examples?

Hundreds. One could write a shelf of novels on the lives of these kids.

There was a boy from Kansas City who, at age 12, was really in bad shape. He hated school. He had nothing that he liked. His self-esteem was low. He was in trouble with the school. We thought he would end up having serious trouble.

Then, in his senior year, when we looked at his booklet, we noticed that he had completely changed. He was happy. He felt strong self-esteem. He'd write that he was especially happy when he was looking for a valve or pipes at the hardware store or when he was carrying some rocks to his truck. When he was doing these things, he felt really positive. And we couldn't understand what he was talking about.

> Challenge gives children vision and direction, focus and perseverance. Support give the serenity that allows them freedom from worry and fear.

In the interviews, we asked him, What is this about looking for a valve or carrying rocks? He told us that he had a business building koi ponds. At some time in his junior year, he saw one of these Japanese fishponds in somebody's garden, and he became so fascinated that he built one in his own yard and one for his neighbor. And then he started building ponds commercially. At age 18, he bought a panel truck for his koi pond business. And he felt tremendous. He had to learn everything from plumbing to biology: how the fish live and what to feed them. He learned chemistry. He learned mathematics to understand water pressure and volume. Senior year he did great in school. He ended up going to a community college and taking technical courses. That is what can happen when a kid makes a connection between something inside and an opportunity outside. To me, that's how education should be. To educate means to lead out. And we don't lead kids out. We kind of stop them. To educate is to expose kids to many possibilities until they find a connection between what's really important to them and the world out there. And then we must nurture and cultivate that connection.

Did the act of writing the journals help the students in your study become more active in their pursuit of learning?

Definitely. Some psychologists use journal writing as therapy. Once you really have an idea of what you're doing, you have a chance to take charge of your behavior. Often kids are put in a dependent state in school; they are not supposed to take any initiative except in what the teachers want them to do. Television puts them in another kind of dependent state. Many come to tacitly believe that they have no say over their own development as human beings.

Writing things down and reflecting on them is one of those things that makes a person ask, Why am I doing these things when I feel so bad when I do them? Why don't I do more of those things that make me happy?

Mihaly Csikszentmihalyi is the D.J. and C.S. Davidson Professor of Psychology at the Drucker School of Management, Claremont Graduate University in Claremont, California. He is the author or coauthor of 15 books, among them *Flow: The Psychology of Optimal Experience* (Harper & Row, 1990) and, with Barbara Schneider, *Becoming Adult: How Teenagers Prepare for the World of Work* (BasicBooks, 2000). **Marge Scherer** is Editor in Chief of *Educational Leadership*; el@ascd.org.

Self-Efficacy

A Key to Improving the Motivation of Struggling Learners

HOWARD MARGOLIS and PATRICK P. McCABE

Self-efficacy . . . influence[s] task choice, effort, persistence, and achievement. Compared with students who doubt their learning capacities, those who have a sense of efficacy for [particular tasks] participate more readily, work harder, persist longer when they encounter difficulties, and achieve at a higher level. . . . Students do not engage in activities they believe will lead to negative outcomes. (Schunk and Zimmerman 1997, 36)

Many struggling learners resist academics, thinking that they lack the ability to succeed, even if they expend great effort. In other words, these struggling learners have low rather than high self-efficacy for academics. It is widely believed that without sufficiently high self-efficacy, or the belief that they can succeed on specific academic tasks like homework, many struggling learners will not make the effort needed to master academics. They will give up or avoid tasks similar to those previously failed (Baker and Wigfield 1999; Bandura 1993; Casteel, Isom, and Jordan 2000; Chapman and Tunmer 2003; Henk and Melnick 1995; Jinks and Morgan 1999; Lipson and Wixson 1997; Lynch 2002; Pajares 1996; Pintrich and Schunk 2002; Schunk and Zimmerman 1997; Walker 2003).

A key to reversing this perspective—getting struggling learners with low self-efficacy to invest sufficient effort, to persist on tasks, to work to overcome difficulties, to take on increasingly challenging tasks, and to develop interest in academics—is for teachers to systematically stress the development of high self-efficacy. Fortunately, research suggests that teachers can often strengthen struggling learners' self-efficacy by linking new work to recent successes, teaching needed learning strategies, reinforcing effort and persistence, stressing peer modeling, teaching struggling learners to make facilitative attributions, and helping them identify or create personally important goals (Ormrod 2000; Pajares 2003; Pajares and Schunk 2001; Pintrich and Schunk 2002; Schunk 1999; Zimmerman

2000a). For these strategies to be effective, however, struggling learners with low self-efficacy must succeed on the very type of tasks they expect to fail. This strongly suggests that classwork must be at their proper instructional level, and homework at their proper independent level (Culyer 1996; Lipson and Wixson 1997). Work should challenge rather than frustrate them (Strickland, Ganske, and Monroe 2002). It should strengthen expectations of success rather than failure. To achieve this, teachers need to (a) give struggling learners work at their proper instructional and independent levels, and (b) adhere to instructional principles likely to improve self-efficacy.

Frustration, Instructional, and Independent Levels

Perhaps the most important academic decision teachers make for struggling learners is determining the levels at which to instruct them. Swanson's (1999) findings support this contention. As part of a larger meta-analysis assessing the effectiveness of interventions for students with learning disabilities, he identified the instructional components that best predicted outcomes. Two of the more important components were controlling task difficulty and sequencing tasks from easy to difficult. His findings reflect recommendations that reading specialists have made for decades—instruct students at their proper instructional and independent levels and avoid the frustration level (Leslie and Caldwell 2001; McCormick 2003; Newcomer 1986).

Criteria for instructional, independent, and frustration level tasks are often defined by objective measures (e.g., the percent of words correctly identified in oral reading) and are influenced by each struggling learner's unique perceptions about what is frustrating or anxiety provoking. What one struggling learner finds challenging, another, with the same skills, can find frustrating and nightmarish. Challenge is also influenced by such factors as a struggling learner's ability to organize, initiate, monitor, and sustain activities. A task that one struggling learner has little difficultly structuring and organizing can overwhelm and frustrate another at the same academic level.

For struggling learners with expectations of failure, teachers should avoid tasks the learners find frustrating or anxiety provoking. If frequently encountered, such tasks will provoke dysfunctional but understandable avoidance reactions: refusal to start or complete work; off-task dawdling; unthoughtful, careless responses; distractibility and fidgetiness. Little learning will occur, and motivation will plummet. As Newcomer (1986) noted: "Continuing to expect a child to read material at his or her frustration level can create serious achievement and emotional problems" (26).

Although perceptions are personal and teachers may need to adjust instructional and independent level criteria for particular struggling learners, teachers should follow well-established guidelines for determining instructional and independent levels. In most cases, these guidelines set the stage for success.

For materials to be at a student's instructional reading level, students should quickly and correctly read aloud 90 to 95 percent of words in context and understand 70 to 89 percent of the text. Instructional level assumes that teachers will work with students, teaching vocabulary, skills, and strategies; monitoring and guiding practice; and structuring independent practice. For independent level materials, which students should find easier than instructional level materials, students should quickly and correctly read aloud 96 percent or more of the words in context and understand 90 percent or more of the text (McCormick 2003). Whenever students work by themselves, at their desks or at home, materials should be at their independent level. Giving instructional level homework to struggling learners is equivalent to giving them frustration level materials, as their independent work habits and skills are often poor and teachers are not there to teach, supervise, and support them.

Commercial informal reading inventories (IRIs) can help identify a struggling learner's instructional, independent, and frustration reading levels (Lipson and Wixson 1997; McCormick 2003). Although such IRIs are easy to administer, and some are supported by extensive validity data (Leslie and Caldwell 2001; McCabe and Margolis 1999), they lack the specificity of Curriculum-Based Assessment (CBA) for determining and monitoring struggling learners' reading levels in specific curriculum (Fewster and Macmillan 2002; Idol, Nevin, and Paolucci-Whitcomb 1999). One CBA strategy for identifying struggling learners' instructional and independent reading levels is to individually administer a hierarchical series of 100-word selections from the books the learners will likely read (Idol, Nevin, and Paolucci-Whitcomb 1999). By having learners read three different selections from each prospective book that matches their estimated reading abilities and comparing each learner's median performance for accuracy (number of words correctly read), rate (correct words per minute) and comprehension (percent of questions correctly answered) to locally derived norms, teachers can get relatively reliable indications of the challenge these books present (Idol, Nevin, and Paolucci-Whitcomb 1999; Fewster and Macmillan 2002).

Teachers also can use the cloze procedure to quickly estimate the learners' ability to understand specific reading materials. The procedure, which has learners silently read passages of 250 to 300 words, can be administered to individual students or whole classes. Unlike the materials from which the cloze passages were copied, the cloze passage replaces every fifth word with a blank space of even length (Lipson and Wixson 1997; Spinelli 2002). Students write in the missing words. Materials on which students accurately identify 44 to 56 percent of the missing words (synonyms are counted as incorrect) represent their instructional level, 57 percent or more their independent level, and 43 percent or less their frustration level (Spinelli 2002). These guidelines can help teachers identify materials that struggling learners can successfully read.

Instructional and independent levels are different for tasks and assignments that do not stress the fluent identification of words in context. Salvia and Ysseldyke (2001) consider correct response rates of 85 to 95 percent challenging and less than 85 percent "too difficult." They caution for "students with severe cognitive handicaps, rates of correct response of less than 90 percent may indicate that the material is too challenging for guided practice" (25).

By adhering to these guidelines and, when they're too demanding, reducing them and the length, complexity, and abstractness of the work to reflect struggling learners' actual difficulties, perceptions of difficulty, and feelings of anxiety, teachers can often strengthen learners' self-efficacy for academics. One strategy for determining the adaptations needed is FLIP (Schumm and Mangrum 1991), which asks students to evaluate materials for friendliness (F), language (L), interest (I), and prior knowledge (P). By using FLIP, or adapting it to different subject matter, materials, and assignments, teachers can design instruction that increases the probability of success.

Whenever instructional or independent level data are unclear and teachers have to choose between more or less difficult levels, they should choose the less difficult. As struggling learners' moderate efforts produce high rates of success, more challenging materials and tasks should replace easier ones. Otherwise, they will have little opportunity to learn anything new, may get bored, and may think that teachers have little confidence in their abilities.

Instructional Principles

Frequently Link New Work to Recent Successes

To effectively link new work to recent successes requires many recent successes. To create many, teachers need to "stack the deck for success" by adhering to the struggling learners' proper instructional and independent levels, "stimulating recall of prerequisite learning" (Borich 2000, 159), shortening and simplifying work, and limiting the number and length of assignments. The key is giving learners moderately challenging work they can succeed at, if they make a moderate effort.

One way to help assure that struggling learners get tasks likely to produce high rates of success is to systematically employ CBA and to continually monitor learners' success rates

FLIP question: "How difficult is the language in my reading assignment?"

Possible student responses:

- Many new words; complicated sentences

- Some new words; somewhat complicated sentences

- No new words; clear sentences

Source: Schumm and Mangrum 1991, 122.

FIGURE 1. Sample FLIP question and possible responses.

(Rieth and Evertson 1988). By administering brief CBA probes several times a month, to assess progress in learners' areas of difficulty (e.g., reading, writing, spelling), and designing instruction and assignments to match their achievement and readiness to handle similar or increasingly challenging tasks, teachers can increase the learners' probability of success (Alper, Ryndak, and Schloss 2001; Galagan 1985; Spinelli 2002).

Once struggling learners have recent successes to draw on, teachers can help them link new work to their previous successes by explicitly showing and asking them how the new work resembles those past successes and then reminding them of what they did to succeed. Examining prior successes also provides teachers an excellent opportunity to employ one or several other self-efficacy enhancing strategies: teaching struggling learners to evaluate their work and chart their successes; teaching them to attribute success to controllable factors like effort, persistence, and correct use of strategies; having them review and annotate portfolios of successful work; helping them identify or develop specific, short-term, realistic goals; and persuading them to keep trying (Henk and Melnick 1998; Ormrod 2000; Pintrich and Schunk 2002; Schunk 2003; Walker 2003).

Teach Needed Learning Strategies

Characteristically, struggling learners do not know how to approach academic tasks. They do not know what learning or cognitive strategies to use or how to use them (Ellis and Lenz 1996; Vaughn, Gersten, and Chard 2000). Thus, teachers need to explicitly and systematically teach them the secrets of learning—the strategies that produce success (Swanson 2000).

Explicit, systematic instruction involves sequencing materials and tasks from easy to difficult; modeling and explaining to struggling learners, in a simple step-by-step fashion what they need to do; providing feedback about what they are doing right and what they need to do differently; providing abundant opportunities for guided practice, with task-specific feedback about how to correct errors; and, when they have achieved a high degree of proficiency (e.g., 96 percent word recognition in context for reading [McCormick 2003] and 85 percent on nonword recognition tasks, such as subtraction problems [Joyce and Weil 1996]), having them practice independently. As

Vaughn, Gersten, and Chard (2000) concluded: "Teaching students how to apply a particular strategy should be overt, and students should have multiple opportunities to practice the strategy under quality feedback conditions before they are expected to use the strategy on their own" (105).

In addition to sequencing, modeling, explicit step-by-step directions, feedback, correction, and practice (Pintrich and Schunk 2002; Swanson 2000), teachers might increase struggling learners' expectations of success by involving them in cooperative learning activities which are well within their ability to achieve. They know they will discreetly get whatever help they need, and they view their group as friendly and internally noncompetitive (Alderman 1999; Henk and Melnick 1998; Schunk and Zimmerman 1997; Vermette 1998). Teachers might also increase struggling learners' expectations of success by giving them strategy reference cards to use whenever they want (Casteel, Isom, and Jordon 2000). Reference cards present and illustrate each step of a strategy in ways struggling learners can readily comprehend. If they use reference cards when learning a strategy, they are apt to feel comfortable with them. Because they determine when to use the cards, they can dispense with them when they want. By putting struggling learners in control of using the cards and modeling the use of the cards themselves, teachers can eliminate any stigma associated with them.

For struggling learners who believe they lack the ability to succeed and who avoid more than superficial involvement in schoolwork, explicit, systematic strategy instruction may lack the power to involve them in meaningful, engaging ways. In such situations, teachers (and in some cases, parents) need to provide extrinsic, age-appropriate reinforcers (e.g., stickers, small toys, free time, computer time) that struggling learners are willing to work for until they become interested in the work and develop a strong, sustaining belief that with moderate effort, they can succeed. To prevent extrinsic reinforcement from backfiring and to reduce or eliminate it within a few months, teachers need to adhere to several basic principles of reinforcement and instruction:

- Use the smallest, most natural reinforcers for which struggling learners will work.

- Vary reinforcers to avoid boredom; change reinforcers that no longer work.

- Start by reinforcing struggling learners every time they correctly apply the strategy; briefly explain why they earned the reinforcer.

- Gradually thin out the frequency of extrinsic reinforcement by reinforcing fewer instances of correct strategy application. Go slow—do not reduce reinforcement too quickly.

- From the beginning, pair tangible, extrinsic reinforcers with common social and verbal reinforcers (e.g., smiles, task-specific praise).

- Reinforce struggling learners in all environments and situations in which they should use the learning strategy and correctly use it (e.g., with different teachers or in different classes, reinforce correct strategy use).

- Listen to struggling learners to learn about their personal goals, values, interests, and problems and link schoolwork to these.
- Stress work that struggling learners find important, interesting, or curiosity arousing.

Reinforce Effort and Persistence

Social cognitive theory predicts that many struggling learners, students who have suffered countless academic difficulties and failures, will have low self-efficacy for academics (Henk and Melnick 1998; Jinks and Morgan 1999; Schunk and Zimmerman 1997; Walker 2003; Zimmerman 2000a). Consequently, they are less prone than successful learners to tackle tasks they perceive as difficult, invest significant effort in such tasks, persist in the face of difficulty, and perform at high levels (Bandura 1997; Ormrod 2000; Pajares 1996; Schunk 1999; Zimmerman 2000a).

To strengthen struggling learners' self-efficacy, teachers need to select tasks well within struggling learners' abilities, sequence tasks from easy to difficult, help struggling learners realize they have the skills to succeed, provide them with help and encouragement whenever needed, show them how to correct their mistakes, and introduce "difficult" tasks only when they are no longer difficult—when struggling learners have mastered the prerequisites on which success depends (Rosenshine 1983; Salvia and Ysseldyke 2001; Swanson 2000). In such situations, resistance will often evaporate, creating legitimate opportunities to reinforce effort and persistence.

Resistance, however, will not evaporate if the initial tasks are too lengthy, too complex, or too difficult. Thus, to create opportunities to reinforce effort and persistence, initial assignments should be challenging but well within the struggling learners' abilities. Success should require reasonable, moderate effort—not Herculean. Struggling learners should view tasks as doable, not impossible.

Doable tasks that struggling learners can successfully complete with moderate effort makes "effort feedback" credible and can enhance self-efficacy, motivation, and achievement (Schunk 2001). Effort feedback, however, can backfire, if struggling learners are frequently reinforced for the effort invested in repeating the same task. They may "doubt their capacities and wonder why they still have to work hard to succeed" (Schunk 2001, 139).

Stress Peer Modeling

Although teacher modeling is highly effective (Swanson 2000), peer models may be particularly effective in strengthening self-efficacy (Alderman 1999; Pajares and Schunk 2001; Schunk 1999, 2003). Fortunately, teachers who give students interesting work at their proper instructional and independent levels usually have several peer models to choose from, as such work encourages proper behavior.

Peer models can be mastery or coping models. Peer coping models have the advantage of showing struggling learners how other students, similar to them, make and overcome mistakes in acquiring and applying new skills and learning strategies. This fosters the belief, "She's like me. If she can do it, I can" (Schunk 2001).

To improve the effectiveness of peer coping models, teachers should

- choose an important skill or strategy that is likely to challenge but not frustrate models and struggling learners;
- break complicated skills and strategies into manageable components;
- select models who resemble the struggling learners and who they respect;
- have models explain their actions, in a simple step-by-step manner, while they work to learn and apply the skill or strategy;
- have models correct their mistakes and verbally attribute failures to controllable factors (e.g., poor effort) and successes to controllable factors (e.g., correctly using a strategy) and ability (e.g., "I read well enough to use the Multipass strategy");
- have struggling learners observe models reinforced, in a variety of appropriate situations, for correctly using the targeted skill or strategy; and
- reinforce struggling learners, in a variety of appropriate situations, for correctly using the targeted skill or strategy.

Teach Students to Make Facilitative Attributions

Attributions are people's explanatory beliefs about why things happen to them. They explain success and failure and influence future actions, including effort, persistence, and choices (Bandura 1997; Pajares and Schunk 2001; Zimmerman 2000b).

> The attributions that people assign to the things that happen to them . . . guide their future behavior. . . . [Students] may attribute their school successes and failures to . . . aptitude or ability (how smart or proficient they are), effort (how hard they tried), other people (how well the teacher taught or how much their classmates like them), task difficulty (how "easy" or "hard" something is), luck, mood, illness, fatigue, or physical appearance. . . . If students erroneously attribute their failures to stable and uncontrollable causes, they are unlikely [emphasis added] to change their future behaviors in ways that will lead to greater success. (Ormrod 2000, 497-98)

To counteract the effects of erroneous attributions that destroy self-efficacy—reducing struggling learners' willingness to try, to make reasonable efforts, and to persist—teachers need to stress accurate, facilitative attributions throughout the day and teach struggling learners to do the same.

Facilitative attributions associate successes with controllable factors, such as effort, persistence, and the correct use of learning or cognitive strategies. They stress what students did (Composite explanation: "I succeeded because I tried very hard. . . . I stuck to it. . . . I followed the steps on my cue cards"). Similarly, they attribute poor performances and failures to the same controllable factors, but stress what students did not do (Composite explanation: "I failed because I didn't try hard enough…. I didn't stick to it…. I didn't follow the steps on my cue cards").

Facilitative attributions also link successes to ability, such as learned intelligence (e.g., "I'm smart about that now. I learned how to use Multipass to understand the tough parts of my science book"). In contrast, they divorce poor performance or failure from ability.

Many experts have recommended combining attribution statements with cognitive strategies (Borkowski, Weyhing, and Carr 1988; Chapman and Tunmer 2003; Fulk 1994; Mushinski Fulk and Mastropieri 1990; Pintrich and Schunk 2002; Schunk and Rice 1993; Shelton, Anastopoulos, and Linden 1985). In a sense, it provides the best of both by giving struggling learners the formula, the secret for achieving success—the strategy—and teaches them to take credit for using and sticking with the strategy. Mushinski Fulk and Mastroprini (1990) designed a model for integrating strategy and attribution instruction.

Help Students Create Personally Important Goals

Perhaps nothing is more motivating than combining personally important goals with the belief that with reasonable effort, they are achievable (Pintrich and Schunk 2002; Schunk 2001; Zimmerman 2000b). But not every goal is motivating. Not every goal will improve low self-efficacy. For goals to positively influence self-efficacy and motivation, they need to be personally important to struggling learners, short-term, specific, and achievable (Alderman 1999; Bandura 1997; Schunk 1999; Stipek 1998). Moreover, to sustain motivation, struggling learners need credible feedback that they are making substantial progress toward achieving their goal (Alderman 1999; Bandura 1997; Pajares and Schunk 2001; Schunk 1999, 2003).

Personally important goals are goals that students want to achieve, goals they think will make an important difference in their lives. Struggling learners are far more likely to work to achieve goals that are important to them (Slavin 1999), and which they think they can achieve, than goals they view as unimportant and beyond their abilities.

Short-term goals (e.g., "Get a B+ on next week's social studies test") work hand in hand with long-term goals (e.g., "Pass social studies so I'm eligible for the hockey team"). Long-term goals, goals that will take months or years to attain, express students' dreams, students' hopes. Short-term goals are subgoals; they are intermediate steps between the present and long-term goals. Struggling learners need short-term goals to prevent loss of motivation, caused by the remoteness of long-term goals. Without frequent, explicit, visible feedback that they are making progress on short-term goals, struggling learners often get discouraged, retreating from academics. Frequently noting progress improves self-efficacy and motivation (Schunk 1999, 2001).

Specific, short-term goals are easily measurable, allowing struggling learners and teachers to frequently evaluate progress against a clear standard. For example, struggling learners can easily judge whether they met these specific, short-term goals:

- Write two compositions that earn a "B" on the class writing rubric.
- Try out for the band.

Step 1: *Explain purpose.* Explain the purpose of the strategy. Make sure the student understands how the strategy will help her. Relate the purpose to the student's frame of reference so she sees value in learning the strategy.

Step 2: *Discuss effort.* Discuss with the student how she controls her own effort and the critical role effort plays in producing successful outcomes.

Step 3: *Model examples.* Apply the strategy correctly and incorrectly. Label the examples correct and incorrect.

Step 4: *Model attributions.* Model controllable attributions while engaging in the strategy (e.g., "I got the right answer because I first skimmed the chapter, read all the headings and subheadings, and tried hard. . . . I got the wrong answer because I rushed and didn't skim the whole chapter. I didn't try hard.")

Step 5: *Provide guided practice.* Give the student ample opportunity to practice the combined strategy-attribution sequence with timely task-specific feedback until she routinely gets the right answer, makes positive attributions about her efforts, and appears comfortable with the strategy (e.g., "Kelly, that's great. You got the right answer because you first skimmed the chapter and worked hard. You told yourself that putting the effort in improves your understanding.").

Step 6: *Provide independent practice.* Give the student ample opportunity to use the combined strategy-attribution sequences by herself. Monitor student behavior and offer task-specific feedback as needed (e.g., "Nice job Kelly. You worked hard and gave yourself credit for skimming the chapter before reading it. Your effort made a difference.").

Step 7: *Conduct formative evaluation.* Assess the student's progress and modify teaching strategies if difficulty is apparent (e.g., if Kelly has trouble skimming full chapters of some twenty pages, reduce skimming to a more manageable fraction and provide more frequent feedback).

Step 8: *Introduce a new strategy.* Once the student routinely uses the strategy correctly and takes credit for making adequate effort and using it correctly, introduce a slightly different strategy appropriate for the student's instructional level. Re-institute attribution retraining sequence with step 1.

Note: Adapted from B. M. Mushinski Fulk and M. A. Mastropieri 1990.

FIGURE 2. General steps for combined attribution retraining and strategy instruction.

Scene: The teacher reads a paragraph aloud to his class. The paragraph, on Martin Luther King's assassination, is projected onto a screen, from an overhead projector. As the teacher reads aloud, he illustrates the Paraphrasing Reading Strategy (Ellis 1996) by saying:

- I'm using the RAP strategy.

- The three steps are "R" for Read a paragraph, "A" for Ask yourself what the paragraph was about, and "P" for Put the main idea and two details in your own words.

- I read the paragraph. I'll check the "R" on my checklist.

FIGURE 3. A teacher think-aloud for a learning strategy checklist.

Although many struggling learners can monitor and evaluate their work, some cannot. Teachers can teach struggling learners to monitor their work by frequently demonstrating think-alouds when evaluating struggling learners' work (Tierney and Readance 2000; Walker 2003; Wilheim 2001), and teaching them to use simple self-evaluation forms, rubrics, learning strategy reference cards, and learning strategy checklists (Casteel, Isom, and Jordan 2000; Lipson and Wixson 1997; Walker 1997, 2003). Figure 3 illustrates how teachers might use a think-aloud with a learning strategy checklist.

Realistic goals, goals that struggling learners can achieve with moderate effort, are more motivating than excessively difficult or excessively easy goals. Excessively difficult goals lead to resistance or despair because struggling learners believe them impossible to achieve. In contrast, excessively easy goals offer no challenge. They are boring; when achieved, struggling learners do not feel more competent. One instance in which excessively easy goals may be appropriate, but only temporarily, is when struggling learners are reeling from sustained difficulty and failure and need successful experiences to begin restoring confidence.

If struggling learners lack personally important goals, or they are vague, teachers should help them formulate precise, personal goals. Otherwise, it is more difficult to meaningfully involve them in academics. Fortunately, many struggling learners appreciate the activity, as they, like most people, want something. The two keys are finding out what struggling learners want and helping them express it in explicit, visible, concrete terms.

One way to get the information needed to help struggling learners formulate personally important goals is to ask them to complete an interest inventory. Another, more personal way is to listen empathetically to them about anything they want to discuss. Teachers can then meet with them and use this information to collaboratively write down the struggling learners' long-term and related short-term goals. One strategy to better understand their goals, and to help them better understand their own goals, is for teachers and struggling learners to circle, discuss, illustrate, and define vague words—words that are difficult to visualize and describe. If the opportunity to help struggling learners develop personally important goals is unavailable, teachers might ask guidance counselors for assistance.

Once struggling learners have defined personally important, specific, realistic, short-term goals, and understand their relationship to their long-term goals and schoolwork, teachers and struggling learners need to frequently assess progress toward achieving these goals (Schunk, 2001). If struggling learners are making good progress, teachers and learners should discuss what they are doing to produce success; if progress is poor, how to improve the situation. Typically, as learners note progress, their self-efficacy and enthusiasm for learning improves.

Incorporate Other Motivational Factors

Motivation, or the willingness to initiate and sustain goal directed activity, is influenced by self-efficacy (Bandura 1993; Henk and Melnick 1998; Jinks and Morgan 1999; Pajares and Schunk 2001; Pintrich and Schunk 2002; Schunk and Rice 1993; Schunk and Zimmerman 1997; Zimmerman 2000b; Zimmerman and Martinez-Pons 1990). "If," as an old saying goes, "people don't think they can, they won't." The converse, however, is not true. Just because people think they can do something, does not mean they will. However, they will likely invest in activities they find interesting or valuable, if their environment is safe and supportive, and if difficulties do not lead to embarrassment or comparisons with more successful peers. Thus, attempts to increase self-efficacy must take place within emotionally safe, secure classes that emphasize motivational principles that create or nurture a desire to learn and achieve. Such classes are usually taught by enthusiastic, optimistic teachers who

- run well-organized classes;

- encourage students to use well-organized, well-stocked learning centers and libraries;

- treat students with respect;

- show interest in students;

- give students choices;

- relate curriculum to students' lives and interests, in and out of school;

- radiate interest in their lessons;

- stimulate and maintain curiosity;

- engage students in collaborative learning activities, such as cooperative learning and peer tutoring;

- encourage sharing;

- use a variety of teaching approaches, appropriate to lesson objectives;

- make expectations clear and realistic;

- provide help, whenever needed, in socially appropriate ways, that avoid student embarrassment;

- compare students' achievements to their past achievements, rather than to other students';

- stress cooperative rather than competitive activities;

- provide frequent, immediate, task-specific feedback, including corrective comments and justified praise;

- ensure that students have the prerequisite knowledge and skill to master new topics and assignments;

- emphasize what is right about students' work; and

- challenge rather than frustrate students.

Caveats

As Linnenbrink and Pintrich (2003) noted, "Psychology and educational psychology are probabilistic sciences. . . . [Because they examine] what occurs, on average, across situations, there may be . . . situations where the principles do not apply. . . . [Thus,] it is important that teachers use psychological research as a guide …rather than a prescriptive device" (134). Consequently, teachers who employ this article's suggestions need to monitor their effects on struggling learners and continue to use and refine those suggestions that work and modify or abandon those that don't. More important than any single suggestion is addressing struggling learners' self-efficacy in informed, systematic ways.

Because self-efficacy is task-specific (e.g., affected by the level and complexity of the task and the social and physical context in which it must be completed), attempts to strengthen it need to focus on the specific task or academic subject in which struggling learners feel incompetent. It is quite possible, for example, that they feel highly confident in one subject (e.g., mathematics) and inadequate in another (reading). The distinction is often finer. In reading, some have confidence in their comprehension abilities with second grade materials but none in their second grade word recognition skills.

No one knows how high self-efficacy must be to improve poor effort, persistence, and academic performance. High self-efficacy, however, is not always good. Overconfident or cocky students may not invest the effort needed to do well (Zimmerman 2000b). Therefore, they need intrinsically interesting tasks that, within reason, challenge their abilities. If they are overconfident and uninterested in tasks, teachers need to link reinforcement to both effort and accomplishment (Pajares 2003; Pintrich and Schunk 2002).

To succeed, struggling learners often need teachers' assistance. If materials and tasks are at the learners' proper instructional and independent levels, the help needed should be minimal. If learners need excessive help, or have to invest a Herculean effort, the task is at their frustration level. In such situations, teachers need to modify tasks so struggling learners need only minimal help.

If teachers often give more help than struggling learners need, they may interpret this as a sign that teachers think they are incompetent (Schunk 2001). Thus, teachers need to carefully assess the amount of help needed and give struggling learners the least amount of help needed to achieve success.

Often, struggling learners' low self-efficacy is part of larger, more complex problems. Although the suggestions in this article can often improve self-efficacy, they will probably be most effective if incorporated into a comprehensive program that systematically addresses the struggling learners' priority needs. Moreover, some struggling learners have had so much failure in their lives, and have so many other problems, that efforts to improve self-efficacy will take a long time and an informed, coordinated, skilled effort on the part of teachers, related service personnel, and parents. Not addressing struggling learners' self-efficacy needs, however, is likely to impede educational progress (Bandura, 1993), as "students' self-beliefs about academic capabilities . . . play an essential role in their motivation to achieve" (Zimmerman 2000a, 89).

Conclusion

For students to meaningfully involve themselves in learning for sustained periods, sufficient self-efficacy is required. Understandably, many struggling learners believe that academics mean failure and frustration—they have low self-efficacy for academics.

To reverse this, teachers must recognize that low self-efficacy is not an immutable, global trait. Rather, it is a modifiable, task-specific set of beliefs derived largely from frequent failures. By matching task difficulty to struggling learners' instructional and independent levels, linking new work to recent successes, teaching them strategies that produce success, reinforcing effort and persistence, using peer models, stressing and teaching facilitative explanations for successes and failures, and helping them understand how schoolwork can help them achieve personally important goals, teachers can often strengthen struggling learners' self-efficacy. By doing so, teachers increase the likelihood that struggling learners will become more motivated, more involved, more persistent, and more successful learners.

REFERENCES

Alderman, M. K. 1999. *Motivation for achievement: Possibilities for teaching and learning.* Mahwah, NJ: Lawrence Erlbaum Publishers.

Alper, S., D. L. Ryndak, and C. N. Schloss. 2001. *Alternative assessment of students with disabilities in inclusive settings.* Boston: Allyn and Bacon.

Baker, L., and A. Wigfield. 1999. Dimensions of children's motivation for reading and their relations to reading activity and reading achievement. *Reading Research Quarterly* 34 (4): 452-57.

Bandura, A. 1993. Perceived self-efficacy in cognitive development and functioning. *Educational Psychologist* 28 (2): 117-48.

Bandura, A. 1997. *Self-efficacy: The exercise of control.* New York: Freeman.

Borich, G. D. 2000. *Effective teaching methods.* 4th ed. Merrill: Upper Saddle River, NJ.

Borkowski, J. G., R. S. Weyhing, and L. A. Carr. 1988. Effects of attributional retraining on strategy-based reading comprehension in learning-disabled students. *Journal of Educational Psychology* 80:46-53.

Casteel, C. P., B. A. Isom, and K. F. Jordan. 2000. Creating confident and competent readers: Transactional strategies instruction. *Intervention in School and Clinic* 36 (2): 67-74.

Chapman, J. W., and W. E. Tunmer. 2003. Reading difficulties, reading-related self-perceptions, and strategies for overcoming negative self-beliefs. *Reading and Writing Quarterly: Overcoming Learning Difficulties* 19 (1): 5-24.

Culyer, R. C. 1996. Making homework work. *Education Digest* 61(9): 52-53.

Ellis, E. S. 1996. Reading strategy instruction. In *Teaching adolescents with learning disabilities: Strategies and methods,* 61-125. Ed. D. D. Deshler, E. S. Ellis, and B. K. Lenz. 2nd ed. Denver: Love Publishing.

Ellis, E. S., and B. K. Lenz. 1996. Perspectives on instruction in learning strategies. In *Teaching adolescents with learning disabilities: Strategies and methods,* 9-60., ed. D. D. Deshler, E. S. Ellis, and B. K. Lenz. 2nd ed. Denver: Love Publishing.

Fewster, S., and P. D. Macmillian. 2002. School-based evidence for the validity of curriculum-based measurement of reading and writing. *Remedial and Special Education* 23 (3): 149-56.

Fulk, B. M. 1994. Mnemonic keyword strategy training for students with learning disabilities. *Learning Disabilities Research and Practice* 9 (3): 179-85.

Galagan, J. 1985. Psychoeducational testing: Turn out the light, the party's over. *Exceptional Children* 52:288-99.

Henk, W. A., and S. A. Melnick. 1995. The reader self-perception scale (RSPS): A new tool for measuring how children feel about themselves as readers. *Reading Teacher* 48:470-82.

———. 1998. Upper elementary-aged children's reported perceptions about good readers: A self-efficacy influenced update in transitional literacy contexts. *Reading Research and Instruction* 38 (1): 57-80.

Idol, I., A. Nevin, and P. Paolucci-Whitcomb. 1999. *Models of curriculum-based assessment: A blueprint for learning.* 3rd ed. Austin, TX: Pro-Ed.

Jinks, J., and V. Morgan. 1999. Children's perceived academic self-efficacy: An inventory scale. *The Clearing House* 72 (4): 224-30.

Joyce, B., and M. Weil. 1996. *Models of teaching.* 5th ed. Boston: Allyn and Bacon.

Leslie, L., and J. Caldwell. 2001. *Qualitative Reading Inventory-3.* NY: Longman.

Linnenbrink, E. A., and P. R. Pintrich. 2003. The role of self-efficacy beliefs in student engagement and learning in the classroom. *Reading and Writing Quarterly: Overcoming Learning Difficulties* 19 (2): 119-38.

Lipson, M. Y., and K. K. Wixson. 1997. *Assessment and instruction of reading disability: An interactive approach.* 2nd ed. NY: Longman.

Lynch, J. 2002. Parents' self-efficacy beliefs, parents' gender, children's reader self-perceptions, reading achievement and gender. *Journal of Research in Reading* 25 (1): 54-67.

McCabe, P., and H. Margolis. 1999. Developing reading programs: How the Qualitative Reading Inventory II can help consultants. *Journal of Educational and Psychological Consultation* 10 (4): 385-93.

McCormick, S. 2003. *Instructing students who have literacy problems.* 4th ed. Englewood Cliffs, NJ: Merrill.

Mushinski Fulk, B. M., and M. A. Mastropieri. 1990. Training positive attitudes. *Intervention in School and Clinic* 26 (2): 79-83.

Newcomer, P. L. 1986. *Standardized Reading Inventory* (manual). Austin, TX: Pro-Ed.

Ormrod, J. E. 2000. *Educational psychology: Developing learners.* 3rd ed. Upper Saddle River, NJ: Prentice Hall.

Pajares, F. 1996. Self-efficacy beliefs in academic settings. *Review of Educational Research* 66 (4): 543-78.

Pajares, F. 2003. Self-efficacy beliefs, motivation, and achievement in writing: A review of the literature. *Reading and Writing Quarterly: Overcoming Learning Difficulties* 19 (2): 139-58.

Pajares, F., and D. H. Schunk. 2001. Self-beliefs and school success: Self-efficacy, self-concept, and school achievement. In *Perception,* 239-66., ed. R. Riding and S. Rayner. London: Ablex Publishing.

Pintrich, P. R., and D. H. Schunk. 2002. *Motivation in education: Theory, research, and applications.* 2nd ed. Englewood Cliffs, NJ: Prentice Hall.

Rieth, H., and C. Evertson. 1988. Variables related to the effective instruction of difficult-to-teach children. *Focus on Exceptional Children* 20 (5): 1-8.

Rosenshine, B. 1983. Teaching functions in instructional programs. *Elementary School Journal* 83:335-51.

Salvia, J., and J. E. Ysseldyke. 2001. *Assessment.* 8th ed. Boston: Houghton Mifflin Company.

Schumm, J. S., and C. T. Mangrum II. 1991. FLIP: A framework for content area reading. *Journal of Reading* 35 (2): 120-24.

Schunk, D. H. 1999. Social-self interaction and achievement behavior. *Educational Psychologist* 34 (4): 219-27.

———. 2001. Social cognitive theory and self-regulated learning. In *Self-regulated learning and academic achievement: Theoretical perspectives,* 125-51., ed. B. J. Zimmerman and D. H. Schunk. Mahwah, NJ: Lawrence Erlbaum Associates.

———. 2003. Self-efficacy for reading and writing: Influence of modeling, goal setting, and self-evaluation. *Reading and Writing Quarterly: Overcoming Learning Difficulties* 19 (2): 159-72

Schunk, D. H., and J. M. Rice. 1993. Strategy fading and progress feedback: Effects on self-efficacy and comprehension among students receiving remedial reading services. *Journal of Special Education* 27:257-76.

Schunk, D. H., and B. J. Zimmerman. 1997. Developing self-efficacious readers and writers: The role of social and self-regulatory processes. In *Reading engagement: Motivating readers through integrated instruction,* 34-50., ed. J. T. Guthrie and A. Wigfield. Newark, DE: International Reading Association.

Shelton, T. L., A. D. Anastopoulos, and J. D. Linden. 1985. An attribution training program with learning disabled children. *Journal of Learning Disabilities* 18 (5): 261-65.

Slavin, R. E. 1999. *Educational psychology: Theory and practice.* 6th ed. Boston: Allyn and Bacon.

Spinelli, C. G. 2002. *Classroom assessment for students with special needs in inclusive settings.* Upper Saddle River, NJ: Merrill.

Stipek, D. 1998. *Motivation to learn: From theory to practice.* 3rd ed. Boston: Allyn and Bacon.

Strickland, D. S., K. Ganske, and J. K. Monroe. 2002. *Supporting struggling readers and writers: Strategies for classroom intervention 3-6.* Newark, DE: International Reading Association.

Swanson, H. L. 1999. Instructional components that predict treatment outcomes for students with learning disabilities: Support for a combined strategy and direct instruction model. *Learning Disabilities Research and Practice* 14 (3): 129-40.

Swanson, H. L. 2000. What instruction works for students with learning disabilities? Summarizing the results from a meta-analysis of intervention studies. In *Contemporary special education research: Synthesis of the knowledge base on critical instructional issues,* 1-30. ed. R. Gersten, E. P. Schiller, and S. Vaughn. Mahwah, NJ: Lawrence Erlbaum Associates.

Tierney, R. J., and J. E. Readence. 2000. *Reading strategies and practices: A compendium.* 5th ed. Boston: Allyn and Bacon.

Vaughn, S., R. Gersten, and D. J. Chard. 2000. The underlying message in LD intervention research: Findings from research syntheses. *Exceptional Children* 67 (1): 99-114.

Vermette, P. J. 1998. *Making cooperative learning work.* Upper Saddle River, NJ: Merrill.

Walker, B. J. 1997. Discussions that focus on strategies and self-assessment. In *Lively discussions: Fostering engaged reading,* 183-204, ed. L. B. Gambrell and J. F. Almasi. Newark, DE: International Reading Association.

Walker, B. 2003. The cultivation of student self-efficiency in reading and writing. *Reading and Writing Quarterly: Overcoming Learning Difficulties* 19 (2): 173-87.

Wilheim, J. D. 2001. *Improving comprehension with think-aloud strategies.* New York: Scholastic Professional Books.

Zimmerman, B. J. 2000a. Self-efficacy: An essential motive to learn. *Contemporary Educational Psychology* 25:82-91.

———. 2000b. Attaining self-regulation: A social cognitive perspective. In *Handbook of self-regulation,* 13-39, ed. M. Boekaerts, P. R. Pintrich, and M. Zeidner. San Diego: Academic Press.

Zimmerman, B. J., and M. Martinez-Pons. 1990. Student differences in self-regulated learning: Relating grade, sex, and giftedness to self-efficacy and strategy use. *Journal of Educational Psychology* 82:51-59.

Howard Margolis is a professor of special education at Queens College of the City University of New York in Flushing. Patrick P. McCabe is an associate professor in the Graduate Literacy Education Program at St. John's University in Jamaica, New York.

From *The Clearing House,* July/August 2004, pp. 241-249. Reprinted by permission of the Helen Dwight Reid Educational Foundation. Published by Heldref Publications, 1319, Eighteenth St., NW, Washington, DC 20036-1802. Copyright © 2004.

Help for Stressed Students

**Through creative strategies, secondary schools can
reduce academic stress and make learning more meaningful.**

Denise Clark Pope and Richard Simon

A high school counselor boasts about the "best and brightest" students in her school. They are motivated and diligent, they enroll in honors and advanced placement courses and achieve high grades and test scores. They play sports, participate in theater and music programs, and serve as community volunteers and school leaders. They "do everything and do it well."

But recent research shows a different, more troubling view. To get ahead, many of these high-achieving students feel compelled to compromise their values and manipulate the system. They admit to scheming, lying, and cheating to get the grades they believe they need for future success. They aren't engaged in meaningful learning experiences. Instead they are busy, in their own words, "doing school."

"Doing School"

This alternate picture of high-achieving adolescents emerged from an in-depth yearlong study of five motivated and successful students—two boys and three girls from diverse ethnic and socioeconomic backgrounds—documented in *"Doing School" How We Are Creating a Generation of Stressed Out, Materialistic, and Miseducated Students* (Pope, 2001). Other large-scale research and news reports have echoed the study's findings (see Hardy, 2003; Roeser & Eccles, 1998).

Instead of thinking deeply about the content of their courses, students who are "doing school" focus on managing their workloads and cutting corners. They memorize facts and figures just long enough to ace the exams and then move on to the next set of tasks. They form classroom alliances to win favors from teachers and administrators, who wield great power as they dole out grades and write college recommendation letters. As one student notes,

> People don't go to school to learn. They go to get good grades, which brings them to college, which brings them the high-paying job, which brings them to happiness, so they think. But basically, grades are where it's at. (Pope, 2001, p. 4)

In addition to the stresses usually associated with adolescence—negotiating relationships with parents and peers and dealing with the many changes of puberty—these college-bound students are often overwhelmed with school, home, and work responsibilities. One honor student in the study takes several advanced placement courses and is involved in numerous school clubs, including School Site Council, Mock Trial, and the Spanish Club. She plays field hockey and badminton and performs in the school band. She reflects on her hectic high school experience:

> I sometimes have two or three days where I only get two hours of sleep per night. I see lots of my friends burned out, but I don't have time to worry about this. Some people see health and happiness as more important than grades and college; I don't. I feel compelled to compete because we have a really smart class, and I am competing with them to get into col-

> **Pressure for high achievement in school has become a significant risk factor for adolescent mental and physical health, academic integrity, and school engagement.**

This student and others like her call themselves "robo-students." They drag themselves through the school day, exhausted and living in a constant state of stress. Some sacrifice sleep, healthy eating, and exercise to pursue high grade point averages. Others suffer from anxiety and depression as they compare themselves with their peers and realize that a *B* grade, once considered good, may now be a liability. They know that more students than ever are applying to selective colleges, and their guidance counselors advise them to take the most rigorous courses available and to get the highest test scores possible to gain admission to these schools.

The students regret the frantic pace and the sacrifices they make, but they see no other way to achieve their goals and meet the often unrealistic expectations of their parents, teachers, peers, and community. Now more than ever before, pressure for high achievement in school has become a significant risk factor for adolescent mental and physical health, academic integrity, and school engagement.

Promising Initiatives

How can schools address the causes and consequences of academic stress and improve the health and well-being of their students? The efforts of one public high school in New York and a research-based intervention at Stanford University yield some strategies.

A Schoolwide Plan

Many students at the Wheatley School, a public high school in the affluent community of Old Westbury, New York, are carbon copies of the five students profiled in *Doing School*. In a course taught by the principal, students used their journal entries to passionately describe the pressure of living in a community that expects all students to go to top-notch four-year colleges. They wrote about plagiarism, sleep deprivation, and test anxiety as well as the use of expensive tutors, therapists, caffeine, and prescription pills. One student described the pressure as "never-ending":

> There is no margin of error. When someone gets a *C* on a quiz, they cry. I received a *C+* in Spanish. My parents were screaming at me, and they said I should get a tutor. They have no idea what it is like to go to school—how much pressure it is.

In response to these concerns, the school gave copies of *Doing School* to each faculty member and all interested students and parents and provided time during the school day for extensive discussion and debate about student stress. Within a few months, the school community agreed to make reducing stress on students a leading goal. A team of faculty members, students, parents, and administrators then developed an action plan that began with seven tasks:

- Measure the level of stress for students and faculty using multiple survey instruments.
- Address the topic of stress in one or more of Wheatley's Community Dialogue Nights.
- Reduce testing during the midterm period.
- Continue a faculty dialogue on ways to reduce student stress.
- Create a new intervention program for students who do poorly in school because they cannot deal with the competition and stress.
- Explore the idea of making lunch mandatory for all students. (Almost 20 percent of students were using the lunch period to take an additional academic course.)
- Hire consultants to teach faculty how to incorporate stress

reduction activities into their classrooms.

The school is currently implementing each of these activities. In addition, teachers have begun to announce homework assignments well in advance, reduce the amount of homework they give (especially on weekends), and offer more extra-credit opportunities. Teachers have also started giving students more choice about the items that they answer on tests and about the test scores that will count toward their final grades. Additional recommendations that have emerged from community meetings include giving more long-term, meaningful assignments, such as culminating unit projects that focus on mastery of skills; making vacations homework-free; teaching students ways to relax in stressful situations; and educating parents about the effects of stress and pressure.

The long-term success of these strategies remains to be seen. Almost two years after discussions began and only a few months into the implementation of the changes, some students continue to report schedules that leave little time for sleep and a belief that a grade of *B* or even *B+* is akin to an *F*. One 10th grader wrote,

> Every kid in our school strives to be the perfect well-rounded student, and to excel at everything. Juggling sports, school, clubs, and various other extracurriculars, it's hard to fit sleep into our busy schedules. Right now as I am typing this, I still have two labs, math, and social studies homework to do.

Some positive results, however, are clear. Staff members now recognize the stress problem as real and feel more empathy toward the students. As all parties become more aware of the issue, teachers and administrators feel empowered to make incremental changes that have the potential to reduce stress—or at least make it more manageable.

A University Initiative

Another promising initiative is under way at Stanford University, where an interdepartmental advisory board responded to nationwide reports of increased anxiety and depression among college students (Benton, Robertson,

Tseng, Newton, & Benton, 2003). The board created the Stressed Out Students (SOS) project, an intervention to counter academic stress at the middle school and high school levels. Inspired in part by Wheatley's approach, the board developed a plan based on stakeholder dialogue and site-based school reform efforts.

> "Some people see health and happiness as more important than grades and college; I don't"

Following a public forum on academic stress to educate schools and community members about the severity and scope of the problem, Stanford hosted 15 local school teams of principals and other administrators, teachers, parents, and students for a one-day workshop devoted to fostering health, school engagement, and academic integrity. Each school team then met at least twice during the summer with an SOS coach to discuss the root causes of academic stress at its school and to develop plans for change. In November, the school teams came together again to share success stories, to determine benchmarks for assessing progress, and to problem-solve together to improve change efforts.

Multiple Strategies

From the experiences of Wheatley and the input from many other schools involved in the SOS project, we offer the following collection of strategies that schools are implementing to reduce student stress and increase engagement.

Collaborate with students and parents. Several schools in the SOS project have noted the benefits of having student and parent representation on their stress reduction teams. Many schools have surveyed students and parents about issues related to academic stress, including student workload, homework time, extracurricular activities, sleep habits, course expectations, and college admissions. The schools use this information to identify the scope of the problem, to effect further change, and to determine progress each year.

Improve students' use of time. Many schools have enacted changes related to students' use of time by eliminating midsemester exams, scheduling final exams before vacation, or eliminating summer assignments to give students some real time off. Some schools are using test and project calendars across grade levels to prevent scheduling conflicts that force students to take several tests or turn in several major projects on the same day. Other schools have created homework guidelines that ask teachers to consider the purpose of each assignment and to track how long each student takes to complete the assignment. Several schools are moving toward block scheduling, realizing that the traditional seven-period day causes undue stress on students as they race from class to class and struggle each night to complete homework for seven courses. And some schools have implemented delayed starts once a week to allow students some extra sleep time and to give teachers some extra planning or professional development time.

Develop mental health initiatives. Schools are working to provide counseling services that prevent stress instead of just reacting to the many cases of anxious and depressed students. Counselors teach classes on time management, stress reduction, yoga, and meditation. Another stress reducer is an advisory system in which teachers work with 15–20 students during a homeroom or tutorial period. Students and adults get to know one another well and can identify appropriate resources for help as problems arise.

Redefine success. To address the assumptions that underlie their competitive climates, schools need to ask themselves, What does real learning look like? How do we define success in school and life? Are we communicating these broad definitions of success to our students?

As a result of reflecting on such questions, some schools in the SOS project are changing the way they publicly honor students so that they celebrate academic excellence without making all students feel unhealthy pressure to compete for the same goals. Many schools have stopped ranking students by GPA or awarding valedictorians. Instead of posting pictures of students who earn a 4.0 grade point average or listing the names of the colleges that seniors will attend, some schools honor students who represent a broader definition of success, such as students who serve their school and community, who excel in athletics or the arts, or who demonstrate dedication to a cause or passion.

Raise parents' awareness. Because unreasonable parental expectations can fuel higher levels of stress, schools have instituted parent education evenings to address the pressures that well-meaning families place on their children. School counselors explain to parents that college should not be considered a status symbol but should represent the best fit between the student and the school. They encourage parents to work with their children to assess which activities and courses to take, keeping in mind the students' interests and passions, not just university admissions criteria.

Change curriculum and assessment policies. Finally, schools are making real strides toward engaging students and fostering motivation. Studies show that students are more likely to engage with school when they care about the subject matter, see that it connects to their lives in some way, and have some autonomy over their studies (see Intrator, 2004). Teachers are developing curriculum around student interests and are replacing traditional unit exams with culminating projects that allow for authentic assessment. Instead of relying mostly on lecture-based instruction, teachers can vary their techniques to include more student-centered approaches, such as small-group discussions and dramatic enactments.

Although difficult to put into place, these classroom-level changes are an integral part of reducing student stress and fostering academic integrity and engagement.

Creating a More Balanced Culture

It won't be easy to change the culture in school and society that places a premium on academic achievement and competition. Yet the experiences of the Wheatley School and the Stressed Out Students project show that when schools work together with parents and students to recognize the problem of academic stress and address its root causes, the process of reforming schools can begin.

The school change strategies described here, however, can only go so far in changing the culture of unhealthy competition in our schools. Colleges and universities need to join this conversation and send different messages to our high school students. Some, like Stanford and MIT, have already grappled with this issue and made changes in their admissions practices. For instance, MIT now limits the number of extracurricular activities a candidate may list on the application and asks students to write an essay about what gets them excited. Stanford posts a letter on its admissions Web site explaining that it will not necessarily admit the students who take the most AP courses.

Changes like these may be outside the purview of K–12 schools. But if we want lasting, fundamental reform, everyone in society must work toward creating a healthier culture for our adolescent learners.

References

Benton, S. A., Robertson, J. M., Tseng, W., Newton, F. B., & Benton, S. L. (2003). Changes in counseling center client problems across 13 years. Professional Psychology: *Research and Practice, 34*(1), 66–72.

Hardy, L. (2003). Overburdened, overwhelmed. *American School Board Journal, 190*(4), 18–23.

Intrator, S. M. (2004). The engaged classroom. *Educational Leadership, 62*(1), 20–24.

Pope, D. C. (2001). *"Doing school": How we are creating a generation of stressed out, materialistic, and miseducated students.* New Haven: Yale University Press.

Roeser, R. W., & Eccles, J. S. (1998). Adolescents' perceptions of middle school. *Journal of Research on Adolescence, 8*(1), 123–158.

Denise Clark Pope is a Lecturer in the School of Education, Stanford University, Stanford, California; 650-736-1779; dclark@sanford.edu. Richard Simon is Principal of the Wheatley School, Old Westbury, New York; 516-333-7846; simon@ewsdonline.org.

When Children Make Rules

In constructivist classrooms, young children's participation in rule making promotes their moral development.

Rheta DeVries and Betty Zan

Sherice Hetrick-Ortman's kindergartners were passionate about block building. These children at the Freeburg Early Childhood Program in Waterloo, Iowa, lavished care on their complex structures and felt justly proud of their creations. Some of the children were concerned, however, about problems in the block area. They discussed the matter at group time and came up with some new rules to post in the block-building area:

- Keep hands off other people's structures.
- No knocking people's structures down.
- Four friends in the block area at one time.

When children care about a classroom problem such as this one and take part in solving it, they are more likely to view the resulting rules as fair. Having *made* the rules, they are more likely to observe them. Just as important, participating in the process of rule making supports children's growth as moral, self-regulating human beings.

Rules in schools have traditionally been made by teachers and given to children. Today, many teachers see the benefits of allowing children to have a voice in developing classroom rules. But if we are not careful, this involvement can be superficial and meaningless. How can we best involve children in making classroom rules?

Morality and Adult-Child Relationships

We speak from a constructivist point of view, inspired by the research and theory of Jean Piaget. In constructivist education, rule making is part of the general atmosphere of mutual respect, and the goal is children's moral and intellectual development (DeVries & Zan, 1994).

Piaget (19832/1965) identified two types of morality that parallel two types of adult-child relationships: one that promotes optimal moral and intellectual development, and one that retards it. *Heteronomous* morality consists of conformity to external rules without question. Overly coercive relationships with adults foster this type of morality and can impede children's development of self-regulation. *Autonomous* morality, by contrast, derives from an internal need to relate to other people in moral ways. Cooperative relationships with adults foster this type of morality and help children develop high levels of self-regulation.

Obviously, children and adults are not equals. However, when the adult respects the child as a person with a right to exercise his or her will, their relationship has a certain psychological equality that promotes autonomy.

Piaget, of course, did not advocate complete freedom, and neither do we. Although constructivist teachers minimize the exercise of adult authority or coercion in relation to children, *minimize* does not mean *eliminate* (DeVries, 1999; DeVries & Edmiaston, 1999; DeVries & Kohlberg, 1987/1990). Rather, we strive for a balance that steadily builds the child's regulation of his or her own behavior.

Norms and Rules in Constructivist Classrooms

To investigate how constructivist teachers use external control and how they develop classroom norms and rules, we interviewed the teachers at the Freeburg Early Childhood Program, a laboratory school serving children ages 3–7 in a predominantly low-income neighborhood. The school's aim is to demonstrate constructivist practices.

Norms Established by Teachers

We define *norms* as specific expectations that teachers establish for children's behavior—ways of behaving that everyone takes for granted as part of the culture of the classroom. A norm is usually unwritten and sometimes unspoken until someone violates it and the teacher takes corrective action. The Freeburg teachers' reflections revealed three kinds of norms that existed in their classrooms:

- *Safety and health norms* ensure children's well-being. Our teachers articulated these as non-negotiables. Examples include "No hurting others," "Lie down at rest time," "Keep shoes on outside," "No crashing trikes or other vehicles," and "Don't throw sand."
- *Moral norms* pertain to respect for people and animals. They often relate to fair treatment or distribution of goods. Examples of these are "Take fair turns," "Talk through a conflict until there is a resolution," "If you bring a live animal into the classroom, try to make it comfortable," and "No hurting animals."
- *Discretionary norms* consist of routines and procedures to make the classroom run smoothly and make learning possible. Kathy Morris, the teacher in the 3-year-olds' class, pointed out that

young children do not like chaos, and they need adults to figure out routines that work so that events run smoothly. Discretionary norms also include societal norms for politeness and individual responsibility that children need to know. Examples include "Sit with the group at group time," "Wait until all are seated at lunch before eating," and "Clean up your place after lunch."

All teachers must sometimes exert external control.

All teachers have safety and health norms, moral norms, and discretionary norms. These norms are acceptable and necessary uses of external authority in a constructivist classroom. But constructivist teachers carefully evaluate their reasons for norms and attempt to minimize the use of external control as much as possible.

Rules Made by Children

We define rules as formal agreements among teachers and children. Constructivist teachers often conduct discussions of problems that relate to their norms and engage children in making classroom rules that arise from these norms.

When teachers first suggest that children make rules, children often parrot such adult admonitions as "Never talk to strangers" or "Raise your hand and wait to be called on." This occurs especially when children are unaccustomed to a sociomoral atmosphere in which they feel free to express their honest opinions. Children may view rule making as another exercise in trying to figure out the right answer or say what they think the teacher wants to hear. The rules that they suggest may not reflect a real understanding of the need to treat others in moral ways. When children only mindlessly restate adults' rules, they have not engaged in true rule making.

Children who engage in true rule making sometimes reinvent rules that elaborate on already established norms. Although these elaborations are not entirely original, they still give the children feelings of autonomy in their power to create rules. For example, Gwen Harmon's 4-year-olds, working within the classroom norm "Don't hurt animals," developed the following practical and concrete rules regarding the chicks that they hatched in the classroom:

- Pick them up safely.
- Don't push them.

- Don't squeeze them.
- Don't put things in their box.
- Don't punch them.
- Don't put them on the light bulb.
- Don't drop them.
- Don't throw them.
- Don't pick them up by their wings.
- Don't color on them.
- Don't pull their heads off.

Reinvented rules demonstrate children's understanding of the moral norm because they translate the norm into children's own words and provide elaborations that make sense to them. Sometimes the elaborations are novel, dealing with situations that the teacher had not considered discussing. For example, in Beth Van Meeteren's 1st grade classroom, where the norm is to treat others with respect, children made the rule, "When people pass gas, do not laugh, or they will be upset or embarrassed."

Sometimes children develop entirely original rules. Unlike reinvented rules, invented rules reflect children's power to make decisions in the classroom. For example, Dora Chen's class of 4-year-olds invented a new rule in response to a problem they saw during one of their classroom routines. One day during clean-up, a child saw another child finishing a snack and felt that no one should eat snacks during clean-up time. He told the teacher, who raised the issue at group time. She asked, "What should our rule be?" After a 17-minute discussion in which the children suggested various possibilities, the teacher clarified the choice between "No snack during clean-up: throw it away" or "Finish snack before going outdoors." The children voted to throw away their unfinished snacks when clean-up started.

The new rule, driven by children's interest and concern, went beyond the teacher's concerns. Although the teacher preferred giving the children more time to finish their snacks, she believed that the children's solution was fair given the one-hour activity time in which to eat snacks.

Guidelines for Exerting External Control

Some people have the misconception that constructivist teachers are permissive and that external control never occurs in constructivist classrooms. In fact, all teachers must exert external control sometimes. From our discussions with teachers and our understanding of research and theory,

we have derived four general guidelines for the use of external control.

Provide a general and pervasive context of warmth, cooperation, and community. We draw inspiration for this guideline from the work of Jean Piaget, especially from *The Moral Judgment of the Child* (1932/1965). Many others, however, have come to this same conclusion starting from different theoretical perspectives (Nelson, 1996; Watson, 2003). In fact, almost all of the recent classroom management programs on the market, with the exception of Assertive Discipline, stress the importance of cooperation and community (Charles, 2002).

Act with the goal of students' self-regulation. A developmental perspective leads us to focus on the long term. We want to contribute to the development of autonomous, self-regulating human beings who can make decisions based on the perspectives of all involved. Therefore, compliance is not our primary goal. Of course, we all wish sometimes that children would be more compliant. But we constantly remind ourselves and one another that developing self-regulation takes time, and we celebrate significant events, such as when an aggressive child actually uses words for the first time to tell another child what he wants instead of slugging him.

Minimize unnecessary external control as much as is possible and practical. Constructivist teachers do use external control; in fact, they use it quite a bit. As Piaget states, "However delicately one may put the matter, there have to be commands and therefore duties" (1932/1965, p. 180). Teachers in constructivist classrooms, however, use external control of children consciously and deliberately, not impulsively or automatically. The teachers with whom we work constantly ask themselves whether the external regulation is absolutely necessary.

Through discussions with teachers Gwen Harmon, Shari McGhee, and Christie Sales, we have identified several situations that can lead to unnecessary control of children. Avoidable control-inducing situations occur when

- The classroom arrangement invites rowdy behavior.
- Children do not know the classroom routine.
- Too many transitions lead to too much waiting time.
- Crowding in a part of the classroom leads to conflicts.

- Group time goes on for too long; children become restless, and some act out.
- Activities are not sufficiently engaging to appeal to children's purposes, and children become aimless.
- The classroom does not contain enough materials, and children compete for what is available.
- Clean-up is poorly organized, and children resist cleaning up after activity time.
- A mismatch exists between the teacher's expectations and the children's competencies.
- The teacher attributes a character flaw to a child who misbehaves.

When external control is necessary, use the least amount necessary to secure compliance. Ideally, the constructivist teacher uses external control judiciously to make sure that the child's experience overall is a mixture increasingly in favor of the child's self-regulation. When external regulation becomes necessary, the teacher must preserve the child's dignity and autonomy—for example, by giving the child a choice and thus returning a degree of autonomy as soon as possible.

Meaningful Rule Making

For many years, we have advocated allowing young children to make classroom rules, arguing that such opportunities are part and parcel of a constructivist, democratic classroom. By encouraging children to make classroom rules, the teacher minimizes unnecessary external control and promotes the development of children's moral and intellectual autonomy.

To genuinely think for themselves and exercise autonomy, children must be given the power to make rules and decisions that both elaborate on classroom norms and break new ground. By actively seeking out appropriate opportunities and recognizing them when they arise in the daily life of the classroom, teachers can create classrooms that are fair and democratic.

References

Charles, C. (2002). *Building classroom discipline* (7th ed.). Boston: Allyn and Bacon.

DeVries, R. (1999). Implications of Piaget's constructivist theory for character education. In M. Williams & E. Schaps (Eds.), *Character education*. Washington, DC: Character Education Partnership.

DeVries, R., & Edmiaston, R. (1999). Misconceptions about constructivist education. *The Constructivist, 13*(3), 12–19.

DeVries, R., & Kohlberg, L. (1987/1990). *Constructivist early education*. Washington, DC: National Association for the Education of Young Children.

DeVries, R., & Zan, B. (1994). *Moral classrooms, moral children: Creating a constructivist atmosphere in early education*. New York: Teachers College Press.

Nelson, J. (1996). *Positive discipline*. New York: Ballantine Books.

Piaget, J. (1932/1965). *The moral judgment of the child*. London: Free Press.

Watson, M. (2003). *Learning to trust*. San Francisco: Jossey-Bass.

Rheta DeVries is a professor and Director of the Regents' Center for Early Developmental Education, University of Northern Iowa, 107 Schindler Education Center, Cedar Falls, IA 50701; (391) 273–2101; rheta.devries@uni.edu. **Betty Zan** is an assistant professor and Research Fellow at the Regents' Center for Early Developmental Education; (319) 273–2101; betty.zan@uni.edu.

The Key to Classroom Management

By using research-based strategies combining appropriate levels of dominance and cooperation and an awareness of student needs, teachers can build positive classroom dynamics.

Robert J. Marzano and Jana S. Marzano

Today, we know more about teaching than we ever have before. Research has shown us that teachers' actions in their classrooms have twice the impact on student achievement as do school policies regarding curriculum, assessment, staff collegiality, and community involvement (Marzano, 2003a). We also know that one of the classroom teacher's most important jobs is managing the classroom effectively.

A comprehensive literature review by Wang, Haertel, and Walberg (1993) amply demonstrates the importance of effective classroom management. These researchers analyzed 86 chapters from annual research reviews, 44 handbook chapters, 20 government and commissioned reports, and 11 journal articles to produce a list of 228 variables affecting student achievement. They combined the results of these analyses with the findings from 134 separate meta-analyses. Of all the variables, classroom management had the largest effect on student achievement. This makes intuitive sense—students cannot learn in a chaotic, poorly managed classroom.

Research not only supports the importance of classroom management, but it also sheds light on the dynamics of classroom management. Stage and Quiroz's meta-analysis (1997) shows the importance of there being a balance between teacher actions that provide clear consequences for unacceptable behavior and teacher actions that recognize and reward acceptable behavior. Other researchers (Emmer, Evertson, & Worsham, 2003; Evertson, Emmer, & Worsham, 2003) have identified important components of classroom management, including beginning the school year with a positive emphasis on management; arranging the room in a way conducive to effective management; and

identifying and implementing rules and operating procedures.

In a recent meta-analysis of more than 100 studies (Marzano, 2003b), we found that the quality of teacher-student relationships is the keystone for all other aspects of classroom management. In fact, our meta-analysis indicates that on average, teachers who had high-quality relationships with their students had 31 percent fewer discipline problems, rule violations, and related problems over a year's time than did teachers who did not have high-quality relationships with their students.

> The quality of teacher-student relationships is the keystone for all other aspects of classroom management.

What are the characteristics of effective teacher-student relationships? Let's first consider what they are not. Effective teacher-student relationships have nothing to do with the teacher's personality or even with whether the students view the teacher as a friend. Rather, the most effective teacher-student relationships are characterized by specific teacher behaviors: exhibiting appropriate levels of dominance; exhibiting appropriate levels of cooperation; and being aware of high-needs students.

Appropriate Levels of Dominance

Wubbels and his colleagues (Wubbels, Brekelmans, van Tartwijk, & Admiral,

1999; Wubbels & Levy, 1993) identify appropriate dominance as an important characteristic of effective teacher-student relationships. In contrast to the more negative connotation of the term *dominance* as forceful control or command over others, they define dominance as the teacher's ability to provide clear purpose and strong guidance regarding both academics and student behavior. Studies indicate that when asked about their preferences for teacher behavior, students typically express a desire for this type of teacher-student interaction. For example, in a study that involved interviews with more than 700 students in grades 4–7, students articulated a clear preference for strong teacher guidance and control rather than more permissive types of teacher behavior (Chiu & Tulley, 1997). Teachers can exhibit appropriate dominance by establishing clear behavior expectations and learning goals and by exhibiting assertive behavior.

Establish Clear Expectations and Consequences

Teachers can establish clear expectations for behavior in two ways: by establishing clear rules and procedures, and by providing consequences for student behavior.

The seminal research of the 1980s (Emmer, 1984; Emmer, Sanford, Evertson, Clements, & Martin, 1981; Evertson & Emmer, 1982) points to the importance of establishing rules and procedures for general classroom behavior, group work, seat work, transitions and interruptions, use of materials and equipment, and beginning and ending the period or the day. Ideally, the class should establish these rules and procedures through discussion and mutual consent by teacher and students (Glasser, 1969, 1990).

Along with well-designed and clearly communicated rules and procedures, the teacher must acknowledge students' behavior, reinforcing acceptable behavior and providing negative consequences for unacceptable behavior. Stage and Quiroz's research (1997) is instructive. They found that teachers build effective relationships through such strategies as the following:

- Using a wide variety of verbal and physical reactions to students' misbehavior, such as moving closer to offending students and using a physical cue, such as a finger to the lips, to point out inappropriate behavior.
- Cuing the class about expected behaviors through prearranged signals, such as raising a hand to indicate that all students should take their seats.
- Providing tangible recognition of appropriate behavior—with tokens or chits, for example.
- Employing group contingency policies that hold the entire group responsible for behavioral expectations.
- Employing home contingency techniques that involve rewards and sanctions at home.

Establish Clear Learning Goals

Teachers can also exhibit appropriate levels of dominance by providing clarity about the content and expectations of an upcoming instructional unit. Important teacher actions to achieve this end include

- Establishing and communicating learning goals at the beginning of a unit of instruction.
- Providing feedback on those goals.
- Continually and systematically revisiting the goals.
- Providing summative feedback regarding the goals.

The use of rubrics can help teachers establish clear goals. To illustrate, assume that a teacher has identified the learning goal "understanding and using fractions" as important for a given unit. That teacher might present students with the following rubric:

4 points. You understand the characteristics of fractions along with the different types. You can accurately describe how fractions are related to decimals and

percentages. You can convert fractions to decimals and can explain how and why the process works. You can use fractions to understand and solve different types of problems.

3 points. You understand the basic characteristics of fractions. You know how fractions are related to decimals and percentages. You can convert fractions to decimals.

2 points. You have a basic understanding of the following, but have some small misunderstandings about one or more: the characteristics of fractions; the relationships among fractions, decimals, and percentages; how to convert fractions to decimals.

1 point. You have some major problems or misunderstandings with one or more of the following: the characteristics of fractions; the relationships among fractions, decimals, and percentages; how to convert fractions to decimals.

0 points. You may have heard of the following before, but you do not understand what they mean: the characteristics of fractions; the relationships among fractions, decimals, and percentages; how to convert fractions to decimals.

The clarity of purpose provided by this rubric communicates to students that their teacher can provide proper guidance and direction in academic content.

Exhibit Assertive Behavior

Teachers can also communicate appropriate levels of dominance by exhibiting assertive behavior. According to Emmer and colleagues, assertive behavior is

the ability to stand up for one's legitimate rights in ways that make it less likely that others will ignore or circumvent them. (2003, p. 146)

Assertive behavior differs significantly from both passive behavior and aggressive behavior. These researchers explain that teachers display assertive behavior in the classroom when they

- Use assertive body language by maintaining an erect posture; facing the offending student but keeping enough distance so as not to appear threatening and matching the facial expression with the content of the message being presented to students.
- Use an appropriate tone of voice, speaking clearly and deliberately in a

pitch that is slightly but not greatly elevated from normal classroom speech, avoiding any display of emotions in the voice.

- Persist until students respond with the appropriate behavior. Do not ignore an inappropriate behavior; do not be diverted by a student denying, arguing, or blaming, but listen to legitimate explanations.

Appropriate Levels of Cooperation

Cooperation is characterized by a concern for the needs and opinions of others. Although not the antithesis of dominance, cooperation certainly occupies a different realm. Whereas dominance focuses on the teacher as the driving force in the classroom, cooperation focuses on the students and teacher functioning as a team. The interaction of these two dynamics—dominance and cooperation—is a central force in effective teacher-student relationships. Several strategies can foster appropriate levels of cooperation.

Provide Flexible Learning Goals

Just as teachers can communicate appropriate levels of dominance by providing clear learning goals, they can also convey appropriate levels of cooperation by providing flexible learning goals. Giving students the opportunity to set their own objectives at the beginning of a unit or asking students what they would like to learn conveys a sense of cooperation. Assume, for example, that a teacher has identified the topic of fractions as the focus of a unit of instruction and has provided students with a rubric. The teacher could then ask students to identify some aspect of fractions or a related topic that they would particularly like to study. Giving students this kind of choice, in addition to increasing their understanding of the topic, conveys the message that the teacher cares about and tries to accommodate students' interests.

Teachers with effective classroom management skills are aware of high-needs students and have a repertoire of specific techniques for meeting some of their needs.

Take a Personal Interest in Students

Probably the most obvious way to communicate appropriate levels of cooperation is to take a personal interest in each student in the class. As McCombs and Whisler (1997) note, all students appreciate personal attention from the teacher. Although busy teachers—particularly those at the secondary level—do not have the time for extensive interaction with all students, some teacher actions can communicate personal interest and concern without taking up much time. Teachers can

- Talk informally with students before, during, and after class about their interests.
- Greet students outside of school—for instance, at extracurricular events or at the store.
- Single out a few students each day in the lunchroom and talk with them.
- Be aware of and comment on important events in students' lives, such as participation in sports, drama, or other extracurricular activities.
- Compliment students on important achievements in and outside of school.
- Meet students at the door as they come into class; greet each one by name.

Use Equitable and Positive Classroom Behaviors

Programs like Teacher Expectations and Student Achievement emphasize the importance of the subtle ways in which teachers can communicate their interest in students (Kerman, Kimball, & Martin, 1980). This program recommends many practical strategies that emphasize equitable and positive classroom interactions with all students. Teachers should, for example,

- Make eye contact with each student. Teachers can make eye contact by scanning the entire room as they speak and by freely moving about all sections of the room.
- Deliberately move toward and stand close to each student during the class period. Make sure that the seating arrangement allows the teacher and students clear and easy ways to move around the room.
- Attribute the ownership of ideas to the students who initiated them. For instance, in a discussion a teacher might say, "Cecilia just added to Aida's idea by saying that...."

- Allow and encourage all students to participate in class discussions and interactions. Make sure to call on students who do not commonly participate, not just those who respond most frequently.
- Provide appropriate wait time for all students to respond to questions, regardless of their past performance or your perception of their abilities.

Awareness of High-Needs Students

Classroom teachers meet daily with a broad cross-section of students. In general, 12–22 percent of all students in school suffer from mental, emotional, or behavioral disorders, and relatively few receive mental health services (Adelman & Taylor, 2002). The Association of School Counselors notes that 18 percent of students have special needs and require extraordinary interventions and treatments that go beyond the typical resources available to the classroom (Dunn & Baker, 2002).

Although the classroom teacher is certainly not in a position to directly address such severe problems, teachers with effective classroom management skills are aware of high-needs students and have a repertoire of specific techniques for meeting some of their needs (Marzano, 2003b). Figure 1 summarizes five categories of high-needs students and suggests classroom strategies for each category and subcategory.

- *Passive* students fall into two subcategories: those who fear *relationships* and those who fear *failure*. Teachers can build strong relationships with these students by refraining from criticism, rewarding small successes, and creating a classroom climate in which students feel safe from aggressive people.
- The category of *aggressive* students comprises three subcategories: *hostile, oppositional,* and *covert.* Hostile students often have poor anger control, low capacity for empathy, and an inability to see the consequences of their actions. Oppositional students exhibit milder forms of behavior problems, but they consistently resist following rules, argue with adults, use harsh language, and tend to annoy others. Students in the covert subcategory may be quite pleasant at times,

but they are often nearby when trouble starts and they never quite do what authority figures ask of them. Strategies for helping aggressive students include creating behavior contracts and providing immediate rewards and consequences. Most of all, teachers must keep in mind that aggressive students, although they may appear highly resistant to behavior change, are still children who are experiencing a significant amount of fear and pain.

- Students with *attention* problems fall into two categories: *hyperactive* and *inattentive.* These students may respond well when teachers contract with them to manage behaviors; teach them basic concentration, study, and thinking skills; help them divide tasks into manageable parts; reward their successes; and assign them a peer tutor.
- Students in the *perfectionist* category are driven to succeed at unattainable levels. They are self-critical, have low self-esteem, and feel inferior. Teachers can often help these students by encouraging them to develop more realistic standards, helping them to accept mistakes, and giving them opportunities to tutor other students.
- *Socially inept* students have difficulty making and keeping friends. They may stand too close and touch others in annoying ways, talk too much, and misread others' comments. Teachers can help these students by counseling them about social behaviors.

The most effective classroom managers did not treat all students the same; they tended to employ different strategies with different types of students.

School may be the only place where many students who face extreme challenges can get their needs addressed. The reality of today's schools often demands that classroom teachers address these severe issues, even though this task is not always considered a part of their regular job.

In a study of classroom strategies (see Brophy, 1996; Brophy & McCaslin, 1992), researchers examined how effective classroom teachers interacted with specific types of students. The study found that the most effective classroom managers did not

FIGURE 1 Categories of High-Needs Students			
Category	**Definitions & Source**	**Characteristics**	**Suggestions**
Passive	Behavior that avoids the domination of others or the pain of negative experiences. The child attempts to protect self from criticism, ridicule, or rejection, possibly reacting to abuse and neglect. Can have a biochemical basis, such as anxiety.	**Fear of relationships:** Avoids connection with others, is shy, doesn't initiate conversations, attempts to be invisible. **Fear of failure:** Gives up easily, is convinced he or she can't succeed, is easily frustrated, uses negative self-talk.	Provide safe adult and peer interactions and protections from aggressive people. Provide assertiveness and positive self-talk training. Reward small successes quickly. Withhold criticism.
Aggressive	Behavior that overpowers, dominates, harms, or controls others without regard for their well-being. The child has often taken aggressive people as role models. Has had minimal or ineffective limits set on behavior. Is possibly reacting to abuse and neglect. Condition may have a biochemical basis, such as depression.	**Hostile:** Rages, threatens, or intimidates others. Can be verbally or physically abusive to people, animals, or objects. **Oppositional:** Does opposite of what is asked. Demands that others agree or give in. Resists verbally or nonverbally. **Covert:** Appears to agree but then does the opposite of what is asked. Often acts innocent while setting up problems for others.	Describe the student's behavior clearly. Contract with the student to reward corrected behavior and set up consequences for uncorrected behavior. Be consistent and provide immediate rewards and consequences. Encourage and acknowledge extracurricular activities in and out of school. Give student responsibilities to help teacher or other students to foster successful experiences.
Attention problems	Behavior that demonstrates either motor or attentional difficulties resulting from a neurological disorder. The child's symptoms may be exacerbated by family or social stressors or biochemical conditions, such as anxiety, depression, or bipolar disorders.	**Hyperactive:** Has difficulty with motor control, both physically and verbally. Fidgets, leaves seat frequently, interrupts, talks excessively. **Inattentive:** Has difficulty staying focused and following through on projects. Has difficulty with listening, remembering, and organizing.	Contract with the student to manage behaviors. Teach basic concentration, study, and thinking skills. Separate student in a quiet work area. Help the student list each step of a task. Reward successes; assign a peer tutor.
Perfectionist	Behavior that is geared toward avoiding the embarrassment and assumed shame of making mistakes. The child fears what will happen if errors are discovered. Has unrealistically high expectations of self. Has possibly received criticism or lack of acceptance while making mistakes during the process of learning.	Tends to focus too much on the small details of projects. Will avoid projects if unsure of outcome. Focuses on results and not relationships. Is self-critical.	Ask the student to make mistakes on purpose, then show acceptance. Have the student tutor other students.
Socially inept	Behavior that is based on the misinterpretation of nonverbal signals of others. The child misunderstands facial expressions and body language. Hasn't received adequate training in these areas and has poor role modeling.	Attempts to make friends but is inept and unsuccessful. Is forced to be alone. Is often teased for unusual behavior, appearance, or lack of social skills.	Teach the student to keep the appropriate physical distance from others. Teach the meaning of facial expressions, such as anger and hurt. Make suggestions regarding hygiene, dress, mannerisms, and posture.

Source: Marzano, R. J. (2003). *What works in schools: Translating research into action* (pp. 104–105). Alexandria, VA: ASCD.

treat all students the same; they tended to employ different strategies with different types of students. In contrast, ineffective classroom managers did not appear sensitive to the diverse needs of students. Although Brophy did not couch his findings in terms of teacher-student relationships, the link is clear. An awareness of the five general categories of high-needs students and appropriate actions for each can help teachers build strong relationships with diverse students.

Don't Leave Relationships to Chance

Teacher-student relationships provide an essential foundation for effective classroom management—and classroom management is a key to high student achievement. Teacher-student relationships should not be left to chance or dictated by the personalities of those involved. Instead, by using strategies supported by research, teachers can influence the dynamics of their classrooms and build strong teacher-student relationships that will support student learning.

References

Adelman, H. S., & Taylor, L. (2002). School counselors and school reform: New directions. *Professional School Counseling, 5*(4), 235–248.

Brophy, J. E. (1996). *Teaching problem students.* New York: Guilford.

Brophy, J. E., & McCaslin, N. (1992). Teachers' reports of how they perceive and cope with problem students. *Elementary School Journal, 93,* 3–68.

Chiu, L. H., & Tulley, M. (1997). Student preferences of teacher discipline styles. *Journal of Instructional Psychology, 24*(3), 168–175.

Dunn, N. A., & Baker, S. B. (2002). Readiness to serve students with disabilities: A survey of elementary school counselors. *Professional School Counselors, 5*(4), 277–284.

Emmer, E. T. (1984). *Classroom management: Research and implications.* (R & D Report No. 6178). Austin, TX: Research and Development Center for Teacher Education, University of Texas. (ERIC Document Reproduction Service No. ED251448)

Emmer, E. T., Evertson, C. M., & Worsham, M. E. (2003). *Classroom management for secondary teachers* (6th ed.). Boston: Allyn and Bacon.

Emmer, E. T., Sanford, J. P., Evertson, C. M., Clements, B. S., & Martin, J. (1981). *The classroom management improvement study: An experiment in elementary school classrooms.* (R & D Report No. 6050). Austin, TX: Research and Development Center for Teacher Education, University of Texas. (ERIC Document Reproduction Service No. ED226452)

Evertson, C. M., & Emmer, E. T. (1982). Preventive classroom management. In D. Duke (Ed.), *Helping teachers manage classrooms* (pp. 2–31). Alexandria, VA: ASCD.

Evertson, C. M., Emmer, E. T., & Worsham, M. E. (2003). *Classroom management for elementary teachers* (6th ed.). Boston: Allyn and Bacon.

Glasser, W. (1969). *Schools without failure.* New York: Harper and Row.

Glasser, W. (1990). *The quality school: Managing students without coercion.* New York: Harper and Row.

Kerman, S., Kimball, T., & Martin, M. (1980). *Teacher expectations and student achievement.* Bloomington, IN: Phi Delta Kappan.

Marzano, R. J. (2003a). *What works in schools.* Alexandria, VA: ASCD.

Marzano, R. J. (with Marzano, J. S., & Pickering, D. J.). (2003b). *Classroom management that works.* Alexandria, VA: ASCD.

McCombs, B. L., & Whisler, J. S. (1997). *The learner-centered classroom and school.* San Francisco: Jossey-Bass.

Stage, S. A., & Quiroz, D. R. (1997). A meta-analysis of interventions to decrease disruptive classroom behavior in public education settings. *School Psychology Review, 26*(3), 333–368.

Wang, M. C., Haertel, G. D., & Walberg, H. J. (1993). Toward a knowledge base for school learning. *Review of Educational Research, 63*(3), 249–294.

Wubbels, T., Brekelmans, M., van Tartwijk, J., & Admiral, W. (1999). Interpersonal relationships between teachers and students in the classroom. In H. C. Waxman & H. J. Walberg (Eds.), *New directions for teaching practice and research* (pp. 151–170). Berkeley, CA: McCutchan.

Wubbels, T., & Levy, J. (1993). *Do you know what you look like? Interpersonal relationships in education.* London: Falmer Press.

Robert J. Marzano is a senior scholar at Mid-continent Research for Education and Learning in Aurora, Colorado, and an associate professor at Cardinal Stritch University in Milwaukee, Wisconsin; (303) 796–7683; robertjmarzano@aol.com. His newest book written with Jana S. Marzano and Debra J. Pickering is *Classroom Management That Works* (ASCD, 2003). **Jana S. Marzano** is a licensed professional counselor in private practice in Centennial, Colorado; (303) 220–1151; janamarzan@aol.com.

Twelve Practical Strategies to Prevent Behavioral Escalation in Classroom Settings

SMITA SHUKLA-MEHTA and RICHARD W. ALBIN

Dan is a first-grade student at Edison Elementary with both academic and behavior problems. Although he has not met the classification criteria for special education eligibility, he does demonstrate high rates of off-task behavior and frequently argues with his teachers and other adults. One day during language arts, one of his peers, Samantha, got out of her seat to sharpen her pencil. Dan told Samantha very loudly that she was not supposed to get out of her seat. The teacher told Dan to mind his own business. Dan asked the teacher why Samantha could get up to sharpen her pencils but he could not do the same. The teacher said to Dan, "You need to copy the sentences from the board." Dan pushed his desk forward, made faces and said, "I don't want to!" The teacher walked up to Dan's desk, grabbed his arms and pulled him up from the chair, looked straight into his eyes and said, "One more word out of that mouth and I will send you to the Behavior Room." Dan said angrily, "I wish I was dead and I wish I could use my knife on you." He looked like he was about to cry. The teacher immediately informed the Principal and Dan was sent to Off Campus Detention (OCD) for 3 days. If he really had a knife, he would have been placed in OCD for the remaining days of the school year. This account of an actual incident is an example of behavioral escalation in the classroom.

When the term "behavioral escalation" is used, most people think of a crisis that involves injury to others or damage to physical property. However, in reality, although not every incident reaches crisis level proportions, it could end with a temporary removal of a student from the classroom or school. Examples of such behavior include: engaging the teacher in an argument, using verbal or gestural threats, coming too close to others, using intimidating tactics to coerce the teacher into withdrawing requests, throwing objects, walking out of the classroom or school without permission, resisting physical blocking or holds, or physically hitting others.

Every adult who has dealt with the problem behavior of students who "escalate," is able to give a physical description of the behavior. However, the task of defining behavioral escalation is a different matter altogether (Baer 1982; Evans, Meyer, Kurkjian, and Kishi 1988; Fox and Hoffman 2002; Shukla-Mehta and Albin 2002). Rarely do people think in terms of the structural pattern or the manner in which the various problematic responses are sequentially organized. For purposes of this article, behavioral escalation is defined as an event where a group of topographically (physically) different problem behaviors occur in a sequential pattern in which successive responses are of increasing severity or intensity (Albin, O'Brien, and Horner 1992; Colvin 1990; Lalli, Mace, Wohn, and Livezey 1995; Shukla and Albin 1996; Wahler and Fox 1982). Such sequences usually begin with less severe problems (e.g., whining, complaining, and arguing), many of which can be dealt with easily whereas others escalate and become more severe responses (e.g., throwing furniture, physical assault) that can even cause injury to people and/or damage to property (Shukla 1994).

Most classroom problems are minor and are easily resolved. Unfortunately, during behavioral escalation where both the teacher and student become engaged in a confrontation, classroom instruction comes to a standstill and other students in class become anxious or curious spectators (Hewitt 1999). Although this is true in both general and special education settings, it is more likely to occur in classrooms where the teacher is not properly trained to manage severe behavioral problems. Understandably, teachers want students to comply with requests rather than giving consequences for noncompliance. However, when both student and teacher escalate, students are eventually removed from the classroom for arguing, consistently challenging the teacher, or refusing to follow directions. In special educational settings, teachers may be more inclined to continue to redirect students to avoid behavioral escalation; however, instruction and engagement does end when someone gets hurt (Gunter and Jack 1994). Therefore, experts urge teachers to focus on preventing behavioral escalation rather than managing crisis situations once they occur. In the following discussion, we describe twelve practical strategies identified as empirically effective in preventing behavioral escalation. The strategies apply to general and special education classroom settings and can be useful across various school and non-school environments and with various age groups of children and adolescents.

Reinforce calm and on-task behaviors. Because most behavior is maintained by virtue of some kind of reinforcement (e.g., teacher attention, peer approval), teachers should immediately reinforce students when they display target behaviors like working calmly and being on-task through verbal praise or task assistance on a consistent basis. Teacher attention is a powerful tool. Teachers should not wait to attend to students until they display disruptive behavior; otherwise, inadvertently, problem behavior will be reinforced and will continue to occur in the future (Kennedy 2000). Teachers can walk around the classroom (i.e., use proximity control) and assist and reinforce students who are engaged in academic work (De Pry and Sugai 2002; Gunter, Shores, Jack, Rasmussen, and Flowers 1995). This will address one of the reasons students may seek to escape a task or access teacher attention by using problem behavior. Similarly, provide students with positive attention through a smile, gesture, touch, or a pleasant comment when they display unprompted socially appropriate behavior (e.g., helping a peer to complete a word problem). This will increase the likelihood of socially appropriate behavior instead of problem behavior (Carr, Bailey, Ecott, Lucker, and Weil 1998).

Know the triggers. Most student behavior is triggered (i.e., set off) by something. For example, students may start putting their books in the backpack when they look at the clock and see that only a few minutes are left until class is over. Anything that prompts an action from others is a trigger. For students, triggers for problem behavior may include difficult academic tasks (e.g., word problems involving fractions), less time available for task completion (e.g., 15 vocabulary words in 15 minutes), particular expressions by a teacher or peer (e.g., "Can't you get anything right?" [Albin et al. 1992; Baer 1997; Harrison and Gunter 1996]), or their own behavior (e.g., anxiety about an upcoming exam, not comprehending instruction, or fear of making mistakes [Skinner 1938]). Whenever possible, teachers should work to reduce or eliminate these triggers. For example, if academic task requests act as a trigger, teachers can make curricular or in-

structional adaptations, such as offering choices, extending the time for completing class assignments, providing assistance before the student gets frustrated, or providing the option of working with a peer buddy, depending on the specific problem situation (Dunlap, Kern-Dunlap, Clarke, and Robbins 1991; Gunter, Denny, and Venn 2000; Jolivette, Wehby, Canale, and Massey 2001; Shukla, Kennedy, and Cushing 1999). The best way to deal with such situations is to make these adaptations before behavior problems occur—proactively, not after the fact (Darch, Miller, and Shippen 1998). To be effective, the student must realize that these options are available and that he does not have to resort to inappropriate behavior to solve problems (Clare and Im 1999).

Similarly, teachers should also recognize events that trigger their own behavior (e.g., being questioned by a student, or excessive demands for help; Taylor and Romanczyk 1994). Knowledge of triggers for teacher behavior will allow them to regulate their own behavior and avoid a confrontation with students instead of being drawn into a verbal conflict when provoked (Colvin 2001; Omer 2001; Wahler and Dumas 1986).

Pay attention to anything unusual about the student's behavior. When the student arrives at school each day, note if the student appears distraught, anxious, or preoccupied. Often, previously unresolved problems (e.g., poor sleep, feeling sick, witnessing a fight between parents, or being anxious about an upcoming event) can undermine the otherwise positive effect of teacher reinforcers like praise (Horner, Day, and Day 1997; Kennedy and Meyer 1996). These events (called setting events) may be upsetting to students, so they are more likely to use problem behavior to access quiet space, rest, or low task demands (Kennedy and Meyer 1996). On such occasions when specific setting events play a role, assignment of low preference tasks, difficult or teacher-selected tasks, are more likely to trigger student behavior initiated to escape task demands (O'Reilly 1995). Again, it makes sense to afford students options before acting-out occurs rather than after its occurrence.

Do not escalate along with the student. When early behaviors in a sequence fail to produce the desired outcome (e.g., to avoid a difficult task or to get peer attention), students are more likely to display severe problem behavior (e.g., draw the teacher into a verbal argument [Hewitt 1999; Walker, Colvin, and Ramsey 1995]). This is especially true when in the past, the use of problem behavior may have resulted in escape from task related teacher requests through teacher capitulation or referring student to the office (i.e., a negative reinforcement history [Colvin 1990; Martens, Bradley, and Eckert 1997; Omer 2001; Patterson 1982; Patterson, Reid, and Dishion 1992; Wahler and Dumas 1986]). If students do succeed in drawing teachers into a verbal conflict, teachers should become cognizant of that fact and not escalate along with students. It is important for teachers to remain calm when provoked, especially if students have already lost self-control. Students try to provoke teachers by making comments like, "You can't make me do this," or "Well, I am done with my sentences and I ain't doing any more!" (Hewitt 1999). If teachers also lose self-control, then both persons will escalate together and act inappropriately (Colvin 2001). Teachers are models for socially appropriate behavior and should maintain that stature. Teachers should disengage (i.e., back off) from the confrontation. Depending on the stage and seriousness of the behavior, tactics such as humor (e.g., "Phew! We almost went to war over this!"), redirecting student attention (e.g., "Please review the punctuation on your sentences"), and giving students time or personal space (e.g., "… I will come back in a little bit to see if you need help") to think about their choices (Walker et al. 1995), may provide a break in the sequence of interactions (i.e., removing triggers). Such a break can succeed in preventing an escalation (Baer 1997).

Offer students opportunities to display responsible behavior. Most behavior is a matter of choice (Mace and Roberts 1993). Students choose to display a given behavior (e.g., complain about a peer) on the basis of their past experiences with using the behavior to obtain specific outcomes (e.g., get the teacher's attention and have the peer reprimanded [Fox and Hoffman 2002]). Thus, if the teacher continues to reprimand or redirect the peer, our student's complaining behavior would be reinforced. Such experiences over time create a "learning history," which affects the students' motivation for engaging in specific behaviors. However, if the teacher did not reprimand the peer following student complaints (i.e., put complaining on extinction), then it is likely that complaining will decrease. Students should be taught to take responsibility for their own behavior by making an informed choice on the basis of their knowledge of consequences for both acceptable and problem behavior. For example, when a student is agitated or difficult to redirect, teachers might offer the choice of moving to a quiet area to work, doing an alternative but related task, or asking for help until he or she feels calmer (Colvin 1993; Darch et al. 1998). Making any demand that the student stay on task or behave appropriately when he or she is very agitated will only serve to further escalate the situation. One option would be to verbally prompt the student regarding the right choice and clarify consequences for both the right and the wrong choices. We can do this successfully only if we have made it clear to students that asking for help or quiet time is preferred to acting out (Jayne, Schloss, Alper, and Menscher 1994).

However, if a student is very agitated or in an accelerated state, rational thinking may be difficult because of physiological arousal (e.g., adrenaline rush [Colvin 1993]). At this time, teachers should not attempt to promote appropriate behavior; instead, they should let the student know about the consequences of severe problem behavior such as physical assault or destruction of property. Later, teachers can debrief with the student privately so that the presence of peers (a potential source of peer attention) is not an issue in attempting to resolve the problem. Knowledge of the consequences at an early stage might prompt some students to make a responsible choice and discontinue problem behavior, but only if they possess the skill.

Intervene early in the sequence. Most students have several types of problem behaviors (e.g., complaining, getting out of seat, arguing), that they use to obtain the desired outcome (e.g., avoiding or escaping task requests). Some of these behaviors will be less severe (e.g., pushing task materials away) and others will be more severe (e.g., throwing or breaking task materials [Shukla and Albin 1996]). When less severe behaviors fail to produce the desired effect, some students will resort to more severe problem behaviors. This is how escalation occurs (Shukla 1994; Shukla-Mehta and Albin 2002). By intervening when less severe problem behaviors occur, teachers can avoid a potentially more serious incident.

Teachers should observe to see if there is an obvious pattern or sequence in which the different behaviors occur. Does a behavioral incident usually begin with one or two of the same behaviors each time (e.g., whining, complaining, or questioning the teacher)? Many times these are the early behaviors in the sequence and should be given our attention. When any of these early behaviors occur, teachers should anticipate the next few behaviors in the sequence and use effective strategies noted above to get the situation under control before the student loses control (Shukla 1994). Research and experience show that appropriate early intervention will usually prevent an escalation of behavior to crisis level proportions (Shukla and Albin 1996). Also, intervening after the occurrence of severe problem behavior by removing the student from the classroom might reinforce the student's escape-motivated problem behavior (Lalli, Casey, and Kates 1995).

Understand how such behavioral incidents ended in the past. Whether an incident is minor or major, how it ends will determine the likelihood of future occurrences. Teachers should evaluate the effectiveness of their strategy on the basis of the effect it has on a student's behavior (Horner, Sugai, Todd, and Lewis-Palmer 1999-2000). For example, if a student continues to disrespect the teacher during instruction by making lewd remarks, many schools require that the student be referred to the office. Temporary removal from the classroom could serve the purpose of escaping classroom instruction. Teachers should ask questions such as: Did I succeed in keeping the student focused on task, or did the student get his or her way (e.g., escape completion of class assignments)? If students got their way, then it is likely that they will continue to display such behaviors in the future because they seem to work—they were successful in producing the desired outcome even if the outcome is undesirable to the teacher (O'Neill et al. 1997).

Know the function of problem behaviors. Most students use problem behavior to either get access to something they find pleasant (e.g., peer or teacher attention, a desired item or activity, internal stimulation, or control of a situation), or to avoid or escape something they find unpleasant (e.g., a difficult task, a series of requests, or an nonpreferred teacher [O'Neill et al. 1997]). They will continue to use problem behavior until the desired outcome (reinforcer) is produced (Shukla-Mehta and Albin 2002). In such an instance, it is logical to assume that the various problem behaviors occur for the same function (or purpose [Sprague and Horner 1992]). The student may argue with the teacher, throw materials, or walk out of a class to escape or avoid the task demands of an assignment. However, the same student may use foul language, bully peers, or pass notes in class to get peer attention. Knowing the functions that problem behaviors serve for students is the key to the effective selection of intervention strategies for managing such behaviors (Day, Horner, and O'Neill 1994; Lalli and Kates 1998; O'Neill et al. 1997).

Use good judgment about which behaviors to punish. It is important to make sure that the consequence matches the severity of the problem behavior. In other words, do not use severe punishment (e.g., verbal humiliation or spanking) for mildly disruptive behavior problems (e.g., walking out of seat or pushing task materials away) (Horner et al. 1990) or the same consequence (e.g., in-school suspension) for all types of problem behavior (e.g., talking, arguing, getting out of seat, or hitting a peer [Sugai, Sprague, Horner, and Walker 2000]). Particularly within special education settings, the use of severe punishment for early occurring, less severe problem behaviors may decrease their occurrence momentarily, but lead to an escalation at some other point in the future—a few minutes, a few hours, or a few days later (Colvin 1993). In such a situation, aggression is induced by punishment (Goh and Iwata 1994). When the needs of students are not met, the problem situation still remains unresolved, increasing the likelihood of an escalation in behavior.

Use extinction procedures wisely. The technical definition of extinction is the withdrawal of the consequent stimulus that previously maintained the problem behavior. In other words, extinction pertains to removing or not delivering a specific consequence following the occurrence of a behavior, that in the past, consistently served to reinforce the behavior (i.e., maintained its occurrence). For example, a student uses foul language (behavior) during instruction and the teacher sends the student to the behavior specialist (consequence) on the assumption that the student will not display similar behavior in future. However, if this behavior continues to occur on a daily basis, it is likely that the consequence (escape from the instructional situation) is reinforcing the student's problem behavior. To illustrate, if the teacher wanted to put foul

language on extinction, she would stop sending the student out of the classroom (i.e., remove the reinforcer). Instead, she would use an alternative strategy, for example, teach the student to request assistance for difficult tasks (Durand and Carr 1992).

Teachers advertently or inadvertently use extinction for less severe behavior problems such as complaining or shouting to reduce its occurrence by ignoring the behavior. They believe that if they ignore such behaviors, the student will stop complaining or shouting. However, if these behaviors are maintained by escape, complaining or shouting will stop but the student will escalate to more severe behavior like throwing books or pushing the desk (Shukla and Albin 1996). This is because extinction for less severe behaviors in the sequence may stop their occurrence but motivate the student to engage in more severe behaviors that have produced the desired outcome (Goh and Iwata 1994), leading to an escalation in behavior.

Most experts agree that it is better to use extinction in combination with differential reinforcement of alternative (communication) responses that are more socially acceptable (Carr and Durand 1985; Lalli et al. 1995; Shukla and Albin 1996). For instance, a student argues with the teacher about a grade assigned for a class project because in the past such coercive tactics resulted in changing to a higher grade. If the teacher does not change the grade (i.e., uses extinction), the student may stop arguing and instead press his or her parents to file a complaint against the teacher (more serious behavior). Before that happens, the teacher should use this opportunity to prompt an alternative and socially appropriate response (e.g., asking questions politely, describing logic) instead of arguing. When the student complies, the teacher should provide immediate reinforcement (e.g., "Thanks for asking so politely") and acknowledge appropriate behavior. (The grade may or may not be changed.) This will help to prevent an escalation in behavior while giving the student an opportunity to communicate effectively with the teacher.

Teach students socially appropriate behavior to replace problem behavior. All of the strategies we have described can be successful in preventing a behavioral escalation, but there is no substitute for teaching students socially appropriate behavior or skills to replace problem behavior (Derby et al. 1997; Day et al. 1994; Durand and Carr 1992; Horner and Day 1991; Lalli, Mace, Wohn, and Livezey 1995; Shukla and Albin 1996; Sprague and Horner 1992). Teachers should use their knowledge of the main reasons for the occurrence of behavioral problems and teach alternative social and communication skills that will succeed in producing the same effect as problem behavior does for the student. For example, teach the student to ask for help instead of complaining when a difficult task is assigned. Then, when the student requests help, the teacher must provide assistance immediately and consistently. If not, the student will revert back to complaining because asking for help does not seem to produce the desired effect.

Teach academic survival skills and set students up for success. There is little question that academic failure is positively correlated with behavioral problems (Bulgren and Carta 1993; Cooper and Speece 1990). Teachers who teach academic survival skills to students (Snyder and Bambara 1997) and promote their active engagement (Martens, Lochner, and Kelly 1992), are less likely to be challenged with disruptive behavior (De Pry and Sugai 2002). Also, the use of effective instructional strategies has been known to increase student success and encourage more socially appropriate classroom behavior. Some examples include the use of response cards (Armendariz and Umbreit 1999), where students have the option to write their response to teacher questions on a dry-erase board and raise it up for the teacher to check. This allows the teacher to know the accuracy of the student's response. Alternatively, teachers may also use index cards with previously prepared answers to specific questions, and the student raises the index card with the correct response. The use of guided notes (Lazarus 1991) is also an effective tool. Guided notes are helpful for students who find it difficult to take notes at the speed at which the teacher lectures. Thus, the teacher provides students with notes from her lectures with key words, terminologies, and summary points left blank. The students are required to fill in the blank spaces by paying attention to the lecture notes on the overhead transparencies. This tool makes it easier to take notes. Teachers could also reduce task difficulty by making adaptations in curricula such as using books on tape, incorporating paragraph or chapter summaries, providing vocabulary lists, and similar such techniques. Teachers should also use proactive instructional methods such as pre-correction (Colvin, Patching, and Sugai 1993). Teachers anticipate the mistakes that students might make, either academically or behaviorally, and present a prompt before the error, making it more likely that the student will attend to that prompt and be successful. For example, if a math teacher knows that one of her students has difficulty figuring out the formula for solving fraction problems, she can provide some prompts (e.g., "Remember the rule about the lowest common denominator"). Such a prompt will guide the student to follow the logical path and determine the correct answer.

The various events surrounding the escalation of student behavior problems can pose significant challenges, but they are preventable. If we study carefully the behavioral patterns of students and identify the purpose of problem behavior, then we will be more successful in implementing proactive and preventive strategies. The key is to anticipate the occurrence of events and to use effective preventive strategies instead of falling into the trap of relying on punishment to control student behavior (Horner et al. 1990). Above all, teaching academic survival skills and social skills, just like any other academic con-

tent, is essential to ensuring successful student outcomes. The higher the rate of student success, the less likely the student is to engage in problem behavior (Todd, Horner, and Sugai 1999).

REFERENCES

Albin, R. W., M. O'Brien, and R. H. Horner. 1992. Analysis of an escalating sequence of problem behaviors: A case study. *Research in Developmental Disabilities* 16:133-47.

Armendariz, F., and J. Umbreit. 1999. Using active responding to reduce disruptive behavior in a general education classroom. *The Journal of Positive Behavior Interventions* 1:152-58.

Baer, D. M. 1982. The imposition of structure on behavior and the demolition of behavioral structures. In *Response structure and organization: The 1981 Nebraska symposium on motivation,* edited by J. Bernstein, 217-254. Lincoln: University of Nebraska Press.

Baer, D. M. 1997. Some meanings of antecedent and environmental control. In *Environment and behavior,* edited by D. M. Baer and E. M. Pinkston, 15-29. Boulder, Colo.: Westview Press.

Bulgren, J. A., and J. J. Carta. 1993. Examining the instructional contexts of students with learning disabilities. *Exceptional Children* 59:182-91.

Carr, E. G., and V. M. Durand. 1985. Reducing behavior problems through functional communication training. *Journal of Applied Behavior Analysis* 18:111-26.

Carr, J. E., J. S. Bailey, C. L. Ecott, K. D. Lucker, and T. M. Weil. 1998. On the effects of noncontingent delivery of differing magnitudes of reinforcement. *Journal of Applied Behavior Analysis* 31:313-22.

Clare, C. M., and A. Im. 1999. Choice vs. preference: The effects of choice and no choice of preferred and non-preferred spelling tasks on the academic behavior of students with disabilities. *Journal of Behavioral Education* 9:239-53.

Colvin, G. 2001. *Defusing anger* [Video]. Available from IRIS Media, 258 East 10th Avenue, Suite B, Eugene, OR 97401.

Colvin, G. 1993. *Managing acting-out behavior.* Eugene, Ore.: Behavior Associates.

———. 1990. Procedures for preventing serious acting out behavior in the classroom. *Association for Direct Instruction News* 9, 27-30.

Colvin, G., B. Patching, and G. Sugai. 1993. Precorrection: An instructional approach for managing predictable problem behaviors. *Intervention in School and Clinic* 28:143-50.

Cooper, D. H., and D. L. Speece. 1990. Maintaining at-risk children in regular education settings: Initial effects of individual differences and classroom environment. *Exceptional Children* 54:117-28.

Darch, C., A. Miller, and P. Shippen. 1998. Instructional classroom management: A proactive model for managing student behavior. *Beyond Behavior* 9:18-27.

Day, H. M., R. H. Horner, and R. E. O'Neill. 1994. Multiple functions of problem behaviors: Assessment and intervention. *Journal of Applied Behavior Analysis* 27:279-89.

De Pry, R. L., and G. Sugai. 2002. The effect of active supervision and pre-correction on minor behavioral incidents in a sixth grade general education classroom. *Journal of Behavioral Education* 11:255-67.

Derby, K. M., D. P. Wacker, W. Berg, A. DeRaad, S. Ulrich, J. Asmus, et al. 1997. The long-term effects of functional communication training in home settings. *Journal of Applied Behavior Analysis* 30:507-31.

Dunlap, G., L. Kern-Dunlap, S. Clarke, and F. R. Robbins. 1991. Functional assessment, curricular revision, and severe problem behavior problems. *Journal of Applied Behavior Analysis* 24:387-97.

Durand, V. M., and E. G. Carr. 1992. An analysis of maintenance following functional communication training. *Journal of Applied Behavior Analysis* 25:777-94.

Evans, I. M., L. H. Meyer, J. A. Kurkjian, and G. S. Kishi. 1988. An evaluation of behavioral interrelationships in child behavior therapy. In *Handbook of behavior therapy in education*, edited by J. C. Witt, S. N. Elliot, and F. M. Gresham, 89-215. New York: Plenum.

Fox, S., and M. Hoffman. 2002. Escalation behavior as a specific case of goal-directed activity: A persistence paradigm. *Basic & Applied Social Psychology* 24:273-85.

Goh, H., and B. A. Iwata. 1994. Behavioral persistence and variability during extinction of self-injury maintained by escape. *Journal of Applied Behavior Analysis* 27:173-74.

Gunter, P. L., and S. L. Jack. 1994. Effects of challenging behaviors of students with EBD on teacher instructional behavior. *Preventing School Failure* 38:35-40.

Gunter, P. L., R. L. Shores, S. E. Jack, S. K. Rasmussen, and J. Flowers. 1995. On the move: Using teacher/student proximity to improve students' behaviors. *Teaching Exceptional Children* 28:12-14.

Harrison, J. S., and P. L. Gunter. 1996. Teacher instructional language and negative reinforcement: A conceptual framework for working with students with emotional and behavioral disorders. *Education and Treatment of Children* 19:183-96.

Hewitt, M. B. 1999. The control game: Exploring oppositional behavior. *Reclaiming Children and Youth* 8:30-33.

Horner, R. H., and H. M. Day. 1991. The effects of response efficiency on functionally equivalent competing behaviors. *Journal of Applied Behavior Analysis* 24:719-32.

Horner, R. H., H. M. Day, and J. R. Day. 1997. Using neutralizing routines to reduce problem behaviors. *Journal of Applied Behavior Analysis* 30:601-14.

Horner, R. H., G. Dunlap, R. E. Koegel, E. G. Carr, W. Sailor, J. Anderson, et al. 1990. Toward a technology of "nonaversive" behavioral support. *Journal of the Association for Persons With Severe Handicaps* 15:125-32.

Homer, R. H., G. Sugai, A. W. Todd, and T. Lewis-Palmer. 1999-2000. Elements of behavior support plans: A technical brief. *Exceptionality* 8:205-15.

Jayne, D., P. J. Schloss, S. Alper, and S. Menscher. 1994. Reducing disruptive behavior by training students to request assistance. *Behavior Modification* 18:320-38.

Jolivette, K., J. H. Wehby, J. Canale, and N. G. Massey. 2001. Effects of choice-making opportunities on the behavior of students with emotional and behavioral disorders. *Behavioral Disorders* 26:131-45.

Kennedy, C. H. 2000. When reinforcers for problem behavior are not readily apparent. *Journal of Positive Behavior Interventions* 2:195-201.

Kennedy, C. H., and K. A. Meyer. 1996. Sleep deprivation, allergy symptoms and negatively reinforced behavior. *Journal of Applied Behavior Analysis* 29:133-35.

Lalli, J. S., S. Casey, and K. Kates. 1995. Reducing escape behavior and increasing task completion with functional communication training, extinction, and response chaining. *Journal of Applied Behavior Analysis* 28:261-68.

Lalli, J. S., and K. Kates. 1998. The effect of reinforcer preference on functional analysis outcomes. *Journal of Applied Behavior Analysis* 31:79-90.

Lalli, I. S., F. C. Mace, T. Wohn, and K. Livezey. 1995. Identification and modification of a response-class hierarchy. *Journal of Applied Behavior Analysis* 28:551-59.

Lazarus, B. D. 1991. Guided notes, review, and achievement of secondary students with learning disabilities in main-stream content courses. *Education and Treatment of Children* 14:112-27.

Mace, F. C., and M. L. Roberts. 1993. Factors affecting selection of behavioral interventions. In *Communicative alternatives to challenging behavior: Integrating functional assessment and intervention strategies*, edited by J. Reichle and D. P. Wacker, 113-133. Baltimore: Paul H. Brookes.

Martens, B. K., T. A. Bradley, and T. L. Eckert. 1997. Effects of reinforcement history and instructions on the persistence of student engagement. *Journal of Applied Behavior Analysis* 30:569-72.

Martens, B. K., D. G. Lochner, and S. Q. Kelly. 1992. The effects of variable-interval reinforcement on academic engagement. A demonstration of matching theory. *Journal of Applied Behavior Analysis* 25:143-51.

Omer, H. (2001), Helping parents deal with children's acute disciplinary problems without escalation: The principle of nonviolent resistance. *Family Process* 40:53-66.

O'Neill, R. E., R. H. Horner, R. W. Albin, J. R. Sprague, K. Storey, and S. J. Newton. 1997. *Functional assessment and program development for problem behavior: A practical handbook*. Pacific Grove, Calif: Brooks-Cole.

O'Reilly, M. F. 1995. Functional analysis and treatment of escape-maintained aggression correlated with sleep deprivation. *Journal of Applied Behavior Analysis* 28:225-26.

Patterson, G. 1982. *Coercive family process: A social learning approach to family intervention*. Eugene, Ore.: Castalia.

Patterson, G. R., J. B. Reid, and T. J. Dishion. 1992. *Antisocial boys*. Eugene, Ore.: Castalia.

Shores, R. E., P. L. Gunter, and S. L. Jack. 1993. Classroom management strategies: Are they setting events for coercion? *Behavioral Disorders* 18:92-102.

Shukla, S. 1994. Escalating sequences of problem behaviors: Analysis and intervention. Unpublished doctoral dissertation, University of Oregon, Eugene.

Shukla, S., and R. W. Albin. 1996. Effects of extinction alone and extinction plus functional communication training on covariation of problem behaviors. *Journal of Applied Behavior Analysis* 29:565-68.

Shukla, S., C. H. Kennedy, and L. S. Gushing. 1999. Intermediate school students with severe disabilities: Supporting their social participation in general education classrooms. *The Journal of Positive Behavior Interventions* 1:130-40.

Shukla-Mehta, S., and R. W. Albin. 2002. Strategies for preventing behavioral escalation: From theory to practice. *Behavioral Development Bulletin* 1:19-33.

Skinner, B. F. 1938. *The behavior of organisms*. New York: Appleton-Century Crofts.

Snyder, M. C., and L. M. Bambara. 1997. Teaching secondary students with learning disabilities to self-manage classroom survival skills. *Journal of Learning Disabilities* 30:534-43.

Sprague, J. R., and R. H. Horner. 1992. Covariation within functional response classes: Implications for treatment of severe problem behavior. *Journal of Applied Behavior Analysis* 25:735-45.

Sugai, G., J. R. Sprague, R. H. Horner, and H. M. Walker. 2000. Preventing school violence: The use of office discipline referrals to assess and monitor school-wide discipline interventions. *Journal of Emotional and Behavioral Disorders* 8:94-101.

Taylor, J. C., and R. G. Romanczyk. 1994. Generating hypotheses about the function of student problem behavior by observing teacher behavior. *Journal of Applied Behavior Analysis* 27:251-65.

Todd, A. W., R. H. Horner, and G. Sugai. 1999. Self-monitoring and self-recruited praise: Effects on problem behavior, academic engagement, and work completion in a typical classroom. *The Journal of Positive Behavior Interventions* 1:66-76.

Wahler, R. G., and J. E. Dumas. 1986. Maintenance factors in coercive mother-child interactions: The compliance and predictability hypotheses. *Journal of Applied Behavior Analysis* 19:13-22.

Wahler, R. G., and J. J. Fox. 1982. Response structure in deviant child-parent relationships: Implications for family therapy. In *Response structure and organization. The 1981 Nebraska symposium on motivation*, edited by D. J. Bernstein, 1-46. Lincoln: University of Nebraska.

Walker, H. M., G. Colvin, and R. Ramsey. 1995. *Antisocial behavior in school: Strategies and best practices*. Pacific Grove, Calif.: Brookes/Cole.

Smita Shukla-Mehta is an associate professor in the College of Education and Psychology at the University of Texas at Tyler, and Richard W. Albin is an associate professor in the Department of Educational and Community Services at the University of Oregon, Eugene.

Corporal Punishment
Legalities, Realities, and Implications

PATRICIA H. HINCHEY

For some time now, I have been talking to practitioners about corporal punishment in schools, especially middle and high schools. Practitioner responses to my questions about the legal status of paddling and other physical discipline in their states have fallen into two categories: surprise that I would ask about the subject as if practices such as paddling still existed anywhere, and surprise that I would ask about the topic as if paddling weren't common in every school in the country. Most teachers appear to assume that the status of corporal punishment in their own school or state is a national standard—a perception that is far from contemporary reality. The following quiz will help readers determine the reliability of their own perceptions relating to this topic:

True or False?

- The issue of corporal punishment has reached the United States Supreme Court, which has upheld the practice as constitutional.

- Military personnel and criminals have the right to due process before corporal punishment can be imposed; as a matter of federal law, schoolchildren, on the contrary, do not.

- Early in his term in office, President George W. Bush promoted legislation that would protect educators who had beaten children form lawsuits. Both teachers' unions, the NEA (National Education Association) and the NFT (National Federation of Teachers), opposed this legislation, intended to protect their members.

- Researchers have demonstrated that corporal punishment can constitute a form of sexual abuse.

However unlikely it may seem to many readers, the answer in every case is "true."

U.S. Courts and Corporal Punishment

The Supreme Court case that now provides the foundation for corporal punishment policies is *Ingraham v. Wright* (1977). Two students, James Ingraham and Roosevelt Andrews, suffered severe paddlings in their Florida junior high school that left Ingraham needing medical attention for severe pain and bruising and Andrews unable in one instance to use his arm for a week. Their suit argued that the paddlings were unconstitutional, in violation of the Eighth Amendment's prohibition of cruel and unusual punishment and also of the Fourteenth Amendment's guarantee of due process. The Court, however, rejected both arguments. Because corporal punishment has long been common among parents and school officials alike, the Court found, it could not be classified as "cruel and unusual." Moreover, the Court found that the Eighth Amendment is intended to protect criminals, not schoolchildren, and that children who suffered severe punishment could gain redress by prosecuting officials on such charges as assault and battery, a recourse thought to be sufficient protection for children.

Although many parents and students have indeed sought legal redress for severe beatings, they rarely win in court—

making it especially difficult to understand why President Bush has supported a legislative effort to prohibit lawsuits against educators (Breaking 2001; Spare 2001). Courts have found in favor of schools and teachers even when the punishment they imposed included paddling a nine-year-old seven times within half an hour; sticking a straight pin into a student's arm; confining children in closets and other small, dark spaces; slamming them into walls; and stuffing and/or taping children's mouths (Hyman and Snook 1999). Parents have also been dismayed to lose cases filed after a child was paddled without parental permission. Unless a school chooses to abide by parental wishes, parents in states where corporal punishment is legal can protect their children from beatings only by removing them from schools that employ paddling.

Sometimes the offenses against children are so egregious that it seems unbelievable that courts would find for schools and against the family, but it routinely happens. For example, one seventeen-year-old female, who was both an honor student and a senior with no prior record of misbehavior, skipped school. This young adult was forced to bend over a desk and submit to several blows inflicted by an adult male coach whom she had trusted until the incident. For the girl, consequences included not only the physical pain of the beating, but also menstrual hemorrhaging and long-lasting emotional trauma. Despite arguments that the case involved not only physical but also sexual abuse, the school won the case (Hyman and Snook 1999). In fact, over and over again corporal punishment has been linked to sexual abuse, although many state legislators who could outlaw the practice apparently remain unmoved by such arguments (see Donahue 2001, for example, or Johnson 1994, and others listed on Project NoSpank's Web page "Spanking Can Be Sexual Abuse," available at <http://nospank.net/ 101.htm >).

Nor is any special consideration offered to students with disabilities, for whom courts have upheld paddling, isolation, and mouth taping as punishments. In one case, a disabled student was forced to do exercise so rigorous that it led to his death (Hyman and Snook 1999). Rather than finding such incidents a cause for restraining corporal punishment, legislators have blithely moved forward toward solidifying educators' legal right to impose physical punishment on students with disabilities. In June 2001, a bill enabling discipline of the disabled was introduced by U.S. Senator Jeff Sessions of Alabama and passed the United States Senate.

As the following examples illustrate, courts rarely punish abusive educators in states that allow corporal punishment.

Worldwide and Nationwide Legality

It is perhaps telling that the United States is one of two countries worldwide that have not yet ratified the Convention on the Rights of the Child, adopted by the United Nations General Assembly in November 1989. The other is Somalia. The document calls for multiple protections of the human rights of children, including the right to be protected from violence.

As other countries of the world move toward greater and greater protection of their children, with Northern Ireland and Scotland strengthening laws against corporal punishment in 2001, the United States retains its dubious distinction of being one of very few developed countries whose national policy allows corporal punishment in schools. Over one hundred organizations joined forces to call this fact to national attention in a widely publicized letter to the president of the United States: "Throughout the developed, industrial world, and in many developing nations, the use of corporal punishment against schoolchildren is forbidden. No European country permits the practice" (Open Letter to the President, available at <http:// nospank.net/endcp.htm>). Organizations signing the letter included the American Academy of Pediatrics, the National Congress of Parents and Teachers Association, the National Mental Health Association, the American Psychological Association, the American Association of Physicians for Human Rights, the National Association of School Psychologists, the American School Counselor Association, and the National Committee for Prevention of Child Abuse.

However, the organizations' plea that the president "instruct the Secretary of the U.S. Department of Education to take expeditious and forceful action to deny federal assistance to any school, school district, or other educational entity that authorizes the use of corporal punishment" has fallen on deaf ears. The effort has also been undermined both by President Bush's support for legislation protecting those who beat children and by Senator Session's efforts to make sure that all children are equally subject to such beatings. A *Houston Chronicle* story reported the case of several Canadian parents who moved to Ohio and Indiana to escape the Canadian law prohibiting the use of such objects as paddles, sticks, and belts to inflict punishment on children. In Ohio and Indiana, parents (and others) are free to strike children with such instruments (Clairborne 2001).

For those concerned about the physical safety and mental health of children, the good news is that legislators in twenty-seven states and the District of Columbia have heeded the research and advice of pediatricians, parents, educators, and others and have passed state laws prohibiting corporal punishment in schools. However, that leaves children in nearly half of all states still subject to the abuses of corporal punishment with little or no practical means of prevention or redress. The box identifies states that continue to allow physical punishment of schoolchildren, despite its dangers.

Although defenders of corporal punishment argue that few incidents are excessive, a review of news reports indicates otherwise—and that the extreme cases are sufficiently horrifying to justify exclusion of corporal punishment, whatever the rate of incidence.

States That Allow Corporal Punishment

*Alabama	*Mississippi
Arizona	*Missouri
*Arkansas	New Mexico
Colorado	North Carolina
Delaware	Ohio
Florida	*Oklahoma
*Georgia	Pennsylvania
Idaho	South Carolina
Indiana	*Tennessee
Kansas	*Texas
Kentucky	Wyoming
*Louisiana	

Note: *States listed in the top ten pupil-battering states in both the 1996–97 and 1997–98 Elementary and Secondary School Civil Rights Compliance Reports.

Source: Danger Zones: States in the U.S. that Permit Pupil-Beating, Jordan Riak, .<http://nospank.net/eddpts.htm>

The Realities of Corporal Punishment in the United States

All of the following incidents were reported in newspapers during 2001. In the context of cases with results as severe as death, some cases seem almost trivial by comparison. Still, it is likely that most parents would be greatly upset by the actions of a California teacher who, despite a ban on corporal punishment, taped a first-grader's mouth shut and threatened to tie her up (McLellan 2001); and of an Arizona teacher who tried to force a sixth-grader to chew gum already chewed by others and saved in a jar for the purposes of this punishment (Mother 2001). Such bodily indignities, however, are the least of what a child may suffer in school, as other reported incidents nationwide reveal.

An Oklahoma Christian school teacher struck a 12-year-old with a 3-foot long dowel because he was passing notes in class and inflicted bruises that hospital doctors characterized as "severe" (Martin 2001). A parent in Louisiana was unsuccessful in filing a criminal action against an assistant principal who broke a paddle on a 13-year-old (Shackleford 2001). A parochial school director in Florida was arrested after using a wooden board to paddle an 8-year-old, leaving a mark some 4 inches wide and 6 inches long and welts as high as a quarter of an inch (Port 2001). In another Florida incident, a dean at an elementary school was found guilty of misdemeanor battery for excessively beating an 8-year-old; he was required to take an anger-management course and subsequently returned to his role as school leader—although after this incident, the school did ban corporal punishment (Hustead 2001). In Michigan, another state where

corporal punishment is legally restricted, a 15-year-old freshman football player did not return to school for weeks after he received 10 blows with a paddle that eventually cracked. Some six or seven other player were also hit, one approximately 12 or 13 times (Potts 2001). In Tennessee, a school employee faced criminal charges after hitting a 15-year-old in the arm with a baseball bat (Armstrong 2001).

A national antispanking group called for a civil rights audit of students in Mobile, Alabama because black children in recent years have received 65 to 70 percent of all paddlings there, although they make up slightly less than half of all students. Statistics also indicated that on the whole, for the 1998–99 school year, 73 percent of paddlings administered statewide in Alabama were to the black students who make up only 41 percent of its total school population (Catalanello 2001).

If all reports related to religious schools and alternative "boot-camp" type schools were included, this list would be much longer.

Implications: What Teachers Can Do

When I work with education students, tomorrow's teachers, I try to impress on them that becoming a professional educator means accepting responsibility for protecting the rights and interests of children in classrooms. To do less is to fall short of the trust placed in us by our students, their parents, and our profession. A classroom teacher who is willing to take even one of the following steps is, on the other hand, acting to meet professional responsibilities.

1. Become familiar with the information made available by Parents and Teachers against Violence in Education (PTAVE) and by Temple University's National Center for the Study of Corporal Punishment and Alternatives (NCSCPA). Web sites sponsored by these organizations offer a complete library of resources, including news and research articles. The more teachers know about corporal punishment, the better they can counter arguments for it with evidence of the danger it poses to children.

- PTAVE's Project No Spank, <http://nospank.net/>
- Temple University's NCSCPA, <http://temple.edu/education/nespca/NCSCPA.html>

2. Become familiar with print resources as well. Among the most important books on corporal punishment is Hyman and Snook's *Dangerous Schools: What We Can Do About the Physical and Emotional Abuse of Our Children.* Although that book is possibly the most important print resource detailing the dangers of physical punishment, there are several others that also can be helpful:

- Greven, P. 1991. Spare the child: The religious roots of punishment and the psychological impact of physical abuse. New York: Random House.
- Straus, M., and D. Donnelly. 1993. Beating the devil out of them: Corporal punishment in American families. San Francisco: Jossey-Bass.
- Males, M. 1996. The scapegoat generation: America's war on adolescents. Monroe, MA: Common Courage Press.

3. Monitor Project No Spank. Because this is one of the most important sources of information for children's advocates, signing on to its mailing list can be an important step in staying informed and involved.

4. Accept the need to be political in a variety of ways, in a variety of arenas. Develop relationships with colleagues, parents, administrators, school board members and politicians who have the power to help change policy and laws. Find allies and work with them to bring change on local and state levels, using voting power judiciously.

Educate your colleagues at every opportunity. Raise your concerns with other teachers and share what you know about the dangers of corporal punishment. Have them read what you have read, and try to enlist their support and build a strong core of opposition.

Promote efforts to be sure your school is safe for children. Research local policy. If corporal punishment is allowed, consider working for change; meanwhile, try to determine if guidelines are being followed and promote compliance if they are not. In schools where corporal punishment is not permitted, try to determine if the reality of classroom life conforms to regulations; if you find discrepancies, do what you can to spark awareness and promote adherence to policy.

Seek union support. If you are in a local union affiliated with the National Education Association (NEA), ask union representatives to begin publicizing the NEA stance against corporal punishment because of its dangers. The NEA was, in fact, the first major national education organization that called for banning corporal punishment in a 1992 resolution (NEA 1998). If you are affiliated with the American Federation of Teachers, work to persuade that union to join in the NEA public stance.

Enlist the help of your parents and teachers association. Be sure that local chapters are familiar with *Corporal punishment: Myths and realities* (National PTA, 1991) <http://nospank.net/pta.htm>. This National PTA document discusses the dangers of corporal punishment.

Parting Thoughts

As teachers, we must always act as advocates for children's welfare. We have many avenues to help ensure that schools are safe for children—or to protest and publicize existing dangers loudly and frequently, seeking a change in policy. To help end the legal beatings of children in schools teachers must become thoroughly educated on the issue and then assume the role of change agents, pursuing restraint and reform at every opportunity. Certainly parents, administrators, and school board members share teachers' commitment to the welfare of children. By learning and then sharing the extensive evidence against corporal punishment, teachers may be able to counter the ubiquitous argument that "a little swat on the behind never hurt anybody." Lawmakers and courts have failed to ensure that schools are safe places for the children entrusted to our care. These children cannot afford teachers to fail as their advocates and protectors as well.

Key words: corporal punishment, teachers as advocates, abuse, child welfare

REFERENCES

Armstrong accused of hitting teen with baseball bat. 2001. Associated Press State & Local Wire. 6 September. Retrieved 28 January 2002, from Lexis-Nexis database.

Bragg, R. 2001. Christian school questioned over discipline for wayward. *New York Times.* 5 July. Retrieved 28 January 2002, from <http://nospank.net/n-i03.htm>

Breaking the hickory stick. 2001. Editorial, *New York Times,* Late Edition (East Coast): A.16. 7 May.

Catalanello, R. 2001. National group seizes on racial disparity in punishment at Mobile schools. *Mobile Register.* 21 July. Retrieved 28 January 2002, from <http://nospank.net/n-i13.htm>.

Clairborne, W. 2001. Canadians from sect flee to U.S. over right to spank. 2 August. *Houston Chronicle:* 7.

Donahue, J. 2001. Spanking as sexualized abuse. *Counseling Today.* May. Retrieved 29 October 2001 from <http://nospank.org/donahue.htm>.

Hustead, J. 2001. "Excessive" spanking gets Dawkins probation. 10 April. *Press Journal* (Vero Beach, FL): A3.

Hyman, I., and P. Snook. 1999. *Dangerous schools: What we can do about the physical and emotional abuse of our children.* San Francisco: Jossey-Bass.

Johnson, T. 1994. The sexual dangers of spanking children. Retrieved 29 October 2001, from <http://nospank.org/s-dngr.htm>

Martin, L. 2001. Teacher charged with injury. *Tulsa World.* 11 October. Retrieved 25 January 2002, from Lexis-Nexis database.

McLellan, D. 2001. Tustin district bars substitute who allegedly taped girl's mouth shut. *Los Angeles Times:* B3. 22 May.

Mother says child was ordered to chew someone else's used gum. 2001. *Associated Press State & Local Wire.* 12 April. Retrieved 28 January 2002, from Lexis-Nexis database.

National Education Association (NEA). 1998. *Child Abuse and Neglect.* Retrieved 20 February 2002, from <http://www.nea.org/issues/safescho/childabus.html>.

Parents and Teachers Against Violence in Education (PTAVE). *Project No Spank.* Retrieved 29 October 2001, from <http://www.nospank.net>.

Port Charlotte school director arrested for paddling student. 2001. *Associated Press State & Local Wire.* 3 July. Retrieved 28 January 2002, from Lexis-Nexis database.

Potts, L. February 5, 2001. Football coach accused of paddling student is suspended. *Associated Press State & Local Wire.* Retrieved January 28, 2002, from Lexis-Nexis database.

Shackleford, C. 2001. Principal won't face charges over paddling. *Chattanooga Times:* B2. 13 September.

Spare the rod: Washington shouldn't encourage corporal punishment, 2001. Editorial in Pittsburgh *Post-Gazette.* 21 May. Retrieved 25 January 2002, from <http://nospank.net/n-h81.htm>.

Stockwell, J. 2001. Boy's death at school a homicide. *Washington Post.* 5 July. Retrieved 28 January 2002, from <http://nospank.net/n-i04.htm>.

Patricia H. Hinchey is an associate professor of education at Penn State University.

UNIT 6
Assessment

Unit Selections

Key Points to Consider

- What fundamental concepts from contemporary learning and motivation theories have specific implications for how teachers assess their students? Are such practices consistent with what is promulgated with standardized tests?

- What are some important principles for using standardized test scores to improve instruction? What are some limitations of standardized tests?

- Many educators believe that schools should identify the brightest, most capable students. What are the assessment implications of this philosophy? How would low-achieving students be affected?

- What principles of assessment should teachers adopt for their own classroom testing? Is it necessary or feasible to develop a table of specifications for each test? How do we know if the test scores teachers use are reliable and if valid inferences are drawn from the scores? How can teachers make time to involve students in self-assessment?

Student Website
www.mhcls.com/online

Internet References
Further information regarding these websites may be found in this book's preface or online.

Awesome Library for Teachers
 http://www.neat-schoolhouse.org/teacher.html
FairTest
 http://fairtest.org
Kathy Schrocks's Guide for Educators: Assessment
 http://school.discovery.com/schrockguide/assess.html
Phi Delta Kappa International
 http://www.pdkintl.org
Washington (State) Center for the Improvement of Student Learning
 http://www.k12.wa.us/

In which reading group does Jon belong? How do I construct tests? How do I know when my students have mastered the course objectives? How can I explain test results to Mary's parents? Teachers answer these questions, and many more, by applying principles of assessment. Assessment refers to procedures for measuring and recording student performance and constructing grades that communicate to other's levels of proficiency or relative standing. Assessment principles constitute a set of concepts that are integral to the teaching-learning process. Indeed, a significant amount of teacher time is spent in assessment activities, and with more accountability there is a greater emphasis on assessment.

Assessment provides a foundation for making sound evaluative judgments about students' learning and achievement. Teachers need to use fair and unbiased criteria in order to assess student learning objectively and accurately and make appropriate decisions about student placement. For example, in assigning Jon to a reading group, the teacher will use his test scores as an indication of his skill level. Are the inferences from the test results valid for the school's reading program? Are his test scores consistent over several months or years? Are they consistent with his performance in class? The teacher should ask and then answer these questions so that he or she can make intelligent decisions about Jon. On the other hand, will knowledge of the test scores affect the teacher's perception of classroom performance and create a self-fullfilling prophesy? Teachers also evaluate students in order to assign grades, and the challenge is to balance "objective" test scores with more sub-

jective, informally gathered information. Both kinds of evaluative information are necessary, but both can be inaccurate and are frequently misused.

The articles in this section focus on two contemporary issues in assessment—the use of high-stakes standardized tests and classroom assessment that is integrated with teaching.

The first article in this unit provides an overview of what we have learned over many years about the impact of standardized testing on teaching and learning. The next two articles discuss the importance of standards-based testing and how this kind of testing may be related to classroom instruction. It has become increasingly clear that high-stakes testing will be required, and understanding the limitations as well as negative consequences of this kind of testing is needed.

W. James Popham, a longstanding expert in testing, argues for much more emphasis on classroom assessment. This suggested emphasis is provided in the next three articles in this unit. The first describes a landmark series of investigations called "Working Inside the Black Box," researchers provide a detailed account of how formative classroom assessment can provide better grading of students, more effective use of student self-assessment, and improved learning. Rick Stiggins, another expert in testing, and Jan Chappuis argue for student self-assessment as a technique that engages students in learning and provides excellent formative feedback to teachers. In the last article James Allen shows how classroom assessment and grading practices can be accomplished to accurately reflect student learning.

The Lessons of High-Stakes Testing

Research shows that high-stakes tests can affect teaching and learning in predictable and often undesirable ways.

By Lisa M. Abrams and George F. Madaus

Today's widespread implementation of standards-based reform and the federal government's commitment to test-based accountability ensure that testing will remain a central issue in education for the foreseeable future. Test results can provide useful information about student progress toward meeting curricular standards. But when policymakers insist on linking test scores to high-stakes consequences for students and schools, they often overlook lessons from the long history of research.

The Current Landscape

The most recent round of high-stakes testing grew out of the standards-based reform movement that began in the early 1990s. This reform effort gave rise to state-level accountability systems characterized by four components (Hamilton, Stecher, & Klein, 2002):

• *Content standards* that communicate the desired knowledge and skills;

• *Tests* designed to measure the progress toward achieving the content standards;

• *Performance targets,* which identify criteria used to determine whether schools and students have reached the desired level of achievement; and

• *Incentives,* such as rewards and sanctions based on the attainment of the performance targets.

Every state has now instituted a statewide testing program and curricular standards or frameworks—except Iowa, where local districts develop their own standards and benchmarks. The state tests vary substantially in difficulty, content, item format, and, especially, the sanctions attached to test performance. For example, Massachusetts, New York, Texas, and Virginia use test results to award high school diplomas. Other states—Missouri, Rhode Island, and Vermont, for example—use students' performance on the state test to hold schools, rather than students, accountable. Still others, including Iowa, Montana, Nebraska, and North Dakota, currently attach no sanctions to test performance (Edwards, 2003).

The 2001 reauthorization of the Elementary and Secondary Education Act, also known as No Child Left Behind (NCLB), carries testing and accountability requirements that will substantially increase student testing and hold all schools accountable for student performance. This legislation marks a major departure from the federal government's traditional role regarding elementary and secondary education. It requires that states administer reading and math tests annually in grades 3-8 and dur-ing one year in high school starting in 2005-2006. These requirements will affect almost 25 million students each school year (National Center for Education Statistics, 2002).

NCLB requires states to meet adequate yearly progress (AYP) goals to ensure school accountability for student achievement on state tests. Schools that fail to achieve AYP goals face demanding corrective actions, such as replacement of school staff, implementation of new curriculum, extension of the school day or academic year, parental choice options, and, finally, complete reorganization.

Lessons We Should Have Learned

The current emphasis on testing as a tool of education reform continues a long tradition of using tests to change pedagogical priorities and practices. In the United States, this use of testing dates back to 1845 in Boston, when Horace Mann, then Secretary of the Massachusetts State Board of Education, replaced the traditional oral exam with a standardized written essay test. Internationally, high-stakes testing extends as far back as the 15th century in Treviso, Italy, where teacher salaries were linked to student examination performance (Madaus & O'Dwyer, 1999).

A 1988 examination of the effects of high-stakes testing programs on teaching and learning in Europe and in the United States (Madaus, 1988) identified seven principles that captured the intended and unintended consequences of such programs. Current research confirms that these principles still hold true for contemporary statewide testing efforts.

Principle 1: The power of tests to affect individuals, institutions, curriculum, or instruction is a perceptual phenomenon. Tests produce large effects if students, teachers, or administrators believe that the results are important. Policymakers and the public generally do believe that test scores provide a reliable, external, objective measure of school quality. They view tests as symbols of order, control, and attainment (Airasian, 1988).

Today's high-stakes testing movement relies on the symbolic importance of test scores. Forty-eight states currently require schools to provide the public with "report cards" (Edwards, 2003). Goldhaber and Hannaway (2001) found that the stigma associated with a school receiving a low grade on the state report card was a more powerful influence on Florida teachers than were the school-level sanctions imposed for poor test results.

Principle 2: The more any quantitative social indicator is used for social decision making, the more likely it will be to distort and corrupt the social process it is intended to monitor. In other words, placing great importance on state tests can have a major influence on what takes place in classrooms, often resulting in an emphasis on test preparation that can compromise the credibility or accuracy of test scores as a measure of student achievement.

We can assess whether this principle still applies today by examining the relationship between rising state test scores and scores on other achievement tests. Both old and new studies of this relationship (for example, Amrein & Berliner, 2002; Haladyna, Nolen, & Haas, 1991; Klein, Hamilton, McCaffrey, & Stecher, 2000; Linn, 1998) show that improvements in the state test scores do not necessarily reflect general achievement gains.

We can also find examples of this second principle in two recent surveys of teachers' opinions. In one national study, roughly 40 percent of responding teachers reported that they had found ways to raise state-mandated test scores without, in their opinion, actually improving learning (Pedulla et al., 2003). Similarly, in a Texas survey, 50 percent of the responding teachers did not agree that the rise in TAAS scores "reflected increased learning and high-quality teaching" (Hoffman, Assaf, & Paris, 2001, p. 488).

Principle 3: If important decisions are based on test results, then teachers will teach to the test. Curriculum standards and tests can focus instruction and provide administrators, teachers, and students with clear goals. A substantial body of past data and recent research, however, confirms that as the stakes increase, the curriculum narrows to reflect the content sampled by the test (for example, Jones et al., 1999; Madaus, 1991; McMillan, Myran, & Workman, 1999; Pedulla et al., 2003; Stecher, Barron, Chun, & Ross, 2000).

New York State, where the state department of education is requiring schools to spend more time on the NCLB-tested areas of reading and math, provides an example of how such pressure encourages schools to give greater attention to tested content and decrease emphasis on nontested content. According to one school principal, "the art, music, and everything else are basically out the window... something has to go" (Herszenhorn, 2003).

Principle 4: In every setting where a high-stakes test operates, the exam content eventually defines the curriculum. Pressure and sanctions associated with a state test often result in teachers using the content of past tests to prepare students for the new test. Several studies have documented that an overwhelming majority of teachers feel pressure to improve student performance on the state test. For example, 88 percent of teachers surveyed in Maryland and 98 percent in Kentucky believed that they were under "undue pressure" to improve student performance (Koretz, Barron, Mitchell, & Keith, 1996a, 1996b). As an outgrowth of this pressure, the amount of instructional time devoted to specific test preparation often increased.

More recent studies have found that teachers are spending a sizable amount of instructional time and using a variety of test-specific methods to prepare students for their state tests (Herman & Golan, n.d.; Hoffman, Assaf, & Paris, 2001). In North Carolina, 80 percent of elementary teachers surveyed "spent more than 20 percent of their total instructional time practicing for the end-of-grade tests" (Jones et al., 1999, p. 201). A national survey found that teachers in high-stakes states were four times more likely than those in low-stakes settings to report spending more than 30 hours a year on test preparation activities, such as teaching or reviewing topics that would be on the state test, providing students with items similar to those on the test, and using commercial test-preparation materials from previous years for practice (Pedulla et al., 2003).

The current emphasis on testing as a tool of education reform continues a long tradition of using tests to change pedagogical priorities and practices.

Principle 5: Teachers pay attention to the form of the questions of high-stakes tests (short-answer, essay, multiple-choice, and so on) and adjust their instruction accordingly. A wide variety of research confirms that test format does influence instruction in both positive and negative ways.

Studies in states that require students to formulate and provide written responses to test questions show an increased emphasis on teaching writing and higher-level thinking skills (Taylor, Shepard, Kinner, & Rosenthal, 2003). For example, in Kentucky, 80 percent of teachers surveyed indicated that they had increased their instructional emphasis on problem solving and writing as a result of the portfolio-based state test (Koretz, Barron, Mitchell, & Keith, 1996a).

In several studies, teachers have reported decreases in the use of more time-consuming instructional strategies and lengthy enrichment activities (Pedulla et al., 2003; Taylor et al., 2003). Further, a recent study found that the format of the state test may adversely affect the use of technology for instructional purposes: One-third of teachers in high-stakes states said that they were less likely to use computers to teach writing because students were required to construct handwritten responses on the state test (Russell & Abrams, in press).

Principle 6: When test results are the sole or even partial arbiter of future education or life choices, society treats test results as the major goal of schooling rather than as a useful but fallible indicator of achievement. Almost 100 years ago, a chief inspector of schools in England described this principle in a way that resonates today:

> Whenever the outward standard of reality (examination results) has established itself at the expense of the inward, the ease with which worth (or what passes for such) can be measured is ever tending to become in itself the chief, if not sole, measure of worth. And in proportion as we tend to value the results of education for their measurableness, so we tend to undervalue and at last to ignore those results which are too intrinsically valuable to be measured. (Holmes, 1911, p. 128)

In the next five years, almost half of U.S. states will require students to pass a state-mandated test as a requirement for graduation (Edwards, 2003). As a result, a passing score on the state test is the coin of the realm for students, parents, teachers, and administrators. The social importance placed on state test scores ensures that students' successful performance on the state test is the ultimate goal for schools. Local press coverage on school pass rates and anecdotal evidence that scores on the state test may influence local real estate sales show the importance of test performance as a surrogate for education quality.

Principle 7: A high-stakes test transfers control over the curriculum to the agency that sets or controls the exam. State standards-based reform efforts leave the details and development of testing programs to state departments of education and whomever the department contracts with to construct the test. This system shifts the responsibility for determining curricular priorities and performance standards away from local school administrators or classroom teachers and often results in a one-size-fits-all curriculum and test.

Falmouth, Massachusetts, provides a recent noteworthy example of how a high-stakes state test can override local control. Under the threat of losing state funding and the licensure of the school principal and superintendent, the Falmouth School Committee reversed a decision to award diplomas to special-needs students who failed the Massachusetts state exam, thus shattering the hopes of a student seeking admittance to a nonacademic culinary degree program (Myers, 2003).

From High-Stakes Tests to Multiple Measures

No one denies the importance of accountability. The relationship between test scores and accountability, however, is not as simple as most people think. The seven principles formulated in 1988 have been acted out in state after state in the past 15 years and clearly reveal the serious flaws in the practice of using a single high-stakes measure to hold all students and schools accountable.

Cut-off scores that place students in such performance categories as *needs improvement, basic, proficient, or advanced* are arbitrary. The subjective methods used to categorize students into performance categories often lack validity (Horn, Ramos, Blumer, & Madaus, 2000). Further, most policymakers and the public do not understand the psychometric underpinnings of the tests. Issues that might seem trivial to them, such as the assumptions made when running computer programs that produce scaled scores, and even basic decisions about rounding, have significant consequences when categorizing students.

> ## We need to enhance state testing programs by including multiple measures of student achievement.

Like any measurement tool that produces a number—such as blood pressure gauges, complex laboratory tests, radar detectors, breathalyzers, and fingerprinting—test scores are fallible. Yet most state laws do not consider margin of error when interpreting a student's scores.

Misguided executive decisions, poorly conceived legislation, understaffing, unrealistic reporting deadlines, and unreasonable progress goals can cause numerous errors in test scores (Rhoades & Madaus, 2003). In addition, scoring or programming errors can result in incorrect scores. Winerip (2003) describes the impact of human error on one Florida 3rd grader. When the tests of 71 3rd grade students who scored below the passing cut-off score were hand-scored, the process unearthed a scoring machine error that marked a question wrong for this student because of an erasure. "Instantly, Raven was transformed from 3rd-grade dufe to a state-certified 4th grader" (p. B9).

In addition, any single test can only sample knowledge and cannot give a full picture of what students know and can do. As an illustration, Harlow and Jones's interviews with students (2003) showed that on the science portion of the Third International Mathematics and Science Study (TIMSS), the students had more knowledge about concepts than their written answers had demonstrated for more than half of the test questions. Conversely, the interviews suggested that for one-third of the items, students lacked a sound understanding of the information assessed even though they had given the correct response.

A fundamental principle in social science research is to always use at least two methods when studying social science phenomena because relying on only one method can produce misleading results. We need to enhance state testing programs by including multiple measures of student achievement. Measuring in a variety of ways does not mean giving students multiple opportunities to take the same test, but rather incorporating other methods of measurement or additional criteria, such as teacher judgments, when making decisions about grade promotion and graduation.

As districts, schools, and teachers respond to federal and state test-based accountability policies, we must step back from a blind reliance on test scores. We need to acknowledge that tests, although useful, are also fallible indicators of achievement. We also need to recognize that when test scores are linked to high-stakes consequences, they can weaken the learning experiences of students, transform teaching into test preparation, and taint the test itself so that it no longer measures what it was intended to measure.

In classrooms, teachers provide many opportunities for students to demonstrate their knowledge and skills. Likewise, we should insist that test scores never be used in isolation, but that schools incorporate other indicators of what students know and can do—especially teacher judgment—before making high-stakes decisions about the education of students.

Teachers are spending a sizable amount of instructional time to prepare students for their state tests.

References

Airasian, P. W. (1988). Symbolic validation: The case of state-mandated, high-stakes testing. *Educational Evaluation and Policy Archives, 10*(4), 301-313.

Amrein, A. L., & Berliner, D. C. (2002). High-stakes testing, uncertainty, and student learning. *Education Policy Analysis Archives, 10*(18). [Online]. Available: http://epaa.asu.edu/epaa/v10n18

Edwards, V. (Ed.). (2003, Jan. 9). *Quality Counts 2003: If I can't learn from you... (Education Week Special Re-*

port), *12*(17). Bethesda, MD: Editorial Projects in Education.

Goldhaber, D., & Hannaway, J. (2001). *Accountability with a kicker: Observations on the Florida A+ Plan.* Paper presented at the annual meeting of the Association of Public Policy and Management, Washington, DC.

Haladyna, T., Nolen, S., & Haas, N. (1991). Raising standardized achievement test scores and the origins of test score pollution. *Educational Researcher, 20*(5), 2-7.

Hamilton, L., Stecher, B., & Klein, S. (Eds.). (2002). *Making sense of test-based accountability in education.* Santa Monica, CA: Rand.

Harlow, A., & Jones, A. (2003, July). *Why students answer TIMSS science test items the way they do.* Paper presented at the annual conference of the Australian Science Education Research Association, Melbourne, Victoria, Australia.

Herman, J., & Golan, S. (n.d.). *Effects of standardized testing on teachers and learning* (CSE Technical Report 334). Los Angeles: National Center for Research on Evaluation, Standards, and Student Testing.

Herszenhorn, D. (2003, July 23). Basic skills forcing cuts in art classes. *The New York Times,* p. B1.

Hoffman, J., Assaf, L., & Paris, S. (2001). High-stakes testing in reading: Today in Texas, tomorrow? *The Reading Teacher, 54*(5), 482-494.

Holmes, E. (1911). *What is and what might be.' A study of education in general and elementary in particular.* London: Constable.

Horn, C., Ramos, M., Blumer, I., & Madaus, G. (2000). *Cut scores: Results may vary.* Chestnut Hill, MA: National Board on Educational Testing and Public Policy, Boston College.

Jones, M., Jones, B., Hardin B., Chapman, L., Yarbough, T., & Davis, M. (1999). The impact of high-stakes testing on teachers and students in North Carolina. *Phi Delta Kappan, 81*(3), 199-203.

Klein, S., Hamilton, L., McCaffrey, D., & Stecher, B. (2000). What do test scores in Texas tell us? *Education Policy Analysis Archives, 8*(49). [Online]. Available: http://epaa.asu.edu/epaa/v8n49

Koretz, D., Barron, S., Mitchell, K., & Keith, S. (1996a). *Perceived effects of the Kentucky instructional results*

information system (KIRIS)(MR-792PCT/FF). Santa Monica, CA: Rand.

Koretz, D., Barron, S., Mitchell, K., & Keith, S. (1996b). *Perceived effects of the Maryland school performance assessment program* (CSE Technical Report 409). Los Angeles: National Center for Research on Evaluation, Standards, and Student Testing.

Linn, R. (1998). *Assessments and accountability* (CSE Technical Report 490). Boulder, CO: CRESST/University of Colorado at Boulder.

Madaus, G. (1988). The influence of testing on the curriculum. In L. Tanner (Ed.), *Critical issues in curriculum* (pp. 83-121). Chicago: University of Chicago Press.

Madaus, G. (1991, January). *The effects of important tests on students: Implications for a national examination or system of examinations.* Paper prepared for the American Educational Research Association Invitational Conference on Accountability as a State Reform Instrument, Washington, DC.

Madaus, G., & O'Dwyer, L. (1999). A short history of performance assessment: Lessons learned. *Phi Delta Kappan, 80*(9), 688-695.

McMillan, J., Myran, S., & Workman, D. (1999, April 19-23). *The impact of mandated statewide testing on teachers' classroom assessment and instructional practices.* Paper presented at the annual meeting of the American Educational Research Association, Montreal, Quebec, Canada.

Myers, K. (2003, July 16). A dream denied: Aspiring chef rethinks her future as Falmouth school board bows to state pressure on MCAS. *Cape Cod Times.* Available: www.capecodonline.com

National Center for Education Statistics. (2002). *Digest of educational statistics 2001.* Washington, DC: Government Printing Office.

Pedulla, J., Abrams, L., Madaus, G., Russell, M., Ramos, M., & Miao, J. (2003). *Perceived effects of state-mandated testing programs on teaching and learning: Findings from a national survey of teachers.* Chestnut Hill, MA: National Board on Educational Testing and Public Policy, Boston College.

Rhoades, K., & Madaus, G. (2003). *Errors in standardized tests: A sys-*

temic problem. Chestnut Hill, MA: National Board on Educational Testing and Public Policy, Boston College.

Russell, M., & Abrams, L. (in press). Instructional uses of computers for writing: The impact of state testing programs. *Teachers College Record*.

Stecher, B., Barron, S., Chun, T., & Ross, K. (2000). *The effects of the Washington state education reform on schools and classrooms* (CSE Technical Report 525). Los Angeles: National Center for Research on Evaluation, Standards, and Student Testing.

Taylor, G., Shepard, L., Kinner, F., & Rosenthal, J. (2003). *A survey of teachers' perspectives on high-stakes testing in Colorado: What gets taught, what gets lost* (CSE Technical Report 588). Los Angeles: CRESST.

Winerip, M. (2003, July 23). Rigidity in Florida and the results. *The New York Times*, p. B9.

Lisa M. Abrams (617-552-0665; abramsli@bc.edu) is a doctoral candidate and a research associate at the Center for the Study of Testing, Evaluation, and Education Policy, and **George F. Madaus** (617–552-4521;madaus@bc.edu) is a professor and Boisi Chair in Education and Public Policy, Boston College, 323 Campion Hall, Chestnut Hill, MA 02467.

From *Educational Leadership,* November 2003, pp. 31-35. Reprinted by permission of the Association for Supervision and Curriculum Development.
Copyright © 2003 by ASCD. All rights reserved. The Association for Supervision and Curriculum Development is a worldwide community of educators advocating sound policies and sharing best practices to achieve the success of each learner. To learn more, visit ASCD at www.ascd.org

Are We Measuring Student Success with High-Stakes Testing?

by Kathleen Anderson Steeves,
Jessica Hodgson,
and Patricia Peterson

A researcher, whether scientific, political, or educational, will tell you that evaluative measures begin with a working theory of the expected outcome. If high-stakes standardized exams and tests of similar ilk are intended to measure student success, why then have we not seen more discussion and careful thought placed on understanding what the outcomes of such testing actually mean and say about our students? What, in effect, do such tests actually set out to measure in our children?

Should we not, as teachers, administrators, and community leaders, be more worried about the measures and results of these annual "intelligence" tests that are increasingly being used to label students? FairTest (2002) recently noted that the United States already tests more children more often than any other nation. As a FairTest (1998) survey concluded, "There are more regulations governing the food we feed our pets than the tests used to make decisions about our children."

Should we not, as educators, insist on the time to step back and answer some fundamental questions? What is a successful student? What constitutes successful student habits, knowledge, abilities, and work? How can high-stakes testing be used more appropriately as a powerful tool for teachers to assist student learning?

Should we not open the debate about whether high-stakes tests, as they currently exist in most states, are accurate measures of what we want our students to be able to do before grade promotion or graduation? Do we want to stay on a path of instruction in which decisions are made about student intelligence, teacher ability, and school value based on a one-time test of general knowledge that has not been clearly defined or examined? As a country adopting more standardized testing, should we not see if its outcomes meet its admittedly high goals?

As educators who see the real effects of the tests on a daily basis, we believe that redefining and reexamination is overdue. Only after reevaluation and setting the parameters for student success can we go on to say definitively that such tests adequately measure the intended variables. This reevaluation must be undertaken before current testing trends, which may label students unfairly and inaccurately, become further entrenched in our society as the all-encompassing measure of a good student.

HISTORICAL DEFINITIONS OF THE SUCCESSFUL STUDENT

Though the specific details of student success have varied throughout the history of education—from the Puritan's scripture-citing prodigy to the Industrial Revolution's well-oiled cog of a learner—certain variables have remained intact (McNergney and Herbert 1995). As Goodlad (1984, 36) stated, there are a "broad array of educational goals in four [predominant] areas that have emerged in this country over more than 300 years." Though not nationally recognized, these four areas have become educationally institutionalized. They represent a logical first step in the search for the "successful" student, including, as Goodlad (1984, 51) noted, "A. Academic Goals (including: 1. Mastery of Basic Skills and Fundamental Processes, and 2. Intellectual Development); B. Vocational Goals; C. Social, Civic, and Cultural Goals; and D. Personal Goals."

According to Goodlad (1984), both parents and teachers have ranked academic goals of schooling as their top priority. These goals consisted of enabling students to: read, write, and solve basic arithmetic problems; acquire ideas from reading and listening; learn to communicate ideas through writing and speaking; utilize available sources of information; employ problem-solving skills, principles of logic, and different modes of inquiry; use and evaluate knowledge through critical and independent skills; accumulate a general fund of knowledge; and develop a positive attitude toward intellectual development.

Of the eight sub-skills constituting academic success, only one—enabling students to "accumulate a general fund of knowledge"—suggests that student success is connected to the mere "knowing" (or testing) of general information. Instead, Goodlad's goals point to a student's ability to "do" as the keystone to academic success. Words like "acquire," "problem-solve," "utilize," "analyze," and "inquire" rest at the helm of a student's successful navigation and eventual completion of school.

Currently, standards in all disciplines *are* academically rigorous. In describing their own standards for student success, national learning organizations have defined success in terms of what the student can "do":

- Apply reflective thinking and decision making when analyzing current civic/social events (National Council for the Social Studies 1993).
- Develop the abilities that characterize science as inquiry (Center for Science, Mathematics, and Engineering Education 1996).
- Investigate, make sense of, and construct meanings from new situations; make and provide arguments for conjectures; and use a flexible set of strategies to solve problems from both within and outside mathematics (National Council of Teachers of Mathematics 1989).
- Apply a wide range of strategies to comprehend, interpret, evaluate, and appreciate texts, including drawing on prior experience, interactions with other readers and writers, knowledge of word meaning of other texts (National Council of Teachers of English 1996).
- Use English to communicate in social settings, to achieve academically in all content areas and in socially and culturally appropriate ways (Teachers of English to Speakers of Other Languages 1997).

Indeed, teacher conceptions of the "successful" student appear to be aligned with those of the community, parents, and employers, each defining success as a student's ability to solve problems, seek solutions, and create and understand meaningful texts. A research study of employers in Oxon Hill, Maryland (Walker 1999), found that employers, like teachers, defined a successful student as one able to acquire and apply knowledge, such as: 1) locating and using meaningful information, 2) deciphering written and spoken language, 3) employing English in a context-appropriate manner, and 4) working with others in a professional manner.

Members of the National Education Goals Panel (1994) imagined successful students as those "practicing the scientific method, solving problems as a group, analyzing data, expressing their findings in writing, and defending their analysis in discussion." Educators such as Theodore R. Sizer and Ernest Boyer have envisioned similar learning environments and roles for the "successful" student. For Sizer (1992, 72), "The residue of serious learning is a mixture of awareness and logic. One exercises qualities of the mind with specifics, but the qualities themselves are the end to be pursued." In short, the goal of learning for Sizer is not the knowledge garnered but rather the process of learning to garner it. As Boyer (in Fiske 1991, 65), former president of the Carnegie Foundation for the Advancement of Teaching, has argued, "The key to problem solving is not to figure out the answer to a question that someone else hands you, but to define the right problem. An educated person

today is someone who knows the right questions to ask." When so many seem to agree on the current definition of a successful student, what's the problem?

HIGH-STAKES TESTING IN PRACTICE

Since U.S. educators first invented the modern standardized norm-referenced test, as Debra Meier (2000, 25) recently declared:

> *Our students have been taking more tests more often than any nation on the face of the earth, and schools and districts have been going public with test scores starting almost from the moment children enter school. From the third- or fourth-grade level (long before any of our international counterparts bother to test children) we have test data for virtually all schools, by race, class, and gender. We know exactly how many kids did better or worse in every subcategory. We have test data for almost every grade thereafter in reading and math, and to some degree in all other subjects. This has been the case for nearly half a century.*

Current trends in testing, though still tentative because there has not been enough time for in-depth study, include: use of multiple-measure assessments, emphasis on reading, and some sort of transitional accountability system as an interim step to mandatory state testing (Anderson, Fiester, Gonzales, and Pechman 1996). According to FairTest (2002), as of 1999, 17 states had graduation tests and five more were planning to implement such tests. Of the 15 states south of the Mason-Dixon line, 11 required students to pass graduation tests. In all, 39 states give either a criterion-referenced or norm-referenced test to determine their students' proficiency level. Almost all states are in the process of implementing proficiency tests of some kind, a process required now by the new federal education legislation. Illustrations from several jurisdictions provide a snapshot of some of the issues for teachers and students in this high-stakes testing trend.

In the District of Columbia, principals' and teachers' evaluations are initially to be based on student scores and improvement on the Stanford-9 (SAT-9) test battery, a multiple choice test adopted in 1996 to measure student achievement in reading and mathematics. A committee that included several teachers argued that the SAT-9 test matched the district's public schools curriculum, which is now aligned with national standards. The SAT-9 is available with various sets of empirical, normative information; ironically, none of the individual tests apply specifically to urban school districts (Harcourt Brace Educational Measurement 1999).

In Maryland, the state's School Performance Assessment Program (MSPAP), established in 1990 as the result of the Governor's Commission on School Performance, tests students' mastery in math, reading, and writing. Tasks require students to respond to questions or directions that lead to a solution to a problem, a recommendation, a decision, an explanation, or a rationale for the students' response to the task or question (Maryland State Department of Education [MSDOE] 1998). Once hailed for offering one of the first "performance-based" school tests in the nation, few states have followed Maryland's lead with MSPAP (Argetsinger and Nakashima 1998), finding such tests to be too expensive and time-consuming. MSPAP critics have complained that the test is used only to rate schools and does not measure individual student performance. An analysis of the 2001 MSPAP scores for the eighth-grade exam showed a dramatic decline in scores that left educators without an explanation. As a result, schools were given an option as to whether to use it or not. Questions were raised about the test's validity and the reliance on one test as a measure of teacher and school success (Shulte 2002). Starting with the class of 2004, high school students will be required to pass the Maryland Functional tests in content courses as a requirement for graduation (MSDOE 1998).

Massachusetts has spent $20 million on the development of the Massachusetts Comprehensive Assistance System, which will be required of all tenth-graders beginning in 2003. The state test will include multiple-choice and open-response questions. A newly formed group, the Coalition for Authentic Reform in Education, is actively opposing the notion that one test should be the only measure of student achievement (Public Broadcasting Service [PBS] 2002).

In Virginia, public schools began using the Standards of Learning (SOL) tests to assess students and schools in 1998. Students are tested in English, mathematics, history/social studies, science, and computer/technology in grades 3, 5, and 8 and at the end of core courses in high school. Beginning with the class of 2004, passing the SOL tests will be a determinant of earning a high school diploma. In addition, by 2006, a school's accreditation will depend on a 70 percent student-passing percentage on the SOL tests (Virginia Department of Education [VDOE] 1999–2001). In the second year of testing, 93 percent of public schools failed to reach the approved benchmark. The state was considering ways to adjust its timetable to implement sanctions (Mathews 1999). At this point, about half of the schools have achieved a passing rate on the required core SOL exams—though ESL students' scores were not included (VDOE 2001). In an effort to comply with expected requirements of President Bush's (2001) "No Child Left Behind" federally backed education legislation, Virginia is moving to expand the SOL testing to grades 4, 6, and 7.

HIGH-STAKES TESTING MAY FAIL STUDENTS AND TEACHERS

If these high-stakes tests are to be the measure of students, as well as of schools, it is imperative that we assess the effect of such testing on student academic success. When our country looks blindly to one test to tell us all we hope to know about students, teachers, and schools, then educators must demand a closer look at the actual meaning of these test results. Many educators know the flaws in the system firsthand. For example, when important consequences—such as student graduation and school accreditation—are linked to high-stakes testing, teachers are likely to respond by "teaching to the test" (Gordon and Reese 1997, 346). To ensure that students pass the assessment, teachers

cover material that they believe will most likely be included on the test. However, teaching to these high-stakes tests has several negative consequences for both teachers and students.

When teaching to the test, the test does not become an assessment of a student's mastery of content; it is, instead, a powerful curricular tool. The teacher is forced to make instructional decisions that are not based on prior professional experience, or what is of academic importance, or what is in the best interest of the student; instead, decisions are based on what is most likely to be included on a standardized test (Shepard 1991). In essence, the test becomes a teacher's filter for making instructional decisions. As the curriculum becomes more narrow, content and skills that are not on the standardized assessment are eliminated. In fact, teachers feel pressure to make sure classroom activities correspond to material on the assessment even though they may know other materials will better prepare students for success in the world.

Gordon and Reese (1997) conducted a study on the effects of high-stakes testing on teachers in Texas. In this case, the high-stakes assessment became the object of instruction rather than the outcome of previous instruction. The Texas Assessment of Academic Skills (TAAS) evaluates schools based on the results of the assessment and gives cash awards to schools with high test scores, while poorly performing schools face "sanctions and intervention" (Gordon and Reese 1997, 348). These researchers found that one way Texas teachers have responded to high-stakes testing is to emphasize skills on the test. Teachers tended to spend more time on "drill and practice" and less time on "hands-on activities" found in the curriculum standards. Teachers in Texas complained that the TAAS made them accountable in terms of teaching TAAS-related content, but it did not make them accountable in terms of being effective teachers (Gordon and Reese 1997). Critics of the state's testing procedures have noted that dropout rates have increased, as has cheating (PBS 2002).

Gary Natriello (in Benning 1999), a professor at Columbia University's Teachers College, has argued that the new emphasis on testing may discourage teachers from entering the field because they really want to shape young minds rather than raise a test score by a point or two. Furthermore, schools—especially in urban settings—already have difficulty filling teaching positions. If the broad application of high-stakes test scores demoralizes the teachers currently working, and discourages potential teachers from applying, student achievement ultimately suffers.

Students are likewise affected by high-stakes testing. One of the most troubling effects of high-stakes testing is that it "can force students to leave school before they have to take the examination, or after failing it" (Madaus 1991, 229). Another effect is that the performance of principals and superintendents is often linked to the number of students who reach the bar set by the state. Unfortunately, this situation may mean it is in an administrator's best interest to eliminate systematically from the test those students who probably wouldn't make the bar and to keep enrolled discipline-problem students who will get high scores on the test. In fact, in efforts to increase school performance on high-stakes testing, some schools have relied on increased special education placement and retention in grade. This system allows schools to control, to some extent, the student population whose test scores are reflected in school scores (Allington and McGill-Franzen 1992).

Whatever philosophical perspective one has toward high-stakes testing, it is clear that these tests have a significant effect on both teachers and students. In narrowing the curriculum, changing instructional strategies, and impacting the classroom and student demographics, high-stakes testing negatively alters the educational environment for teachers and students.

There is no evidence that passing the current tests equates to student success. Actually, for many, it may even mean the opposite.

Overall, educators understand that the emphasis these tests place on lower-level skills is not in line with what discipline-based organizations are asking their teachers to do in meeting content standards. Given the increased focus on nationwide standards, it must be asked whether schools *are* supplying their students with the skills and knowledge necessary to become "successful." There is no evidence that passing the current tests equates to student success. Actually, for many, it may even mean the opposite. These questions must then be asked: Are we producing students who can problem-solve, analyze, and ask the right questions? Are we evaluating them accordingly? Are these popular and increasingly endorsed "high-stakes" tests, which neatly tell us who has succeeded and who has failed, attuned to our definition of a successful student or to the philosophy of success that shapes current practice?

RETHINKING HOW WE MEASURE SUCCESS

With the current rush toward adoption of high-stakes testing forms that align with state standards, we must encourage important and necessary public discussion about the outcomes and what we are actually trying to assess in our students today (U.S. Department of Education 1998). As schools hurriedly move toward the narrow use of standardized tests to determine eligibility for graduation and school and teacher evaluation, we argue that it still has not been made clear what these tests really measure and if they actually come close to identifying our society's agreed-upon definition of a successful student.

It is necessary to reopen the discussion on testing, not as a measure to be removed, but as something that must be reexamined for what test results actually do mean and how the billions in testing dollars could be spent best in assessing our students. We must begin a discussion about what a successful student is and whether a revamped test or a restructured system of accounting for the results could more accurately measure this success.

As part of the call to reenergize this important discussion, various issues must be considered. The discussion has begun in a number of states, but it must be expanded.

How do we increase the validity of these tests? Most research employs a margin of error. Why is that not true in high-stakes tests? A student scoring one point below the cut-off score (defined in no logical way) gets no credit, while the student scoring at the cut-off point or one point above gets full credit and is promoted.

Which standards are we using to measure success? All content areas include important skills and knowledge, but what consistent measure of comparison is being used (state, county, district, or national standards)?

What are the long-term effects of high-stakes testing on students who do not graduate or drop out before they fail yet again? Do we have the collective will across the board in urban, suburban, and rural schools to use the test data to make a difference and assist students who need additional instructional time and resources to achieve the standards?

In the end, we must ask one another if we have developed a clear, agreed-upon definition of a successful student so that we may really put required resources into achieving success for all students. We must be certain that the promise to "leave no child behind" is not just overlooked by current community leaders and politicians who herald the tests unchanged. We must insist that high-stakes, standardized testing becomes less a political tool for finger pointing and assessing student and school failure and more of a reasoned way to help pinpoint why these students are failing and where resources are needed to produce the truly successful students we all want!

REFERENCES

Allington, R. L., and A. McGill-Franzen. 1992. Does high-stakes testing improve school effectiveness? *ERS Spectrum* 10(2): 3–12.

Anderson, L., L. Fiester, M. Gonzales, and E. Pechman. eds. 1996. *Improving America's schools: Newsletter on issues on school reform* (Spring). Washington, D.C.: Improving America's Schools Association. Available at: *http://www.ed.gov/pubs/IASA/newsletters/standards.*

Argetsinger, A., and E. Nakashima. 1998. In Md., the 'bubble' test has burst: Analytical exam gains favor over multiple-choice format. *Washington Post,* 11 May, A1.

Benning, V. 1999. Teachers wary of new exams. Poll finds support for D.C. program. *Washington Post,* 5 July, A1.

Bush, G. W. 2001. No child left behind. Washington, D.C.: U.S. Department of Education. Available at *http://www.ed.gov/offices/OESE/esea/nclb/titlepage.html.*

Center for Science, Mathematics, and Engineering Education, 1996. *National science education standards.* Washington, D.C.: National Academy Press.

FairTest: The National Center for Fair & Open Testing. 1998. FairTest applauds National Research Council report opposing high-stakes tests and endorsing tougher regulation of exam use. Press release, 3 Sept. Cambridge, Mass.: FairTest. Available at *http://www.fairtest.org/pr/nrc-pr.htm.*

FairTest:The National Center for Fair & Open Testing. 2002. Will more testing improve schools? Fact sheet. Cambridge, Mass.: FairTest. Available at: *http://www.fairtest.org.facts/Will%20More%20Testing%20Improve%20Schools.html.*

Fiske, E. B. 1991. *Smart schools, smart kids. Why do some schools work?* New York: Simon & Schuster.

Goodlad, J. I. 1984. *A place called school: Prospects for the future.* New York: McGraw-Hill.

Gordon, S. P., and M. Reese. 1997. High-stakes testing: Worth the price? *Journal of School Leadership* 7(4): 345–68.

Harcourt Brace Educational Measurement. 1999. Stanford-9 Achievement Test Series: It's like nothing you've ever seen before. San Antonio: HBEM.

Madaus, G. F. 1991. The effects of important tests on students. *Phi Delta Kappan 73*(3): 226–31.

Maryland State Department of Education. 1998. Maryland school performance report, 1998: State and school systems. Annapolis: MSDOE. ERIC ED 429 348.

Mathews, J. 1999. Va. schools may get reprieve on standards. *Washington Post,* 16 September, B1.

McNergney, R. F., and J. M. Herbert. 1995. *Foundations of education: The challenge of professional practice.* Boston: Allyn & Bacon.

Meier, D. 2000. *Will standards save public education?* Boston: Beacon Press.

National Council for the Social Studies. 1993. Social studies online: Standards and position statements. Washington, D.C.: NCSS.

National Council of Teachers of English. 1996. *Standards for the English Language Arts.* Urbana, Ill.: NCTE and the International Reading Association.

National Council of Teachers of Mathematics. 1989. Curriculum standards for grades 9–12. Reston, VA: NCTM. Available at *http://standards.nctm.org/Previous/CurrEvStds/currstand9-12.htm.*

Public Broadcasting Service. 2002. Frontline: Testing our schools. Television program, 28 March.

Shepard, L. A. 1991. Will national tests improve student learning? *Phi Delta Kappan 73*(3): 232–38.

Shulte, B. 2002. County questions drop in MSPAP scores: Despite new initiatives, district's results decline. *Washington Post,* 31 January, T14.

Sizer, T. R. 1992. *Horace's School: Redesigning the American high school.* Boston: Houghton Mifflin.

Teachers of English to Speakers of Other Languages. 1997. ESL standards for pre-K–12 students. Alexandria, Va.: TESOL. ERIC ED 420 991.

U.S. Department of Education. 1998. Turning around low-performing schools. A guide for state and local leaders. Washington, D.C.: USDE. ERIC ED 420 119.

Virginia Department of Education. 1999–2001. Standards of learning discussion forum. SOLs unfair to students. Richmond: VDOE. Available at: *http://www.vdoe.vipnet.org/messages/23/36.html?996190534.*

Virginia Department of Education. 2001. Spring 1999 Standards of Learning test results. Richmond: VDOE. Available at: *http://www.pen.k12.va.us/sol99.*

Walker, L. 1999. A community case study. GWU class, Teacher Education, SPED #233, Professor West, Washington, D.C.

Kathleen Anderson Steeves is Associate Professor of History/Social Studies Education at George Washington University in Washington, D.C. Her research interests include secondary history and social studies, education reform and standards, teacher leadership, and the history of education.

Jessica Hodgson teaches social studies at Chantilly High School in Fairfax County, Virginia. She is currently involved in research on using writing as a learning tool in the history classroom.

Patricia Peterson teaches 7th- and 8th-Grade English at Garner-Patterson Middle School in Washington, D.C. Her focus is on literacy development through poetry, music, and service learning. Ms. Peterson recently established a student Poetry Club connecting students with community artists and writers.

From *The Educational Forum*, Spring 2002, pp. 228-235. © 2002 by Kappa Delta Pi, International Honor Society in Education. Reprinted by permission.

The Seductive Allure of Data

Most state accountability tests fail to produce the kinds of data that will improve teaching and learning. Teachers can get the data they need from classroom assessments—if they know how to design instructionally useful tests.

W. James Popham

The word *data*, at least to most educators, simply reeks of goodness. Although probably less heart-warming than *children, smaller classes*, and *summer vacation*, the term *data* inclines most educators to think good thoughts laced with notions of evidence, science, and rigor. Indeed, the theme of this issue of *Educational Leadership* reflects educators' belief that data play a central role in improving student achievement. In any education lexicon these days, the term *data* is inarguably one of our most positively loaded nouns.

Data Scorned?

But *data* shouldn't elicit automatic obeisance from right-thinking educators. Indeed, we should spurn some data. In the following analysis, I intend to dismiss certain sorts of data. I want educators to realize that the wrong kinds of data, even if warmly applauded by many, can actually stifle teachers' pursuit of accurate evidence regarding their students' achievement.

Currently, teachers are buffeted by messages that the often undecipherable test results they receive are, in fact, the data they need to make instructional decisions. Is it any wonder when, after trying in vain to make sense of such opaque test data, many teachers simply quit believing in the instructional utility of data? To avoid becoming disillusioned with all data, teachers must learn how to distinguish between instructionally delightful and instructionally dismal data.

At the Top of the Heap: Test Data

Although all sorts of data might help to improve instruction, the most important data in the United States these days are *test data*—particularly data describing students' performance on achievement tests. That's because schools increasingly employ those data to evaluate educators' effectiveness.

State-determined achievement tests increasingly serve as the centerpiece of state accountability systems. But data from most states' accountability tests, unfortunately, have almost no value for improving teaching and learning. More dangerously, such tests lull educators into believing that they have appropriate data when, in fact, they do not. As a consequence, many educators fail to ask for more meaningful, instructionally valuable data that would help them teach students better.

Instructionally Beneficial Data

Instructionally beneficial data can only come from instructionally useful tests. Here are five attributes of an instructionally useful test, which apply to large-scale assessments as well as to teacher-made classroom assessments.

Significance. An instructionally useful test measures students' attainment of a worthwhile curricular aim—for instance, a high-level cognitive skill or a substantial body of important knowledge. It makes no sense to assess students' mastery of such trifling knowledge as esoteric scientific terms or dates associated with obscure historical events. (I suppose that someone might come up with a cogent argument for asking students to memorize state capitals. I've never been able to.)

Teachability. An instructionally useful test measures something teachable. Teachability means that most teachers, if they deliver reasonably effective instruction aimed at the test's assessment targets, can get most of their students to master what the test measures. For instance, an instructionally useful test should not measure students' innate intelligence. In standardized achievement tests, we frequently encounter items requiring students to engage in such spatial visualization tasks as mentally "folding" letters or geometric shapes into two equal halves. Such tasks clearly depend on a student's inherited visualization aptitude.

Similarly, certain high-level inference skills are extraordinarily difficult to teach because the cognitive processes central to those skills usually depend on the idiosyncratic nature of a particular student's prior experiences. It simply makes no sense to assess students' mastery of essentially unteachable outcomes.

Describability. A useful test provides or is directly based on sufficiently clear descriptions of the skills and knowledge it measures so that teachers can design properly focused instructional activities. These descriptions must not only be provided in plain language, but must also be sufficiently succinct so that they are not off-putting to busy teachers.

If a test is based on an already clearly described set of content standards, and if teachers can tell which of those content standards the test will cover, then no further descriptive information is needed. But if the content standards are not clear enough to unambiguously let teachers identify those curricular targets, then lucid descriptions of what the test will assess must accompany any instructionally useful test. A content standard such as "Students will read a variety of different types of texts" communicates little of instructional value to the teacher.

It makes no sense to assess students' mastery of ill-defined curricular targets or to force teachers to play an annual guessing game about which of the state's content standards the statewide accountability tests will assess.

Reportability. An instructionally useful test yields results at a specific enough level to inform teachers about the effectiveness of the instruction they provide. A national commission has urged that any education accountability test report its results on a standard-by-standard basis for individual students (Commission on Instructionally Supportive Assessment, 2001). Such per-standard reporting of results would enable teachers to identify those parts of their instruction that were successful or unsuccessful on the basis of students' post-instruction test data.

It makes no sense to provide teachers with data so general that those teachers cannot evaluate and improve their own instructional efforts. Similarly, it makes no sense for assessors to contend that they have assessed the complete array of a state's content standards when, in fact, they have measured some standards either by only a handful of items or by no items at all.

Nonintrusiveness. In clear recognition that testing time takes away from teaching time, an instructionally useful test shouldn't take too long to administer—it should not intrude excessively on instructional activities. For instance, if a state-level test of students' reading skills is administered each spring, it should be administrable in one, or at most two, class periods. Longer tests simply soak up too much instructional time. It makes no sense to test students interminably, diverting several weeks of precious instructional time each year to assessment.

In review, we are most likely to obtain instructionally useful data through the use of instructionally useful tests. The five attributes of an instructionally useful test are its significance, teachability, describability, reportability, and nonintrusiveness. The data derived from an instructionally useful test will enable teachers to do a better job of instructing their students. And that, after all, should be the reason we test students in the first place.

Detecting Dismal Data

As suggested earlier, tests that don't produce instructionally useful data can disincline educators to demand data that are instructionally beneficial. In the following three common assessment situations, the wrong kinds of data—provided by the wrong kinds of tests—have diminished the quality of education that we provide to our students.

Nationally Standardized Achievement Tests

Today's nationally standardized tests miss the mark dramatically with respect to three of the attributes of instructionally useful assessment:

- *Describability.* All nationally standardized achievement tests have been constructed according to a traditional measurement approach aimed at providing a comparative picture of students' relative performances. The developers try to devise a "one-size-fits-all" test and describe it in a manner that will make it attractive to many potential purchasers. As a result, nationally standardized tests don't include properly tied-down descriptions of what they assess. Teachers can't aim their instruction accurately if they have murky assessment targets.

- *Teachability.* In order to produce the score spread on which comparative score interpretations depend, nationally standardized tests contain many instructionally insensitive items that are linked to students' socioeconomic status or inherited academic aptitudes. It is particularly difficult for teachers to increase students' performance on such items.

- *Reportability.* Nationally standardized achievement tests almost always report their results at levels of generality altogether unsuitable for teachers' day-to-day instructional decision making. Some national tests do a better job than others when it comes to reporting students' results. But in no case do these tests provide data that teachers can easily use to appraise their own instructional effectiveness.

I believe that nationally standardized achievement tests have a role in education. Both parents and teachers can benefit from data indicating a student's relative strengths and weaknesses. But the genuine instructional yield of nationally standardized tests is much more modest than the publishers of these tests would have us believe.

Standards-Based Tests

There is a charade currently going on in the way the United States carries out its education assessment activities. Its name is "standards-based assessment." Standards-based tests supposedly measure students' mastery of a state's officially approved content standards—the skills and knowledge constituting the state's curricular aims. Yet because most states have adopted too many content standards and stated them too vaguely, most states' standards-based tests just don't do a decent job determining a student's mastery of those standards.

Pretending that a one- or two-hour state test can provide a meaningful fix on a student's mastery of myriad, often fuzzy content standards is patently hypocritical. Today's standards-based assessments constitute a serious violation of any sort of truth-in-advertising precept. Standards-based tests don't measure what they pretend to measure.

The data yielded by today's standards-based tests have another equally serious shortcoming. Those data almost never provide any indication of *which* content standards a student has or hasn't mastered. In the absence of such data, how can teachers tell which parts of their instruction they need to modify?

Teachers don't learn much of instructional value when the standards-based test results tell them that Johnny is "not proficient" with respect to his mastery of a set of 17 language arts content standards. Teachers cannot discern which of the 17 content standards their students have mastered (hence, which standards have been well taught) and which of the 17 content standards their students have not mastered (hence, which standards have not been well taught).

So most of today's standards-based tests fall down seriously on several attributes of an instructionally useful test. They often lack significance because, in a fruitless effort to measure all of a state's sprawling content standards, they simply do not assess students' mastery of the most important content. Standards-based tests also get low grades on describability—they usually fail to describe their assessment targets satisfactorily, because these tests are based on a plethora of too many, insufficiently clear content standards. And perhaps most seriously, standards-based tests often lack reportability—they fail to provide standard-by-standard reports to teachers, students, or students' parents.

Teachers' Classroom Assessments

Given the enormous pressure placed on teachers these days to boost their students' scores on external exams, teachers understandably tend to give less attention to their own classroom assessments. That's a mistake—but only if the teacher's classroom tests are instructionally useful.

Teachers can judge the instructional utility of their classroom assessments by using the same five attributes of an instructionally useful test that I just applied to large-scale external exams. Teachers should ask themselves the following questions:

- Do my classroom assessments measure genuinely worthwhile skills and knowledge?
- Will I be able to promote my students' mastery of what's measured in my classroom assessments?

- Can I describe what skills and knowledge my classroom tests measure in language sufficiently clear for my own instructional planning?
- Do my classroom assessments yield results that allow me to tell which parts of my instruction were effective or ineffective?
- Do my classroom tests take up too much time away from my instruction?

Clearly, the answers to these questions will vary from teacher to teacher. Generally, teachers who employ their classroom assessments most appropriately adopt a "less is more" approach. They focus on measuring only a modest number of curricular aims, but make certain that those aims deal with genuinely significant outcomes that students can master with adequate instruction. As a dividend of focusing on a smaller number of significant outcomes, those outcomes can then be clearly described to help the teacher target instruction and assessment.

Teachers must deal with one additional consideration if they intend to use their classroom data to supplement results from external exams: Unless classroom tests provide credible data, skeptics will rush to dismiss the results as "self-interested home cooking." I'm not talking about tests that teachers use only to inform themselves about their ongoing instruction, but rather about the more significant sorts of data that schools use to judge a teacher's instructional effectiveness.

One straightforward way for teachers to collect credible evidence of their own effectiveness is to use a pretest/posttest design in which they give identical assessments at the start of a semester and again at its conclusion. Students must use the same kind of paper if the test calls for a constructed response (such as writing an essay). Students do not date their responses. The teacher codes the pretests and posttests so they can be subsequently identified, and then mixes them all together so that a scorer cannot discern which responses are pretests and which are posttests.

Data from most states' accountability tests, unfortunately, have almost no value for improving teaching and learning.

At this point the teacher calls on a nonpartisan scorer (for instance, another teacher or a parent) to blind-score the students' responses. Only after all the shuffled papers have been scored does the teacher sort them into pretests and posttests. The improvement between the pretests and posttests constitutes credible evidence of the teacher's instructional success (Popham, 2001).

What Can Educators Do?

In response to today's increasingly important assessment concerns, I suggest a two-stage course of action. First, educators should disregard data from any test that isn't instructionally useful. Second, they should push for the installation of instructionally useful tests so that the data that those assessments yield will lead to better-taught students.

Although most of today's standards-based tests are not instructionally useful, that need not be the case. A national commission recently described how to create accountability tests that are both accurate and instructionally useful (Commission on Instructionally Supportive Assessment, 2001). Many states assess students' written composition competence by requiring students to generate original writing samples, which are then evaluated according to scoring guides (rubrics) based on teachable criteria. Almost all of today's writing samples are instructionally beneficial. If you live in a state where such instructionally useful tests do not exist, lobby aggressively for their introduction.

If you live in a state that uses nationally standardized achievement tests for accountability purposes, try your hardest to get them replaced with more appropriate, instructionally useful accountability tests.

Teachers should also bring common sense to the scrutiny of their own classroom assessments. In general, a quest for assessment sanity will lead teachers to adopt a less-is-more measurement approach. However, if the resultant data will be used for instructional evaluation, then teachers must collect those data in a manner sufficiently credible to persuade even non-believers of the data's validity.

To educators, the wrong data can often be seductively appealing. But the right data will, in fact, help teachers do a better job with students. *Those* are the data we need.

References

Commission on Instructionally Supportive Assessment. (2001). *Building tests that support instruction and accountability: A guide for policymakers*. Washington, DC:

Author. [Online]. Available: www.nea.org/accountability/buildingtests.html

Popham, W. J. (2001). *The truth about testing: An educator's call to action*. Alexandria, VA: ASCD.

W. James Popham is a professor emeritus at the University of California, Los Angeles, Graduate School of Education and Information Studies; wpopham@ucla.edu.

Working Inside the Black Box:

Assessment for Learning in the Classroom

In their widely read article "Inside the Black Box," Mr. Black and Mr. Wiliam demonstrated that improving formative assessment raises student achievement. Now they and their colleagues report on a follow-up project that has helped teachers change their practice and students change their behavior so that everyone shares responsibility for the students' learning.

BY PAUL BLACK, CHRISTINE HARRISON, CLARE LEE, BETHAN MARSHALL, AND DYLAN WILIAM

IN 1998 "Inside the Black Box," the predecessor of this article, appeared in this journal.[1] Since then we have learned a great deal about the practical steps needed to meet the purpose expressed in the article's subtitle: "raising standards through classroom assessment."

In the first part of "Inside the Black Box," we set out to answer three questions. The first was, Is there evidence that improving formative assessment raises standards? The answer was an unequivocal yes, a conclusion based on a review of evidence published in over 250 articles by researchers from several countries.[2] Few initiatives in education have had such a strong body of evidence to support a claim to raise standards.

This positive answer led naturally to the second question: Is there evidence that there is room for improvement? Here again, the available evidence gave a clear and positive answer, presenting a detailed picture that identified three main problems: 1) the assessment methods that teachers use are not effective in promoting good learning, 2) grading practices tend to emphasize competition rather than personal improvement, and 3) assessment feedback often has a negative impact, particularly on low-achieving

students, who are led to believe that they lack "ability" and so are not able to learn.

However, for the third question—Is there evidence about how to improve formative assessment?—the answer was less clear. While the evidence provided many ideas for improvement, it lacked the detail that would enable teachers to implement those ideas in their classrooms. We argued that teachers needed "a variety of living examples of implementation."

THE JOURNEY:
LEARNING WITH TEACHERS

Since 1998, we have planned and implemented several programs in which groups of teachers in England have been supported in developing innovative practices in their classrooms, drawing on the ideas in the original article. While this effort has amply confirmed the original proposals, it has also added a wealth of new findings that are both practical and authentic. Thus we are now confident that we can set out sound advice for the improvement of classroom assessment.

THE KMOFAP PROJECT

To carry out the exploratory work that was called for, we needed to collaborate with a group of teachers willing to take on the risks and extra work involved, and we needed to secure support from their schools and districts. Funding for the project was provided through the generosity of the Nuffield Foundation, and we were fortunate to find two school districts—Oxfordshire and Medway, both in southern England—whose supervisory staff members understood the issues and were willing to work with us. Each district selected three secondary schools: Oxfordshire chose three coeducational schools, and Medway chose one coeducational school, one boys' school, and one girls' school. Each school selected two science teachers and two mathematics teachers. We discussed the plans with the principal of each school, and then we called the first meeting of the 24 teachers. So in January 1999, the King's—Medway-Oxfordshire Formative Assessment Project (KMOFAP) was born.

Full details of the project can be found in our book, *Assessment for Learning: Putting It into Practice.*[3] For the present purpose, it is the outcomes that are important. The findings presented here are based on the observations and records of visits to classrooms by the King's College team, records of meetings of the whole group of teachers, interviews with and writing by the teachers themselves, and a few discussions with student groups. Initially, we worked with science and mathematics teachers, but the work has been extended more recently to involve teachers of English in the same schools and teachers of other subjects in other schools.

SPREADING THE WORD

Throughout the development of the project, we have responded to numerous invitations to talk to other groups of teachers and advisers. Indeed, over five years we have made more than 400 such contributions. These have ranged across all subjects and across both primary and secondary phases. In addition, there has been sustained work with some primary schools. All of this gives us confidence that our general findings will be of value to all, although some important details may differ for different age groups and subjects. Furthermore, a group at Stanford University obtained funding from the National Science Foundation to set up a similar development project, in collaboration with King's, in schools in California. Extension of our own work has been made possible by this funding. And we also acknowledge support from individuals in several government agencies who sat on the project's steering group, offered advice and guidance, and helped ensure that assessment for learning (see "Assessment for Learning," below) is a central theme in education policy in England and Scotland.

THE LEARNING GAINS

From our review of the international research literature, we were convinced that enhanced formative assessment would produce gains in student achievement, even when measured in such narrow terms as scores on state-mandated tests. At the outset we were clear that it was important to have some indication of the kinds of gains that could be achieved in real classrooms and over an ex-

---

ASSESSMENT FOR LEARNING

▲ Assessment for learning is any assessment for which the first priority in its design and practice is to serve the purpose of promoting students' learning. It thus differs from assessment designed primarily to serve the purposes of accountability, or of ranking, or of certifying competence. An assessment activity can help learning if it provides information that teachers and their students can use as feedback in assessing themselves and one another and in modifying the teaching and learning activities in which they are engaged. Such assessment becomes "formative assessment" when the evidence is actually used to adapt the teaching work to meet learning needs.

---

tended period of time. Since each teacher in the project was free to choose the class that would work on these ideas, we discussed with each teacher what data were available within the school, and we set up a "mini-experiment" for each teacher.

Each teacher decided what was to be the "output" measure for his or her class. For grade-10 classes, this was generally the grade achieved on the national school-leaving examination taken when students are 16 (the General Certificate of Secondary Education or GCSE). For grade-8 classes, it was generally the score or level achieved on the national tests administered to all 14-year-olds. For other classes, a variety of measures were used, including end-of-module-test scores and marks on the school's end-of-year examinations.

Many teachers do not plan and conduct classroom dialogue in ways that might help students to learn.

For each project class, the teacher identified a comparison class. In some cases this was a parallel class taught by the same teacher in previous years (and in one case in the same year). In other cases, we used a parallel class taught by a different teacher or, failing that, a nonparallel class taught by the same or a different teacher.

When the project and the control classes were not strictly parallel, we controlled for possible differences in prior achievement by the use of "input" measures, such as school test scores from the previous year or other measures of aptitude.

This approach meant that the size of the improvement was measured differently for each teacher. For example, a grade-10 project class might outperform the comparison class by half a GCSE grade, but another teacher 's grade 8 project class might outscore its control class by 7% on an end-of-year exam. To enable us to aggregate the results, we adopted the common measuring stick of the "standardized effect size," calculated by taking the difference between the scores of the experimental and control groups and then dividing this number by the standard deviation (a measure of the spread in the scores of the groups).

For the 19 teachers on whom we had complete data, the average effect size was around 0.3 standard deviations. Such improvements, produced across a school, would raise a school in the lower quartile of the national performance tables to well above average. Thus it is clear that, far from having to choose between teaching well and getting good test scores, teachers can actually improve their students' results by working with the ideas we present here.

HOW CHANGE CAN HAPPEN

We set out our main findings about classroom work under four headings: questioning, feedback through grading, peer- and self-assessment, and the formative use of summative tests. Most of the quotations in the following pages are taken directly from pieces written by the teachers. The names of the teachers and of the schools are pseudonyms, in keeping with our policy of guaranteeing anonymity.

QUESTIONING

Many teachers do not plan and conduct classroom dialogue in ways that might help students to learn. Research has shown that, after asking a question, many teachers wait less than one second and then, if no answer is forthcoming, ask another question or answer the question themselves.[4] A consequence of such short "wait time" is that the only questions that "work" are those that can be answered quickly, without thought—that is, questions calling for memorized facts. Consequently, the dialogue is at a superficial level. As one teacher put it:

> I'd become dissatisfied with the closed Q & A style that my unthinking teaching had fallen into, and I would frequently be lazy in my acceptance of right answers and sometimes even tacit complicity with a class to make sure none of us

had to work too hard. … They and I knew that if the Q & A wasn't going smoothly, I'd change the question, answer it myself, or only seek answers from the "brighter students." There must have been times (still are?) where an outside observer would see my lessons as a small discussion group surrounded by many sleepy onlookers.
> —*James*, Two Bishops School

The key to changing such a situation is to allow longer wait time. But many teachers find it hard to do this, for it requires them to break their established habits. Once they change, the expectations of their students are challenged:

> Increasing waiting time after asking questions proved difficult to start with due to my habitual desire to "add" something almost immediately after asking the original question. The pause after asking the question was sometimes "painful." It felt unnatural to have such a seemingly "dead" period, but I persevered. Given more thinking time, students seemed to realize that a more thoughtful answer was required. Now, after many months of changing my style of questioning, I have noticed that most students will give an answer and an explanation (where necessary) without additional prompting.—*Derek*, Century Island School

One teacher summarized the overall effects of her efforts to improve the use of question-and-answer dialogue in the classroom as follows:

Questioning

• My whole teaching style has become more interactive. Instead of showing how to find solutions, a question is asked and pupils are given time to explore answers together. My year 8 [grade 7] target class is now well-used to this way of working. I find myself using this method more and more with other groups.

No hands

• Unless specifically asked, pupils know not to put their hands up if they know the answer to a question. All pupils are expected to be able to answer at any time even if it is an "I don't know."

Supportive climate

• Pupils are comfortable with giving a wrong answer. They know that these can be as useful as correct ones. They are happy for other pupils to help explore their wrong answers further.
—*Nancy*, River-side School

Increasing the wait time can help more students become involved in discussions and increase the length of their replies. Another way to broaden participation is to ask students to brainstorm ideas, perhaps in pairs, for two to three minutes before the teacher asks for contributions. Overall, a consequence of such changes is that teachers learn more about the students' prior knowledge and about any gaps and misconceptions in that knowledge, so that teachers' next moves can better address the learners' real needs.

To exploit such changes means moving away from the routine of limited factual questions and refocusing attention on the quality and the different functions of classroom questions. Consider, for example, the use of a "big question": an open question or a problem-solving task that can set the scene for a lesson and evoke broad discussion or prompt focused small-group discussions. However, if this strategy is to be productive, both the responses that the task might generate and the ways of following up on these responses have to be anticipated. Collaboration between teachers to exchange ideas and experiences about good questions is very valuable. The questions themselves then become a more significant part of teaching, with attention focused on how they can be constructed and used to explore and then develop students' learning. Here's one teacher's thinking on the matter:

> I chose a year-8, middle-band group and really started to think about the type of questions I was asking—were they just instant one-word answers—what were they testing—knowledge or understanding—was I giving the class enough time to answer the question, was I quickly accepting the correct answer, was I asking the girl to explain her answer, how was I dealing with a wrong answer? When I really stopped to think, I realized that I could make a very large difference to the girls' learning by using all their answers to govern the pace and content of the lesson. —*Gwen*, Waterford School

Effective questioning is also an important aspect of the impromptu interventions teachers conduct once the students are engaged in an activity. Asking simple questions, such as "Why do you think that?" or "How might you express that?" can become part of the interactive dynamic of the classroom and can provide an invaluable opportunity to extend students' thinking through immediate feedback on their work.

Overall, the main suggestions for action that have emerged from the teachers' experience are:

• More effort has to be spent in framing questions that are worth asking, that is, questions that explore issues that are critical to the development of students' understanding.

• Wait time has to be increased to several seconds in order to give students time to think, and everyone should be expected to have an answer and to contribute to the discussion. Then all answers, right or wrong, can be used to develop understanding. The aim is thoughtful improvement rather than getting it right the first time.

• Follow-up activities have to be rich, in that they create opportunities to extend students' understanding.

Put simply, the only point of asking questions is to raise issues about which a teacher needs information or about which the students need to think. When such changes have been made, experience demonstrates that students become more active participants and come to realize that learning may depend less on their capacity to spot the right answer and more on their readiness to express and discuss their own understanding. The teachers also shift in their role, from presenters of content to leaders of an exploration and development of ideas in which all students are involved.

FEEDBACK THROUGH GRADING

When giving students feedback on both oral and written work, it is the nature, rather than the amount, of commentary that is critical. Research experiments have established that, while student learning can be advanced by feedback through comments, the giving of numerical scores or grades has a negative effect, in that students ignore comments when marks are also given.[5] These results often surprise teachers, but those who have abandoned the giving of marks discover that their experience confirms the findings: students do engage more productively in improving their work.

Many teachers will be concerned about the effect of returning students' work with comments but no scores or grades. There may be conflicts with school policy:

> My marking has developed from comments with targets and grades, which is the school policy, to comments and targets only. Pupils do work on targets and corrections more productively if no grades are given. Clare [Lee] observed on several occasions how little time pupils spent reading my comments if there were grades given as well. My routine is now, in my target class, i) to not give grades, only comments; ii) to give comments that highlight what has been done well and what needs further work; and iii) to give the minimum follow-up work expected to be completed next time I mark the books.
> —*Nancy*, Riverside School

Initial fears about how students might react turned out to be unjustified, and neither parents nor school inspectors have reacted adversely. Indeed, the provision of comments to students helps parents to focus on the learning issues rather than on trying to interpret a score or grade. We now believe that the effort that many teachers devote to grading homework may be misdirected. A numerical score or a grade does not tell students how to improve their work, so an opportunity to enhance their learning is lost.

A commitment to improve comments requires more work initially, as teachers have to attend to the quality of the comments that they write on students' work. Collaboration between teachers in sharing examples of effective comments can be very helpful, and experience will lead to more fluency. There is, however, more involved because comments become useful feedback only if students use them to guide further work, so new procedures are needed.

> After the first INSET [inservice training meeting] I was keen to try out a different way of marking books to give pupils more constructive feedback. I was keen to try and have a more easy method of monitoring pupils' response to my comments without having to trawl through their books each time to find out if they'd addressed my comments. I implemented a comment sheet at the back of my year-8 class' books. It is A4 [letter] in size, and the left-hand side is for my comments, and the right-hand side is for the pupils to demonstrate by a reference to the page in their books where I can find the evidence to say whether they have done the work. . . . The comments have become more meaningful as the time has gone on, and the books still take me only one hour to mark. — *Sian*, Cornbury Estate School

We have encountered a variety of ways of accommodating the new emphasis on comments. Some teachers have ceased assigning scores or grades at all, some teachers enter scores in their own record books but do not write them in the students' books, others give a score or grade only after a student has responded to the teacher's comments. Some teachers spend more time on certain pieces of work to ensure that they obtain good feedback and, to make time for this, either do not mark some pieces, or look at only a third of their students' books each week, or involve the students in checking the straightforward tasks.

A particularly valuable method is to devote some lesson time to rewriting selected pieces of work, so that emphasis can be put on feedback for improvement within a supportive environment. This practice can change students' expectations about the purposes of class work and homework.

As they tried to create useful feedback comments, many of the project teachers realized that they needed to reassess the work that they had asked students to undertake. They found that some tasks were useful in revealing students' understandings and misunderstandings, while others focused mainly on conveying information. So some activities were eliminated, others modified, and new and better tasks actively sought.

Overall the main ideas for improvement of feedback can be summarized as follows:

• Written tasks, alongside oral questioning, should encourage students to develop and show understanding of the key features of what they have learned.

• Comments should identify what has been done well and what still needs improvement and give guidance on how to make that improvement.

• Opportunities for students to respond to comments should be planned as part of the overall learning process.

The central point here is that, to be effective, feedback should cause thinking to take place. The implementation of such reforms can change both teachers' and students' attitudes toward written work: the assessment of students' work will be seen less as a competitive and summative judgment and more as a distinctive step in the process of learning.

PEER ASSESSMENT AND SELF-ASSESSMENT

Students can achieve a learning goal only if they understand that goal and can assess what they need to do to reach it. So self-assessment is essential to learning.[6] Many teachers who have tried to develop their students' self-assessment skills have found that the first and most difficult task is to get students to think of their work in terms of a set of goals. Insofar as they do so, they begin to develop an overview of that work that allows them to manage and control it for themselves. In other words, students are developing the capacity to work at a metacognitive level.

In practice, peer assessment turns out to be an important complement to self-assessment. Peer assessment is uniquely valuable because students may accept criticisms of their work from one another that they would not take seriously if the remarks were offered by a teacher. Peer work is also valuable because the interchange will be in language that students themselves naturally use and because students learn by taking the roles of teachers and examiners of others.[7] One teacher shared her positive views of peer assessment:

> As well as assessing and marking (through discussion and clear guidance) their own work, they also assess and mark the work of others. This they do in a very mature and sensible way, and this has proved to be a very worthwhile experiment. The students know that homework will be checked by themselves or another girl in the class at the start of the next lesson. This has led to a well-established routine and only on extremely rare occasions have students failed to complete the work set. They take pride in clear and well-presented work that one of their peers may be asked to mark. Any disagreement about the answer is thoroughly and openly discussed until agreement is reached.
> —*Alice*, Waterford School

The last sentence of this teacher's comments brings out an important point: when students do not understand an explanation, they are likely to interrupt a fellow student when they would not interrupt a teacher. In addition to this advantage, peer assessment is also valuable in placing the work in the hands of the students. The teacher can be free to observe and reflect on what is happening and to frame helpful interventions:

> We regularly do peer marking—I find this very helpful indeed. A lot of misconceptions come to the fore, and we then discuss these as we are going over the homework. I then go over the peer marking and talk to pupils individually as I go round the room.
> —*Rose*, Brownfields School

However, self-assessment will happen only if teachers help their students, particularly the low achievers, to develop the skill. This can take time and practice:

> The kids are not skilled in what I am trying to get them to do. I think the process is more effective long term. If you invest time in it, it will pay off big dividends, this process of getting the students to be more independent in the way that they learn and to take the responsibility themselves.
> —*Tom*, Riverside School

One simple and effective idea is for students to use "traffic light" icons, labeling their work green, yellow, or red according to whether they think they have good, partial, or little understanding. These labels serve as a simple means of communicating students' self-assessments. Students may then be asked to justify their judgments in a peer group, thus linking peer assessment and self-assessment. This linkage can help them develop the skills and the detachment needed for effective self-assessment.

Another approach is to ask students first to use their "traffic light" icons on a piece of work and then to indicate by hands-up whether they put a green, yellow, or red icon on it. The teacher can then pair up the greens and the yellows to help one another deal with their problems, while the red students meet with the teacher as a group to deal with their deeper problems. For such peer-group work to succeed, many students will need guidance about how to behave in groups, including such skills as listening to one another and taking turns.

In some subjects, taking time to help students understand scoring rubrics is also very helpful. Students can be given simplified versions of the rubrics teachers use, or they can be encouraged to rewrite them or even to create their own. Again, peer assessment and self-assessment are intimately linked. Observers in several language arts classrooms saw children apply to their own work lessons they had learned in peer assessment. A frequently heard comment was "I didn't do that either" or "I need to do that too."

Students' reflection about their understanding can also be used to inform future teaching, and their feedback can indicate in which areas a teacher needs to spend more time. A useful guide is to ask students to "traffic light" an end-of-unit test at the beginning of the unit: the yellow and red items can be used to adjust priorities within the teaching plan. Our experience leads us to offer the following recommendations for improving classroom practice:

- The criteria for evaluating any learning achievements must be made transparent to students to enable them to have a clear overview both of the aims of their work and of what it means to complete it successfully. Such criteria may well be abstract, but concrete examples should be used in modeling exercises to develop understanding.
- Students should be taught the habits and skills of collaboration in peer assessment, both because these are of intrinsic value and because peer assessment can help develop the objectivity required for effective self-assessment.
- Students should be encouraged to keep in mind the aims of their work and to assess their own progress toward meeting these aims as they proceed. Then they will be able to guide their own work and so become independent learners.

The main point here is that peer assessment and self-assessment make distinct contributions to the development of students' learning. Indeed, they secure aims that cannot be achieved in any other way.

THE FORMATIVE USE OF SUMMATIVE TESTS

The practices of self-assessment and peer assessment can be applied to help students prepare for tests, as in tackling the following problem:

> [The students] did not mention any of the reviewing strategies we had discussed in class. When questioned more closely, it was clear that many spent their time using very passive revision [reviewing] techniques. They would read over their work doing very little in the way of active revision or reviewing of their work. They were not transferring the active learning strategies we were using in class to work they did at home.
> —*Tom*, Riverside School

To remedy this situation, students can be asked to "traffic light" a list of key words or the topics on which the test will be set. The point of this exercise is to stimulate the students to reflect on where they feel their learning is secure, which they mark green, and where they need to concentrate their efforts, in yellow and red. These traffic lights then form the basis of a review plan. Students can be asked to identify questions on past tests that probe their "red" areas. Then they can work with textbooks and in peer groups to ensure that they can successfully answer those questions.

The aftermath of tests can also be an occasion for formative work. Peer marking of test papers can be helpful, as with normal written work, and it is particularly useful if students are required first to formulate a scoring rubric—an exercise that focuses attention on the criteria of quality relevant to their productions. After peer marking, teachers can reserve their time for discussion of the questions that give widespread difficulty, while peer tutoring can tackle those problems encountered by only a minority of students.

One other finding that has emerged from research studies is that students trained to prepare for examinations by generating and then answering their own questions outperformed comparable groups who prepared in conventional ways.[8] Preparing test questions helps students develop an overview of the topic:

> Pupils have had to think about what makes a good question for a test and in doing so need to have a clear understanding of the subject material. As a development of this, the best questions have been used for class tests. In this way, the pupils can see that their work is valued, and I can make an assessment of the progress made in these areas. When going over the test, good use can be made of group work and discussions between students concentrating on specific areas of concern.
> —*Angela,* Cornbury Estate School

Developments such as these challenge common expectations. Some have argued that formative and summative assessments are so different in their purpose that they have to be kept apart, and such arguments are strengthened when one experiences the harmful influence that narrow, high-stakes summative tests can have on teaching. However, it is unrealistic to expect teachers and students to practice such separation, so the challenge is to achieve a more positive relationship between the two. All of the ways we have described for doing so can be used for tests in which teachers have control over the setting and the marking. But their application may be more limited for tests in which the teacher has little or no control.

Overall, the main possibilities for improving classroom practice by using summative tests for formative purposes are as follows:

• Students can be engaged in a reflective review of the work they have done to enable them to plan their revision effectively.

• Students can be encouraged to set questions and mark answers so as to gain an understanding of the assessment process and further refine their efforts for improvement.

• Students should be encouraged through peer assessment and self-assessment to apply criteria to help them understand how their work might be improved. This may include providing opportunities for students to rework examination answers in class.

The overall message is that summative tests should become a positive part of the learning process. Through active involvement in the testing process, students can see that they can be the beneficiaries rather than the victims of testing, because tests can help them improve their learning.

REFLECTIONS: SOME UNDERLYING ISSUES

The changes that are entailed by improved assessment for learning have provoked us and the teachers involved to reflect on deeper issues about learning and teaching.

LEARNING THEORY

One of the most surprising things that happened during the early INSET sessions was that the participating teachers asked us to run a session on the psychology of learning. In retrospect, perhaps we should not have been so surprised at this request. After all, we had stressed that feedback functioned formatively only if the information fed back to the learner was used by the learner in improving performance. But while one can work out after the fact whether or not any feedback has had the desired effect, what the teachers needed was a way to give their students feedback that they knew in advance was going to be useful. To do that they needed to build up models of how students learn.

So the teachers came to take greater care in selecting tasks, questions, and other prompts to ensure that students' responses actually helped the teaching process. Such responses can "put on the table" the ideas that students bring to a learning task. The key to effective learning is then to find ways to help students restructure their knowledge to build in new and more powerful ideas. In the KMOFAP classrooms, as the teachers came to listen more attentively to the students' responses, they began to appreciate more fully that learning was not a process of passive reception of knowledge, but one in which the learners were active in creating their own understandings. Put simply, it became clear that, no matter what the pressure to achieve good test scores, learning must be done by the student.

Students came to understand what counted as good work through exemplification. Sometimes this was done through focused whole-class discussion around a particular example; at other times it was achieved through the use of sets of criteria to assess the work of peers.

Engaging in peer assessment and self-assessment is much more than just checking for errors or weaknesses. It involves making explicit what is normally implicit, and thus it requires students to be active in their learning. As one student wrote:

> After a pupil marking my investigation, I can now acknowledge my mistakes easier. I hope that it is not just me who learned from the investigation but the pupil who marked it did also. Next time I will have to make my explanations clearer, as they said "It is hard to understand."...
> I will now explain my equation again so it is clear.

The students also became much more aware of when they were learning and when they were not. One class, which was subsequently taught by a teacher not emphasizing assessment for learning, surprised that teacher by complaining: "Look, we've told you we don't understand this. Why are you going on to the next topic?" While students who are in tune with their learning can create difficulties for teachers, we believe that these are exactly the kinds of problems we should want to have.

SUBJECT DIFFERENCES

From hearing about research and discussing ideas with other colleagues, the teachers built up a repertoire of generic skills. They planned their questions, allowed appropriate wait time, and gave feedback that was designed to cause thinking. They ensured that students were given enough time during lessons to evaluate their own work and that of others.

However, after a while it became clear that these generic strategies could go only so far. Choosing a good question requires a detailed knowledge of the subject, but not necessarily the knowledge that is gained from advanced study in a subject. A high level of qualification in a subject is less important than a thorough understanding of its fundamental principles, an understanding of the kinds of difficulties that students might have, and the creativity to be able to think up questions that stimulate productive thinking.[9] Furthermore, such pedagogical content knowledge is essential in interpreting responses. That is, what students say will contain clues to aspects of their thinking that may require attention, but picking up on these clues requires a thorough knowledge of common difficulties in learning the subject. Thus, while the general principles of formative assessment apply across all subjects, the ways in which they manifest themselves in different subjects may differ. We have encountered such differences in making comparisons between teachers of mathematics, science, and language arts.

In mathematics, students have to learn to use valid procedures and to understand the concepts that underpin them. Difficulties can arise when students learn strategies that apply only in limited contexts and do not realize that they are inadequate elsewhere. Questioning must then be designed to bring out these strategies for discussion and to explore problems in understanding the concepts so that students can grasp the need to change their thinking. In such learning, there is usually a well-defined correct outcome. In more open-ended exercises, as in investigations of the application of mathematical thinking to everyday problems, there may be a variety of good solutions. Then an understanding of the criteria of quality is harder to achieve and may require joint discussion of examples and of the abstract criteria that they exemplify.

In science, the situation is very similar. There are many features of the natural world for which science provides a "correct" model or explanation. However, outside school, many students acquire different ideas. For example, some students come to believe that animals are living because they move but that trees and flowers are not because they don't. Or students may believe that astronauts seem almost weightless on the moon because there is no air present. Many of these "alternative conceptions" can be anticipated, for they have been well documented. What has also been documented is that the mere presentation of the "correct" view has been shown to be ineffective. The task in such cases is to open up discussion of such ideas and then provide feedback that challenges them by introducing new pieces of evidence and argument that support the scientific model.

There are other aspects for which an acceptable outcome is less well defined. As in mathematics, open-ended investigations call for different approaches to formative assessment. Even more open are issues about social or ethical implications of scientific achievements, for there is no "answer." Thus such work has to be "open" in a more fundamental way. Then the priority in giving feedback is to challenge students to tease out their assumptions and to help them to be critical about the quality of any arguments.

Peer assessment and self-assessment have a long history in language arts. Both the nature of the subject and the open outcome of many of the tasks characteristically make such practices central to one of the overall aims of the discipline, which is to enhance the critical judgment of the students.

A second important function of peer assessment and self-assessment was introduced by Royce Sadler, who argued that criteria alone are unhelpful in judging the quality of a piece of work or in guiding progression, because there will always be too many variables.[10] The key lies in knowing how to interpret the criteria in any particular case, which involves "guild knowledge." Teachers acquire this knowledge through assessing student work, and it is this process that allows them to differentiate between grades and to gain a sense of how progress is achieved. Peer assessment and self-assessment provide similar opportunities for students to be apprenticed into the guild, provided the criteria of quality are clearly communicated.

The priority in giving feedback is to challenge students to tease out their assumptions and to help them be critical about the quality of arguments.

In language arts, as in science and mathematics, attention needs to be paid to the central activities. Those that are the most successful are those rich tasks that provide students with an opportunity either to extend their understanding of a concept within the text or to "scaffold" their ideas before writing. Characteristically, these include small-group and pair work, with the results often being fed back into a whole-class discussion. Again, this type of work is not uncommon in language arts, the skill being to make the task sufficiently structured to scaffold learning but not so tightly defined as to limit thinking. Such activities not only provide students with a chance to develop their understanding through talk, but they also provide the teacher with the opportunity to give feedback during the course of a lesson through further questioning and guidance. The better the quality of the task, the better the quality of the interventions.

Differences between learning tasks can be understood in terms of a spectrum. At one end are "closed" tasks with a single well-defined outcome; at the other are "open" tasks with a wide range of acceptable outcomes. Tasks in language arts—for example, the writing of a poem—are mainly at the open end. But there are closed components even for such tasks—for example, the observance of grammatical or genre conventions. Tasks in, say, mathematics are more often closed, but applications of mathematics to everyday problems can require open-ended evaluations. Thus, in varying measure, the guidance needed for these two types of learning work will be needed in all subjects.

Despite these differences, experience has shown that the generic skills that have been developed do apply across subjects. One of the project's science teachers gave a talk to the whole staff about his experiences using some of the generic skills that we've been discussing and subsequently found how such practices distributed themselves throughout the disciplines:

> Art and drama teachers do it all the time, so do technology teachers (something to do with open-ended activities, long project times, and perhaps a less cramped curriculum?). But an English teacher came up to me today and said, "Yesterday afternoon was fantastic. I tried it today with my year 8s, and it works. No hands up, and giving them time to think. I had fantastic responses from kids who have barely spoken in class all year. They all wanted to say something, and the quality of answers was brilliant. This is the first time for ages that I've learnt something new that's going to make a real difference to my teaching."
> —*James*, Two Bishops School

MOTIVATION AND SELF-ESTEEM

Learning is not just a cognitive exercise: it involves the whole person. The need to motivate students is evident, but it is often assumed that offering such extrinsic rewards as grades, gold stars, and prizes is the best way to do it. However, there is ample evidence to challenge this assumption.

Students will invest effort in a task only if they believe that they can achieve something. If a learning exercise is seen as a competition, then everyone is aware that there will be losers as well as winners, and those who have a track record as losers will see little point in trying. Thus the problem is to motivate everyone, even though some are bound to achieve less than others. In tackling this problem, the type of feedback given is very important. Many research studies support this assertion. Here are a few examples:

- Students who are told that feedback "will help you to learn" learn more than those who are told that "how you do tells us how smart you are and what grades you'll get." The difference is greatest for low achievers.[11]

- Students given feedback as marks are likely to see it as a way to compare themselves with others (ego involvement); those given only comments see it as helping them to improve (task involvement). The latter group outperforms the former.[12]

Students given marks are likely to see it as a way to compare themselves with others; those given only comments see it as helping them to improve. The latter group outperforms the former.

- In a competitive system, low achievers attribute their performance to lack of "ability"; high achievers, to their effort. In a task-oriented system, all attribute performance to effort, and learning is improved, particularly among low achievers.[13]

- A comprehensive review of research studies of feedback found that feedback improved performance in 60% of the studies. In the cases where feedback was not helpful, the feedback turned out to be merely a judgment or grade with no indication of how to improve.[14]

In general, feedback given as rewards or grades enhances ego involvement rather than task involvement. It can focus students' attention on their "ability" rather than on the importance of effort, thus damaging the self-esteem of low achievers and leading to problems of "learned helplessness."[15] Feedback that focuses on what needs to be done can encourage all to believe that they can improve. Such feedback can enhance learning, both directly through the effort that can ensue and indirectly by supporting the motivation to invest such effort.[16]

THE BIG IDEA: FOCUS ON LEARNING

Our experiences in the project all point to the need to rethink a teacher's core aim: enhancing student learning. To achieve this goal calls for a willingness to rethink the planning of lessons, together with a readiness to change the roles that both teacher and students play in supporting the learning process.

A LEARNING ENVIRONMENT: PRINCIPLES AND PLANS

Improvement in classroom learning requires careful forethought.

> Actually thinking about teaching has meant that I have been able to come up with ideas and strategies to cope with whatever has arisen and has contributed greatly to my professional development. I now think more about the content of the lesson. The influence has shifted from "What am I going to teach and what are the pupils going to do?" toward "How am I going to teach this and what are the pupils going to learn?"
>
> —*Susan*, Waterford School

One purpose of a teacher's forethought is to plan to improve teaching actions. So, for example, the planning of questions and activities has to be in terms of their learning function.

> I certainly did not spend sufficient time developing questions prior to commencing my formative training. . . . Not until you analyze your own questioning do you realize how poor it can be. I found myself using questions to fill time and asking questions which required little thought from the students. When talking to students, particularly those who are experiencing difficulties, it is important to ask questions which get them thinking about the topic and will allow them to make the next step in the learning process.
>
> —*Derek*, Century Island School

Of equal importance is concern for the quality of the responses that teachers make, whether in dialogue or in feed-back on written assignments. Effective feedback should make more explicit to students what is involved in a high-quality piece of work and what steps they need to take to improve. At the same time, feedback can enhance students' skills and strategies for effective learning.

There is also a deeper issue here. A learning environment has to be "engineered" to involve students more actively in the learning tasks. The emphasis has to be on students' thinking and making that thinking public. As one teacher put it:

> There was a definite transition at some point, from focusing on what I was putting into the process, to what the students were contributing. It became obvious that one way to make a significant sustainable change was to get the students doing more of the thinking. I then began to search for ways to make the learning process more transparent to the students. Indeed, I now spend my time looking for ways to get students to take responsibility for their learning and at the same time making the learning more collaborative.
>
> —*Tom*, Riverside School

Collaboration between teachers and students and between students and their peers can produce a supportive environment in which students can explore their own ideas, hear alternative ideas in the language of their peers, and evaluate them.

> One technique has been to put the students into small groups and give each student a small part of the unit to explain to [his or her] colleagues. They are given a few minutes' preparation time, a few hints, and use of their exercise books. Then each student explains [his or her] chosen subject to the rest of the group. Students are quick to point out such things as, "I thought that the examples you chose were very good as they were not ones in our books. I don't think I would have thought of those." Or "I expected you to mention particles more when you were explaining the difference between liquids and gases." These sessions have proven invaluable— not only to me, in being able to discover the level of understanding of some students, but to the students too.
>
> —*Philip*, Century Island School

An additional advantage of such an environment is that a teacher can work intensively with one group, challenging the ideas and assumptions of its members, knowing that the rest of the class members are also working hard.

So the main actions to be taken to engineer an effective learning environment are:

• Plan classroom activities to give students the opportunity to express their thinking so that feedback can help develop it;

• formulate feedback so that it guides improvement in learning;

• use activities that demand collaboration so that everyone is included and challenged and train students to listen to and respect one another's ideas; and

• be sure that students are active participants in the lessons and emphasize that learning may depend less on their capacity to spot the right answer and more on their readiness to express and discuss their own understanding.

A LEARNING ENVIRONMENT: ROLES AND EXPECTTIONS

It is one thing to plan new types of classroom activity and quite another to put them into practice in ways that are faithful to the aims they were developed to serve. Here there are no recipes to follow in a uniform way. *Inside the Black Box* was clear in stating that the effective development of formative assessment would come about only if "each teacher finds his or her own ways of incorporating the lessons and ideas that are set out above into her or his own patterns of classroom work."

A second principle is that the learning environment envisaged requires a classroom culture that may well be unfamiliar and disconcerting for both teachers and students. The effect of the innovations implemented by our teachers was to change the "classroom contract" between the teacher and the student—the rules that govern the behaviors that are expected and seen as legitimate by teachers and students.

The students have to change from behaving as passive recipients of the knowledge offered by the teacher to becoming active learners who can take responsibility for and manage their own learning.

For the teachers, courage is necessary. One of the striking features of the project was that, in the early stages, many participants described the new approach as "scary" because they felt they were going to lose control of their classes. Toward the end of the project, they spoke not of losing control but of sharing responsibility for the students' learning with the class—exactly the same process but viewed from two very different perspectives. In one perspective, the teachers and students are in a delivery/recipient relationship; in the other, they are partners in pursuit of a shared goal:

> What formative assessment has done for me is made me focus less on myself but more on the children. I have had the confidence to empower the students to take it forward.
> —*Robert*, Two Bishops School

What has been happening here is that everybody's expectations—that is, what teachers and students think that being a teacher or being a student requires you to do—have been altered. While it can seem daunting to undertake such changes, they do not have to happen suddenly. Changes with the KMOFAP teachers came slowly and steadily, as experience developed and confidence grew in the use of the various strategies for enriching feedback and interaction. For example, many teachers started by using questions to encourage thinking. Then they improved their oral and written feedback so that it brought thinking forward and went on to develop peer and self-assessment.

To summarize, expectations and classroom culture can be changed:

• by changing the "classroom contract" so that all expect that teacher and students work together for the same end: the improvement of everyone's learning;

• by empowering students to become active learners, thus taking responsibility for their own learning;

• by incorporating the changes in the teacher's role one step at a time, as they seem appropriate; and

• by sustained attention to and reflection on ways in which assessment can support learning.

WHAT YOU CAN DO

To incorporate some of the ideas about formative assessment into your own practice, the first step is to reflect on what you are now doing. Discussion with colleagues and observation of one another's lessons can help spark such reflection.

A next step must be to try out changes. Wholesale change can be too risky and demanding, so it is often best to think of one thing you feel confident to try—be it "traffic lights," peer assessment, improved questioning, whatever—and simply try it. If you are a teacher in a middle school or high school, try it with just one group. Or if you are an elementary teacher, try it in just one subject area. We found that, as teachers gained confidence in the power of allowing students to say what they know and what they need to know, the teachers decided that they should extend assessment for learning to the whole of their teaching.

Taking on further strategies will then lead to further progress. When several colleagues are collaborating, each starts with a different strategy and then shares findings. This process should lead to the explicit formulation of an "action plan," comprising a range of strategies to be used, in combination, preferably starting with a class at the beginning of the school year. The first reason to start at the beginning of the year is so that there can be time to accustom both teacher and students to a new way of working. The second is that it can be very difficult to change the established habits and routines in the middle of a year. The experience of a year's sustained work, with only a few classes, preferably alongside similar efforts by colleagues, can provide a firm basis for subsequent adoption of new practices on a wider scale.

Collaboration with a group trying out similar innovations is almost essential. Mutual observation and the sharing of ideas and experiences about the progress of action plans can provide the necessary support both with the tactics and at a strategic level. Support for colleagues is particularly important in overcoming those initial uncertainties when engaging in the risky business of changing the culture and expectations in the classroom.

As for any innovation, support from administrators is essential. One way administrators can support change of this kind is to help peer groups of teachers find time to meet on a regular basis. Opportunities should also be found for teachers to report to faculty and staff meetings.

The work of any group experimenting with innovations is an investment for the whole school, so that support should not be treated as indulgence for idiosyncratic practices. Indeed, such work should be integrated into a school improvement plan, with the expectation that the dissemination of fruitful practices will follow from the evaluation of a group's experiences.

There may be a need to review school policies: an example would be a policy that, by demanding a grade on every piece of homework, prevents the serious use of comments.

At the same time, there may be a need to review current school policies because such policies can actually constrain the use of formative assessment. A notable example would be a policy that, by demanding that a score or grade be given on every piece of homework, prevents the serious use of comments. Five of the six schools in the KMOFAP project have, following the experience of their science and mathematics teachers, modified their policies to allow "comment only" marking; for two of these, the modification was that no scores or grades be given on homework throughout the school. In another example, a "target setting" system that required very frequent review was inhibiting any change in learning methods that might slow down immediate "progress" in order to produce medium-to long-term gains in learning skills. Those engaged in innovations may need formal exemption from such policies.

Thus support, evaluation, and subsequent dissemination of innovation in assessment for learning will be planned in a coherent way only if the responsibility for strategic over-sight of the development is assigned to a member of the school leadership team. Our experience supports the view that to realize the promise of formative assessment by leaving a few keen individuals to get on with it would be unfair to them, while to do it by imposing a policy that requires all teachers to immediately change their personal roles and styles would be absurd.

What is needed is a plan, extending over at least three years, in which a few small groups are supported for a two year exploration. These groups then form a nucleus of experience and expertise for disseminating their ideas throughout the school and for supporting colleagues in making similar explorations for themselves.

Notes

1. Paul Black and Dylan Wiliam, "Inside the Black Box: Raising Standards Through Classroom Assessment ," *Phi Delta Kappan*, October 1998, pp. 139-48. A version of this article has been published and widely sold in the United Kingdom. A booklet, published in 2002, has also been widely distributed in the UK. It covers the same issues as the article and bears the same title with the same authors. Both booklets, and further booklets in this series, are published by NFER-NELSON.

2. Only a few references to the literature are given here. Further information about publications and other resources can be obtained on the King's College website in the pages of the King's Formative Assessment Group. Some of the publications can be downloaded from this site: www.Kel.ac.uk/education/research/Kal.html.

3. Paul Black and Dylan Wiliam, "Assessment and Classroom Learning," *Assessment in Education*, March 1998, pp. 7-71.

4. Paul Black, Christine Harrison, Clare Lee, Bethan Marshall, and Dylan Wiliam, *Assessment for Learning: Putting It into Practice* (Buckingham, U.K.: Open University Press, 2003).

5. Mary Budd Rowe, "Wait Time and Rewards as Instructional Variables , Their Influence on Language, Logic, and Fate Control," *Journal of Research in Science Teaching*, vol. 11, 1974, pp. 81-94.

6. Ruth Butler, "Enhancing and Undermining Intrinsic Motivation; The Effects of Task-Involving and Ego-Involving Evaluation on Interest and Performance," *British Journal of Educational Psychology*, vol. 58, 1988, pp. 1-14.

7. Royce Sadler, "Formative Assessment and the Design of Instructional Systems," *Instructional Science*, vol. 18, 1989, pp. 119-44.

8. Royce Sadler, "Formative Assessment: Revisiting the Territory," *Assessment in Education*, vol. 5, 1998, pp. 77-84.

9. See, for example, Paul W. Foos, Joseph J. Mora, and Sharon Tkacz, "Student Study Techniques and the Generation Effect," *Journal of Educational Psychology*, vol. 86, 1994, pp. 567-76; and Alison King, "Facilitating Elaborative Learning Through Guided Student-Generated Questioning ," *Educational Psychologist*, vol. 27, 1992, pp. 111-26.

10. See, for example, Mike Askew et al., *Effective Teachers of Numeracy: Final Report*(London: King's College London, School of Education, 1997). In this study, there was no correlation between the progress made by elementary school students in arithmetic and the highest level of mathematics studied by the teacher. Indeed, there was a nonsignificant negative correlation between the two. The students who made the most progress were taught by teachers without high levels of subject knowledge, but who emphasized the connections between mathematics concepts.

11. Sadler, "Formative Assessment and the Design of Instructional Systems."

12. Richard S. Newman and Mahna T. Schwager, "Students' Help Seeking During Problem Solving: Effects of Grade, Goal, and Prior Achievement," *American Educational Research Journal*, vol. 32, 1995, pp. 352–76.

13. Ruth Butler, "Task-Involving and Ego-Involving Properties of Evaluation: Effects of Different Feedback Conditions on Motivational Perceptions, Interest, and Performance ," *Journal of Educational Psychology*, vol. 79, 1987, pp. 474-82.

14. Rhonda G. Craven, Herbert W. Marsh, and Raymond L. Debus, "Effects of Internally Focused Feedback on Enhancement of Academic Self-Concept," *Journal of Educational Psychology*, vol. 83, 1991, pp. 17-27.

15. Avraham N. Kluger and Angelo DeNisi, "The Effects of Feedback Interventions on Performance: A Historical Review, a Meta-Analysis, and a Preliminary Feedback Intervention Theory," *Psychological Bulletin*, vol. 119, 1996, pp. 254-84.

16. Carol S. Dweck, "Motivational Processes Affecting Learning," *American Psychologist* (Special Issue: Psychological Science and Education), vol. 41, 1986, pp. 1040-48.

17. Carol S. Dweck, *Self-Theories: Their Role in Motivation, Personality, and Development* (Philadelphia: Psychology Press, 2000).

PAUL BLACK *is a professor emeritus, Department of Education and Professional Studies, King's College London, where* CHRISTINE HARRISON *is a lecturer in science education.* CLARE LEE *is a teacher advisor for the Warwickshire County Council.* BETHAN MARSHALL *is a lecturer in English education, Department of Education and Professional Studies, School of Education, King's College London.* DYLAN WILIAM *is director of the Learning and Teaching Research Center, Educational Testing Service, Princeton, N.J. They wish to thank the Medway and Oxfordshire local education authorities and the schools directly involved in the project described here, especially the teachers who shouldered the greatest burdens. The work on which this article is based was supported by grants from the Nuffield Foundation and from the U.S. National Science Foundation, as part of the Stanford University Classroom Assessment Project to Improve Teaching and Learning (CAPITAL). But the opinions expressed are those of the authors.* © 2004, Dylan Wiliam.

From *Phi Delta Kappan,* September 2004, pp. 9-21. Copyright © 2004 by NFER Nelson. Reprinted by permission.

Using Student-Involved Classroom Assessment to Close Achievement Gaps

The authors argue that the failure of 60 years of total reliance on assessment via standardized tests to help reduce achievement score gaps must compel us to rethink the role of assessment in this endeavor. They advocate rebalancing assessment priorities to bring classroom assessment into the equation. Evidence gathered over decades from around the world reveals strong achievement gains and reduced achievement score gaps when teachers implement student-involved classroom assessment practices in support of student learning in their classrooms. Five standards of sound classroom assessment practice are described which, if put in place, would permit teachers and schools to draw upon a heretofore untapped reservoir of motivation in ways that benefit students, especially low performers.

Rick Stiggins

Jan Chappuis

From their very earliest school experiences, our students draw life-shaping conclusions about themselves as learners on the basis of the information we provide to them as a result of their teachers' classroom assessments. As that evidence accumulates over time, they decide if they are capable of succeeding or not. They decide whether the learning is worth the commitment it will take to attain it. They decide if they should have confidence in themselves as learners and in their teachers—that is, whether to risk investing in the schooling experience. These decisions are crucial to their academic well-being. Depending on how they decide, their teachers may or may not be able to influence their learning lives.

Because of individual academic difficulties, some students can land on the wrong side of these decisions. If we are to help them—if we are to close achievement gaps—we must help them believe they are capable of succeeding and that success is worth the investment.

The results of a decade of research and development (cited later) help us understand how to use the classroom assessment process and its results to help students become confident learners. Strong achievement gains are within reach for all students, especially those who have experienced little success before. To gain access to these results, we must (a) fundamentally redefine the relationships among assessment, student motivation, and effective schools, and (b) provide teachers with a set of classroom assessment competencies that historically has been denied them. This article describes such a new vision and the conditions that must be in place to attain it.

The Challenge

In motivating low-performing students to want to learn, our collective challenge comes in two parts. First, we must prevent students from giving up in hopelessness at the outset, by engendering confidence from their earliest experiences. Second, we must rekindle hope among those students who have lost faith in themselves as learners already.

It's tempting to conceive of the latter challenge as an issue of self-concept, that is, as a personal-emotional concern. If we can raise these students' self-concept, they will become capable learners. But this approach puts the cart before the horse. Rather, we conceptualize the problem far more productively if we conceive of the first challenge in light of effective classroom assessment.

If these students are to believe in themselves as productive learners, then they must first experience credible forms of academic success as reflected in the results of what they understand to be rigorous assessment. A small success can spark confidence, which, in turn, encourages more effort. If each attempt brings more success, their academic self-concept will begin to shift in a more positive direction. Our goal then is to perpetuate this cycle.

The direction of this effect is critical. First comes achievement and then comes confidence. With increased confidence comes the belief that learning is possible. Success must be framed in terms of academic attainments that represent a significant personal stretch. Focused effort with an expectation of success is essential. Students must come honestly to believe that what counts here—indeed the only thing that counts here—is learning that results from the effort expended.

Such evidence kindles students' faith in themselves as learners. Feedback delivered once a year from standardized district, state, national, or international assessments is far too infrequent and broadly focused to be helpful. The evidence must come to students moment to moment through on-going classroom assessment. This places the classroom teacher at the heart of the relation between assessment and school effectiveness.

Thus, the essential school improvement question from an assessment point of view is this: *Are we skilled enough to use classroom assessment to either (1) keep all learners from losing hope to begin with, or (2) rebuild that hope once it has been destroyed?*

Successful students enjoy the rewards of their own success at learning. These keep them striving (typically on the upper side of achievement score gaps), and teachers can continue to rely on those motivators. But what of those students who have not experienced success? What do we do when the traditional reward- and punishment-driven behavior-management system has lost its motivational power in the eyes of the student?

The Insufficiency of Accountability Testing

Over the decades, we have attempted to motivate by holding schools accountable for scores on standardized tests and by intensifying the stakes associated with low test scores. This began in the 1940s with college admissions tests. Next came district-wide standardized tests in the 1950s and 1960s. The 1970s was the decade of the state assessment. In the 1980s and 1990s, we added national and international assessments. During these latter decades, we have seen fit to attach truly dire consequences to low test scores. For individual students these can include promotion/retention, as well as graduation decisions. Surely, policymakers believe, this will compel everyone involved to strive for academic excellence.

But alas, not only is there little evidence that these multiple layers of externally imposed tests have improved school quality or reduced achievement score gaps, but some contend that they have exacerbated the problem by forcing increases in dropout rates and declines in graduation rates, especially among minorities (Amrein & Berliner, 2002). These high-stakes tests have caused as many chronic low achievers to give up in the face of what they believe to be unattainable achievement standards as they have spurred high achievers to try even harder. So test score averages flatline, with gaps between different subgroups of our student population apparently cast in stone.

The Case for Student-Involved Classroom Assessment

Ongoing classroom assessments can be used in far more productive ways to encourage student confidence. Three categories of powerful tools, taken together, permit us to tap a wellspring of motivation that resides within each learner. These tools in-

clude student involvement in the assessment process, student-involved record keeping, and student-involved communication. Together, they redefine how we use assessment to excite students about their learning potential. Here's why:

The teacher's *instructional task* is to take students to the edge of their capabilities, to encourage growth. From the point of view of some students, stepping off that edge can be frightening. "When I have stepped off the edge in the past, I have disappeared into the chasm below, crashing in a cloud of dust. Thanks much, but not again." In such instances, the teacher's *instructional challenge* is to help students face their personal edge with confidence, trusting that their teacher will help them learn from their initial mistakes. Students must understand that, when they try to grow academically, at first, they may not be very proficient, and that is all right. The trick is to help them know that failures hold the seeds of later success, but only if we keep going.

In other words, we must stop delivering the message to students that low-level performance is always and necessarily a bad thing. Sometimes low performance is inevitable, such as when they are trying something new. Everyone makes halting progress as a writer at first. Wise teachers use the classroom assessment process as an instructional intervention to teach the lesson that small increments of progress are normal. Success is defined as continual improvement over the long haul. We can use student involvement in the assessment, record keeping, and communication processes to teach these lessons.

Student-involved classroom assessment opens the assessment process and invites students in as partners, monitoring their own levels of achievement. Under the careful management of their teachers (who begin with a clear and appropriate vision of what they want their students to achieve), students are invited to play a role in defining the criteria by which their work will be judged. They learn to apply these criteria, identifying the strengths and weaknesses in their own practice work. In short, student-involved assessment helps learners see and understand our vision of their academic success. The result will be classrooms in which there are no surprises and no excuses. This builds trust and confidence.

Student-involved record keeping encourages learners to monitor improvements in their performance over time through repeated self-assessment. For example, as students build growth portfolios of evidence of their success over time, they can reflect on the changes they see. In effect, we use such repeated formative classroom assessments as a mirror permitting students to watch themselves grow. As they chart progress, they gain a sense of control over their own learning. This can be a powerful confidence builder.

Student-involved communication invites learners to share their self-assessments with others. Student-involved parent/teacher conferences—a significant breakthrough in communicating about student achievement—illustrate this concept in action. When students are prepared well over an extended period to tell the story of their own success (or lack thereof), they experience a fundamental shift in their internal sense of responsibility for that success. The pride that students feel when they have a positive story to tell, and then tell it convincingly, engenders commitment to further learning. And, students feel an immense sense of personal responsibility when they know that they might have to face the music of telling their parents about the specifics of their nonachievement. They will work very hard to avoid that eventuality; that prospect can drive them to productive work.

In these three ways, we can use student involvement to help them see, understand, contribute to, and appreciate their own journey of achievement success. This is exactly what teachers must do to help their students understand the achievement expectations, find and follow the path of success, and feel in charge of, rather than victimized by, the assessment process.

Research Evidence of Reduced Achievement Gaps

In 1984, Bloom published a summary of his research on the impact of mastery learning models on student learning, comparing standard whole-class instruction (the control condition) with two experimental interventions, a mastery learning environment and one-on-one tutoring of individual students. One hallmark of both experimental conditions was the extensive use of classroom assessment in support of, and not merely to check for, learning as a key part of the instructional process. The analyses revealed significant differences in student achievement favoring the experimental conditions that relied on classroom assessment to support learning (effect sizes ranged from one to two standard deviations).

In their 1998 research review, Black and Wiliam examined the research literature on assessment worldwide, asking if there is evidence that improving the quality and effectiveness of use of student-involved formative assessments raises student achievement as reflected in summative assessments. They reviewed more than 250 articles that addressed the issue. On pooling the information on the estimated effects of student-involved classroom assessment on summative test scores, they too uncovered positive effects, reporting effect sizes of a half to a full standard deviation. Further, Black and Wiliam report that "improved [student-involved] formative assessment helps low achievers more than other students and so reduces the range of achievement while raising achievement overall" (p. 141). *This result has direct implications for districts seeking to reduce achievement gaps between and among subgroups of students.*

The work of the Education Trust (Jerald, 2001) revealed that one key to promoting very high levels of achievement in traditionally low-performing schools was the effective use of day-to-day classroom assessment as an integral part of a healthy teaching and learning process.

More recently, Meisels, Atkins-Burnett, Xue, and Bickel (2003) revealed how student involvement with work sample-based performance assessments yields similar gains on standardized test performance when compared with students who did not experience the embedded performance assessment (effect sizes ranged .75 to 1.5 standard deviations).

In 2004, Rodriguez reported similar size achievement gains when examining the relationships among student characteristics, teachers' classroom assessment practices, and student achievement as measured in the Third International Math and Science Study (TIMSS). Specifically, he concluded that "There are areas in which teachers have a potential to affect students: developing self-efficacy regarding their potential of mastering mathematics and discouraging the uncontrollable attributions students make in the classroom" (p. 20). In other words, teachers can help all students, but especially low performers, come to believe that they can control their own success in learning mathematics.

Taken together, the evidence provided in these studies suggests that achievement gains and reductions in score gaps are within reach if classroom assessments (1) focus on clear purposes, (2) provide accurate reflections of achievement, (3) provide students with continuous access to descriptive feedback on improvement in their work (versus infrequent judgmental feedback), and (4) bring students into the classroom assessment processes. These four findings, then, frame the necessary conditions that must be satisfied to gain access to the achievement effects reported.

Classroom Assessment to Reduce Achievement Gaps

These four conditions must be satisfied to ensure the effective use of any assessment in any context (Stiggins, 2005)—but especially to close achievement gaps. Part of the reason our nation has experienced difficulty in improving student achievement overall and in reducing achievement gaps, we contend, is that the vast majority of teachers and administrators practicing in the United States today have never been given the opportunity to understand, let alone learn to satisfy these conditions:

Condition #1: Assessment Development Must Always Be Driven by a Clearly Articulated Purpose.

That is, the information needs of the intended user(s) must be considered in designing, developing, and using the assessment. Sometimes those users and uses center on assessment to support learning—to inform teachers about how to help students learn more and to inform students themselves about how to maximize their success. We call these assessments FOR learning (Assessment Reform Group, 1999; Stiggins, 2002). Other times assessments serve to verify that learning has occurred (or not). These may inform school leaders about program effectiveness or provide agents of accountability with evidence to the community. We label these assessments OF learning.

The research evidence cited herein reveals that paying careful attention to the former, assessment FOR learning via sound classroom assessment, will yield significant school improvement and reduced score gaps. Students need more information about their learning destination and progress than they typically get. Assessment FOR learning practices remedy that by helping students answer three questions: *Where am I going? Where am I now? How can I get there from here?* In other words, students need to know what the intended learning or expected standard of quality is. They need to know how to judge and monitor their own progress. And they need to know what to do to get themselves from where they are to where they need to be (Black & Wiliam, 1998; Sadler,

1989). Assessment FOR learning engages students in thinking about themselves as learners. It is a new idea for many teachers to understand that formative assessment can and should be done *for and by* students, and yet it is crucial to students becoming effective learners.

Condition #1 calls on educators to understand students' information needs and to plan assessments purposefully to meet those needs along with the information needs of adult instructional decision makers.

Condition #2: Assessments Must Arise From and Accurately Reflect Clearly Specified and Appropriate Achievement Expectations.

In any assessment context, we must begin assessment development by defining a clear vision of what it means to succeed. In assessment OF learning contexts, we identify state, local, or classroom achievement standards and devise assessments reflective of those. In assessment FOR learning environments, teachers deconstruct standards into the enabling classroom targets students must master on their journey to meeting state standards. To meet any standard, students must master subject matter content, meaning to *know and understand*. Some standards demand that they learn to use knowledge to *reason* and solve problems, whereas others require mastery of specific *performance skills*, where it's the doing that is important, or the ability to create *products* that satisfy certain criteria of quality. Student success hinges on the clarity of these expectations in the minds of teachers and then of their students.

Students need to know where they are headed to participate actively in their own learning; when they don't know the learning destination, they are at best just along for the ride. Teacher and students cannot partner effectively without a shared vision of the enterprise. And the effectiveness of subsequent student involvement in the assessment process depends on their knowing what the achievement expectations are.

Condition #2 requires that teachers become clear themselves about the intended learning, teach intentionally to it, and let students in on the secret up front.

Condition # 3: Assessment Methods Used Must Be Capable of Accurately Reflecting the Intended Targets and Are Used as Teaching Tools Along the Way to Proficiency.

Teachers have a variety of assessment alternatives from which to select as they focus on the valued leaning targets. Accurate assessment conclusions are dependent on the selection or development of proper assessment tools. The options include *selected response* (multiple choice, true/false, matching, and fill in), *extended written response, performance assessments* (based on observation and judgment), and direct *personal communication* with the student. The challenge in all contexts is to match an assessment method with an intended achievement target. Bad matches yield inaccurate assessments.

The teaching challenge is to use the assessment, in advance of the graded event, as a vehicle to deepen the learning and to reveal to students their developing proficiencies. Figure 1 provides a sampling of strategies using different assessment methods as teaching tools. (Stiggins, Arter, Chappuis, & Chappuis, 2004).

Classroom Assessment in Service of Learning

1. Engage students in reviewing strong and weak samples to determine attributes of a good performance or product.
2. Before a discussion or conference with the teacher or peer, students identify their own perceptions of strengths and weaknesses on a specific aspect of their work.
3. Students practice using criteria to evaluate anonymous strong and weak work.
4. Students work in pairs to revise an anonymous weak work sample they have just evaluated.
5. Students write a process paper, detailing the process they went through to create a product or performance. In it they reflect on problems they encountered and how they solved them.
6. Students develop practice test plans based on their understanding of the intended learning targets and essential concepts in material to be learned.
7. Students generate and answer questions they think might be on the test, based on their understanding of the content/processes/skills/they were responsible for learning.
8. A few days before a test, students discuss or write answers to questions such as: "Why am I taking this test? Who will use the results? How?" "What is it testing?" "How do I think I will do?" "What do I need to study?" "With whom might I work?"
9. Teacher arranges items on a test according to specific learning targets, and prepares a "test analysis" chart for students, with three boxes: "My strengths," "Quick review," and "Further study." After handing back the corrected test, students identify learning targets they have mastered and write them in the "My strengths" box. Next, students categorize their wrong answers as either "simple mistake" or "further study." Then, students list the simple mistakes in the "Quick review" box. Last, students write the rest of the learning targets represented by wrong answers in the "Further study" box.
10. Students review a collection of their work over time and reflect on their growth: "I have become a better reader this quarter. I used to. . . , but now I . . ."
11. Students use a collection of their self-assessments to summarize their learning and set goals for future learning: "Here is what I have learned . . . Here is what I need to work on . . ."
12. Students select and annotate evidence of achievement for a portfolio.

In addition, all assessments rely on a relatively small number of exercises to permit the user to draw inferences about a student's mastery of larger domains of achievement. Accurate assessments rely on a representative sample of all those possibilities that is large enough to yield dependable inferences about how the respondent would have done if given all possible exercises.

But even if we devise clear achievement targets, transform them into proper assessment methods, and sample student performance appropriately, there are still factors that can cause a student's score on a test to misrepresent his or her real achievement. Problems can arise from the test, the student, or the environment where the test is administered.

For example, tests can consist of poorly worded questions, place reading or writing demands on respondents that are confounded with mastery of the material being tested, have more than one correct response, be incorrectly scored, or contain racial or ethnic bias. The student can experience extreme evaluation anxiety or interpret test items differently from the author's intent, as well as cheat, guess, or lack motivation. Any of these could give rise to inaccurate test results. Or the assessment environment could be uncomfortable, poorly lighted, noisy, or otherwise distracting. Part of the challenge of assessing well in the classroom is to be aware of the potential sources of bias and to know how to devise assessments, prepare students, and plan assessment environments to deflect these problems before they ever impact results.

Condition #3, then, demands accuracy of assessment results and intentional involvement of students to deepen the learning.

Condition #4: Communication Systems Must Deliver Assessment Results Into the Hands of Their Intended Users in a Timely, Understandable, and Helpful Manner.

The central question of the first condition, "What is the purpose for the assessment?" guides the development of effective communication systems. In assessments OF learning, where the assessment purpose is to report how much students have learned at a particular point in time, our communication systems consist of grade reports, standardized test reports, parent-teacher conferences, and the like. These systems are firmly in place (indeed, they may be the only systems in place), and although ensuring their timeliness and clarity is important, developing communication systems in service of assessment FOR learning is required to close the achievement gap.

In assessments FOR learning, the assessment purpose is to provide teachers and students with information they need along the way, during the learning process, to make decisions that will bring about more learning. In this side of the assessment house, an effective communication system provides regular diagnostic information to the teacher and frequent descriptive feedback to the learner. Grades (numbers and letters) do not provide the detail needed to function effectively as feedback in this setting. Furthermore, evaluative, "high-stakes" grades—those destined for the report card—are often counterproductive while students are in the process of learning, for judgment offered too soon can shut learning down. Bloom, Black, and Wiliam, and other researchers, strongly support the use of criterion-based feedback, instead, to keep the learning process going. Such comments reflect student strengths and areas for improvement relative to established standards, but do not insert a summative judgment. They are most powerful when they identify what students are doing right, or have learned, as well as what they need to work on (Black & Wiliam, 1998; Bloom, 1984).

Students also play an important role in a communication system designed to support learning. When they are involved in collecting evidence of their achievement, charting their growth, and setting goals for future learning, students develop insight into themselves as learners. In addition, both the achievement and their commitment to learning increase (Covington, 1992). Such practices prepare students to become active participants in sharing their achievement with parents and other teachers.

Condition #4, then, requires careful attention to meeting the communication needs of audiences in both assessment OF and FOR learning contexts.

Conclusion

Students' decisions about their academic capabilities are formulated on the basis of classroom assessment evidence. In contexts where wide gaps appear in test score results between and among different subgroups of the student population, the chances are high that low performers have judged themselves to be incapable of succeeding. In this presentation, we propose the use of student-involved classroom assessment to turn their thinking in more positive directions. The evidence reveals that there is no question about what will happen to their achievement and score gaps when we do so.

References

Amrein, A. L., & Berliner, D. C. (2002). High-stakes testing, uncertainty, and student learning. *Educational Policy Analysis Archives*, 10(8) 70 pp. Retrieved May 2004 from `http://epaa.asu.edu/epaa/v10n18/`.

Assessment Reform Group. (1999). *Assessment for learning: Beyond the black box*. Cambridge, UK: University of Cambridge Press.

Black, P., & Wiliam, D. (1998). Assessment and classroom learning. *Educational Assessment: Principles, Policy and Practice*, 5(1), 7–74. Also summarized in an article entitled, Inside the black box: Raising standards through classroom assessment. *Phi Delta Kappan*, 80(2), 139–148.

Bloom, B. (1984). The search for methods of group instruction as effective as one-to-one tutoring. *Educational Leadership*, 41(8), 4–17.

Covington, M. (1992). Making the grade: A self-worth perspective on motivation and school reform. New York: Cambridge University Press.

Jerald, C. D. (2001). *Dispelling the Myth Revisited*. Washington DC: Education Trust.

Meisels, S., Atkins-Burnett, S., Xue, Y., & Bickel, D. D. (2003). Creating a system of accountability: The impact of instructional assessment on elementary children's achievement scores. *Educational Policy Analysis Archives*, 11(9) 19 pp. Retrieved January 2004 from `http://epaa.asu.edu/eapp/v11n9/`

Rodriguez, M. C. (2004). The role of classroom assessment in student performance on TIMSS. *Applied Measurement in Education*, 17, 1–24.

Sadler, R. (1989). Formative assessment and the design of instructional systems. *Instructional Science*, 18, 119–144.

Stiggins, R. J. (2002). Assessment crisis! The absence of assessment FOR learning. *Phi Delta Kappan*, 83(10), 758–765.

Stiggins, R. J. (2005). *Student-involved assessment FOR learning* (4th ed.). Columbus, OH: Merrill Prentice Hall.

Stiggins, R., Arter, J., Chappuis, J., & Chappuis, S. (2004). *Classroom assessment for student learning: Doing it right—using it well*. Portland, OR: Assessment Training Institute.

Rick Stiggins and ***Jan Chappuis*** *work at Assessment Training Institute.*

Requests for reprints can be sent to Rick Stiggins, Assessment Training Institute, 317 SW Alder Street, Suite 1200, Portland OR 97204. E-mail: ati@assessmentinst.com

From *Theory Into Practice*, vol. 44, no. 1, Winter 2005. Copyright © 2005 by Lawrence Erlbaum Associates. Reprinted by permission.

Grades as Valid Measures of Academic Achievement of Classroom Learning

JAMES D. ALLEN

What is the purpose of grades? In this article I present one answer to this question from a perspective that many educators might see as somewhat radical or extreme. The perspective that I take is based on the fundamental educational psychology assessment principle of validity—the validity of what learning is being assessed and the validity of the communication of that assessment to others. I believe most teachers fail to give grades to students that are as valid as they should be. Because grading is something that has been done to each of us during our many years as students, it is hard to change the invalid "grading" schema that has become embedded in our minds. Now, as educators often required to grade students, and because of this embedded schema, we often grade students in invalid ways similar to how we were graded. Inadequate education in valid assessment and grading principles and practices is a reason many teachers continue to perpetuate invalid grading practices with students. Since educational testing and assessment is a major content knowledge area in educational psychology, the issues regarding assessment and grading that I address in this article could well be addressed in an educational psychology course. If our preservice and inservice teachers are going to learn appropriate assessment and grading practices then educational psychologists need to provide the relevant information in their classes.

The most fundamental measurement principle related to meaningful assessment and grading is the principle of validity (Gallagher 1998; Gredler 1999; Linn and Gronlund 2000; Stiggins 2001). Although there are many validity issues involved in classroom assessment that classroom teachers should consider, such as making sure the way they assess students corresponds to the type of academic learning behaviors being assessed (Ormrod 2000), the focus here is on the valid assessment and communication of final class grades as summaries of students' academic achievement of content knowledge of a subject. Validity addresses the accuracy of the assessment and grading procedures used by teachers (Gallagher 1998; Gredler 1999; Linn and Gronlund 2000). Do the assessment procedures and assignment of grades accurately reflect and communicate the academic achievement of the student? Validity is important because the sole purpose of grades is to accurately communicate to others the level of academic achievement that a student

has obtained (Snowman and Biehler 2003). If the grades are not accurate measures of the student's achievement, then they do not communicate the truth about the level of the student's academic achievement. Unfortunately, as stated by Cizek, even as "grades continue to be relied upon to communicate important information about [academic] performance and progress ... they probably don't" (1996, 104).

Assigning grades to students is such a complex (and sometimes controversial) issue that some educators have proposed their abolition (Kohn 1999; Marzano 2000). Although I find this an interesting proposal, especially if one is trying to establish a classroom learning environment that is student-centered and encourages self-regulation and self-evaluation, the current reality for most teachers is that they are required to assign grades indicating students' academic achievement in the subjects they teach. Therefore, grading should be as valid as possible. Not only is grading a major responsibility of classroom teachers, but it is also a practice with which they are often uncomfortable and that they find difficult (Barnes 1985; Lomax 1996; Thorndike 1997). The sources of the discomfort and difficulty for teachers regarding the grading of students seem to be threefold. First, the student activities that teachers think should constitute "academic achievement" and how to handle ancillary features of achievement such as students' efforts varies tremendously from teacher to teacher. Although ancillary information such as effort and attitude could be part of an overall student report, they should not be part of a grade that represents academic achievement (Tombari and Borich 1999). Second, teachers often seem to be unsettled regarding the communication function of grades, and they often try to communicate multiple pieces of information about students that can not possibly be contained within a single academic mark. This is an issue of making sure the grade is accurate as a valid communication to others. Third, because of the first two issues, many teachers assign grades that are invalid and not built on a solid principle of measurement (Cizek 1996; Marzano 2000). In addition, partially due to their long career as students experiencing invalid grading practices, as well as inadequate preservice and inservice education on assessment and grading, teachers continue to perpetuate invalid grading practices. Let us consider each of these points in greater depth.

Miscommunication and Confusing Purposes of Grades

Although students learn many things in the classroom, the primary objective is for students to learn academic content knowledge of a particular subject. In order for teachers to know if students are achieving this academic knowledge, they generally are required to not only assess students' knowledge in some way, but eventually summarize that assessment into a letter or numerical grade. This is known as "summative" evaluation. Hopefully, teachers are also gathering nongraded "formative" assessments of students to provide feedback to students as they learn, as well as considering how to motivate students to learn and encouraging them to be self-regulated learners. However, generally, teachers have to eventually place a grade on a grade sheet indicating what level of content knowledge a student has achieved in the subject listed. But why do we place a grade on a grade sheet, report card, or transcript? Why do we create a permanent written record of the grade? And why is the grade listed next to a name of an academic course such as English, U.S. History, Algebra, or Educational Psychology?

As illustrated by the title of the 1996 Yearbook of the Association for Supervision and Curriculum Development, Communicating Student Learning to interested parties is an important function of schools and teachers (Guskey 1996). Although there are various means to communicate student learning, currently a single report card grade for each academic subject is the most common and generally accepted system in middle and secondary schools (Bailey and McTighe 1996; Lake and Kafka 1996). Bailey and McTighe argue that as a communication system, "the primary purpose of secondary level grades and reports [is] to communicate student achievement" so that informed decisions can be made about the student's future (1996, 120). Similarly, authors of major texts devoted to classroom assessment suggest that the major reason for assigning grades is to create a public record of a student's academic achievement that can accurately and effectively communicate to others the level of mastery of a subject a student has demonstrated (Airasian 2000; Gallagher 1998; Gredler 1999; Linn and Gronlund 2000; Nitko 2001; Oosterhof 2001; Stiggins 2001). Nitko points out that: "Grades... are used by students, parents, other teachers, guidance counselors, school officials, postsecondary educational institutions, and employers. Therefore [teachers] must assign grades with utmost care and maintain their validity" (2001, 365). However, according to Marzano, in contrast to teachers', students', parents', and community members' assumption that grades are valid "measures of student achievement ... grades are so imprecise that they are almost meaningless" (2000, 1). Due to the wide variability in the criteria used in grading practices from teacher to teacher, the validity of student grades is unknown and they have limited value as guides for planning the academic and career futures of students (Thorndike 1997). Thus, if a single grade on a report card or transcript is to effectively communicate information to all these varied parties, then that single grade has to have some shared and accurate meaning (O'Connor 1995).

This lack of shared meaning seems to be found throughout our education system. A study by Baron (2000) shows that there is lack of coherence in the beliefs about grades held by parents and students and those held by the education community. Even in the same school, teachers often hold very different views about the purpose of grades and fail to communicate with their colleagues about their grading practices (Kain 1996). Grading practices by teachers rarely follow the measurement principles and grading practices recommended in measurement textbooks (Cross and Frary 1996; Frary, Cross, and Weber 1993). New teachers often work independently and are left to figure out their own grading policies, gradually adhering to the school's norms. There is a similar lack of coherence and communication among college teachers (Barnes, Bull, Campbell, and Perry 1998). Friedman and Frisbie (1995, 2000) make a particularly strong argument for making sure that report card grades accurately report information to parents about a student's academic progress and that teachers and administrators share a common understanding of what information a grade should communicate. They suggest that since grades become part of a students' permanent record, the purpose of these grades must be to communicate a valid summary of a student's academic achievement in the subject that is listed next to the grade on the record.

Grading systems used by teachers vary widely and unpredictably and often have low levels of validity due to the inclusion of nonacademic criteria used in the calculation of grades (Allen and Lambating 2001; Brookhart 1994; 2004; Frary, Cross, and Weber 1993; Olson 1989). Teachers have been found to make decisions about grades related to student effort in attempts to be "fair" in their grading practices (Barnes 1985). Studies have found that two out of three teachers believe that effort, student conduct, and attitude should influence final grades of students (Cross and Frary 1996; Frary, Cross, and Weber 1993). It has also been shown that grades are used as a motivational tool as well as to develop good study habits (Oosterhof 2001) and desirable classroom management behaviors (Allen 1983). Grades should not be a hodgepodge of factors such as student's level of effort, innate aptitude, compliance to rules, attendance, social behaviors, attitudes, or other nonachievement measures (Friedman and Frisbie 2000; Ornstein 1994). Although these factors may indirectly influence students' achievement of content knowledge, subjective—and often unknown to the teacher—factors such as these complicate the ability to interpret a grade since these factors may directly conflict with each other and distort the meaning of a grade measuring academic achievement (Cross and Frary 1996; Guskey 1994; Linn and Gronlund 2000; Nitko 2001; Stiggins 2001; Stumpo 1997). Nonacademic factors are often used as criteria for assigning grades because some teachers consider the consequences of grades more important than the value of clear communication of information and the interpretability of the grades (Brookhart 1993). It follows then that instead of the grade being a function of what a student has learned it has become a function of many variables. Simply put, it would appear that grades are often measures of how well a student lives up to the teacher's expectation of what a good student is rather than measuring the student's academic achievement in the subject matter objectives.

A grade can not be a teacher's "merged judgment"[1] of these factors, since as a single letter or numeric mark, the reported grade must communicate a single fact about the student if it is to be a valid or accurate source of information coherently shared between the reporter of the grade and the grade report's audience. How is the reader of a student's single grade on a transcript to know which factors are included and how much each unknown factor was weighed by the grade-giver to determine the grade? Also, since many of these factors such as effort, motivation, and student attitude are subjective measures made by a teacher, their inclusion in a grade related to academic achievement increases the chance for the grade to be biased or unreliable, and thus invalid. The purpose of an academic report is to communicate the level of academic achievement that a student has developed over a course of study. Therefore, the sole purpose of a grade on an academic report, if it is to be a valid source of information, is to communicate the academic achievement of the student. If other factors about the student are deemed important, such as a student's attitude, level of effort, or social behavior, then other appropriate forms of reporting these factors must be made available and used. If a multidimensional view of the student is desired, then a multidimensional system of reporting is required. Using a single grade as a summary of a teacher's "merged judgment" of a student leads to miscommunication, confusion, and a continuation of the lack of coherence among stakeholders about what a grade represents.

Since important decisions are often based on a student's grade, invalid grades may result in dire consequences for the student. Grades can open up or close down important learning opportunities for students (Jasmine 1999). With high grades, students get admitted to colleges and universities of their choice and receive scholarships and tuition assistance, since grades are a major selection criterion in the college admission process. The reverse is also true. It is very difficult for students to get admitted to some schools if their grades are not sufficiently high. Invalid grades that understate the student's knowledge may prevent a student with ability to pursue certain educational or career opportunities. Also, based on principles of attribution and social cognitive theories, if students receive grades lower than ones that accurately depict their true level of academic knowledge, it may lead students to believe they lack the ability to succeed academically and lower their sense of self-efficacy as well as their motivation to learn (Pintrich and Schunk 2002).

Grading and Lack of Professional Training

Cizek argues that the "lack of knowledge and interest in grading translates into a serious information breakdown in education" and that "reforming classroom assessment and grading practices will require educators' commitment to professional development, [and] classroom-relevant training programs" (1996, 103). Cizek's statement implies that an important area that needs to be addressed is the training of teachers in grading practices based on sound measurement principles relevant to their classroom lives.

This lack of knowledge about measurement theory and application to grading practices is a pervasive problem with preservice teacher training at the college level (Goodwin 2001;

Schafer 1991; Stiggins 1991, 1999). One of the goals of a teacher education program should be to prepare preservice and in-service teachers to develop effective methods to assess students and to communicate clearly and accurately through their grading practices that assessment to others. However, very few teacher education programs include measurement or assessment courses. Allen and Lambating (2001) found in a random sample of teacher education programs that less than one-third required an assessment course, and many of those that did were courses focused on "informal" assessments, or standardized assessment of students with special needs and not focused on classroom assessment and grading. Fewer than half of the fifty states require specific coursework on assessment for their initial certification of teachers (Lomax 1996; O'Sullivan and Chalnick 1991; Stiggins 1999).

Although assigning grades is probably the most important measurement decision that classroom teachers make, the coverage of grading in assessment textbooks is often not as fully developed as other measurement topics that are less relevant to teachers' day-to-day assessment practices (Airasian 1991; Lomax 1996). According to Stiggins (1999), how the concepts of "reliability" and "validity" are related to classroom grading practices is not addressed in the courses which introduce these terms to our preservice teachers. It is important to look at this issue because validity and reliability are considered the most fundamental principles related to measurement and therefore important to classroom assessment and grading (Gallagher 1998; Gredler 1999; Linn and Gronlund 2000).

Some argue that even when teachers are provided with some measurement instruction, they still use subjective value judgements when assigning grades (Brookhart 1993). Undergraduate teacher education majors, when asked about the criteria that should be used for their own grades, believe that "effort" is more important than amount of academic content learned (Placier 1995). One contributing factor may be that after sixteen years of obtaining grades based on factors other than academic achievement, teachers-in-training have a difficult time accepting theoretical principles that do not match with their personal experience. Many beliefs about school practices are well established before students enter college and often are resistant to change (Britzman 1986, 1991; Ginsberg and Clift 1990; Holt-Reynolds 1992; Pajares 1992; Richardson 1996). They form many of their perspectives about teaching from their years of observing teachers and their teaching practices (Lortie 1975). They have been recipients of hundreds of grades from their K–12 teachers and college professors before taking on the responsibility of assigning grades to their own students. Their perception regarding grades comes from their own long experience as students.

Brookhart (1998) suggests that classroom assessment and grading practices are at the center of effective management of classroom instruction and learning. Through the use of real classroom scenarios, preservice teachers need to be taught assessment strategies in relationship to instruction and not as decontextualized measurement principles. As the past president of the American Educational Research Association, Lorrie Shepard has stated: "The transformation of assessment practices cannot be accomplished in separate tests and measurement courses, but rather should be a central concern in teaching methods courses" (2000, 4). In addition to instruction on how to assess and grade using sound principles of measurement, research suggests that preservice teachers need hands-on experience in grading students and how to work with cooperating teachers who assess and grade in ways different than those learned by the preservice teachers (Barnes 1985; Lomax 1996).

What the literature suggests is that educators at all levels make decisions when assigning grades that are not based on sound principles of validity that ensure the grade is a meaningful communication of a student's level of academic achievement. The literature also suggests that students in teacher education programs may be more influenced by the grading practices they have experienced as students in the past, as well as in their current courses taught by their education professors, than by what they learn about assessment and grading in their courses. Additionally, teachers in the field, as products of teacher education programs, seem to exhibit grading practices that confirm that they have not been influenced by measurement courses (Lambating and Allen 2002). This may be because they did not take any assessment courses, or because their long-held beliefs about grading were left unchallenged and the courses did not focus on assessment and grading issues related to measuring classroom learning.

Educational Implications and Conclusion

Concerns about the validity and reliability of grades for communicating meaningful information about students' academic progress have been raised for a long time (see Starch and Elliot 1912, 1913a, 1913b; Adams 1932). In addition, trying to help teachers to understand the purpose and effective functions of grades in the overall evaluation system has been addressed repeatedly in the literature (Airasian 2000; Brookhart 1993; Cross and Frary 1996; Gredler 1999; Guskey 1996; Linn and Gronlund 2000; Marzano 2000; O'Connor 1995; Stiggins 2001). However, there seems to be little progress being made in this area in actual classroom practice.

Two major thrusts need to occur in reforming grading practices. First, if factors such as effort, attitude, compliance, and behavior are to be noted about a student on a report card, then they should be reported with a separate mark and not figured in as part of a grade for academic achievement of content knowledge. However, as in most situations, if a teacher must summarize and communicate a student's classroom progress in an academic subject through a single report card grade, then there must be a consensus that the grade represents the most accurate statement of the student's academic achievement, and only academic achievement. This is the essence of valid assessment. To include nonacademic criteria, such as the student's effort, compliance, attitude, or behavior, makes the grade impossible to interpret in any meaningful way. Perhaps, a simple way to reach this consensus is to teach ourselves and those we prepare to be teachers to reflect on the following question: "If I was given a student's transcript with a single letter grade listed next to the subject I teach, what would be the most logical interpretation I could make about what the grade represents about the

student's knowledge of that academic subject?" Therefore, that is what I should try to have my grades communicate to whomever will read and interpret them in the future.

In order for teachers to act consistently in assigning valid grades based only on appropriate achievement criteria, a second major initiative needs to be undertaken to help teachers understand how to make good grading decisions. This initiative is best addressed through teacher education programs taking on the challenge to improve the assessment training of their students and improve their own grading practices. This entails several dimensions.

First, students' long-held beliefs about the purpose and use of grades need to be challenged by teacher educators. Students' beliefs and value systems related to grades need to be exposed and examined to help them understand the unscientific basis of their grading beliefs. Second, once these beliefs are exposed, instructors must provide students with the theoretical base for good assessment and grading practices as explicated by measurement experts that would replace students' naive notions of assessment and grading. This could be either through self-contained measurement courses taught in a relevant manner by educational psychologists, or integrated into methods courses through collaboration between educational psychology and teacher-education specialists. It would help if more teacher-education programs required adequate instruction on classroom assessment and grading practices. There also needs to be more effective and meaningful grading practices addressed in-depth in measurement textbooks. Third, teacher education students need to be provided with opportunities to encounter grading activities before they are placed into student teaching, in order to practice applying assessment principles and theory to classroom grading issues. Finally, during student teaching experiences, education majors must be given the opportunity, in conjunction with their cooperating teachers and the support of their college supervisors, to actually develop and implement a valid evaluation and grading plan. Schools of education need to work with school district teachers to help improve the communication system for which grades function. Providing in-service "assessment and grading" workshops for practicing teachers, especially those operating as cooperating teachers, might help to establish a consensus of what is appropriate criteria to use for determining and assigning valid grades to indicate academic achievement.

One way to accomplish many of the above steps is through the use of case studies that focus on assessment and grading dilemmas often faced by real teachers. Discussion of case studies can help students to reflect on and expose their belief systems about grades and grading, and analyze them in relationship to educational psychology assessment principles such as validity. One example is the Sarah Hanover case which focuses on a grading dilemma a teacher must deal with when the question of the validity of a student's grade is raised by the student's parent (Silverman, Welty, and Lyon 1996).

However, the area that may be the most difficult to address is the change in the grading practices that teacher educators use in evaluating students. As long as preservice and in-service teachers take classes from education professors who base grading decisions on more than academic achievement, they will have little reason to either believe what we say or practice what we preach about assessment and grading. As teacher educators, we need to model sound grading practices in our own courses in which grades accurately communicate students' achievement of content knowledge learned in our courses, and not how hard they work or how often they attend our classes.

My intention in this article has been to suggest that by giving serious reflection to the meaning of the educational psychology measurement principle of validity, grading practices can improve and the grades we assign to students as teachers can be more accurate and educationally meaningful. We need to begin to break the cycle of invalid grading practices that prevail throughout the education system, and the only behaviors we as teachers can truly control are our own.

Key words: grading, education system, assessment

NOTE

1. The author has borrowed this phrase from an anonymous reviewer.

REFERENCES

Adams, W. L. 1932. Why teachers say they fail pupils. *Educational Administration and Supervision* 18:594–600.

Airasian, P. W. 1991. Perspectives on measurement instruction. *Educational Measurement: Issues and Practice* 10 (1): 13–16, 26.

———. 2000. *Assessment in the classroom: A concise approach.* 2nd ed. Boston: McGraw-Hill.

Allen, J. D. 1983. Classroom management: Students' perspectives, goals and strategies. Paper presented at the annual meeting of the American Educational Research Association, Montreal, Canada, April.

Allen, J. D., and J. Lambating. 2001. Validity and reliability in assessment and grading: Perspectives of preservice and inservice teachers and teacher education professors. Paper presented at the annual meeting of the American Educational Research Association, Seattle, April.

Bailey, J., and J. McTighe. 1996. Reporting achievement at the secondary level: What and how. In Guskey 1996, 119–40.

Barnes, L. B., K. S. Bull, N. J. Campbell, and K. M. Perry. 1998. Discipline-related differences in teaching and grading philosophies among undergraduate teaching faculty. Paper presented at the annual meeting of the American Educational Research Association, San Diego, April.

Barnes, S. 1985. A study of classroom pupil evaluation: The missing link in teacher education. *Journal of Teacher Education* 36 (4): 46–49.

Baron, P. A. B. 2000. Consequential validity for high school grades: What is the meaning of grades for senders and receivers? Paper presented at the annual meeting of the American Educational Research Association, New Orleans, April.

Britzman, D. P. 1986. Cultural myths in the making of a teacher: Biography and social structure in teacher education. *Harvard Educational Review* 56 (4): 442–56.

———. 1991. *Practice makes practice: A critical study of learning to teach.* New York: State University of New York Press.

Brookhart, S. M. 1993. Teachers' grading practices: Meaning and values. *Journal of Educational Measurement* 30 (2): 123–42.

———. 1994. Teachers' grading: Practice and theory. *Applied Measurement in Education* 7 (4): 279–301.

———. 1998. Teaching about grading and communicating assessment results. Paper presented at the annual meeting of the National Council on Measurement in Education, San Diego, April, 1998.

———. 2004. *Grading.* Upper Saddle River, NJ: Pearson/Merrill/Prentice Hall.

Cizek, G. J. 1996. Grades: The final frontier in assessment reform. *NASSP Bulletin* 80 (584): 103–10.

Cross, L. H., and R. B. Frary. 1996. Hodgepodge grading: Endorsed by students and teachers alike. Paper presented at the annual meeting of the National Council on Measurement in Education, New York, April.

Frary, R. B., L. H. Cross, and L. J. Weber. 1993. Testing and grading practices and opinions of secondary teachers of academic subjects: Implications for instruction in measurement. *Educational Measurement: Issues and Practice* 12 (3): 2330.

Friedman, S. J., and D. A. Frisbie. 1995. The influence of report cards on the validity of grades reported to parents. *Educational and Psychological Measurement* 55 (1): 5–26.

———. 2000. Making report cards measure up. *Education Digest* 65 (5): 45–50.

Gallagher, J. D. 1998. *Classroom assessment for teachers.* Upper Saddle River, NJ: Merrill/Prentice Hall.

Ginsburg, M. B., and R. T. Clift. 1990. The hidden curriculum of preservice teacher education. In *Handbook of research on teacher education*, ed. W. R. Houston, 450–65. New York: Macmillan.

Goodwin, A. L. 2001. The case of one child: Making the shift from personal knowledge to informed practice. Paper presented at the annual meeting of the American Educational Research Association, Seattle, April.

Gredler, M. E. 1999. *Classroom assessment and learning.* New York: Longman.

Guskey, T. R. 1994. Making the grade: What benefits students? *Educational Leadership* 52 (2): 14–20.

———. 1996. *ASCD Yearbook, 1996: Communicating student learning.* Alexandria, VA: Association for Supervision and Curriculum Development.

Holt-Reynolds, D. 1992. Personal history-based beliefs as relevant prior knowledge in coursework: Can we practice what we preach? *American Educational Research Journal* 29 (2): 325–49.

Jasmine, T. 1999. Grade distributions, grading procedures, and students' evaluations of instructors: A justice perspective. *Journal of Psychology* 133 (3): 263–71.

Kain, D. L. 1996. Looking beneath the surface: Teacher collaboration through the lens of grading practices. *Teachers College Record* 97 (4): 569–87.

Kohn, A. 1999. Grading is degrading. *Education Digest* 65 (1): 59–64.

Lake, K., and K. Kafka. 1996. Reporting methods in grades K–8. In Guskey 1996, 90–118.

Lambating, J., and J. D. Allen. 2002. How the multiple functions of grades influence their validity and value as measures of academic achievement. Paper presented at the annual meeting of the American Educational Research Association, New Orleans, April.

Linn, R. L., and N. E. Gronlund. 2000. *Measurement and assessment in teaching.* 8th ed. Englewood Cliffs, NJ: Merrill/Prentice Hall.

Lomax, R. G. 1996. On becoming assessment literate: An initial look at preservice teachers' beliefs and practices. *Teacher Educator* 31 (4): 292–303.

Lortie, D. 1975. *Schoolteacher: A sociological study.* Chicago: University of Chicago Press.

Marzano, R. J. 2000. *Transforming classroom grading.* Alexandria, VA: Association for Supervision and Curriculum Development.

Nitko, A. J. 2001. *Educational assessment of students.* 3rd ed. Upper Saddle River, NJ: Merrill/Prentice Hall.

O'Conner, K. 1995. Guidelines for grading that support learning and student success. *NASSP Bulletin* 79 (571): 91–101.

Olson, G. H. 1989. On the validity of performance grades: The relationship between teacher-assigned grades and standard measures of subject matter acquisition. Paper presented at the annual meeting of the National Council on Measurement in Education, San Francisco, March.

Oosterhof, A. 2001. *Classroom application of educational measurement*. Upper Saddle River, NJ: Prentice Hall.

Ormrod, J. E. 2000. *Educational psychology: Developing learners*. 3rd ed. Upper Saddle River, NJ: Merrill/Prentice Hall.

Ornstein, A. C. 1994. Grading practices and policies: An overview and some suggestions. *NASSP Bulletin* 78 (561): 55–64.

O'Sullivan, R. G., and M. K. Chalnick. 1991. Measurement-related course work requirements for teacher certification and recertification. *Educational Measurement: Issues and Practice* 10 (1): 17–19, 23.

Pajares, M. F. 1992. Teachers' beliefs and educational research: Cleaning up a messy construct. *Review of Educational Research* 62 (3): 307–32.

Pintrich, P. R., and D. H. Schunk. 2002. *Motivation in education*. 2nd ed. Upper Saddle River, NJ: Merrill/Prentice Hall.

Placier, M. 1995. "But I have to have an A": Probing the cultural meanings and ethical dilemmas of grades in teacher education. *Teacher Education Quarterly* 22 (1): 45–63.

Richardson, V. 1996. The role of attitudes and beliefs in learning to teach. In *Handbook of research on teacher education*, 2nd ed., ed. J. Sikula, T. Buttery, and E. Guyton, 102–19. New York: Macmillan.

Schafer, W. D. 1991. Essential assessment skills in professional education of teachers. *Educational Measurement: Issues and Practice* 10 (1): 3–6, 12.

Shepard, L. A. 2000. The role of assessment in a learning culture. *Educational Researcher* 29 (7): 4–14.

Silverman, R., W. M. Welty, and S. Lyon. 1996. *Case studies for teacher problem solving*. 2nd ed. New York: McGraw-Hill.

Snowman, J., and R. F. Biehler. 2003. *Psychology applied to teaching*. 10th ed. Boston: Houghton Mifflin.

Starch, D., and E. C. Elliot. 1912. Reliability of grading of high-school work in English. *School Review* 20:442–57.

———. 1913a. Reliability of grading work in mathematics. *School Review* 21:254–59.

———. 1913b. Reliability of grading work in history. *School Review* 20:676–81.

Stiggins, R. J. 1991. Relevant classroom assessment training for teachers. *Educational Measurement: Issues and Practice* 10 (1): 7–12.

———. 1999. Evaluating classroom assessment training in teacher education programs. *Educational Measurement: Issues and Practice* 18 (1): 23–27.

———. 2001. *Student-involved classroom assessment*. 3rd ed. Upper Saddle River, NJ: Merrill/Prentice Hall.

Stumpo, V. M. 1997. 3-tier grading sharpens student assessment. *Education Digest* 63 (4): 51–54.

Thorndike, R. M. 1997. *Measurement and Evaluation*. 6th ed. Upper Saddle River, NJ: Merrill/Prentice Hall.

Tombari, M., and G. Borich. 1999. *Authentic assessment in the classroom*. Upper Saddle River, NJ: Merrill/Prentice Hall.

James D. Allen *is a professor of educational psychology in the Department of Educational and School Psychology at the College of Saint Rose in Albany, New York.*

Index

Index

Test Your Knowledge Form

We encourage you to photocopy and use this page as a tool to assess how the articles in *Annual Editions* expand on the information in your textbook. By reflecting on the articles you will gain enhanced text information. You can also access this useful form on a product's book support Web site at *http://www.mhcls.com/online/*.

NAME: _____   DATE: _____

_____

TITLE AND NUMBER OF ARTICLE:

_____

BRIEFLY STATE THE MAIN IDEA OF THIS ARTICLE:

_____

LIST THREE IMPORTANT FACTS THAT THE AUTHOR USES TO SUPPORT THE MAIN IDEA:

_____

WHAT INFORMATION OR IDEAS DISCUSSED IN THIS ARTICLE ARE ALSO DISCUSSED IN YOUR TEXTBOOK OR OTHER READINGS THAT YOU HAVE DONE? LIST THE TEXTBOOK CHAPTERS AND PAGE NUMBERS:

_____

LIST ANY EXAMPLES OF BIAS OR FAULTY REASONING THAT YOU FOUND IN THE ARTICLE:

_____

LIST ANY NEW TERMS/CONCEPTS THAT WERE DISCUSSED IN THE ARTICLE, AND WRITE A SHORT DEFINITION:

We Want Your Advice

ANNUAL EDITIONS revisions depend on two major opinion sources: one is our Advisory Board, listed in the front of this volume, which works with us in scanning the thousands of articles published in the public press each year; the other is you—the person actually using the book. Please help us and the users of the next edition by completing the prepaid article rating form on this page and returning it to us. Thank you for your help!

ANNUAL EDITIONS: Educational Psychology 06/07

ARTICLE RATING FORM

Here is an opportunity for you to have direct input into the next revision of this volume.
We would like you to rate each of the articles listed below, using the following scale:

1. **Excellent: should definitely be retained**
2. **Above average: should probably be retained**
3. **Below average: should probably be deleted**
4. **Poor: should definitely be deleted**

Your ratings will play a vital part in the next revision.
Please mail this prepaid form to us as soon as possible.
Thanks for your help!

RATING	ARTICLE	RATING	ARTICLE
	1. A Learner's Bill of Rights		27. Implementing a Research-Based Model of Cooperative Learning
	2. Teachers as Leaders		28. Teachers Bridge to Constructivism
	3. What Urban Students Say About Good Teaching		29. Constructivism and Block Scheduling: Making the Connection
	4. Helping Children Cope With Loss, Death, and Grief: Response to a National Tragedy		30. Using Data to Differentiate Instruction
	5. A National Tragedy: Helping Children Cope		31. Do Students Care About Learning? A Conversation with Mihaly Csikszentmihalyi
	6. Shaping the Learning Environment: Connecting Developmentally Appropriate Practices to Brain Research		32. Self-Efficacy: A Key to Improving the Motivation of Struggling Learners
	7. The Importance of Being Playful		33. Help For Stressed Students
	8. What Empathy Can Do		34. When Children Make Rules
	9. The Biology of Risk Taking		35. The Key to Classroom Management
	10. Differing Perspectives, Common Ground: The Middle School and Gifted Education Relationship		36. Twelve Practical Strategies to Prevent Behavioral Escalation in Classroom Settings
	11. Normalizing Difference in Inclusive Teaching		37. Corporal Punishment: Legalities, Realities, and Implications
	12. Into the Mainstream: Practical Strategies for Teaching in Inclusive Environments		38. The Lessons of High-Stakes Testing
	13. Challenges of Identifying and Serving Gifted Children With ADHD		39. Are We Measuring Student Success With High-Stakes Testing?
	14. Raising Expectations for the Gifted		40. The Seductive Allure of Data
	15. Celebrating Diverse Minds		41. Working Inside the Black Box: Assessment for Learning in the Classroom
	16. Creating Culturally Responsive Schools		42. Using Student-Involved Classroom Assessment to Close Achievement Gaps
	17. Successful Strategies for English Language Learners		43. Grades as Valid Measures of Academic Achievement of Classroom Learning
	18. Students Remember…What They Think About		
	19. Beyond Learning By Doing: The Brain Compatible Approach		
	20. Metacognition: A Bridge Between Cognitive Psychology and Educational Practice		
	21. Successful Intelligence in the Classroom		
	22. It's No Fad: Fifteen Years of Implementing Multiple Intelligences		
	23. Caution—Praise Can Be Dangerous		
	24. Constructing Learning: Using Technology to Support Teaching for Understanding		
	25. Creating a Culture For Learning		
	26. Promoting Academic Achievement Through Social and Emotional Learning		

(Continued on next page)

BUSINESS REPLY MAIL
FIRST CLASS MAIL PERMIT NO. 551 DUBUQUE IA

POSTAGE WILL BE PAID BY ADDRESEE

McGraw-Hill Contemporary Learning Series
2460 KERPER BLVD
DUBUQUE, IA 52001-9902

NO POSTAGE
NECESSARY
IF MAILED
IN THE
UNITED STATES

ABOUT YOU

Name _____   Date _____

Are you a teacher? ☐   A student? ☐
Your school's name _____

Department _____

Address _____   City _____   State ___   Zip ___

School telephone # _____

YOUR COMMENTS ARE IMPORTANT TO US!

Please fill in the following information:
For which course did you use this book?
_____

Did you use a text with this ANNUAL EDITION? ☐ yes ☐ no
What was the title of the text?
_____

What are your general reactions to the *Annual Editions* concept?
_____

Have you read any pertinent articles recently that you think should be included in the next edition? Explain.
_____

Are there any articles that you feel should be replaced in the next edition? Why?
_____

Are there any World Wide Web sites that you feel should be included in the next edition? Please annotate.
_____

May we contact you for editorial input? ☐ yes ☐ no
May we quote your comments? ☐ yes ☐ no